JAY TO BEE

JAY TO BEE

JANET FRAME'S LETTERS TO WILLIAM (BILL) THEOPHILUS BROWN
1969–1971

— Edited by Denis Harold —

COUNTERPOINT • BERKELEY, CALIFORNIA

Copyright © 2016 Janet Frame Literary Trust

Excerpts from Bill Brown's letters © Estate of William Theophilus Brown

All rights reserved under International and Pan-American Copyright Conventions. No part of this book may be used or reproduced in any manner whatsoever without written permission from the publisher, except in the case of brief quotations embodied in critical articles and reviews.

Library of Congress Cataloging-in-Publication Data is Available

Cover design by Kelly Winton
Interior design by Neuwirth & Associates

ISBN 978-1-61902-728-2

Counterpoint
2560 Ninth Street, Suite 318
Berkeley, CA 94710
www.counterpointpress.com

Printed in the United States of America
Distributed by Publishers Group West

10 9 8 7 6 5 4 3 2 1

CONTENTS

Introduction

vii

USA

November 1969 to March 1970

1

New Zealand

March 1970 to January 1971

87

Acknowledgements

387

Appendices

389

Dramatis Personae 391
Concepts and Nicknames 395
Quotations 397
Works by Janet Frame 399
Excerpts from Brown's Letters to Frame 401

INTRODUCTION

Janet Frame's letters to Bill Brown (William Theophilus Brown), the Californian painter, written over two decades, are humorous and wide-ranging, revealing little known aspects of her creativity. She felt she had met her match in Brown, a painter, classical pianist and confidant of famous writers, musicians and artists. They met at the MacDowell artist colony in New Hampshire, USA, in late 1969, beginning a friendship that lasted until her death in 2004.

Frame wrote over 500 letters to Brown, from a rate of at least two a week in the first year to one a week for several years, dwindling to one every couple of months by the mid 1980s. The letters include observations of events and people, art and politics, philosophy and comedy, quotes from and parodies of poets such as Walt Whitman and Emily Dickinson, all intertwined with drawings, doodles and collages.

The bulk of the correspondence spans the decade of the 1970s during which Frame published *Daughter Buffalo* in 1972 and *Living in the Maniototo* in 1979. She poured so much dynamism and invention into this correspondence that it together with the novel *In the Memorial Room* (written in 1974 but not published until 2013) constitute the previously unknown masterpieces that fill what had seemed to some academic commentators to be a seven-year dry spell in Frame's middle period. The swift changes of tone and structure of these letters arguably relate to and even prefigure the style of these novels. The letters also provide insights into her ideas and life, thus complementing her three volumes of autobiography published in the first half of the 1980s.

Frame's letters to Brown combine many styles and registers of prose, poetry, drawings, illustrations, typographical flourishes and quotations. She implied they had the characteristics of collages when on thanking Brown in late June 1970 for his 'lovely letter and its enclosures' she quoted a passage from W.H. Auden's long poem 'Letter to Lord Byron' that describes how 'exciting letters' are full of enclosures such as gossip, cuttings and maps: they are a 'collage that you will read.' Frame as early as her student years in the mid 1940s at Dunedin Teacher Training College was interested in the possibility of collage. A project entitled 'The Growth of Cities' bored her until she realised that 'my only hope was to write (and illustrate) the long essay in my own way' by fitting together various texts and images.

Frame's friendship with the very well-read artist-musician Brown was a catalyst to her imagination. Her drawings and collages in her letters to him are most prolific during the early years, especially the first, the period of *Jay to Bee*. She sometimes claimed that she lacked any talent as an artist, but in these letters she expresses a personal style of drawing and design. Brown's letters to her are similarly enlivened by humorous drawings. In later years, she did less art but sometimes included photographs in her letters to Brown, especially of her various houses and cats.

MACDOWELL AND YADDO ARTIST COLONIES

Frame first met Brown at MacDowell in New Hampshire, one of the most famous American artist colonies, where she stayed from mid-September to late November in 1969. She had a lot of fun as a member of a group that included Brown and the writers Jo Carson and Elnora Coleman. They dined and joked together as a reprieve from the earnest seriousness of other guests. They referred to themselves as 'the baby table' and all kept in touch when they left. Two months after leaving MacDowell, Frame stayed a month at another major American artist colony, Yaddo, near Saratoga Springs in northern New York State.*

After leaving MacDowell and before going to Yaddo, Frame flew to California in early December to spend a week with Brown, then on to

---

* This was her third visit there: her first stay was in May 1967, then subsequently from mid February to mid June 1969, October to December 1971, and February-March 1982. During the years 1967 to 1982, she spent a total of twelve months spread over six separate visits at these two artist colonies.

Baltimore to stay with her friend, John Money, a New Zealand born sexologist at Johns Hopkins University, whom she had known in New Zealand in the 1940s. She went to Yaddo in January 1970 and within a fortnight penned word portraits for Brown of fellow guests such as the composers Ned Rorem and Douglas Allanbrook, writers Ann Kazin and Norman Podhoretz and the critic Kenneth Burke. She formed a rapport with Burke, who one evening asked to see some of her poems and the next morning presented her with two pages of incisive critique. She was stimulated by these interactions but compared to the atmosphere of MacDowell felt, as she described in a letter to Brown, that

> 'the formality of Yaddo makes it difficult for people to be themselves among one another—yet this is no great disadvantage for one's work, and I think maybe it is an advantage; it means, though, that people get quickly 'stir crazy'.'

She wrote that she left Yaddo early, accompanying the literary critic Alfred Kazin, husband of her fellow guest Ann Kazin, on the bus down to New York, where she dined that evening with the Kazins at their apartment. She wrote to Brown:

'I was glad to see the Kazins in 'real life' because at Yaddo Ann was very-too-brilliant and witty, and Alfred seemed shyly disapproving, but in their home they were warm and happy—it's marvellous not to be conscious all the time that one's a 'writer'.'

During this period, she stayed with Elnora Coleman in her apartment in New York, then travelled to Baltimore to see John Money, whom she found 'less crabby than when I was last here—I think he is pleased with his series of lectures to the Medical students on Pornography'.

RETURN TO NEW ZEALAND

In early March Frame flew to California for three weeks with Brown and his partner and fellow artist Paul Wonner, before continuing on the long trip back to New Zealand. Understandably, there was no correspondence during this time so there is a gap in the narrative of *Jay to Bee*, but the intense delight and stimulation of this visit can be inferred by the subsequent mutual flow of letters across the Pacific. On arrival in Auckland after a rough flight, she wrote to Brown in order 'to keep in touch, to remind myself of much happiness found at Hermosillo Drive: when I fall asleep I dream of it'.

After a week with her sister June and her family on Auckland's North Shore, Frame arrived home in Dunedin on the first day of April. A creative but often solitary period of eight months ensued that at times felt like exile from the excitements of North America, especially her friendship with Brown. She wrote to him of her loneliness: 'It's a new experience for me to miss people'. Dunedin was no substitute for the Californian 'live oaks', which was one of her most frequent endearments for Brown, Wonner and Ned (their cat):

'Life is pretty barren here for me, socially, because everyone is so bloody staid and straight-laced. I'm getting to rely more and more on the under-population I meet when I go out walking—the numerous cats sitting on fences, absorbing everything with their uncensored gaze . . .'

In May, Frame gave an interview on a national radio programme about her experiences at Yaddo and MacDowell entitled 'Artists' Retreats'*:

'It was a rich experience, for me, to feel for the first time in my life that I was among my own kind, so to speak, living and working and playing with them unselfconsciously.'

She gradually became involved with Dunedin activities and friends such as Charles Brasch, Ruth Dallas and Dorothy White, and visited an elderly relative in hospital. Her correspondence with Brown continued, full of musings, wit and poetry. She commented on the frequency of her letters: 'Another hailstone in my storm of correspondence—dodge it if you wish.' Her letters were an imaginative projection: 'I don't look on my letters to you as letters, not really, they're just a way, for me, of *being there* from time to time with the three live and lively oaks.' The phrase *being there* was most powerfully explored in the long poem On Not Being There† that she wrote in early June. This brilliant poem operates on several levels: the theme of desire underlies a description of a concert that the narrator does not attend.

---

* New Zealand Listener, 27 July 1970

† First published in the posthumous volume of Frame's poetry, *The Goose Bath* (Random House, Auckland, 2006)

Frame occasionally entertained the possibility, encouraged by Brown and Wonner, that some arrangement might be worked out for her to live with them. Soon after she returned to Dunedin, she wrote, 'as soon as you get that small servant-kennel built on to the kitchen let me know'. Several months later she exclaimed, 'Do you really mean that there will be a little place for me with you? I can try it, anyway, and leave it very open as all living is'. Another time, she admitted it was a fantasy: 'I will shatter this fantasy because it is unendurably not true (who said fantasies ever were?)'

CHARACTERS

There are many scenarios and themes that interweave throughout the letters. Many of the characters would have originated in conversations between Frame, Brown and Wonner.

A major picaresque narrative involves a cast of characters who live on the patio at 'Live Oak Inn' in Hermosillo Drive, Santa Barbara, California—Brown and Wonner's address. One of these 'characters' is a carnivorous plant, *Carnie*, which sometimes eats people. *Carnie* transplants a slip of itself to New Zealand from where it occasionally writes 'home'. Mostly, though, it is *Jay*, sometimes called *Jaybird* or *J*, who writes the letters. *Jay* writes to *Bee*—i.e. B, the initial of Bill; Paul is *Pee*. These were nicknames for each other that the three friends often used in the correspondence. The title of the introduction to this book captures this witty interplay.

Other leading characters are *Ned*, an actual cat (whose servants are *Bee* and *Pee*) and *Steinie*, a Steinway piano that *Bee* owns and plays. Other characters and cats visit periodically, for example *Dame Mary Margaret*, an alter-ego of Paul's, a formidable pantomime-dame figure reminiscent of Margaret Rutherford the actor or Princess Margaret, sister of the British monarch who features in some of Frame's collages. Originally, this dame was a character in the asylum in Frame's novel *Faces in the Water*: 'the original Dame M.M. who used to broadcast to Egypt'. Frame kept track of her 'characters' amidst all their adventures that frequently paralleled what Brown and she were doing or dreaming.

Some of the characters retain some mystery, such as *The Mortal Enemy*, which is identified in an April letter as Frame's 'new novel [that] wavers (it is my mortal enemy)' but at other times is something else. The concept had developed since its first appearance in January as a reference to the novella by Willa Cather: 'my short novel (*Mortal Enemy* style) which remains out of reach like a tame chickadee that's decided it won't settle on my hand after all.' She illustrates the interrelationships between a number of these characters in one of her final letters before she returns to the USA:

> 'Hi. I'm just moving, still in imagination only (having left that crumby motel in Offing) out of one horse Focus Town into the pretty little resort of Foreground where I'm staying at the Foreplay Inn before I take the plane to Live Oak Inn. Quite a complicated journey, as complicated as a bee's dance at the entrance to the hive, at sundown.'

Frame's trips to and musings upon 'The Place of the Stone Bees'—the image of a bee carved on the facade of Ajax Bee Supplies near the Dunedin railway station—is one of many fascinating sub-plots. Just before leaving Dunedin at the end of 1970, she describes to Brown a walk

> 'to the place of The Stone Bees, to photograph them, and when I came to them I was confronted by my own imagination and memory, for they were so small I had to search for the carvings and I don't think my photographs will show them.'

This particular image of a bee inspired one of the poetry sections of her next novel, *Daughter Buffalo*.

Possibly the most curious and pervasive character is the *peedauntal*, which appeared in Frame's first correspondence to Brown, a postcard from MacDowell on November 15, 1969:

> 'The Management of Peedauntals Ltd thanks you for your visit to the East and reminds you that it wishes to keep close to its valued client. It moves shortly to lonely premises in Baltimore. Singing opera you need never be peedauntally underprivileged or under-achieved with our late model Peedauntals.'

Several months later Brown sent a drawing of a prototype of the peedauntal, a device whose intended function was to enable people not to 'have to pee down their leg', but whose design was fraught with problems. Frame commented on his prototype:

> 'Alas sir, the Peedauntal model as illustrated has no sex appeal whatsoever, unless of course the buckles fastening it to the leg are diamond or snakeskin. I had in mind something less like an attached bagpipe—'

On another occasion she acknowledged that 'of course I never forget, Ace Bee, that you [. . .] were the originator of the Peedauntal Principal'. The Peedauntal Saga evolved through more than twenty of Frame's letters. She wrote in early July:

> 'Tonight I am going to Charles B's place for dinner after which we are going to see/hear the Opera Company's *The Impresario* and *Il Pagliacci*. It will be a very good opportunity for me (as co-director of the Peedauntal Company N.Z. Ltd.) to see how the product actually works.'

'The Peedauntal Report', spliced with a collage of text from newspapers, is the climax of this particular saga. There are a number of sagas of other 'characters' that intersperse the correspondence with hilarity and poignancy: *Steinie* (a Steinway piano), *Carnie* (a carnivorous plant) and *A Sweater*. And then there is *Lucas*.

LUCAS

Early in August 1970, midway through her ten months back in New Zealand, Frame adopted a kitten for a couple of months that became the focus of emotions ranging from joy to grief. In Frame's correspondence with Brown, cats are cats but also familiars, surrogates, confessors, mysteries, metaphors. She found the kitten 'exceedingly refreshing as he hides nothing and is not ashamed of any of his feelings'. She named it Lucas after the character Lucas Burch in William Faulkner's novel *Light in August*, referring to the cat after it left as the hero of an apocryphal novel, *Cat in August*. She summed up this interlude:

> 'I'm fighting fit but so sad, so sad. I learned so much from Lucas. It was an ideal situation for studying learning between woman and beast. Cats

are so full of knowing on (to us) invisible evidence and I think they could teach us a way of reaching the invisible evidence.'

In October 1970, Frame attended the rehearsal of a play adapted from her novel, *A State of Siege*. Her letters now included practical details of her planned return to the United States. This year, spent in two contrasting places, was proving to be a period of transition for while in one place she was thinking of the other, ruminating on loss and longing, of 'not being there'.

She considered Brown and Wonner's suggestion that she seek a teaching position in the States and enquired about a work visa, but nothing was finalised by the time she returned there early the following year. She posted Brown a copy of a satirical letter she sent to 'To J. J. Smith, Immigration Dept., Wishington', thanking him for his letter and the 'test' he had sent her to fill in. She queried one of the questions, which she shared with Brown:

'There's a question of colour. I am Blue—it does not appear in the photograph I enclosed with my application. I believe, however, that the Blue disappears when one sets foot on U.S. soil.'

Though Frame had the resources to return to the USA, her plans were boosted when Brown offered to pay the airfare and her friend Sue Marquand, the wife of writer John Marquand whom she had met on her first visit to Yaddo in 1967, offered her the long term use of an apartment in New York.

RETURN TO THE USA

In one of Frame's last letters to Brown before she left New Zealand, she exclaimed, 'What a year's history is being written in my letters' thus acknowledging their significance. She flew to Auckland early in December where she based herself at her sister June Gordon's family home. In early January, she took the train to Wellington to spend a week with her friend, Jacquie Baxter*, and on January 29 flew to California where she stayed

---

* New Zealand poet and short story writer (1927-2009), widow of poet James K Baxter

several weeks with Brown and Wonner. She then flew on to the East Coast where she spent the rest of the year living and writing intensively, several times revisiting Brown in California. From October to December, she stayed at Yaddo. The year 1971 was Frame's American year.

Frame's correspondence with Brown continued, though much diminished in volume, up until 1989 when she was shocked to learn that he had sold her letters to a collector, who on-sold them to Pennsylvania State University library. Brown explained that he had been anxious that the collection was cared for. Though troubled by the incident, she forgave him but rarely wrote letters from then on, preferring the telephone, postcards and eventually email.

EDITING *JAY TO BEE*

Jay to Bee preserves the integrity, atmosphere and narrative drive of the first fourteen months of Frame's correspondence with Brown by excluding only repetitious and inconsequential material from a total of 136 letters (including eight postcards) for this period.

The layout of the correspondence is chronological. Given that about half the items are undated, we rigorously scrutinised and cross-checked to establish the sequence, which is slightly different to the order in the catalogue at Penn State University Library in the USA where the originals are lodged.

Frame wrote to Brown an average of twice a week, with Brown writing about half as many times. Most of her letters include drawings and or collages, and many of his include drawings with the occasional collage. Most of hers are typewritten, although there are many hand-written inclusions. She wrote about one fifth completely by hand, usually when she was travelling and away from her typewriter. Almost all of Brown's are handwritten on both sides of blank note paper (about A5 size). Frame also corresponded several times with Wonner: for example in late December 1970, just prior to her return to the USA, she wrote as Dame F.C. [Frame Clutha] to Dame M.M. [Mary Margaret].

Our primary aims with the layout of the letters have been to preserve their integrity and show the relationship of Frame's images to her words by placing them as close as possible to their place in the original text—several facsimiles of this interplay are included. As the images vary considerably in scale, we have resized them so that, for the readers' benefit, they relate more seamlessly to the text. This book, of course, can only be a reasonably faithful and coherent translation of the visceral materiality of the original letters that encompass many kinds and sizes of paper, writing methods and image production.

Frame generally wrote her letters in orthodox sentences with punctuation and spelling according to the standard of the time. We have formatted the paragraphs with regular indents in a way that was not possible with a typewriter, but otherwise we have made minimal edits. We have preserved the lines of asterisks that Frame and Brown jokingly called 'stars'. Some collages that were less striking than the best, or that were somewhat obscure from a present-day perspective, have been omitted.

Frame variably dated and addressed her letters—fewer than half are dated with the day's date. She sometimes wrote her full or partial current address and sometimes her forwarding address. We have standardised the heading to each letter so as to give the location, the exact date or month, and any comment she may have added. For clarity's sake, Frame's verse is rendered in italics while other verse is within quote marks. Footnotes are used sparingly. This is a reader's edition. *Jay to Bee* is not an academic work but is the uncensored revelation of a great writer's imagination at play.

Denis Harold
29 January 2016

USA

November 1969 to March 1970

Dear Bill,

1. MacDowell November 15 1969 (postcard)

The Management of Peedauntals Ltd thanks you for your visit to the East & reminds you that it wishes to keep close to its valued client. It moves shortly to lonely premises in Baltimore. Singing opera you need never be peedauntally underprivileged or under-achieved with our late model Peedauntals. You are missed greatly around the factory especially by the management who sends this postcard.

?

2. November 17

Dear Bill,

The day in Boston was strange and sad and vivid, from the drive in sunlight and clear air and the arrival over Mystic Bridge near Storrow (I thought it was *Sorrow*) Street to the bizarre farewell in the lounge of the Y.W.C.A. In my mind it is like a lived piece of fiction or film. I can see you in your black coat and black cap standing larger than life like a monument against the clear blue sky, as if I had been a child gazing upward; Elnora like a figure from a painting in her bright strong colours and dark face; the scarf-stripes gashing downwards; Jo with a kind of pearl-coloured vivacity; I, squirrel-bulky in my coat, clutching my sweater as a child away from home clutches its favourite toy; the smiling man with the brief-case; the city benevolent because we were there. And all day was a journey with the four of us performing some kind of ritual dance, person to person to person to person, a long long journey to say au revoir; it would have been impossible to say goodbye.

I have never known such a mysterious sad strange day. It was like waiting to be executed, with the execution taking place in a scene from a painting. The lounge. The sailors sprawled asleep in the chairs. The tight-lipped woman guarding the messages and keys in their brown boxes—the striped shadows the striped scarf the striped sailors. And then, after the time in the Museum, all the paintings that had accompanied us, the image of them in our minds, their after-image projected mysteriously in the lounge of the Y.W.C.A. Boston.

Well, it was a dream. Was it a dream?

In lighter vein I have uncovered from the secret manuscripts of Emily Dickinson a letter from a blue jay to a bee which reads as follows:

> *B you are gone away!*
> *even au revoir only*
> *was hard to say.*
> *We are lonely.*
>
> *Jo's in New York this week.*
> *We're settled and at work—*
> *the others are mostly back—*
> *your sweater's warm and thick.*
>
> *You'll get my letter, say,*
> *Friday. Reply straightaway*
> *or better, be with me—*
> *Yours, blue J.*

I don't want to embarrass you with these notes; I don't mean to.

J

3. MacDowell November 22

Dear Bill,

I'm relieved to know you're alive and well and living in California. I (and we) were beginning to think you were dead and to mournyia. (and from there, with a swift turn of a phrase she steered into a
   limerick)

> *The pecker of Harrison Kinney*
> *was so excessively skinny*
> *that like a Greek statue*
> *his balls stared back at you*

a. (classical) *Let's unGreek our leak, go Roman with Pliny.*
b. (classical) *as if you were Pallas Athene.*
c. (pseudo-contem porary) *Like matics without their cine.*
d. (vulgar) *'twas a miracle he had had any.*
e. (") *so teeny so meeny so mini.*
f. (novelistic) *How mean is the thorn in our spinney!*
g. (low) *If you were a horse you'd whinny.*
h. (anthropomorphic) *with little eyes, nosy, and chinny.*

How about that?
*****+++++++++++===========###########*****"""""""""
!!!!!!!!!!!!
@@@@@@@@*******++++
&&&&&***++(*+*(+*)

Now you are back on the city scene you might be interested in the model P[eedauntal] which carries with it a special *testimonial* from Al Bean, Moon-Man whose wife uses it. It is our Supermarket P designed for those who must spend time shopping in one supermarket without being able to get past the barrier. It's an audio model. The user can select Snap-Crackle-Pop of breakfast food for Environmental Harmony; Mood Music for unexpected social encounters; and many other sounds which have to be heard to be believed. And remember, it carries a *testimonial* from Al Bean.

It is no mean accomplishment to serve those who now, their minds at peace, need never urinate in the Magic Flute, nor in the Frozen Foods.
******+++++¼¼¼**)))))++++
"&&_%$#'#$%&'( )**'#$%&'( )*+@'#$$$$$$$$%%%%%%_&&&&
*******+*+*+==-=-=

---------===-=-0-

> There once was a fellow named Lionel
> whose pecker was made of vynil
> while trying to warm it
> he did swiftly unform it
> it melted—in fact—that was final.
>
> Who finds himself beholden
> to satisfy poor Eunice Golden

*must measure his tool
with a thirty foot rule*

*The astronaut, Al Bean
said space is a lousy scene
once my orbit of fame
was from coming to came
but now I'm just Al has-been.*

. . . .

Completion of the last line wins a fabulous tour of the Eastern United States. Visit the MacDowell Colony. Play anagrams and other games with the famous

Elnora the Morer

Jo the pro

Janet the never-ban-it.

Mingle with the MacDowell Elite! Journey inside the Biological Time Bomb! Experience James Thurber! Play Losing Sweaters with Simon! Pedal uphill with Jill!

The range of experience is unparalleled. Spend one free morning in Mrs Crocket's pocket!

One evening in the Specially cooled Jaffrey cinema!

Taste Rose Hips, diluted or concentrated.

This brochure cannot describe the numerous attractions of the fabulous Eastern Seabored.

Take a trip to Baltimore, half a mile to a mile from the Maryland State Prison and the Baltimore Jail. Walk down East Madison Street to the broken-down Laundrette and the writing on the wall

*City to city
state to state
boys this girl
don't need no date.*

And more! Get your teargas gun in Johns Bargain Store, the Monumental Five and Ten Cent. Return to the lonely house. Play Schubert on the unplayed Steinway!

. . . . . .*****++++++=====---7786655443322222

Switch on the radiator
human beings must be kept warm.
Open the window on the attainable and the unattainable heaven
Schubert is home.

★★★★★★+++++★★★★★+++++++++++++++++++++

In Schubert despair sits yearning on a bed of roses
a child full of warm dreams and wishes
lies asleep on the rain-rotted boards of a prepared grave.

★★★★★★★★★

Play a Schubert Impromptu for me.
¢¢¢¢★★★★★★★★★★★★★★★★;;;;
And a Beethoven Bagatelle.
★★★★★★★★★★★★★★
and that musical gossip, Bach, writing an aural manual of erotic technique between man and silence/God.
★★★★★★★★★★★★★★★★★
My chickadee is alive and well. I read *Jude the Obscure*, a book of unrelieved gloom and power. May Sarton's *Plant Dreaming Deep* is a wise generous book. I saw her, briefly, in town and said I would write her a letter. I am now reading *The Idiot* (rereading).
★★★★★★★★★★★★★★★★★★★★★★★
Your absence is terrible.
★★★★★★★★★★★★★★★★★★★★★★★★★★★★★★★★★★★★★★★
The baby table is grim without you and—this week—without Jo. Basil has taken command of B.T. John Brooks also sits there. And Simon and/or Harrison who has discovered Eunice Golden who gives him a moon—(heartbeat). Elnora has been dieting & thus satisfying the maternal instincts of Sylvie (Who is, What is etc. After Shakespeare & Schubert) & of Jackie.

The Pornograph is back!

The library feels like a tomb. You gave so much, Bill! Look after yourself.

J

4. Baltimore November 26

Dear Bill,

   Meanwhile, back in Baltimore . . .

It is half past five and I'm in the sitting-room in a rocking chair listening to the pornograph play the eight Schubert Impromptus. Beside me on one of the slabs of marble filched some years ago from an old cemetery being demolished in downtown Baltimore, are the complete piano works of Schubert which I've been reading as I listen. And thus I've spent my first day in Baltimore.

   The house, once an old shop, is two floors and a basement with the old shop window made into a garden. The rooms are filled with paintings, sculptures, objets d'art. In this room there's the black Steinway taking up much of the space, the pornograph with its speaker, chairs, daybed, a tree made of golden wire set in a tub of white river-stones, several paintings including a huge one of the X-Ray of a deformed foetus, an Abyssinian mural, African spears and shields, New Guinea carved heads, a ceiling-high cabinet of loot from Thailand, Mexico, Peru. There are musical instruments from the Pacific Islands; an Australian aboriginal pipe, a digiridoo, about three feet long from which it's hard to get a sound. ('Put in your digiridoo,' my mother used to say to my brother when he was little and his thing was hanging out.) There's also a fine sculpted head of a negro done by a negro sculptor; camel-bells; and odds and ends of various old houses including Scott Fitzgerald's old mantelpiece. (When several old Baltimore homes were being demolished years ago John Money took out a demolition licence which enabled him to visit the sites and take away anything he cared to have.)

   My own small room has three paintings done by one of John M's former close friends; a Thai Buddha; a row of Peruvian fertility charms, little men with erect penises: seven.

   The house has a characteristic smell which I can't quite describe—it's the smell of absence; nobody spends the day or much of the evening here and I suppose all the objects have their special kind of breath and sweat with no human smell to mask it. John M sometimes has people to stay, and sometimes throws a party but for the most part he spends his time in his hospital office trying to solve other people's sex problems.

Now your 'heartbreaker' is being played. I am back in the Savidge Library*.

My last hours at MacDowell were smooth and uneventful. I had turned in my pepper and salt and cutlery the previous day and thus severed my culinary cord. Jo, Elnora, Sylvie (who left after one game, her quota) and I spent the evening playing anagrams at Mansfield. We made a communal limerick about the Australian arrival† (quote—'the moratorium is a communistic plot')

Now Colebrook came from down under
hoping to be rent asunder
but all she could do
was sit on the loo
and make wild Australian thunder.

****

Earlier in the day I had played the pornograph by myself in the library.

*****

Harrison drove me to the bus stop, I went to Boston to find the Museum of Fine Arts is closed on Mondays, I repaired to the Y and enclose the fruits thereof and will not bore you with a recitation of my thoughts.

****

I was sitting on one of the pew-like seats in the Boston station when I looked up and saw Henry Chapin in cold blood and real life standing with a small hazel-nut of a woman, evidently his wife. It was a strange experience. His wife looked quite old, like a kind of permanent measurement of Henry. We stood talking a while and he carried my bags for me. What rule is it that says people must stop 'being' when they leave places like MacDowell where they have freedom to 'be'? Henry said that he missed the life at MacDowell and he frowned as if he had changed lives, as if the one he wears now is cramping and doesn't fit.

Enough of that but it was one of those interesting encounters that stay in mind and return later as fiction.

---

* library at MacDowell

† The writer, Joan Colebrook, who had been born in Australia, had just arrived at MacDowell

★★★★★

It is late in the evening now, half-past ten. John M and one of his research assistants, Paul, came home and had a small meal and a large drink and went back to the hospital and won't be back until past midnight. While they are away I put an iron bar across the door as this is a wild neighbourhood with bottles being smashed around outside and a few street fights.

I wish you and Jack Daniels would walk in now to say hello.

I wonder how your work is going.

I'm wearing your sweater to shreds.

★★★★★★   ★★★★★   ★★★★★★

It is now Thanksgiving Day, half-past ten in the morning and I am back in the sitting-room. I have played the pornograph, softly, so as not to disturb my host who is working on a paper in the adjoining room. I have been sorting out my MacDowell writings ready for retyping and I come across lines such as

> *in the sour taste of morning*
> *we shovel bran-bits into our mouths*
> *and look out of the window at the trees*
> *whose defeat is showing.*

Doggerel.

It is hot, airless, quiet here. I wish I could say hello to you.

★★★★★   ★★★★★★★###

As stylistic relief I enclose a little clean pornography.

Now back to the heartbreakers.

J

5. Baltimore November

Y.W.C.A. revisited.

THE PIONEER · YWCA
410 STUART STREET
BOSTON, MASSACHUSETTS 02116
All lights and dildos out by midnight.

****

A marksman without comparison
was our midnight cowboy Harrison.
    With his weapon uptight
      he'd shoot all night
at Eunice Golden's garrison.

**********! !

Though the women desired to gorge
at the smithy of Andrew St. George
    there wasn't a doubt
    his furnace was out
and he had no tools in his forge.

****

Though I'm painter rather than pieman
this menu is tempting, said Simon.
    Balls cantaloupe,
    crème de cunt soup
Crocket's casseroled hymen.

****

A writer named Basil the Gloom
kept waiting and waiting for doom.
    When it came, 'It's a boy!'
    he cried with joy.
'Now who's been fucking whom?'

****

6. Baltimore November

From the factory to you untouched by human hand.
****

A frightened young tailor of Boston
whose needle had melted the frost in
a lady's French seam
cried, This is extreme,
It's haystacks that needles get lost in!

The lady who lay with the tailor
had read Roth and Norman Mailer
but could not catch on
where the needle had gone
while the tailor grew paler and paler.

This experience is bewitching,
My needle keeps poking and pitching,
I'd never have sewn
such a seam on my own
and how happily I am stitching!

At last as the light was growing
there dispersed the 'cloud of unknowing',
the dawn it is coming
the lady said humming,
I too said the tailor still sewing!

7. Baltimore November

Dear Bill,

Another letter from my supply, just to say hello as if you were not absent and to try to make news of no news except it may snow tonight and outside I hear the sound of dogs that sound like wolves and a wind snarling around the house. I'm up in my small room where I've moved everything as I've decided to work here instead of in the basement. The room looks out over the small backyard with a garden as big as a cemetery plot, and beyond that an alley, then a school with its high encircling fence of concrete topped with pieces of broken glass. Beside the house is another alley and across from that another school, similarly forbidding, with a high wire fence which, of course, the children manage to climb to play in the yard as they have nowhere else to play. The lights are bright in the alley and cast a white glare on the pavement as if snow had been falling.

Did you know that Edgar Allan Poe who lived in Baltimore collapsed in the street and was taken dying to one of the big hospitals, and that one of his stories about a howling dog is based on a legend of howling wolves from one of the Baltimore Cemeteries?

I have just written to May Sarton saying a few words about her book; hoping that I didn't sound false, because I'm inclined to be so self-conscious about everything I say (less about what I write) that my words seem to turn to oatmeal and dust. I sent her a cat, and I'm sending you one too, though I didn't know I would until I began this letter. It's a beautiful cat.

The dogs howl again. In the daytime I never see them but at night they howl especially when the wind is whining and snarling.

It feels like a prison here. I find the day passes without my doing much work yet I cannot account for the hours. John Money usually goes off to his work at half-past eight and has been coming home at a quarter past one in the morning and though I need not stay up, I do, because there's a heavy iron bar I put against the door and I have to be awake to remove it. I miss the outside world of MacDowell! Theoretically, I have all day and evening to work without interruption, entirely on my own; and yet the hours go by remote from me without my making any impression on them: it is most curious.

Some time during the day I play the pornograph, usually in the morning as soon as John M has gone to work, and then around six-thirty in the evening. One evening I read a medical journal in which Daudet, Heine, De Maupassant were diagnosed as having had syphilis (sp?) and the extracts from Daudet's Diary and the Goncourt Journal were nightmarish. In his last days De Maupassant had a terrible sense that his thoughts were escaping from his head and abandoning him and he used to wander about the hospital where he was confined asking if anyone had seen his thoughts. And then he felt that his face was escaping from him, and his smile and frown—Have you seen my smile?

These are fit topics for Basil the Gloom . . .

Enough for now, on this grim note. Another instalment tomorrow. First, extempore,

> *A psychologist named John Money*
> *once combed his tool with honey*
> > *when it erected*
> > *the bees objected*
> *but the beekeeper thought it funny.*

Goodnight.

THURSDAY.

Nice to get your letter today, Bill. I'll hold off posting this for a few days otherwise you won't know whether you're *going or coming* with all my hellos. You'll be pleased to know that I've just sold *three dozen* deformed foetuses as Christmas hampers; and all I did was lift the iron bar from the door, unchain the chain, unlock the inner door, open it, unlock the outer door, and, foetuses in hand announce, Lovely Christmas hampers, lovely deformed foetuses seventy-five cents apiece. Truly, I didn't know there was such a market for them; they went like hot cakes, and here I am having earned as much or twice as much as I get for a poem. On the other hand the Peedauntals are terribly slack. No-one in Baltimore is interested. I'm thinking maybe of Rental Peedauntals, though the drycleaning and wet-cleaning costs would be astronomous (anonymous and astronomical as they are always cleaned in secret).

*******   ***** FIVE STARS FOR COMFORT

Alas there is no record of the Schubert Sonata in B flat major but the music is here! I've managed by picking out a few chords to know which one it is—it's magnificent; hearing even a few chords one feels as if one's inside is being torn out. It's a new experience for me to hear sounds like this so close to the source. In my brief term of learning the piano as a thirteen-year old (and we didn't even have a piano at home) I learned 'Puck' (which sounds nice and dirty), 'Robin Adair', 'Londonderry Air',

A Curious Story, The Waltz from the Opera of Faust, the Chopin Prelude which goes de/dee de de ??????? Wagner's Star of Eve, Handel's Largo, and a piece called The Shepherd Boy, which was prefaced by the lines, 'Like some vision of far off times lonely shepherd boy/

What song art thou singing in thy youth and joy?'

That was the end of my private musical education. Music (i.e. singing only) was a big thing at school with a festival each year in which little-medium-sized-big-bigger girls sang 'Oh have you seen my lady go down the garden singing' and 'Where'er you walk' and played Moment Musical, Fantasy Impromptu, Marche Militaire, various lullabys, the Moonlight Sonata—*all day.*

****

Another instalment next week.

******

As I was saying it's a new experience for me to hear music so close. The music of all the pieces I ever played had 'safe' sounds, though one or two phrases were a bit shattering; it was fairly safe and neat and self-contained; plaintive and poetic in parts; but each chord was not so clearly part of a tremendous whole. Oh My! (as Elizabeth Ames of Yaddo used to exclaim).

So you see how my MacDowell experience affected me! One of the ways, at least.

*****   *****   *****   *****
*****   *****   *****   *****

FOUR STARS NO TV IN ROOM

****   ****   ****
***   ***   ***

THREE STARS NO BATHROOM OR TV

****   ***   *****

Glad you liked the Y limericks. I sent them to Jo and Elnora too, and today had a brilliant letter from Jo, and I'll go down in history as being driven to despair by her brilliance. It's snowing in New Hampshire! Maybe it's just as well I'm not there as I'd be writing verse about the snow. Yes, Elnora snored at the Y and thus will go down in history. She made a noise like a factory with all its machines working. I was in such a state of shock at having said au revoir to you that I didn't mind but Jo kept whispering urgently to her, while outside the contractors decided to get to work in the middle of the night on the new parking lot they are building near the Y. We were all pretty much in a state of shock, I think, and the temperature in the room was eighty-five and the radiators hissed all night (they didn't really, I'm just inventing this), and before we went to sleep we had one of those confessional chats that women have when they're taking off their make-up and fixing their hair, their glass eyes, their false teeth; and washing their dildos.

     ★★X ★★X

NO MEALS, NO TV NO BATHROOM.

★X   ★   ★   ★

ROOM ONLY AND BOARD PINE OR WALNUT
GROAN BONUS INFLATABLE
PRESIDENT KENNEDY OR CHOICE WHICH MUST BE
MADE WHEN BOOKING
??????????????????

The moonlit evenings, the stars and the palms sound like Auckland New Zealand in the summer; with beach not far away. I had that impression too from the light in your paintings. The light in Dunedin is luminous, slightly blue like snow-light, clear and untouchable, sometimes hostile—what nonsense this is but this is what it seems to me. The light in the subtropical north is more invading, intimate, catastrophic; diffused yet the whole daylight is so brilliant one is constantly blinking and closing one's eyes against it.

★★★★★★

★★★★★+++++++++++++++++++++++++++
 &&&&&&&&&&&&&&&&&&&&&&&&

FRIDAY.

I'm sending you a New Zealand quarterly of five years ago. I have something in it—a part of a series N.Z. writers were doing called *Beginnings*.

 I feel less homesick when I read your letters.

 Blah

 You will know this limerick?

> *Young man, said the countess at tea*
> *Is it true you fart when you pee?*
> *I replied with some wit*

> '*Do you fart when you shit?*
> *If you do then you're one up on me.*'

I didn't make this up, it's in a book. I'm sure we should get our literary gems printed somewhere, even where you suggest, and you, certainly, should make the illustrations.

Goodbye for now.

> *A parking lot near the Y?*
> *I'm afraid that I'm much too shy.*
> *A quarter a time*
> *is a swindling shime*
> *it's far too cheap at the pri*

That limerick shows how my battery has run out!

J

DECEMBER

8. Baltimore December 1

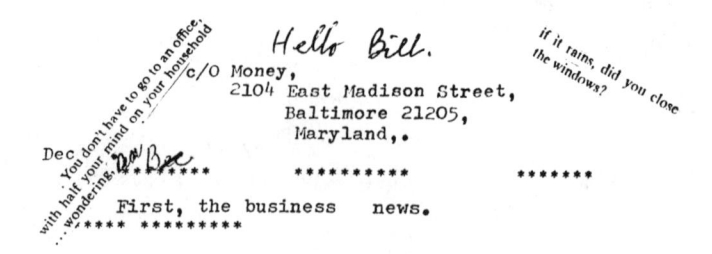

Hello Bill.

c/o Money,
2104 East Madison Street,
Baltimore 21205,
Maryland,.

You don't have to go to an office.
You don't have your mind on your household
with half your mind wondering.

Dec **** ********

if it rains, did you close the windows?

********** *******

First, the business news.

Dear Bee,

First, the business news.

We decided to adopt the conservative approach: to call for and print selected testimonials with photographs if possible, in a nation-wide advertising campaign. The response so far is fair-good although we expect a rise in sales towards the Christmas Season. We are glad that our clients on the West Coast are solidly behind us and we affix a sample of our advertising technique.

> We poured everything we know into a new kind of course
> which trains you at home in your free time. You begin with the fundamentals

> "Your training paid off. I've had four children"

> "Your Course helped me"

> They started

> Very carefully.
> Very beautifully.
> And they have been doing it for 178 years.

> You may. But there is no obligation.

******* ***************** **************

The paintings are beautiful. I can't decide which is my favourite as my preference changes. I had *Ride in the Desert* and *Pedestrian Crossing* propped where I could see them. *Ride in the Desert* is so fluid, poetic and full of light that falls not, as in many paintings, where the artist chooses it shall fall but where the light itself decides and that means of course that the conspiracy of painter and light is total—one becomes the other; maybe this sounds silly.

I'm not a painter, mister, but I know what I like and what I feel. I remember I used to think that people's thoughts came startlingly out of the back of their head and when I suggested this I was laughed at; but how pleased I was many years later to read in a Chekhov story that when a person has his back to you, if you know him, you know the thoughts from glancing at the back of his head—well, not thoughts, feelings. One knows the rider here as one knows the character in a good novel and one sees so much in the back view and shape. I like the way you treat people and their environment as equals, as beings with no barriers* [footnote: Without barriers natural digestion, with barriers, cannibalism.] between them. This painting is sad, I think, but it's also full of the bliss of being in a world where man, rock, tree, sky spring from the same source and are untroubled by trying to separate themselves, rather feeding one from the other. This is in all the paintings in the catalogue (I mean for me) with sometimes a suggestion that plants, rocks, deserts were in the world first and have the right to change man more than he has the right to change them, and the form of change they impose is to make man become them.

The Pedestrian is quite a menacing story. From one angle the hills and slopes resemble benign capes that will protect the pedestrian where man and his machines never will. Yet in another light or view (I felt this after I had looked at the painting for some time) there is a grim suggestion—Look at the pedestrian taking such care in crossing the road and avoiding the traffic when the real terror is in the hills that seem to be following, to overtake and engulf.

There is this movement in all the paintings; nothing is still; nothing is now; it's all a swirl of yesterday and tomorrow. For instance *The White Dog* makes one (me) feel that the woman was sitting quietly reading when her right breast suddenly became a little nipple-nosed white dog while she pretended not to notice, while the white dog in its suddenly being claims all the attention.

Well—I could go on and on in this way but I'll give you a rest, and not mention the other paintings though I like them all and I love having them, or likenesses of them.

[in margin: *take no notice of this crazy stuff*]

✶✶✶✶✶✶   ✶✶✶✶✶✶✶

////¢¢¢¢¢¢¢¢¢¢¢¢¢

333333333333

Meanwhile back in Baltimore . . . I continue to use the pornograph as there is a small collection of records, and to sort my papers including one suitcase full of script from the novel I wrote this year and when I see it, so much of it, typed and retyped and reduced I am overpowered—now—with the amount of work I did then.

I'm hoping to go to New York at the end of December and will stay with Elnora some days before I go to Yaddo on the 5th January. I think Jo and Mark are coming to town then, also. I'd give anything for a quick trip to California to restore me before the Yaddo days begin; and with an advance coming up I could make myself afford it.??!!????

        ★   ★   ★   O

     star   star   star   moon

No limericks this time. They're no fun on your own. Your Dunedin and Golden attempts were perfect—what talents we MacDowellites exhibit when there is no-one looking.

    Blue Jay

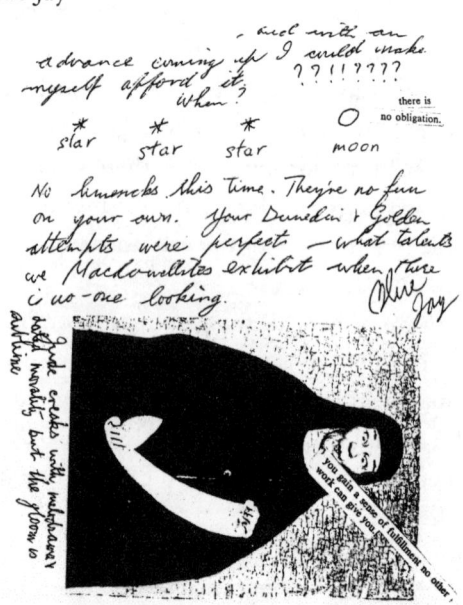

9. Baltimore December

Dear literate live oak, to continue my story,

It's half-past five in the evening and I'm in the sitting room sitting with my typewriter before me, the Steinway and the foetus on my left, the front door on my right, and I've just finished packing a tiny Care Parcel, emergency rations for you to use in the Earthquake or Tidal Wave; and outside it is snowing.

The flight was surprisingly calm considering that the plane's engines failed on take-off and we were transferred to another plane and then chased by an eighty-five mile an hour wind all the way to Baltimore. The pilot who was old with white hair and probably with furlined arteries, made a marvellous job of flying and landing. I dozed, whiskey-soured, most of the way, with daydreams of my wonderful week in Santa Barbara, and though I've been in Baltimore nearly two days now I refuse to relinquish Pacific Time.

A letter from May Sarton was waiting for me. She's had the 'flu and was feeling groggy, and maybe a bit ethereal: she said nice things about my writing. Elnora also has had a kind of 'flu—I phoned her yesterday to cheer her up by telling her I had a gift for her from you. Also I had a note from Charles Neider who is actually back home after his whirlwind visit to Antarctica.

Last night I played Funeral Music by Hindemith and the Brahms Clarinet Quintet, and today I bought a book to teach me the notes and I'm up to page 30, new broom sweeping clean, and it's an interesting exercise in self-knowledge, a disillusionment to find that as usual I want everything for nothing and at once. There's one of the 'Cinq Doigts' pieces by Stravinsky here.

Letter is now interrupted. John Money has a visitor from Sumatra and he has just phoned to say they are arriving.
★★★★★★#######++++++++++
It is now ten p.m. and I've 'retired' to my little room. I tried to call Jo at MacDowell this evening but they must have been so busily eating they heard nothing but their jaws. So I'm sitting here in my bed wishing I were in the world of the live oaks.

The East seems oxygen-starved and murky after California with the blue skies and the butterflies and beautiful Ned with his fur like feathers. Wherever you live, I think it is naturally a place of many blessings, just because you are there.

Forgive this disconnected (as usual) letter, I am tired, and the clock is ticking in my ear, the phone is ringing but everyone is asleep, everyone is tired, the boardinghouse is full tonight, for the visitor is staying a few days, ah how my battery is worn; it comes from not having had my Vitamins! And to make things worse all the people from the Peedauntal Factory have gone off for the holidays just when a big order has come in from both the White House and the MacDowell colony and I'm nearly crazy trying to decide priorities, whether it's better for their work and their country for artists or for statesmen to have to pee down their leg. And worst of all, Nixon wants a Peedauntal in the shape of Santa Claus. I know it's not very businesslike of me but I've never really studied how the stupid things are made, I've just let the foreman and the workers take over, and now I'm racking my brains to make a paper pattern and threading needles and even trying to knit purl and plain to turn out something. I do know a tailor in Boston who might help . . . except that his needles are apt to go astray.

More of this at the crack of dawn (so to speak) tomorrow before I post this and your Care Parcel.
★★★★★★★★★★★%%%&&&&&&
Dawn has broken. I'm posting this immediately
        Love to Paul & Ned & yourself—   J

       ('to divide is not to take away')

10. Baltimore December

Dear Bill,

Hello. It's midday and I've just had a boiled egg for lunch. John M and his Sumatran(?) visitor who has spent the past five years studying at Michigan for his Physics Doctorate, have gone to Washington and from there to a round of Christmas cocktail parties which I declined, as I remembered the boredom of the one and only medical staff party I went to—and of course there was the old problem of describing how long and wide is New Zealand . . . some blockage prevents me from remembering. It seems that when people are 'in' the world of an establishment some part of their mental territory becomes a waste land that unlike a normal wilderness that becomes a sanctuary for ideas and feelings 'of passage', can support no form of life.

I miss you.

I'm playing a Bach flute suite on the pornograph . . . and now I am playing Fugue in C Minor.

I've nothing to say in this letter except that my thoughts are in the little house in Hermosillo Drive and I'm permanently on Pacific Time.

★★★★★★@@@@@@½½½½½+++++++++++++++++=====
------⊔⊔⊔⊔⊔⊔⊔⊔⊔⊔⊔⊔⊔⊔⊔⊔⊔⊔⊔⊔⊔⊔⊔⊔⊔⊔⊔⊔⊔⊔⊔⊔
         ⊓⊓⊓⊓⊓⊓⊓⊓⊓⊓⊓⊓⊓⊓⊓⊓⊓⊓⊓⊓⊓⊓⊓⊓⊓⊓⊓⊓⊓⊓⊓⊓

No limericks today.

$$⊔⊔⊔' '++' ' ' ' '
  ⊓⊓⊓

A small parody.

> *We are the front-end loaders*
> *we are the movers of earth,*
> *wheel-deep in drainage odours*
> *assisting at bungalow's birth.*
> *We are the grim foreboders*
> *of a treeless tasteless earth.*
> =======+++++++++==========

You will be having lunch now, sitting outside under the butterflies, and Paul will be there, and Ned will be lounging around with his fur sticking out—I've never seen a cat whose fur sticks out in so many directions at once, he looks like a black and white thistle-ball, the kind that we used to call 'robbers', and 'one o'clocks'. I suddenly remember that in my little house in Dunedin I'm not entirely catless—there's a neighbour's cat comes to visit me, and when I am downstairs doing my washing in the oldfashioned washing-tubs the cat climbs on the edge of the tub and hits at the water with his paws. I thought at first it was a materialized dream-cat and I was disappointed when I discovered it belonged to a neighbour.

I'm looking forward to Yaddo where I shall be able to walk outside in the woods in the snow and I expect that my new novel will be filled with snow. I am comforted and enclosed by my preliminary vision and I shall try desperately to keep it whole while I reach out to find the words but I know from experience its depressing fragility. Did you ever read a story by William Saroyan, 'The Sunday Zeppelin', in which some children see an advertisement trying to sell a zeppelin with an illustration of two children away up in the sky inside their zeppelin, calling out, Goodbye World. And when they send for the actual thing it turns out to be made of tissue-paper and it tears the first time they try to use it.

++++%%%%★★★★★★★★★

Lolo (the Sumatran visitor) said that for many many years his tribe was forbidden to make any music. Music and dancing were exclusively religious and when the Dutch missionaries came to the country, as they forbade the practice of animism they also forbade the practice of music, and dancing. One can't believe that the missionaries were entirely obeyed, but the story is still of desolation and murder.

★★★★★★★★★★★★★★★★★★★★★★

No limericks today.

‹‹‹‹‹‹‹‹‹‹‹‹‹‹‹‹‹‹‹‹‹‹‹‹‹

I look often at your and Paul's catalogue—I wish I had seen all the photographs in the gallery. More of this in another letter: I mean that I am trying to describe their effect in words, just because I like to do this. I hope an angel continues to guard your work.

★★★★★★★★★★★★

I'm enclosing a Dunedin picture, not very good. It's near where I live.

J

11. until 30th December, c/o Money, (Baltimore) from January 3rd until February 18th, c/o Yaddo after that whoopee.

Dear Bill,

Hello again. It was wonderful to hear your voice in the wilderness. It's very early morning, outside is cold with a sprinkling of snow with more promised, inside is too warm.

John Money is getting ready to fly away for Christmas. His Sumatran friend flew away yesterday—he was a nice gentle quiet man, a nuclear physicist who will return in a couple of years to his village and tribe and primitive living. I wonder what will become of him. Indirectly, you have made his life more fruitful, Bill. I've been spending much time listening to music and tinkering (ghastly word but accurate description) at the piano—I do miss your music (and you) terribly—and Lolo joined in the interest, and now he is returning to his midWestern University and its pretty lonely life, he is going to study the piano in his spare time.

I have received what is usually called the 'Yaddo information'. It is so full of dire warnings and promises of peril that I wonder if this is not a psychological device to prepare the artists to do their best work?

Quote:

in this bad weather it is important for guests to get there no later than three. Taxis, in bad driving weather, often refuse to come inside the grounds and this makes for real difficulties . . . we ask guests who are in the early stages of a cold to please delay their arrival until there is no danger to other guests . . .

And so on. A dangerous place, Yaddo. I shall have a little more privacy than when I was there before as they are giving me an artist's (painter's) studio outside.

I've had an eloquent fan letter from a French student who is writing a thesis on my work. It is hard to know what to say in reply, particularly as one always has in mind the perfection of Rilke's replies to the young poet. This young man is now inspired to become a writer. He asks me—'If you could send me an advice which could be put across the untrue and traffic-jammed roads of literature, pointing to the darkest lanes leading to the essential and deepest part of man it would be a landmark, a milestone, a witness tree in my future . . .' What can one say to that?

I've also had a letter from the representative of the 'anonymous business group' in New Zealand, reminding me that my budget seems very strictly minimal . . .

*******   *********

I'm still on Pacific Time. Ewig.*

★★★★★★★   ★★★★★★★★★★

I played a Hindemith Horn Concerto; and of course every day I play [in margin: Lili Kraus plays it!] a little Schubert. The only Sonata here, the A Major is beautiful. I play the Impromptus over and over and each time I discover so much in them and I change my allegiance from one to the other. They are true poems. Instead of having total allegiance to the feelings aroused by the music I now feel moved by special groups of notes and by the silence between changes from one note-mass to another. Well, they're all heartbreakers. I remember that when my sister's small son began to learn to play the piano he said, Mummy why do my eyes get all prickly when I play the piano and hear the music?

★★★★★★

Down with sentiment. Up with so much.

★★

More later. I must wash.

I'll even look around for *The Heart of Darkness* . . .

I have just received a cable from N.Z. telling me that *Pocket Mirror* has won the yearly award for literary achievement—200 dollars.

Blah blah

> What are you doing what are you
> painting how is the piano are there
> still butterflies is the new fir
> tree growing does the Pacific
> still flow Ned likewise
> are you alive and real is my
> constant communication too
> constant say hello to Paul
> who is very wise have you
> had your laughter ration
> every day
>
>   That was a lovely walk
> we 3 had in the hills among

---

* German word for eternity—common in Rilke and Goethe

the mountain lions and the
live oaks and I think often
of it and I like your paintings on the wall. The nude group in
a circle on a hill top—is it twilight

12. as from Yaddo, but really now from Baltimore where the wind is raging outside

Hello Bill,

    I was very happy to get the letters and to know that your work is—well I don't know how to finish that sentence . . . I like to hear about it and I really do study the catalogues I have here. I agree with most of what Jo says in her write-up, except the idea that it is 'devoid of the tragic view of life': for instance the painting, *Muscatine Diver*, is full of agony and helplessness. There is the trust that Jo writes of but it is the trust of man in his own helplessness, and surely this is a view into or out of a place of tragedy . . . don't mind my inflated meanderings. I feel this, though. I suppose you have to bear with what people say of your work. Remember we were talking of Francis Bacon and his distorted mirror-faces? It occurs to me that they're also people caught in a world without gravity (g), in wind-tunnels of outer space—are there winds in outer space?

    In your paintings people grow like plants out of their surroundings, they *are* their surroundings, and as with the woman and the dog (this is how I see that) they divide into different species and still be part one of the other. In the scene of the woman and the deer the woman is the deer and the deer is the tree.

    In Paul's paintings the objects seem to be gifts or visitors out of the sky, perfectly formed as the egg is perfectly formed, a life-gift or visitor. Gifts stay or are retrieved by the giver; visitors leave. Paul traps them in bottles and glasses and in a human skull; in postcards and books and sometimes just in an area of colour—or on a crucifix: I think this is very exciting.

Now read on:

Christmas came and went. I was alone in the house with a cheesecake and every few hours I hacked at it until it gradually diminished. I enjoyed the quietness. Jo called from South Hadley and as usual had a delightful tale—how Rural Violence trapped her in the basement when she was hanging out her undies, offered her a huge glass of whisky which she drank and then she was drunk for three days . . . Elnora called from Philadelphia where she was surrounded by people, I think, a nephew of eight and a niece of four. She seemed to be engaged in playing chasing games and my imagination quailed at the thought of her rushing up and down the stairs chasing and being chased, as she said was happening. I'm going to New York on Tuesday and I'll be with Elnora until I'm due at Yaddo on January 5th.

I look forward to getting a New Year portrait! Mine may be delayed—well I don't know how long they take to print & I haven't put in my choice yet.

You're right about F. in the W. (my way of saying *lewdly* Faces in the Water). I mean it's written & that's that. Were I writing it today I should make many changes. You may not believe this but I purposely omitted much & 'toned' it down so as not to make it too grim. I haven't read it for years but I remember the people I wrote of and thinking of them from time to time I am still moved by their plight. I think that was hardest—to see so much *suffering*.

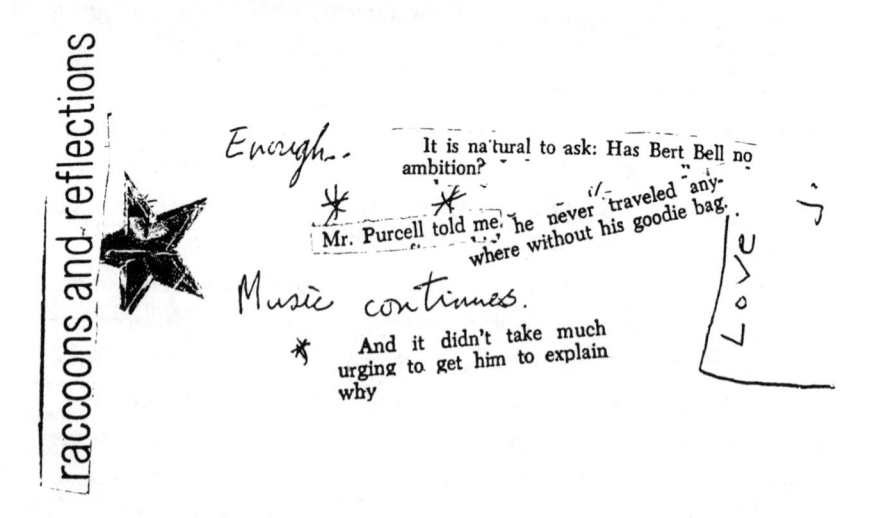

Enough.

It is natural to ask: Has Bert Bell no ambition?

Mr. Purcell told me he never traveled anywhere without his goodie bag.

Music continues.

And it didn't take much urging to get him to explain why

raccoons and reflections

Love

Enough.

I'm sending you a copy of the story that will be in the *New Yorker* some time, I don't know when. The funny marks, including the E at the top are merit marks, I suppose, & E is lowest. They're holding it because it is not a fashionable story—I think.

   ★ ★ ★ ★

O to be in Santa Barbara, not in Baltimore,
for whoever wakes in Santa Barbara sees through the patio door,
dear cunning Ned about to shower
his urine on the paradise flower.

And after morning when mid-morning follows
& the vitamins have been taken in swift swallows,
see where the apricot-cat becomes a menace
to Ned as he contemplates the stones of Venice.

 Love

  J

   ★ ★ ★ ★

JANUARY/YADDO

The arrival of Janet's muse, part man, part woman, part bird, part cat, made in a collage drawing game.

"Thank you for the inspired drawing of my muse . . ." [Letter 19]*

---

* Illustration based on a parlour game that involved several participants drawing on a folded sheet of paper.

13. Elnora's Place January 1970 (handwritten)

Dear Bill,

Your curious (black & white) drawing arrived today and shall be appropriately framed whereupon you & Paul & collaborators go down in history. Your letter was a delight, also the communication from the Alters Art Gallery, also the extraordinary evidence that Ned is beginning to express himself in English & that his number work (as his calendar sensitivity) is commendable. The rewards of your training him must be uplifting to your body and soul.

Meanwhile I write from New York in a bit of a daze and haze from Elnora's womb-like apartment where she lies most hours enveloped in sleep, in human hibernation—I guess the only way to resist the world & its pressures. We've had fun, in her waking hours; her New Year meal was delicious & it was when I was sodden with black-eyed peas, corn bread & salt pork hocks, collard greens, that I whispered my timid hello into the N.Y.—L.A. telephone line. O to be in . . . . etc.

My publisher has given me a copy of one of his magnificent books, for Christmas: *Les Très Riches Heures du Duc de Berry* & as Braziller was the only one in his office I was able to help myself to some of my books which he fetched from the store room: 2 *Pocket Mirrors*. I gave one to Elnora. Would you like one? And another I'll give to Jo. Next week I get the galleys of my 'shocking, wildly comic, lyrical, tragic,' etc. etc. etc. book & if I can I will treat the editor who wrote the blurb with my new kind of Death Ray—I'm awfully sorry but the bottom has fallen out of the Peedauntal Business and I can't for the life of me understand why, or what happened, or whether it was my business acumen that failed or simply the cheap material used in the manufacture of the peedauntals.

I've gone into the Death & Thought-Ray business, quite modestly, and I still offer the deluxe limited line of Peedauntals. My Death Ray will be useful for editors who write blurbs and, later, for critics. It may help at Yaddo also. I know it's not a very original product but my advisers recommend (through a spokesman of course) that I be conservative in my business interests. Thought-Rays, Feeling Rays, Death-Rays have (apparently) a steady market. So far, I'm the only one I know who uses them—at least my model which has many extras & a hi-fi tuning device & people-selector. It can fit, of course, like any small object or animal—say, raccoons & suchlike—into any pocket or recess & that's the beauty of it, the users say.

 ★   ★   ★

Enough of news of the dull work-a-day world. Here is a curious (handwritten) verse.

> *He wore gold braid. His blood shone*
> *like urine in the sun. He was afraid*
> *of water, fire and heart transplant,*
> *of mountains higher than seven thousand feet.*
> *Yet unbuttoning his handmade overcoat,*
> *he rode furiously down Thrillstreet.*

 ★   ★   ★   ★   ★

New York has a special chill in its air, & skies today were high, clear and blue & I rode the bus downtown and back & that's the local colour and now I'll sleep for it is past midnight.

 ★   ★   ★   ★   ★   ★

Elnora gave me her autobiographical manuscript to read. It's very moving in its detailed record of the indifference & insensitivity shown by otherwise 'nice' people, & its account of her father's struggle to die.

 ★   ★   ★   ★   ★   ★

These stars represent my broken thought-processes. Elnora's family is arriving from Philadelphia today & her daughter will be home too & peaceful (?) Yaddo beckons.

 ★   ★   ★   ★   ★   ★

I'm posting Jo's rock (glittering) to her today. As Elnora may have told you she loved the ring.

 ★   ★   ★   ★   ★   ★   ★

a typographical fixation

 ★   ★   ★   ★

Love to Paul

 ★   ★   ★   ★

Love to Ned the sly one

 ★   ★   ★   ★   ★   ★   ★   ★

 ★   ★   These are also suns and pine-needles and mutilated spokesmen, cords of wood & thistledown-heads & tumbleweed going nowhere. I had in mind to write you a slick New York verse ('I sit in one of the dives of 52nd St.' W.H.A.) and may, from Yaddo where I will read the Mallarmé poem also.

[handwritten: blug xx!⊙≡feeling-ray at work.   J.]

14. New York January 4 (postcard)

This is a reminder from Elnora and me.
    Written in haste. More from Saratoga Springs, in detail.
    Nice phone call but phones scare me.

[handwritten: Hello. ☺—smile. J.]

15. Yaddo January 6

Hello Bill,
    First, the monotonous theme without variations—I miss you, miss you.
    Next, I've just disposed of my lunch, at eight forty-five a.m., and look forward to a long day's work with perceptions sharpened by increasing hunger, or that is how it should happen, except that some time during the day I'll probably fall asleep on the cane chaise longue, blanketed and sheeted and pillowed, in the corner of this vast light studio. Oh, I am so privileged—I have a wall thermostat to adjust room heat; I have five tables and one small long low table, chairs, book cases, an adjustable easel of the kind that Hyde Solomon told me he introduced to Yaddo (he has been a kind of adviser for many years on art, artists and equipment) and another easel like the one you had in your studio at MacDowell where you could pin sheets of paper to work on; numerous lights from all angles; a washbasin and john/can or whatever you call it, with, so far, no mice working lace patterns on the toilet paper.
    You could be here painting.

Over in West House I have a nice bedroom and bathroom with my window looking out on the woods a few feet away and the deep deep snow—I walk through snowbanks five feet high to get to my studio fifteen yards from the house. The snow squeaks like icing sugar when you walk on it, and it is full of sparkles.

There are six guests here, none of whom I've met before: a raving old man who arrived yesterday and spoke in a loud voice throughout dinner (served at one table where the Secretary and the Director and his wife also dine); a smooth dark plump man who described his son's third birthday and decided the human race will not become extinct (a Basil the Gloom topic hung around the dinner-table), a woman, maybe in her forties, personable, intelligent, dull; another woman, a *Sylvia*, rather like an alternative version of Sylvie—as if there'd been many cast and put out at stations and colonies through the world—she seems more thoughtful and less jovial than the other guest; and a young painter (black) whose first one-man show has just opened in New York. And J.F. Oh for the babies of MacDowell!

Meanwhile, back in New York . . . I enjoyed being at Elnora's place though her constant hibernation is rather alarming and she seems to have got herself a massive escape through sleep and tranquillisers and sleeping pills. I'm quite a keen sleeper myself so I enjoyed the rest, especially after my rather nasty Baltimore life, but I couldn't help worrying about Elnora's condition. I'm hoping she'll be able to get the last fifty pages of her very moving book finished. I think it's good, and real, and it's clearly been harrowing to write. Her daughter, by the way, in answer to my question about what replaces 'groovy' has said, 'out-a-site' is the word. So now you and Paul can be with it, groovy, turned on and in by labelling everything 'out-a-site' . . .

Jo called on my last night at New York and Elnora and I were delighted. Jo said she had been trying to get to Yaddo for March but there's no probable vacancy until May. She would make the place live a lot. I felt pretty depressed to think, suddenly, that as soon ahead as then, and before, I'll be 'out of this world'; it's a grim thought.

Meanwhile, back in Yaddo, I've robbed the poetry shelves and set myself up very comfortably here and I'll be able to enjoy the music on the pornograph and read through Art News that goes back to the early nineteen fifties, and other journals. I've put Ned's photo near, and the little cream-man from South America also stands near—maybe I'm out-a-site but who cares—if you send me your photo I won't display it of course but it would be nice to have . . . rush across and drop it in the Santa Barbara P.O. . . . I have washed, and walked in the sparsely-falling snowflakes. Don't mind my writing letters to you! My thoughts are more often than not in Hermosillo Drive.

The kind of snow falling today is that where the snowflakes are so isolated they don't know what to do except twirl round and round and melt before they land on the pavement, the wind blowing them in a distracted way. I love the grey in the sky.

Goodbye now.

Love J

The photos Basil sent are proofs only and I must write to the photographer for any I want. They're not very good but there will be one or two fair ones. I look forward to your photos, I'm sure they're a good bargain. I'll look around for a cut-out body in exchange.

16. Yaddo January 8 — 518-584-0746 (just in case)*

[footnote: *at 7. – 7.15 p.m. (the time of going to the other room for conversation)]

Dear Bill,

A morning letter. The photos are a delight—you're an angel to send them. Need I say more?
(Breakfast: choice of cereal, raisins, wheat germ. Orange juice. Eggs anyhow. Coffee. Toast etc.)

The 'raving old man' I referred to in my last letter is Kenneth Burke the illustrious critic. He sleeps in the room above me, he's an insomniac, and he has a preference for listening to allnight radio. He has a sly sense of humour, an unusually humble appraisal of his work, a voice that's inclined to explode, and one eye that stays in its place while the other rolls around and around.

Already I've begun my 'count-down' of dinners—only so many left! They're an ordeal. I just can't bear dining in the presence of authorities—in this case the new director and his wife. Everything is so formal, everybody so bloody well-behaved, and after dinner we seem to be expected to go to the small room off the diningroom and sit and make conversation. So far I haven't said a word—oh yes I said one or two last night and regretted them immediately. I almost spoke at dinner when the discussion was about repairing cars and washing machines and so on, the cost, the shoddy workmanship . . . and everyone had spoken—after all, the topic is not intellectually demanding and even MacDowell babies might be expected to speak a line . . . and I had in mind my experience of inserting a new ball-cock into my plumbing at home, and so, with heart beating fast at the contemplation of my daring, I framed, mentally, my opening sentence—'I once spent all day putting in a new ball-cock', but every time an opportunity came for me to contribute I panicked and said nothing and so the Yaddo meal-table never heard of my indelicate experience. Later, as we sat staring at each other in the anteroom, with everyone talking except me, I spoke a sentence. The topic was Marisol whom someone described as a disconcerting person because she would go to a party and sit and never speak all evening. I had been reading an article on the (socalled) 'Tenth Street Painters' and I murmured, too softly for anyone to hear, 'There's a description of her in that article on the Tenth Street Painters'.

'What? What? What did you say? What? What? What?'

Oh my God! I didn't have the courage to speak another sentence so I just mumbled and blushed and resolved never to speak again . . .

(Dinner: Pork chops, apple sauce, whipped creamed potatoes, cauliflower, Brussels sprouts, carrots. Indian pudding and Ice cream. Coffee and cream.)

Two composers are arriving soon. Douglas Addenbrooke (?) and ?? Rorum which means they will have to open the front library where the grand piano is as the only other piano is in the *Pink Room* where one composer will live and work. (There are grand pianos of course in the mansion and two other studios which are all closed for the winter.) The Pink Room is Katrina Trask's former bedroom and overlooks the line of yew trees (I think they're yew) that lead to her grave.

★★★

> *How does it feel, Bee,*
> *now you're immortalized,*
> *so prized*
> *by Emily?*
>
> *A 'burnished carriage' put by.*
> *'Delirious' incense.*
> *A mad correspondence*
> *with Fly?*
>
> *A poetic fling,*
> *Clover, Capitals,*
> *Peeps at pistils,*
> *two wings and a sting?*
>
> *How does it feel, Bee,*
> *to bed a lily?*

We of Saratoga Springs and formerly of MacDowell are glad you're Billy.
★★★★★   ★★★★★★★★★★★★★★★★★★★★   ★★★★★★★★★★★★★★★

> *Bee! Your photos two*
> *arrived. Was saying yesterday*
> *to myself at Yaddo*
> *that they were due—*
>
> *I arrived here this week—*
> *I'm settled and at work—*
> *I'm an Awful Hack*
> *— Not only your sweater's warm and thick—*
>
> *You'll get this letter, say,*
> *next week. Reply,*
> *Bee, over rose-hip tea—*
> *Yours, Jay.*

......★★

I'm shameless.
★★

(Dinner: chicken, cranberry sauce, rice with mushrooms, olives, asparagus, salad and hot rolls. Cream puffs. Coffee and cream.)

I was saving this for my photos but they haven't arrived.

Goodbye for now & el mismo to you and all at 131 H. Drive.

More again soon!

17. Yaddo January 9

Bee, bear with me—you'd better—
for writing you another letter.
(How's your 'burnished carriage', by the way?
Did you get to visit Fly?)
Alas my battery's not in its prime
and I can't keep up this rhyme
—perhaps another time.

I'm sending two scruffy photos—what a bad bargain you're getting after your own magnificent photos. The one of me in the mirror's the only one that turned out O.K., and that's because I'm in shadow. The other is one I took early early in the morning on Grand Central Station after leaving Elnora's and while I was waiting for the train and I'm still half asleep. At least the MacDowell photo gives you a reminder of Bill Brownia, with sweater and cake-tin and monkey. The flower drawing on the extreme right was made by the fifteen-year old son of the poet* who wrote the 'Tom Cat' poem.

To try to make up the difference I'm sending you a few pages I don't want from the proofs of my new novel which I've been correcting. Just a taste.

Now.

Now.

I'm preparing my dedication for this book *Intensive Care*, and I'm thinking of dedicating it to the person who made possible my visit to

---

* James K. Baxter

this country, and the person who will farewell me when I leave. I'm writing to the two people to ask if they mind and whether they want to be initials only or first names or full names.

If the people approve the dedication will read,

To Sue
       or S.M.   who made my visit possible
          or Sue Marquand   or who welcomed me
and   who
      B (you)   or will say au revoir
      (or whatever)
             (I was thinking of saying 'Who will make it difficult to leave' but that might sound too public and horrible, though it's true.)

If you would be pleased rather than embarrassed or unpleasantly apprehensive do let me know how you would like to appear—as one or two initials or in name? Or what?

I want to get you into a dedication withour embarrassing you (or do I mean without embarrassing myself?) and I think this is the way to do it.

Or I could say something like (if you'd rather not be named) To Sue who made my visit possible, and the live oaks who sheltered me . . . and then you would have to explain now and again to the few people who might read my book that you are actually a live oak!

Any objections, ideas, etc?

(Dinner last evening, pot roast, horseradish sauce, green peas; salad and hot rolls (the salad and hot rolls appear every evening; sometimes it is cornbread); apricot whip which is apricots folded into whipped cream and other riches.)

Ned Rorem the composer arrives today. He has been quoted as saying that Yaddo is a luxurious concentration camp where he could neither camp nor concentrate.

I like also his quote about Beethoven and his wife (though I'm sure Beethoven didn't have a wife).

Beeth: Don't leave me darling, you're my inspiration.

Wife: Me your inspiration? That's a laugh!

Even I can read that music! *[musical notation] Ha ha ha ha!*

***** ************** *******************

With great self-discipline I was going to wait a few days before posting this but I have to know about the dedication.
 Therefore
  goodbye
  & all kinds of thoughts (fantastic) for you & a helping for
   N
   & P
    from J

18. Yaddo January

Dear B,

Bliss to get your letter which I'll answer slowly, in instalments so as not to explode your mailbox with my feeling-rays . . . it's snowing big flakes where this morning it snowed pinhead snow, I ate my lunch here seven hours ago (it is now four o'clock) and like a horse I'm nibbling lumps of sugar.

So the scene is set.

Meals are out-a-site—huge steaks, turkey (wild), salads of olives and dates embedded with cream cheese and coconut, ginger soufflé with whipped cream, coffee-iced cake with strawberries and ice cream . . . squash and green peppers in a swirl of tomato . . .

 ** *******   *********
      real asterisks

***** *******   ************

 ******* ******** to Absorb Salivation ****************

No I did not know that the F. Bacon painting was called *Dread Walking*. To myself I had called it The Scapedog (I have it pinned on the wall here) as it seemed to be receiving more dread and terror than it could cope with; but if it *is Dread* then it must exude Dread upon its surroundings. I've thought now that the dread is the dread of being Dread [in margin: 'not the thing but the effect of it?'], and that is why it is in such anguish. I find it very powerful.

★★★★

Thank you for the Rilke Poems. I don't think his French poems are here but they may be in the local library, and they're certainly in the local college (Skidmore) library which Yaddo guests sometimes use. I do want to read them. I've had a whole world of feeling overturned or unburied by reading in the story of Rilke in Paris—how R. was influenced by Valery's 'Le Cimetière Marin', which he read and translated less than a year before he wrote the elegies and sonnets; he and the Muse, I mean. 'Le Cimetière' seems to have overwhelmed him.

It is strange to look back to myself as a schoolgirl and remember the pale green book, *Ils Ont Chantés*, which I loved and read over and over, especially the poem by Valéry, 'Le Cimetière Marin'. You may observe, even from *Yellow Flowers*, that I am hooked on cemeteries by the sea. Maybe I'm a necrophiliac: I collect cemeteries as I collect (through necessity) public 'comfort stations' which, I suppose, are only another variation of comfort. Rilke liked the poem because to him it was a 'perfect poem'; I liked it because I liked it and it moved me—but the French are marvellous with sea cemeteries—dead sailors, fishermen. Ici repose.

· · ·

TUESDAY.

Snowing it was and is not now. The tree-branches seem to have arranged themselves in all kinds of elaborate poses just to show off the shapes of snow lying along them; in one there's a huge mound of snow like a snow-lion.

I'm not happy here. I haven't laughed—real laughter—for ages and ages. [in margin: since Santa Barbara] Everything is so formal and serious and everyone is so determined not to spill a clue of irrationality or disorder, and one is reminded all the time that one is a Writer, an Artist—When you are writing do you . . . is this a problem you come across when you're writing . . . you as a writer would have something to say on this . . . (you're telling me!)

The Director and his wife (harmless and pleasant in themselves) have before-dinner cocktails with us and dine with us and have after-dinner conversation with us, and everyone chats happily except me. Oh my, it's grim. [in margin: Hello to Paul] Working conditions in this big studio, however, are excellent. (Last evening beneath the formal after-dinner conversation Walter Aebacher (sp?) a—the?—sculptor told me he read of a Queen of England who built a scaffold so she could copulate with a horse.)

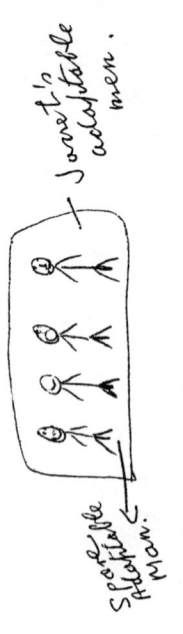

I keep imagining what the portrait of Santa Barbara will be like. It is such a rich idea—how much richer to have a city named after a Saint than after a General, yet I suppose the portrait of a city named after a general would yield much that was unexpected and mysterious and terrible; and Saints, too, have their surprises. The Muse is in this somewhere, emerging from *Hérodiade* and Muzot and the live oaks and the oil derricks and the gaunt hills and the bird of paradise flower. How lucky you are to have a Muse to guard you and prevent you from destroying your own vision! I've never cared for the Muse myself—I think of her as a bitch—I think my muse is either an angel—a stray one—a choice of angels or perhaps Pluto, God of the Underworld who carried off Persephone and I'm Persephone transferred from flower-gathering to higher or lower things, mostly lower.

42 | JAY TO BEE

I hope you got the *Pocket Mirror* I sent. I have a spare ADAPTABLE MAN (title only) and if you like I'll give you my spare *Adaptable Man*—it's a very bad novel but it has a dentist in it—I think I told you about this—based on a dentist I saw only once in my life and inspired by one sentence he spoke to me, 'Rinse whilst I'm gone'. It also has a minister who is obsessed with St. Cuthbert (as I have been since I met him in Anglo Saxon prose). And not much else.

I tried to get *Snowman Snowman* and *The Reservoir* (they're together handsomely 'boxed') when I was at the Braziller office but George B couldn't find one. I did not know that Alan Lelchuk was very fond of *Snowman Snowman*. It's the only book of mine (apart from Faces and Y Flowers, I think) that he's read. He did say, though, that he'd like a copy of these stories. He's a 'fucking arrogant' young man (Philip Roth's description of him, quoted by Alan) but I like him. He's really all trembling sensitivity (or sexitivity, pretty much the same).

I hope Ned has yielded his little cupful by now and is able to go out and about in the garden again.

I called Elnora to say hello. She's been asleep mostly but I think she will get her book finished when she goes to MacDowell.

I love the little sketches in your letter. More.

'Un cigne avance sur l'eau . . .'

[sketch of a heart with rays, annotated: "Not for mink", "+ positive rays"]

Our exclusive heart-ray model, transplanted at no extra cost (admittedly, the initial cost is high!) Can be converted instantly for killing (distance no object). A thousand uses, much in little, even your best friends are deceived by it, wear it on your sleeve, in bed, at parties. Do not, however, bend spindle fold or mutilate, use only as directed. Do not burn when empty. Shake before using. Keep in a *warm* place. Pierce before use. Tear only where indicated. Do not inhale.

[in margin: It is dangerous to exceed the stated dose.]

J

19. Yaddo January

⟨ Page One ⟩

Dear B,

Dear literate graphic numerate semi-live oaks, Thank you for the inspired drawing of my muse and the inspired collage. Paul, how did you know that I, my other self, (e.g. my muse) was thus exactly conglomerately constituted? I had an impression you were wise but not as wise—as clairvoyant—as that! Though my face is not a cat's. It is rather more like the face in the collage . . . Hi, it's me again. The photo is nice and thanks for sending it, though I do look as if I'm holding a false hand and your gestures, Bill, indicate headache or a longing for acromegaly.

Anyway, it was a lovely bonus in the mail, and it cheered me up and made it easier for me to bear, at dinner, (the mail arrived before dinner) the superior snappy tone Granville Hicks adopted when I ventured—*ventured* to say something. The tone implied, What a moron you are! I really don't know why I stick it out here—meaning why I put up with it; habit I suppose, and comfort; but I just hate this constant presence of the Directors—oh for the infant days of MacDowell. Maybe I'm in Hell and MacDowell was the First Circle (lulled to happiness) and Yaddo is the Second Circle, and so on. I suppose it's partly my own constitutional dislike of the presence of institutional authority which makes it difficult.

(My new book will be called *Headache or a Longing for Acromegaly*.)

⟨ Page Two ⟩

When I get some Elmers* I will make a poem collage to send you, also a secrets of Yaddo Collage including Instant Measurements of Members (of the Executive). The housekeeper is a True Character. Yaddo is her life. Like Miss Gee in Auden's poem she wears 'a purple mac for wet days' or its equivalent. She has a new deep blue coat especially for wearing to and from West House for her daily work. She is a fierce bedmaker and (to quote a witty guest), 'You have to get into her bed as if you were a letter getting into an envelope'. She tucks and folds and smoothes.

---

* Brand name of an American glue

The equivalent here of MacDowell's *Rural Violence* is a tall dark woodsy-looking fellow called *Milton*. The staff here are all interesting characters. From time to time Miss Woods, the housekeeper, who, if you make the mistake of calling her *Mrs* is apt to say with a pitch of excitement in her voice, 'Excuse me, madame, I'm *Miss Woods*, I'm a virgin', will confide in me as a kindred spirit (she comes from Liverpool England and regards me as English too), and says darkly, 'They're going to *weed out* all those who don't work'. With emphasis on the 'weed out'. 'Oh yes, madame, there's going to be a lot of weeding out before next summer. They won't be allowed to lounge around the swimming pool all day instead of working as they're supposed to do. They'll be weeded out.'

The 'They' of course are the artists. Temporarily when Miss Woods talks to me, I become 'We'.

She is fearful of the guests whom she calls 'The Men'. Although it is 'the men' she likes to do things for while the women guests get short shrift, as they say. In the morning she approaches me, looking cautiously about her in case someone might overhear, 'Miss Frame, madame, have the men gone (to breakfast?). You know madame I don't like to go to their bathrooms when they're there. They might be embarrassed. What if they came in and found me!'

Yaddo could be such a fine place if only it did not have this tradition and the determination to keep the tradition of formality. Even one's thinking is organized by the many notices. One can't go to the lavatory without being reminded,

This is a small bore plumbing system

and then one is assailed by all kinds of frightful doubts as to whether one is a bore, whether one is a small bore to use the plumbing system, or maybe that somewhere on the estate there are places for large bores to pee. Or one could be a small bore but have a large bore peeing system . . . the possibilities are endlessly confusing.

How warm and soft green the pines are now, with all their snow suddenly washed away in the overnight thaw that brought great blocks of ice as big as automobiles crashing down from the roof. The pines have a spring softness. And the treetrunks are brown instead of that utter black which snowlight gives them.

So goodbye now.

How was Jerry's show?

And

Love. Fragile. This Way Up.
    Open at Above Room Temperature.
        Do not Inhale Dispose of Wrappers Carefully.

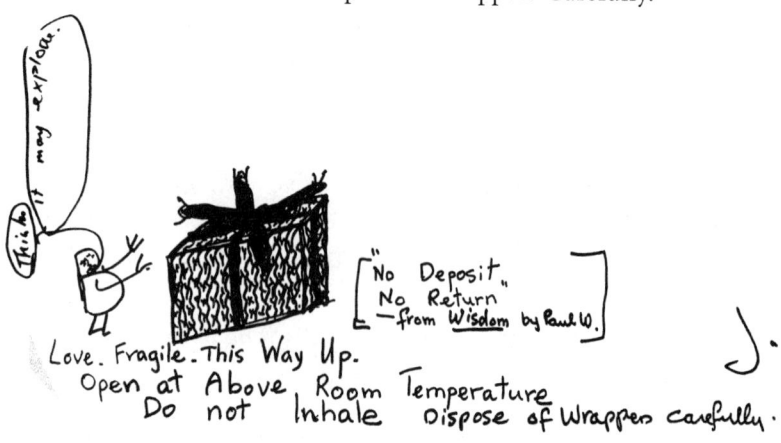

20. Yaddo January (handwritten)

Dear Bill,

    Another letter on my now endless supply of novel writing paper, with 1,000,000,000 thanks for yours & your permission, Bob Battersby, Benedict Beehaven, Ben Beezknee, Brendan Budgeknot. My dedication will read, 'To Sue Marquand & Bill Brown for the possible & impossible greeting & parting'. Does it sound too crazy? I was going to say, With thanks for the *coming and going*, but that might have been misinterpreted, or, should I say, interpreted correctly!

    How is Santa Barbara behaving at her sittings? I have decided that my muse is half-Pluto & half some God of Light—not that he's any help to me, he just *is* & is there to be pondered on. I found May S's book *Mrs S hears the Mermaids Singing* & I found it very moving and wise & brave—all emotional words that say nothing much. I like the way her mind works, I like to follow her explorations & insights. Jim Baxter (who wrote the Tom Cat poem) once asked me, Who does a woman *use for a Muse?* & we had an interesting discussion (I think at that time my mind was on Orpheus—maybe it's still there). In JB's poems his wife (a dear friend of mine) becomes the bad witch, the hag, the shrew etc. while his Muse is a mixture of Mary (he is a Roman Catholic convert) and Venus & various Maori goddesses (his wife is Maori).

How did I come to this topic?

Oh. Your portrait of Santa Barbara while your Muse hovers/lurks near to protect you. I wrote some verses about Santa Barbara and I'll quote a little if you promise not to think it's too bad which it is!

⋆ ⋆ ⋆ ⋆ ⋆

Desert is near encroaching,
 habitual. Painters paint
riders, naked, setting out to challenge
 the sun
aware or unaware
of the blade of light already
 deep in the back between
  the blades of bone.
Painters paint men with
 their faces buried in darkness
diving unobserved, alone, into
 baptismal darkness
for food they trust is benevolent
 just as they believe in
the benevolence of their skin,
 the membrane blessed
to meet the onslaught of
 water, air, fire
when reasoned evidence
 believes not.

⋆ ⋆ ⋆ ⋆ ⋆

Pause for station identification.

Later

⋆ ⋆ ⋆ ⋆ ⋆

Contrast: The blue sky. Alarming fires leap.
Butterflies drift from the broken
    windows of cathedrals,
their lung-wings divining
    the light. A cat
knowing, unknowing, following
    a dream in its mazed
        world collides occasionally
with human concern. Shapes
    of cloth and skin descend
to ignite the purr-spark,
    setting the engine going, but
it's fairly glad to escape
    from the medicinal downpour
        the human shovel-stroke
the heavy word-chains of possession, to spring
    out, out through the hole in the world
up like a black and white fountain into the tree
to lie in the fork of the tree,
    eyes narrowed with sun,
fur ruffled, looking down
    like a big black and white bean-blossom.

        ★   ★   ★   ★

Undisciplined writing

        ★   ★   ★   ★   ★

Yaddo continues to feed luxuriously. With the arrival tomorrow of Dan Curley (where?) a writer who will have the painter's studio adjacent to mine, we shall be full up no vacancies! Dinner at one table (eleven people, counting the secretary & the director & his wife) is too formal still, but there is quiet wit occasionally with Ned R. making dry observations about face-lifting, the Beatles and Helena Rubenstein. Ann Kazin is also witty. I say nothing but I laugh in the appropriate places my hollow laugh. I who have a dislike of all authority find the presence of authority crippling to the serene blossoming of my organic ego (an organic apple such as I tasted at Santa Barbara).

Last evening, however, I achieved some recognition—nay, call it fame—because I have a sprained wrist which the doctor (in Saratoga) has said (dramatically) I must *immobilize* & my fingers won't type until it is better; and thus I joined the ranks, I became an insider, for Ned R has arthritis in his back, Ann K has a sore toe & others have various ailments . . . all acceptable as long as there is no suggestion of 'germs'.

★ ★ ★ ★

disused dentists' drills
or
dentists' disused drills

★ ★ ★ ★ ★

'My Sad Captains'
By Thom Gunn
[quotation of first stanza]

★ ★ ★ ★ ★

capillaries of disused dentists

★ ★ ★ ★ ★

I liked the proboscis monkey very much. Everyone in the world—including the proboscis monkey—must miss you, and that, to me, seems natural.

Fortunately before I hurt my tendons (!?) I had typed 75 poems, all bad, really, for a book: about 10 written since I came here. This is a preliminary as it always is for my short novel (*Mortal Enemy* style) which remains out of reach like a tame chickadee that's decided it won't settle on my hand after all although it can't resist sunflower seeds.

. . .

[margin note: mouse escaping & ↑]

It goes over in my mind though (settles I mean) & becomes grimmer & grimmer & more like a hawk—nightingale—mocking-bird.

I miss the music. Goodnight (it is really morning but goodnight sounds closer) & thoughts for everyone in your household & for you.

"now cracks a noble heart."

Love
J.

21. Yaddo January (handwritten)

Dear Bill,

Hello again, without restraint while it snows powdery snow & the trees appear to have been visited in the night by Old Age.

I'm enjoying my big light studio very much and now that the missing link, Dan Curley, writer, has arrived I shall work here in the evening away from crowded West House which becomes (yes, Bee) a hive of activity with balls (ping-pong) knocking to & fro & pawns being surrendered or captured 'en passant' etc. The sitting-room-library reminds me, then, of Games Night in the looney bin—as the term was.

Last evening when everyone had left the diningroom & the small adjoining 'conversation' room I stayed alone to hear Sonata 32 op 111 Beethoven played by Schnabel, on the repaired pornograph.

Ned Rorem who leaves on Tuesday is giving us drinks in his Pink Room on Monday evening. I suspect that he finds Yaddo too formal. I find it even more formal than when Elizabeth Ames was Director, as the new Director & his wife are *there* among us, from the moment we leave our studios, & though, as I said, they are pleasant people their presence creates its own formality. They have a tendency to want to 'inspect' work & here the painters & sculptors, maybe composers, would be most inconvenienced. The young black painter (he's 22) was disconcerted when the directors asked would he make an appointment for them to visit his studio to see his painting. 'They mean well . . .'

Tomorrow it has been arranged that we play 'Charades' in the evening.

Good God.

Good God.

Good God.

To be fair to the directors, they did say, 'It must never be said that anyone at Yaddo was forced to play Charades'. The pressure is there, though.

The 'raving old man', Kenneth Burke, talks often to me & I like to hear him because I have always respected his scholarship. He translated *Death in Venice* which is being re-issued. He translated it as a labour of love because he was so overcome by the story. His mind at 75 is agile, full of unusual & exciting analogies; he roves in a rich landscape of ideas.

I can't help thinking of poor old Harrison K[inney] who seemed to be so limited & struggling with only Thurber as his life-line.

(I had a note from Jean Boudin—remember her frightful niece & the forced 'poetry' session?—Arnold Dobrin's wife has left him. End of gossip transmitted by Steve (the subway fiend) to Jean B)

I am just about to receive 3500 dollars in advance & royalties (this is after 2300 have been deducted in U.S. tax and agent's commission—gross 5800!)—more than I've ever had.

There's an important Arts Conference in New Zealand in April. It's part of a National Development Conference to plan the way the country should go & I feel very guilty because having received a special invitation (I'm not going) I've been given a chance to help to decide government policy in the Arts & I'm doing nothing about it. I have a remit form & on it I may suggest a place for N.Z. like Yaddo or MacDowell, unrestricted by nationality, where painters, composers, writers etc. can meet & write limericks together, play anagrams, drink rose hip tea and go to bed if they feel like it, AC & DC & all other currents switched on.

I hope you & Paul are at peace with your work & Ned with his stones. Ned really does look more like a blossom than a cat; probably he harbours rubies black & white and Dr Gilbride (a Thomas Mann surname, surely) is an international *jool* thief, cultivating stones as oyster-farmers cultivate pearls.

Beware!

It's strange not to be using my typewriter. I had forgotten that words arrive so quietly; their soundlessness has impressed me over the past 3 days; and yet I miss their shape; their shape in writing is too close to myself.

How is Santa Barbara? How is everything, the sky & the live oaks & the hills & the people, the people & the animals? And the piano with its shiny bones? A worn shine as if it had been kissed by pilgrims.

Goodbye; I mean Au Revoir.

And love AC, DC, 12v (harmless as a torch battery).

Cheese cake last night. Tonight strawberries and ice-cream.

And love

22. Yaddo January

Dear — let me out, I am Santa Barbara, tra-tra-tra.

Hello, the trees are iced with Royal Icing, the snow is several inches deep and squeaks like new shoes and chickadees when you walk on it, and the air is filled with a white mist, and it is Monday morning and I have just written a poem called 'The Dead', of which the last two lines read, 'I smile to see them now,/how contentedly they are clothed with sun'.

After I had written my verse I collected your letter with its lovely dissolved illustrations—I hope there was no mistake in reassembly or rejelling. I'm glad you heard from Jo. Her brilliance makes me bow my head and grow as an irritation in my mind or heart a minute pearl of envy. No, jealousy. Her mind has an anagrammatic pounce.

Meanwhile, at Yaddo, home of delicious desserts, we are quite a small family. *Dan Curley writer. Ann Kazin, writer*, who leaves tomorrow, and later in the week her husband *Alfred Kazin* arrives. *Malcolm Bailey, painter*, who is looking forward to the arrival of a *young poet, female, described as a Viking with red hair*; *Kenneth Burke*; and J.F. Also to arrive soon are *Normon Podorovitz* (?) the edirot of Commentary and *Douglas Alanbrooke the composer.*

Now read on:

J.F. no longer attends the cocktail sitting (complete with Director and wife—how much more acceptable she would feel them to be if they were not *critics*), nor does she stay for the after-dinner conversatione to spend the time discussing 'who's in, who's out in the artistic world'. Her absence is described by Kenneth Burke as playing hookey.

Dear Kenneth who gave me the impression of being a 'raving old man' proved true to form the other night after he had a little too much to drink and after he had written a poem about his lately dead wife. He went insane for several hours and our fear was that he would not emerge from it. The Director and his wife panicked and went home leaving Kenneth in charge of Dan who managed him very well; it was very sad; we all love Kenneth; he is miles above everyone else in intellectual gifts and dreaming power. Dan wrote a poem about the episode and gave us a copy: it's very moving.

Meanwhile I'm trying to work out how I can leave earlier than planned and go to Elnora's apartment in New York where I hope Jo and Elnora will be able to visit me. I can't think of any funerals to attend; the only other emergency is the act of claiming from the Inland Revenue the 3000 dollars or more they owe me; I could ask someone in New York to send me a cable *Come at once*, and leave it lying open in the snow when I've had breakfast.

My Mortal Enemy remains absent. I fancied there had been some kind of connection but I must have been on the literary pill, and that has had the side effect of clotting my ideas into oldfashioned verse so I daresay I'll just go on writing verse while I'm here. I hope you don't suffer too much discomfort over Santa Barbara—you may even be painting her now as you paint Paul's student. I keep adding to my verse about it/her.

> *Feet walk here from time to time.*
> *Not often. The foot*
> *is apt to be caught deep*
> *in the carpeted swamp of the supermarket.*
> *In an easy way nobody cares*
> *that a smoky breath above the Deep Freeze*
> *is all that remains*
> *of the sunken walker.*

I love your decorated letters—could you not illustrate a book of Hours, of limericks, with fanciful L's and O's and so on? And how elaborate your bee is—I count at least four surcingles!

> I lived among great houses
> in the grey wastes of dread;
> laughter not time destroyed my voice;
> *Droop droop no more, nor hang the head.*
>
> I saw this day sweet flowers grow thick
> if as a flower doth spread and die.
> O blissful light, of which the bemes clere.
> *Lord, the snowful sky.* ·
>
> Hath sorrow ever a fitter place
> O Heart small urn,
> Drop drop slow tears
> *Tears pouring from the face of stone.*
>
> I lived among grey houses
> in the grey wastes of dread;
> laughter not time destroyed my voice;
> *droop droop no more nor hang the head.*

How do you like my collage poem filched from first lines of the great? Rather too many tears.

I love the photograph of the drawing; it's immediate and complete. I think that in drawing one must have an awful lot of courage just to make a line and reject the temptation to hide it or blur it. In that way, maybe, drawings resemble poems where you can't hide between the words, where everything *shows*.

The trees outside look like those Christmas trees for sale in the Santa Barbara supermarket.

Battery has run out.

As I told you we're trying desperately to save our Peedauntal business from ruin. For a time we ceased manufacturing. Then one of the shareholders suggested branching into *Rays* but this has not been the success the management hoped for. Next, the idea of Peedauntal Scholarships was put forward; this may help; so far, unfortunately, there have been few applications (we had hoped to have an article at least in *Time* or *Life* featuring interviews with the *Fellows*. We are now working day and night in the utmost secrecy on the *Eternal Peedauntal* which we hope to distribute to Morticians as well as to the breathing and peeing public. Also a contrapuntal peedauntal which opera singers may favour more than they have favoured the usual model. Other variations suggest themselves—the parental (3 sizes), the Continental, the Departmental, the Accidental, the Frontal, . . . battery expired

Please recharge by return and a dessert of love to you 1st and 2nd helpings also Paul & Ned.

J

a dessert of love

P.S. once more—I love the drawing photograph. It *is* like a poem because you have to start with belief in yourself when you make a mark on blank paper.

23. Yaddo January 20

Dear Bill,

Hello, so nice to hear your voice on the phone. I wish it were time for me to 'pass through' Santa Barbara on my dread way to New Zealand. Hurry up please it's time.

I'm testing a Yaddo typewriter which has been lent to me as my own is being repaired while I have my strained/sprained wrist, and the Yaddo authorities and I want to find out if my wrist is better, as they are paying the bills for it (the wrist), as it was their nasty Yaddo door which inflicted it. This typewriter goes like a dream, so smoothly, it's (I declare) granulated, velvetized, enzyme-coated, defatted, defrosted, globulized, saturated, irradiated . . .

I'm glad you don't mind, in fact approve of, having a dedication. I've enjoyed my own slight experience of this, or of being 'mentioned'. Years ago when I was staying with Frank Sargeson there was a constant visitor, a young poet (Frank used to take young poets under his wing) who later wrote a book of verse in which there was a Letter to F.S. where one line read,

'And walk in on you telling Janet lies.'

I felt immortal!

I've never had a poem written to me, though, as you have. Jim Baxter who dedicated a book of essays on poetry to me (Janet Clutha—and I had to keep explaining to people that it was *me*—though if it had been initials only I would have had heavenly competition!) once said that the only realities in New Zealand were Rugby football, masturbation, Wilder* (a murderer confined to the frightful Auckland Security Gaol, who is yet able to escape now and again and is viciously hunted, and who has taken up painting and with the help of local artists had a one-man show); and the other reality—yours truly . . . !

So you see Brendan Budgeknot, Barry Bracegirdle, how my ego blossoms . . . And I, too, feel for Velma Weeper and others. Most of my book dedications, if I've had any, have been to the kind psychiatrist in London, R.H.C. which some people have confused with Royal Holloway College!

* George Wilder was not a murderer; he was a burglar.

```
※※※※※※※※※※※※※※※※※  stars.
##################   The Dance of the Stilts.
%%%%%%%%%%%%%%%%,         ööööööö '
" "ЯЯЦНЯЯЦНЯЯАААНЯЯНЯ      6000000
      ? ННЯННННННН         ΰΰΰΰΰΰΰΰ
      ΰΰΘΰΘΰΘΰΘΰΘ    tttttt  ΙΙΙΙΙΙΙΙ
      ππππππππππππ
      K KKKKKKK     8888888888
                               8888888880000000
                               WWWWWWWWWWW bbbbb
  ※※※※※ ππππππππ               00000000
        oopyut ¡ jkkkkkkkkkkkkkkkkk
※※※※※※※※※  stars to close unsuccessful episode.
```

You asked about Ned Rorem. He seemed to me to be in not very good health, but that's just my impression. At Yaddo he's been rather subdued, withdrawn, I should say rather depressed. He's witty and he doesn't waste words; also he's kind. He leaves today. I told him I knew a cat named indirectly after him. I got the impression that (maybe like us all) he is being gnawed from the inside out like the Spartan boy.

Ann Kazin (Ann Bernstein) Alfred Kazin's wife is nice. So is Dan Curley, a farmer-type from Illinois with a similar stance to Tom Frederickson—was that his name—the composer at MacDowell. As I said before, though, the formality of Yaddo makes it difficult for people to be themselves among one another—yet this is no great disadvantage for one's work, and I think maybe it is an advantage; it means, though, that people get quickly 'stir crazy'.

(Pause while I undo my lunch, slices of turkey, cheese, lettuce, chocolate-iced cake . . .)

★★★★★★

The Director Granville Hicks
was up to his usual tricks.
 He bought some hormone
 from a Yaddo crone
and grew himself triple pricks.

★★★★★★★★★★★★

A funny thing happened said Rorem
today on my way to the forum.
 The thing was my own.

> *It stood up full grown*
> *and laughed without sense or decorum.*

★★★★★★★★★★

Needless to say no-one dreams I have composed these limericks. I might be expelled.

★★★★★★★★★★★★★★★★★

More later.

★★★★

Hurry Up please it's time.

★★★★★★★★★★★★

I'm glad you received *The Pocket Mirror* at last. I posted it on 3rd January! It must have touched down or been laid up for Refuelling at Fergus Falls Minnesota or some other place. It's full of misprints. Also it lacks dignity and beauty—I long to write a dignified beautiful poem; my tone lapses into banality, I tend to leave the dark places where poems are best made and loiter around in the stereotypes and trivialities.

Quote from *Anatomy of Melancholy*:

'Great travail is created for all men: Men's thoughts and fear of their hearts and the imagination of things they wait for and the day of their death.'

★★★★★★★★★★

End of darkness.

★★★★★★★★★★

'Bees are black with gilt Surcingles—
Buccaneers of Buzz.'*

How nice of Emily to describe your surcingles—what are they?

★★★★★★★★★★ Wild Honey.

★★★★★★★★★★★★★★★★★★★★★★★

More later.

When would it be convenient for me to touch down at Santa Barbara (Los Angeles?). And shall I stay $1^2, 2^2, 3^2, 4^2, n^2 \ldots$ days? or a^2, b^2, c^2, n^2 days where $(a^2 - b^2) = (a-b)(a+b)$ where $\sin^2 A$ plus $\cos^2 A$ equals 1 and sin is *not* opposite over hypotenuse . . .

★★★★★★★★★★★★★★★★★★★★★★★★ ★★ stars for seeing.

I've just had my mail letters from Jo, Sylvie and May Sarton: all very

---

* lines by Emily Dickinson

nice indeed. Jo received your glittering rock, as she'll no doubt tell you or has told you. Both she and Elnora (who's back at MacDowell) would like me to stay—Jo in South Hadley for a week after Yaddo 'springs' me; and Elnora in the N.Y. apartment—oh oh oh oh oh oh oh oh oh. Jo wishes you would come East for us to have a reunion before I go away . . . And I'm very eager to go to Santa Barbara, as Blue Jay seeks reunion with Bee in his own Clover attended by Butterfly, Rose, Bird of Paradise, Paul, Pacific, Ned (the Red) and all the live oaks one two three of Hermosillo Drive plus the mountain lions with their gaping golden bones. Maybe I'll make a break-out from Yaddo earlier than I thought.

Dear Brendan Budgeknot, Barry Bracegirdle, enough of this crazy letter which you are under no obligation to answer, I mean not each one of these daily thoughts which fill your mailbox and accompany (with piano) your peanut butter delicacies.

Love for yourself Paul and Ned

J

24. Yaddo January

Dear Bill,

Hello from Bill-less Yaddo that (except for the composer, delayed by a funeral until tomorrow) now has its full complement of winter guests all settling down to write and paint in the mornings and afternoons and to have their scrumptious meal in the evenings at the ten-place table presided over by Granville Hicks (Pricks for Kicks!) and Dorothy Hicks, to whom, as I said on the telephone when I talked to you (I happening to be passing by the telephone at the time), I must now render charity. Their post is a temporary one, for a year until the new permanent director is appointed, and they have the difficult task of trying to change a few of the Yaddo traditions, against opposition from the army of housemaids and perhaps tradition itself. They too are appalled by the warning notices everywhere—Danger. Do Not. Beware.—and are even trying to change the tradition of having all the doors locked. Their custom of arriving at five thirty for cocktails at which we are more or less expected to appear arises from their natural delight in having a drink before dinner (don't we all? Ah, sweet charity) and as Granville has to drive here (they have an apartment in Saratoga) and prefers not to be a drunken driver—well they must drink here. The after-dinner conversation which I now no longer attend is still in force. I'm glad though that I have struck (I think) a blow for individuality. Now when the Hicks say the formal phrase, 'Shall we take our coffee into the other room?' Dorothy adds, knowing there is at least one who will not be taking her coffee into the other room—'at least those of you who would like to'. My absence is accepted now, and others, I'm sure, feel more free about leaving.

Cheers for Pioneer Janet, the innovator of the planet. Groans. Groans.

To continue with sweet charity, where was I—oh the prospective new directors had dinner with us on Sunday evening and (thank god they are not retired critics, though I think he ran a small press for the C.I.A. . . . in the days when everyone was doing things for the C.I.A . . . .) he seems a good type, quiet, practical, a good grasp of facts and needs—something in the style of George Kendall. I don't know if he will be the permanent director. His wife rather resembles someone out of the film *The Manchurian Candidate*.

What a snob-place this is. Last week my story 'Winter Garden' appeared in the *New Yorker* and ever since then G Hicks has been very sweet to me; his wife too . . .

Yesterday Norman Podhoritz, editor of *Commentary* arrived. Also Freya Manfred, a young poet (as company for the young only painter), an unsophisticated Midwestern version of Alan's Frankie; very pleasant. It's so fascinating to see all the artists' shyness (artists are terribly shy people aren't they?) rise to the surface when new people arrive. You could even detect it in Kenneth B. He became a diffident elderly man who glanced apprehensively from time to time (as we all did) at the newcomers. I like Alfred Kazin, as I also liked his wife Ann.

Jo and Elnora called the other evening—one on each of the MacDowell phones and with much giggling we arranged that I would come up to Peterborough-South Hadley (Mark driving me from Springfield) on 15th from New York, stay overnight and return the next day to New York with Jo who has some business there; and I'd see Elnora too on my visit. I'm leaving here on the 11th to stay in Elnora's apartment, and I've told Elnora I won't receive mail there (she would have had to make complicated mail arrangements as all mail is forwarded to her at MacDowell), so I'll be letterless (though not phoneless) in New York. I'll be there until 20th Feb when I go down to Baltimore (staying with J Money) for a medical check with a doctor in town there; and wait around some days for results and so on, I suppose. If I can afford it I'll go back to New York . . . but it would be best to fly from Baltimore early in March—but I will let you know exactly—it depends on my female physical complications, as the Victorian ladies would say. How coy and charitable I have become during my stay at Yaddo!

I phoned Jo and Elnora last evening (also as I happened to be passing by the telephone) and they seem indestructible. I caught Jo (and perhaps Elnora) in the act of playing pool with the suave gentleman who first answered the phone, so it looks as if they are anagramless in MacDowell. Jo says she has finished her play or will finish it before she leaves; that is marvellous. She said Alan Lelchuk called at MacDowell a few days ago bringing Philip Roth with him and they spent a while in Jo's studio.

I've sent away a selection of 70 poems to my publisher; they're not much good, and need to be worked at; some were written here, many at MacDowell. Kenneth Burke asked to see some poems of mine and I showed him three (the first time in my life I've ever shown poems to a critic) and he read them so carefully and wrote a detailed two-page note which in itself reads like a poem e.g. (quote) 'the last two lines are as quintessential as a Delphic Oracle' (he was probably drunk . . .). I had included one about The Dead as a kind of message to him because that is his problem just now and I was heartened to see that he wrote, 'And the closing two lines are good emotional bookkeeping. As long as we have to live, that's the best we can ask for, as regards the past'. It was presumptuous of me, I suppose, because he's such a rich man intellectually that I'm sure grief for him is not so much a loss as a gain, a kind of bookkeeping, to use his own term, where he makes an emotional and intellectual profit. And when he read my story in the *New Yorker* he brought me a poem he had written about his dead wife.

I love the idea of trying to translate the French poem! You must be telepathic.

I made a very free sort of translation of the swan poem; not very competently.

A swan glides upon the water
as on a shimmering mirror
accompanied by its image.

Thus in certain moments a loved
being mirrored like the swan moves
upon the restless waters of

our soul, becoming as it glides
our joy casting its inseparable
shadow of dark dread.   [in margin: Rewrite—teacher.]

Very corny, with the 'as it glides' pretty irrelevant, and the references to soul not made complex enough.
★★★★★★★★★★★★★★★★ stars for comfort.
I have sent separately a spare Adaptable Man and a spare Scented Gardens.

        Crazy love— J

25. Yaddo January 31

Dear Bill,

Hello on Schubert's birthday. Hello with an enclosure of infantile pornographia which, because I am infantile and enjoy being infantile, I had fun doing.

Thaw is here, I'm weary, and I'm leaving here now on February 11th, early morning, having had courage to say that business matters called, which they do, but it is wonderful to know I have seven fewer dinners to sit at and pre-dinner cocktails to be more or less obliged to attend. It really is awfully stuffy having literary people around all the time discussing this and that book—at dinner Malcolm, the young black painter who is dying of boredom began, 'There was a young man from Venus', and someone said, 'Now now Malcolm that's not nice' and the subject was quickly changed to How Writers Can Make a Living, with Granville Hicks lecturing me fiercely, so fiercely I blushed and looked scared, on being willing to send stories to the *New Yorker* when they ask for them. I stammered and stuttered, but if I had burst out with, 'A frightened young tailor from Boston' . . . !

I hope I'm going to Elnora's apartment to stay about ten days and I hope I'll see both Jo and Elnora in New York. I'm making a visit to Baltimore for a medical check-up and then returning to Elnora's apt. I'll let you know when I'm flying West—it will probably be from Baltimore as it's easier to use the airport and take off in time—it will be early March, I daresay. Dare I? I dreamed last night that I came to Santa Barbara and the sky was filled with butterflies and as I watched them the colour fell from their wings, they turned grey and white, and they began to devour me . . . interpret at your peril . . .

. . .

Excuse my stupidity today.

Love from moron J

President Nixon, And The exacting demands of *Sex*

Certainly his physical daring has been highly publicized: he has swum the Bosporus, climbed mountains, undertaken canoe expeditions in the Arctic and earned a brown belt in judo. This month, escaping temporarily from public affairs, he spent a week showing two teen-age girls where the goodies go.

He says he enjoyed it, but he doesn't think he could do it again.

"Time was, when a guy slipped and you'd consider it an accident and let him slide." he commented. "I think we should encourage stiffer members. Loose balls slip away through fog and snow, anonymous, silent, suddenly poignant with melancholy. The movement without the ball becomes a metaphor for all the visions of social interaction in which men don't just sacrifice themselves to the group but actually get their kicks from what they do together.

a compensation, for his small stature and uncomely visage.

Newly snugged in by long, lean curves, flipped out by a front pleat, eye-beep LARGE about them that it's what you will do PART.

ATTENTION! President Nixon DO YOU

ORGANS
NEW AND USED
TRADE IN SPECIALS
FREE LESSON AND WARRANTY
INCLUDED

His achievements in office up to now reflect this key to his character.

WHY NOT → Meet Mrs. Crandall's HEAVY LONG Seventy Foot legs,

not to push too hard or at the wrong time, however.... Be careful

There is a minimal level of daily physical activity which should be performed.

More recently, with "fire in his belly." he slides down banisters to demonstrate he is physically fit.

[Keep Frames where they belong]

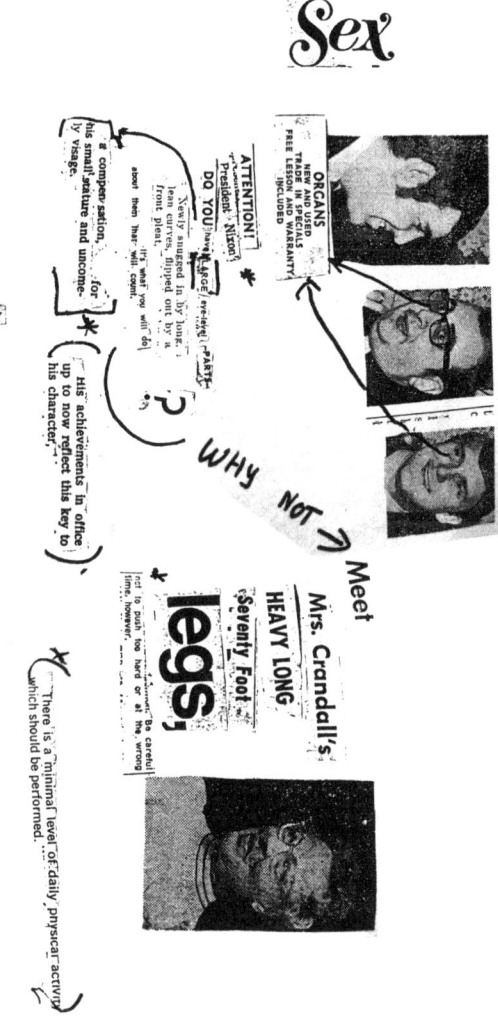

USA: NOVEMBER 1969 TO MARCH 1970 | 65

PIXIE PAGE *DEAR PIXIES,*

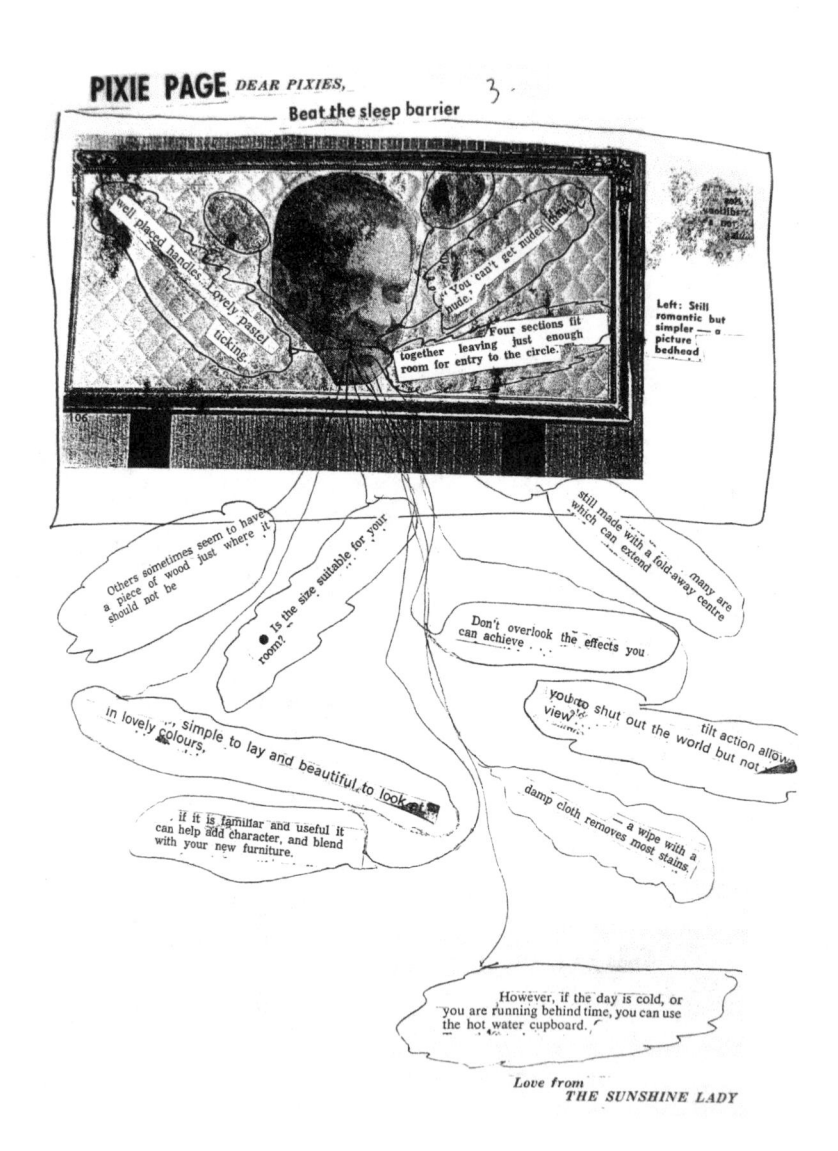

Beat the sleep barrier

3.

well placed handles ... Lovely pastel ticking.

You can't get under them

Four sections fit together leaving just enough room for entry to the circle.

Left: Still romantic but simpler — a picture bedhead

Others sometimes seem to have a piece of wood just where it should not be

Is the size suitable for your room?

still made with a fold-away centre ... many are which can extend

Don't overlook the effects you can achieve

you shut out the world but not view? ... tilt action allows

... simple to lay and beautiful to look at, in lovely colours,

... if it is familiar and useful it can help add character, and blend with your new furniture.

... a wipe with a damp cloth removes most stains.

However, if the day is cold, or you are running behind time, you can use the hot water cupboard.

Love from
THE SUNSHINE LADY

FEBRUARY

26. Yaddo February

Unrestrained letter.

O Western Bee
So Far Far Away
'Gilt-Surcingled, Burnished'
—I'm Faint
with Incense of Absence!
Would I Were
in thy Home Clover
Furnished
with thy Comb Honey—
Yours Blue Jay
(who's taken Over
the mad Correspondence
of the Late Fly.)

(Bee,
Ignore that Rhyme.
Fly is alive and Well
Buzzing to Tell
of Time
and Eternity
—Yours, Emily

As for Blue Jay—A Crow
in a Blue Overcoat
a Bone in Her Throat
a Cry like a Hornblast
the Vanity to Know
that a million Blue Jays
are the Blue Light Cast
by Falling Snow.

Believe me,
Bee,
Yours from the Grave,
Emily.)

   ★★★★★★ ★★★★★★★★★★

Meals at Yaddo
– Director Granville Hicks—
Chocolate Cream Puff—
the Overthrow
of the Politics
of Enough—

Anarchic Appetite—
Diet Dethroned—
Seize the Bright
Gobful Life-Prop
– Stomach Moaned—
Miserable—Stop!

   ★★★★★★★★ ★★★★★★★★★★★

(Bee,
(by the Way)
how's the Hive today?
Does Paul still paint
the Creation of the Butterfly?
Ned Blossom (bean-pretence)
in the Pine Tree?)

mountains	and/or	volcanoes
(snow-capped)		(extinct)
(cloud-shrouded)		(dormant)
(lion-haunted)		(active)

     of
    love

        J.

How's that for lack of (paper) restraint?

Applications invited for PeeDauntal Scholarships.
Canine, feline, leonine, bovine, humine applicants welcome.

27. Yaddo February 5

The Coordinator,
Non- and Sub-Think Feelies,
Santa Barbara

Dear Coordinator,

How pleased—ah more than pleased I was to receive your recent letter which was delayed in the Midwest while it was scrutinised by C.I.A. I am eager to join your group and have only a few business ends to tie up (space for lewd drawing) before I fly westward (??) It is now February 5th. I prepare to leave the Super-Think-Tank, just in time forsooth because pshaw! pshaw! the edirot of *Commentary* has suggested we have reading sessions in the evening . . . of our works.

To be fair and charitable, I'll say that last evening was enjoyable (how could it not have been as I had received your prospectus?), with Kenneth Burke reading, soberly, his talk on Creativity which he is giving at the end of this month in Yakema (sp?) Washington State (he returns to Yaddo then to spend a few more months here); a brilliant talk full of brilliant ideas and passion. Unfortunately his audience now consisted of two critics who at question-time needled him rather and did not have the sense to see he was tired—he'd been working hard all day—; after he left, the discussion continued and I did find it interesting—I like good high-class-high-think talk (though I can't participate myself) especially if what is said reveals the speaker as a thinkie on the surface, by force of circumstance, habit, inclination, but an out-and-out feelie underneath. Besides, I always find it a pleasure to listen to articulate people because I am the most unverbal person.

That is why, sir, I hasten to join the Feelies, and sub-thinkies. Thinking for me is something completely internal; sometimes I wonder how I ever became a (socalled) writer; again that is why I, an inveterate subthinkie, cannot wait to be welcomed into your exclusive society; and how happy I am to realise that butterflies and cats and mountain lions and even plants and trees are quite naturally a part of that society. Watch Ned and see all the internal thinking that's going on and not a messy word spoken.

********   ******************   ***********

When I was a child I once had a dress with that pattern; blue;

**********   ******************   ***************

I was quite horrified at the idea of the destruction of the paintings. You could have photographed yourself and called the result an avant garde work of art: fire and knife-works instead of earth-works. I thought of Dorian Gray which I read when I was very young as my father had just happened to have bought all O.W.'s books at an auction where he really went to buy a diningroom clock which chimed the quarter-hours.

******   ***********   ********

Alas, sir, the Peedauntal model as illustrated* has no sex appeal whatsoever, unless of course the buckles fastening it to the leg are diamond or snakeskin. I had in mind something less like an attached bagpipe—though this of course could add to the musical potentiality of the opera which could be written for baritone and peedauntal—a new wind instrument which combined with the natural wind resulting from the glorious High P in the famous aria might bring the house down . . ..
I had in mind something less surgical in appearance—though again the surgical element might appeal to rather more people than I suppose; I had thought of a kind of cosmetic accessory, especially in the modern dress version where the peedauntal would be the only dress.
It looks as if we'll have to give up the whole enterprise and return to the days of peeing down the leg.

**********   ******************   ***************

What a beautiful little blue jay you drew. Not at all predatory; rather hesitant-looking.

******   ***********   ********

I've just had a fan letter from someone who read my story in the *New Yorker*—yes, it's from a man whose wife died. He writes from the Yale

---

* See Brown's drawing on page 75

Club in New York—a touching letter which assumes that my name is a nom-de-plume and I am writing from my own experience. He identifies himself so completely with the character in the story that he describes some of the difficulties of his marriage and adds, 'You seem to have sensed all this'—which indeed I did not do. Such confidences are touching and one feels first of all that their privacy must be respected at all costs. It's a worry. I understand how some writers burn fan letters without opening them. I'm sure May S would never do this; she would sit down, with the habit learned from her father, as she described it in *Plant Dreaming Deep*, and answer the letter the same evening. And here I am in a turmoil because I've lost that letter from the young man in France, and so haven't even his address. Oh hell.

Talking about letters. Any word from you is mountainous to me (forgive the confidence and treat it as a fan-confession).

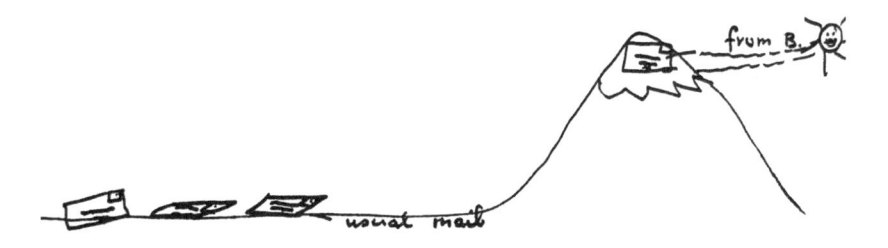

[drawing of a mountain with a letter labelled "from B." at the peak, and smaller letters labelled "usual mail" at the base]

I too have notions of Rilkean correspondence but I'd give it up for peanut-butter-feelie in the patio.

I'll have to live by correspondence when I get back to New Zealand and I'll attach a snapping device to my mail box so that the letters are seized immediately the mailman (postman) puts them towards the box, and are thus not blown away in the high winds that sometimes blow in the hilly place where I live. I have ideas of writing long verse letters.

I've had to be thinking more and more about my return to New Zealand, readjusting myself so to speak, and I've been trying to imagine what my life will be like. I'm going to miss you terribly—I can't explain why (internal thinking)—there'll be a kind of loss around as there is now and as there used to be at MacDowell when B was absent (fan-confession). I see myself in my little house and am cheered by the thought that I like my study and it's a good place to work and the changing light is magnificent to watch (but only butterflies are nourished on the changing light); and I have my solitude and my books, I mean *books*, and I'll have to get some kind of music. Dunedin is a beautiful place of sky and light. I live there chiefly by the sky and the light!

My contact with people will be pretty meagre. The chief problem will be where to get my necessary supply of laughter: Dunedin is a prim place and my friends are on the sedate side. Limericks, frustrated sex—good heavens no. I remember I was very daring to make up a riddle about the English Professor whose name is Alan Horsman and the Psychology Professor whose name was Stephen Grew.

Q: Why was Alan Horsman?

A: Because Stephen Grew.

But I had no-one to tell it to!

I have a friend*, a poet, whom I shall see about once in ten days. She lives with her niece about fifteen minutes walk from where I live, a walk through the Botanical Gardens. She lives a very retired life (she rather resembles early photos of May Sarton, though she's approaching her mid-fifties, a decade older than I). She has leanings to Buddhism and she speaks Japanese (having recently learned it) and lives entirely for her garden, poetry, music, art. She exudes such purity that whenever I visit her I feel positively as if I'm unclean. For many years she was the Secretary to the Editor† of *Landfall* who retired, and their association was very close. I shall see him too. He is a pure earnest bachelor in his early sixties; also a poet, a scholar, Doctor of Literature, Advisor to the Art Museums and the Queen Elizabeth Arts Council. Until his mid-fifties he led a shatteringly lonely life, as far as his relationships with people went, but suddenly around his mid-fifties people were saying they had seen him smile! Someone even made a joke with him! Most people were naturally frightened of him. I remember very vividly when I was a waitress at the Grand Hotel (!) accepting an invitation to afternoon tea—this would be fifteen years ago—it was a dull day and I had no coat to wear and one of the waitresses, when she knew I was going to a grand place on the hill, said, –Perhaps he will give you a coat.

---

* Ruth Dallas

† Charles Brasch

I arrived in fear and trembling, and was greeted by a beautiful white cat. I remember the afternoon and the conversation but I won't bother to recount it. We had slices of seed-cake. When I was leaving and C saw it was raining he said innocently, –Would you like a coat? I can give you a coat!

(I don't mean that the beautiful white cat and I had slices of seed cake!)

At that time of his life he was not known to laugh . . .

During my year as Burns Fellow he welcomed me to the city by taking me to various concerts and plays until Dunedin hostesses began (embarrassingly to me and no doubt to him) to include us as partners in small select dinners. I would arrive to find him as the only other guest.

I gave up going to dinner parties—as a Burns Fellow I had felt obliged. About once in six or seven weeks C invites me to dinner and after a suitable interval I invite him to my place and cook a meal or make tea with my specialties of cookies and hot date scones and freshly baked bread . . .

The other people I may see are my aunt's niece[*] who lives near and whose husband is Economics Professor at the University. She, by the way, would be a perfect Peedauntal wearer should I try to promote the product in Dunedin. She was a source of much envy to us when we were children because she and her cousin used to sing in public and win Rose-bowls (secret pedauntals) for performing arias. Her mother was an old horse, sharp-lipped, and she didn't seem to have any father around; perhaps he died or never was.

(I hope this letter's not too boring.)

I also have another friend[†] upon whom I rely to feel the pulse of the city. She is an immensely talented woman who in her youth (she's in her mid-fifties) studied in America on a Carnegie Fellowship. She has raised two children and buried one husband (always an old old man who seemed to be living in the Victorian era) and now has acquired another husband. I should think she is the most verbally literary woman in New Zealand. She lives conventionally completely within the society of the city. She goes to church regularly, she keeps abreast of local politics, she knows what's going on, particularly in Arts, 'in Wellington'—the

---

[*] Iona Livingston

[†] Dorothy Ballantyne

equivalent of what's going on 'in Washington'; and she's very exhausting to spend time with.

Can't think of anyone else I know in Dunedin.

O there's R*, whom I don't know at all and have seen rarely. He used to live with C†. He's a dwarf, very bright, a university lecturer whose impulses keep getting him in trouble with the police and everyone (his friends) in Dunedin sees to it that he isn't put in prison. He gives allnight dinners and parties but at the only one I've been to I was kept in a corner all night by the wife of a psychiatrist who was confiding that she'd 'done a little writing herself'. R was living at this time with a surgeon who had just returned from being in Tibet with Edmund Hillary and who wore a magnificent Tibetan robe . . .

And then there's my former landlady‡, a grand old lady living in the house built for her by her father, the first Professor of Education. I stayed in an apartment above her house. She is eighty-seven, she is rereading Henry James, she was once a teacher of piano and singing, and every day she plays her piano. All her old friends (mostly unmarried like herself) are in local homes for old people, or dead; and she visits both the hospital and the cemetery to commune with them. She has lace covers on all her furniture.

Well Bill I think I'll stop boring you with this letter because I may be dropping into a story. I guess I'm trying to prepare myself for the return to N.Z.

I won't be able to have any letters from you until 23rd Feb, when I have to be in Baltimore. I want to stay in Baltimore as short-short a time as possible.

Are you really alive and well and living out west—Bill the Brave and Paul the Proud and Ned the Nebulous.

Forgive me, I'm dotty.

feely love from Inner-thinkie-outer-feelie   J

---

* Rodney Kennedy

† Charles Brasch

‡ Ida White

feely love from Inner-thinkie-outer-feelie

THE ILLUSTRATED PEEDAUNTAL

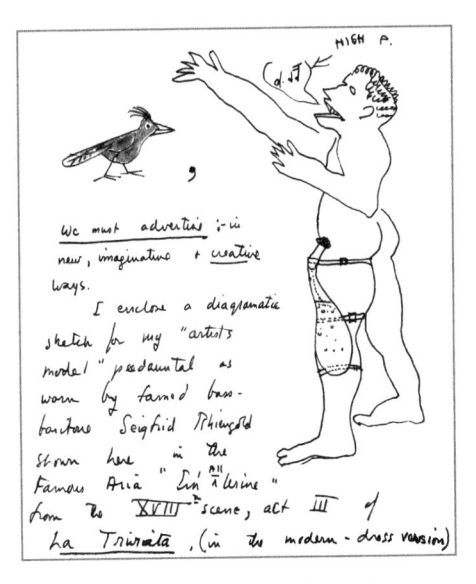

[Brown to Frame, February]   [Frame to Brown, April]

28. Yaddo February (postcard)

Bee small letter large thought-space
peedauntally apace the day drains away
the sun is warm with multicoloured spring alarm
how much simpler to be (bee) nothing-shadow
on the blank page of snow; dig that crazy
urine and sun running down the sky into well and
stream, dig sun sun yellow sun and its saying
its pronominal simplicity; I think I will shut
the door fast keep rainbows and such out retain
the wide white screen for the heart's reeling Kodak,
attend the ceremony some day soon of the final
utter amputation of leaves fatally bloodshot in wars
peedauntally yours, jay.

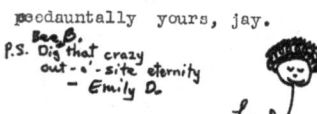

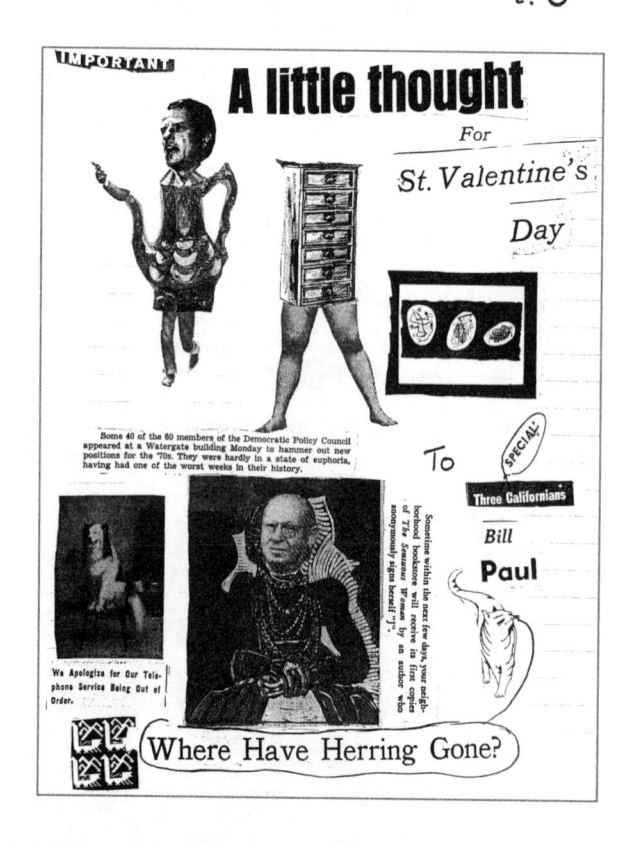

29. Yaddo Pigeon Barn West, with Blue Jay in Residence February

Dear Bill,

A small square letter, probably my last from Yaddo, though who knows what impulse may seize me within the next few days to say another Hello. Sun, and the snow old and speckled like ageing skin, not the brand-new snow I thought I would find here. The sun's shining through a mist this morning and the trees are silver.

Our composer, Douglas Alanbrooke, has arrived. He arrived so secretly that we did not realise it and last evening, glancing around the dinner table, I thought,—What ho, here's a bank manager, and it turned out to be Alanbrooke who is nice, I think, rather like our MacDowell composer Tom but his skin has the peculiar shine that teachers get who teach all day and every day of their lives, as he does, at a girls' College.

Such wild generalisations.

Our mid-West writer went home yesterday, much to Kenneth's dismay, for K has relied quite a lot on his patience and support, and so the day was rather a turmoil with Kenneth drinking from the early hours and then falling into a depression about his wife, then drinking some more, then mourning the loss of his companions 'just as everything was getting normal again'. By his companions he means the Midwestern writer and myself who walked him to the gate each evening. I think the composer will be kind to him. How people tear at one's heart—that's the disadvantage of being a pure feelie as I am; I don't know how people exist if they're feelies and have no way of making art out of it, or trying to. One feels K Burke's greatness and it is appalling to me to think that when next I hear of him it will be through reading his death notice, most likely in a New Zealand newspaper. That is not strictly so, however, for he will write me a letter from time to time.

USA: NOVEMBER 1969 TO MARCH 1970

I have mentally packed up from here ages ago, and am anxious to leave. Norman Podhoretz and Granville Hicks are trying to make me 'read something' before I leave but I insist that if I do it shall be the work of others. I would not dare read my own work—particularly as there is a collection here of writers reading their work on record; Faulkner reading *Light in August*, poets reading their work; and a marvellous recording of Eudora Welty reading two beautiful stories—'A Memory', and 'A Worn Path', in a rich Southern accent. My own work seems of no substance yet I am inspired to improve it.

Liquor here is good these days—everyone seems to have a bottle of something rare and recommended and people appear in the evening clutching their special 'bottle'. I went to the predinner cocktail gathering last evening (I go every second or third evening and omit every evening the after-dinner conversation gathering in the small room off the dining-room) and I quite enjoyed it because Kenneth's unhappy state took a humorous turn as he plunged into sexual reminiscences in front of the usually prim gathering. A couple of evenings ago it was very serious and searching with Dorothy Hicks enquiring conversationally of Alfred Kazin (conversationally and innocently) –Do you often come here? Last evening Kenneth described in detail his visits to the movies when he was from 15-22 and his enjoyment in the girl sitting next to him. 'I used to come,' he shouted, looking positively joyous. And then went on to describe it, while Dorothy Hicks murmured, Oh Kenneth; and I saw or thought I saw Alfred Kazin glancing at me because I'm the shy one and might not know about these things!

Both Alfred and Ann Kazin had been to MacDowell and prefer it to Yaddo, chiefly because of its lack of formality.

How's Santa Barbara? Still with the sailors? She will appear when you least expect her.

The day is too blue and green for me to stay inside. Perhaps I will walk around the lake. This winter that I hoped for here with deep deep snow is a fraudulent season.

Follows my J.F. one-track pornography: J.

30. New York February

Dear Bill,

Hello from Elnora's quiet womblike apartment where I lazed most of yesterday recovering from a hangover which hasn't quite gone, or maybe it's the foul New York air.

First, I loved your letter and the translations and the illustration of the angel descending upon the meal table and you and Paul and Ned hastily rearranging the tablecloth and getting out your usual fare—ninetynine and seventy ninety-ninths pure champagne. I'm interested to see these poems and to try to translate them, with you the teacher.

The time at Las Vegas sounds like fun; reminds me of the old poem of Louis MacNeice about the movies, 'Enter the dream-house, brothers and sisters, Leaving your debts asleep, your history at the door.'*

A N.Z. trip? You say that if you made the trip it wouldn't mean that I'd have to 'put you up' or 'put up with' you. I'd be very sad if you didn't visit and stay but of course you must do what your Muse dictates (portrait of B with brush (?) poised with Muse nearby dictating). It is always nice to be free to come and go . . . You are going to put up with me at Santa Barbara.

How pleasant it is to be out of Yaddo. I had a martini at ten o'clock in the morning of my departure, so did Kenneth B and Freya had nothing (but finished my half-finished martini), and Douglas Allanbrooke just sat and looked silver-haired which he is, and Alfred Kazin had a martini because he had decided overnight to leave also—I've not known people leave early at Yaddo before—their stay is usually extended at their request; Kenneth was persuaded not to drive us to the bus stop (he had planned a royal farewell, taking everyone with him). It was nice to be met, if only inadvertently (I can't think of the word) at New York, for Ann had come to meet Alfred who was also on the bus, and they asked me to dinner so I rushed my bags to Elnora's apartment and returned twenty blocks down West End Avenue to have a very pleasant family evening (they have a daughter of fourteen) but I had rather too much to drink. Another martini to celebrate being out of Yaddo, then wine at dinner, then chocolate liqueur, and I'm afraid I still have the

---

* The quote is from 'Newsreel' by Cecil Day-Lewis (1904–1972).

hangover. I was glad to see the Kazin's in 'real life' because at Yaddo Ann was very-too-brilliant and witty, and Alfred seemed shyly disapproving, but in their home they were warm and happy—it's marvellous not to be conscious all the time that one's a 'writer'...

Elnora's phone seems to be out of order or perhaps 'cut off'. This is the third letter I've written you since I posted my last one but it will be the first I send as I must exercise restraint, old bean.

I must get out now to a phone, will drop this in the box, am dying to see the blue skies of California and what lies beneath them, in the small concentration of 131 H. Drive and the hills—oh my hangover, oh the foul air. Enough.

Yet it was a pleasant welcome to New York and my faith in humankind, in New York humankind, has been restored a little, for yesterday when I had to get a taxi from downtown to up here the taxi-man stopped to buy him and me a hotdog and he almost refused my meagre tip, and at first I was suspicious of his friendliness as one gets in N.Y.C.

Goodbye.   Love

(Hasty—tasty)   J

31. Elnora's Boutique February

Dear Bill,

You mean real butterflies and real humming-birds and real jonquils? And a real **Bill**

I loved your Valentine Card.

I don't know where my time in New York has gone. I rushed north in a blizzard to Springfield, I was met by Mark and Jo, we dined at Holyoke in a small restaurant which had *Bear Steak* on the menu (we had sandwiches), we came to South Hadley Mass, a lovely place deep in snow, full of scarred birches (this is part fiction) and then to Jo's house, painted inside a raw colour as if the wood were being returned to its tree state (and this is precious, a literary whimsy). Only yes, it was newly raw with a strong smell (and here I could delve into childhood when we moved into five different houses before I was five years old but I shan't delve because New York is not a place for delving (not now when I've been rushing uptown and downtown—in one place, though, there was a big empty paint-smelling house surrounded by silver birches). Food again, talk, anagrams and guess who won although Mark and I had surprising resurgences of battery power.

MacDowell was almost unrecognizable under snow. Elnora waited, her eyes fox-bright. And it was nice to be there and say hello. Elnora seemed well and much happier and we laughed a lot but the scene was new and you were not there, so except for Elnora and Jo and the Eaves [women's dormitory at MacDowell] colour against the snow and the whiter than white Colony Hall and the rumour that the tenant of Omicron is being visited by a monstrously fat chickadee, the place seemed far away and strange and when the 'new people' returned to the Eaves from their studios and wandered in and out sharing our rose hip tea and peppermint tea I thought Ugh Ugh as the novelists say and was glad I'd been sprung from MacDowell. The birches though, like salt-washed stone, and the snow!

I'm caught in my own narrative, another state which New York city does not allow.

It was all fun and happy. I slept in Elnora's studio which has a Steinway and if pianos were to appear in Before and After Advertisements it would be the neglected waif side by side with your shining cared-for piano. I'm sorry that Elnora didn't play as she was going to. I had been describing to her how Douglas Allanbrook invited me to his room one evening at Yaddo to play for me and ply me with drinks and hearing he was a good pianist I went to listen (and to drink a little) but when he began his playing was nothing, nothing, nothing. Notes, yes. (I think I told you this.) Notes and gloss and feeling but not feeling for the music, at least it revealed itself as feeling for D.A. playing the music. To make a long repetitive story short it was just not Bill playing and Bill's presence; it was a cardboard half-hour.

Embarrassing aren't I?

It's breakfast time. O to join the Inner-thinkies, feelies in Santa Barbara! I'll let you know when. I had booked for March 2nd but I may be able to get away a few days earlier.

I've done nothing in New York except travel hundreds of blocks by bus and recover from pollution of the air while submitting to pollution of the intelligence and spirit—states which I couldn't define and mention only because I'm sure they exist. Bee, you're right

the bomb has fallen

....

....................pollen

complete and win Dozens of saints, rascals, nuns, picaroons, inquisitors, heretics, bishops, whores and humble people!

Bee, you're right
the bomb has fallen
....
..............pollen

(morning-fresh flavor-sealed)

Love

32. Down Baltimore Way February

Dear **special** Amazing real Bill

Dear special Amazing real Bill,

I miss you and I'm writing a hasty letter to say so. Baltimore is now blue sky, snow sometimes, cold with a *mistral* blowing the pieces of glass and torn cartons and wrappers up and down the street—yesterday was Trash Day in East Madison Street. The plants in the small backyard garden are still grey with no sign of green yet.

So much for local colour. John Money is less crabby than when I was last here—I think he is pleased with his series of lectures to the Medical students on Pornography. I find him much much too serious about everything and even in ordinary conversation he lectures, which is an occupational hazard, I suppose, of lecturers.

In New York I spent a frantic last couple of days rushing around and doing nothing and not going where I wanted to and missing out people I'd promised to say au revoir to. I went to Ann's apartment for a quick dinner (the L.A. Ann) and it was good to see her again, also to have a link with the west coast and to have real messenger news of the live oaks*. [footnote: * species found in Santa Barbara known as Bill, Paul & Ned (a mutant oak, furred)] She had two friends with her, one a young sculptor; the other had recently spent time in New Zealand: both bright. From there I went to the Marquands and spent time with Sue and John and returned to Elnora's apartment in the early morning, slept about three hours, then caught the train to Baltimore and here I am missing **YOU** while I listen to the pornograph and write this letter.

I searched and found the Rilke poems. I'm looking forward to trying to translate them (you will be doing most of the work) (and Paul too). George Braziller will publish my book of poems next year—it frightens me that he has not yet refused to publish my work.

This is not the kind of letter I dream of writing you. It is what we used to call, in our family, an 'On the Monday' letter, derived from my father's habit when he was away from home of recording almost every move in sentences which began, On the Monday . . . . On the Tuesday . . . .

I should know on Wednesday or Thursday when I'll be flying to L.A. Could be the weekend sometime. No later than Monday 2nd March. In the meantime au revoir.

   Basic love

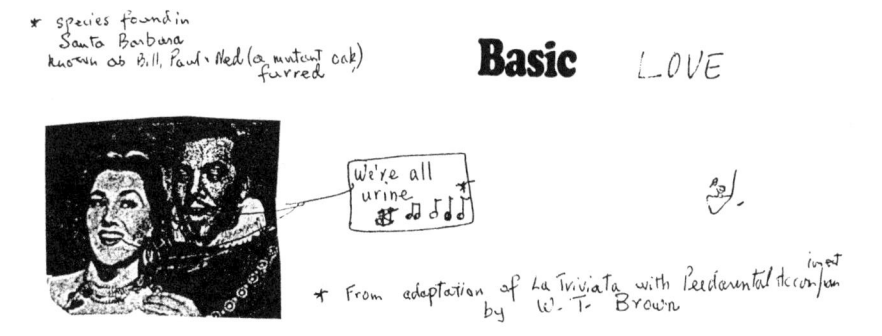

     J

33.

Real ARTIST!

Down Baltimore Way.
Tuesday.

Dear Bill,

> Tiger Shocked
>
> To a grown man—even a man who was raised in Texas, eating a dozen hot females at one sitting is traditional.

Your letter today is so nice and comforting to me in downtown Baltimore, Maryland. This letter will be the last I write to you before I fly on Saturday, American Airlines F.045 leaving Baltimore noon, arriving L.A. at 2.18 Pacific Time—I'll be phoning you tonight to tell you. I wanted it to be Friday but the medical checkup has turned out more complicated than I thought and I'm sitting here in downtown Baltimore Maryland with all kinds of wild apprehensions flying through my mind. I shall have to spend the next two days being radioisotoped, for five hours tomorrow and about three hours the next day and then on Friday hearing the results which I've no reason to expect will not be O.K. but you know what Authors Imagination Inc. does to one. I also have to submit again to one of those immodest internal examinations where one has no control over one's secretions and therefore makes oneself apparently ready to receive the smoothie doctor with all his goods. What shame. For 'one' read 'I'.

It will be good to leave Baltimore and I truly can't wait to land in L.A. It's like a dream. Perhaps it is.

Elnora phoned last evening and she will be finished her book this weekend—very wonderful news, I think, and I'm sure it will help her. I'm glad you like *The Adaptable Man*. I did try to reread it but I found it rather boring from time to time. I did enjoy the way the characters (for me, anyway) became people, especially the dentist whom I built up from that one visit to the dentist. My characters are not really people to the reader—to the critic, I mean.

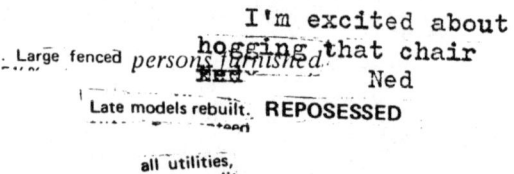

I'm excited about hogging that chair

Ned

Large fenced *persons furnished*

Late models rebuilt. REPOSESSED

all utilities,

I'm excited about flying west and I see myself on the patio hogging that chair while the hummingbirds hum near by and Ned blossoms in Op Art colours, and you and Paul munch p.b. sandwiches.

Here, in downtown Baltimore, my consolation has been the music, and though I can't play the big Steinway it's been something wonderful for me to be alone with a black Steinway most of the day. I've been listening to the pronograph also.

Hasty finish to post →

Love x Love J

MARCH

34. Santa Barbara March 6 (postcard)

By the time you read this I shall have been swallowed by a carnivorous plant which you have been sheltering unbeknownst in your otherwise paradisal garden. I have strength only to write this card which I gave to Ned to post (mail) & pray that he does so. I've not even space to tell the location of the plant. Farewell.

    Your loving Janet.

NEW ZEALAND

March 1970 to January 1971

Dear B.,

35. New Zealand March 23 (postcard)

Dear Ned,

    I often think of you & wonder when you, my distant cousin, will come to visit me. I've quite a nice apartment here at the Zoo but there's nothing much to do all day. I hope you like my hippie-style hair-do. How's life in Santa Barbara these days! I hear you're sweet on Dr Gilbride?

    Love—Felis?

36. Auckland March

Monday.
Dear Bill,   *Bes in antipodes*

Dear Bill,

    I miss you and Paul and Ned and the piano (*your* playing) very much and I wish you were here in this fresh blue world of sea and sky and sun. How clear and sparkling the light is! Ah, but the spaces! Sadly, though, so much of the human furniture of living—the buildings etc.—reminds me of the Blue Chip* Shop and forces me to the conclusion that we are a Blue Chip people. And yet there is such an expanse of sky and sea and light that our Blue Chipness seems irrelevant.

    It has been a long hot summer and the temperature is about or above that of Santa Barbara sunny days. I am sitting in the small caravan-room which my sister hired for a few days to accommodate me. It is noon and I have eaten my peanut butter lunch, with apples and coffee. I have played the tape of the poems—you recite or read them beautifully, Bill. I am alone—my sister is at college, my nephew (who looks like someone from the Steak House) is at University, the other nephew (who also looks

---

* Blue Chip was an American system of redeemable stamps issued by shops

like a waiter, smaller version, at the Steak House) is at his job at the radio station where he is technician, recording etc—I'd forgotten this—he will advise me about a phonograph—my brother-in-law is at his job at the newspaper, and my niece is at school; and I am partially and ever in Santa Barbara.

The flight was very rough for six hours and felt very much like a ship at sea in a storm, which meant that my internal headlines read—Plane buffeted. Engine drops from Plane. Plane Disappears in Pacific. Shortly before the disappearance the pilot radioed that severe turbulence was being encountered. There were no survivors . . . Frogmen are expected to scour the *bed* of the Pacific to recover a valuable tape recording which may give some clue to life in ancient California among the live oaks.

A red butterfly has just flown into the room. This is very much an On-the Monday letter as I shan't be writing a *real* letter until I get back to Dunedin which will be on the 1st April; and this note is to keep in touch, to remind myself of much happiness found at Hermosillo Drive: when I fall asleep I dream of it.

Is the mail strike over? Have you received the book? I think often of the Prisoner and the Frog Prince who are clear in my mind and when I look at the Prisoner I read into the colouring of the figure and the background some crisis of identity and camouflage.

When I get to Dunedin I will 'wake and read and write long letters'*.

Much love, antipodean style—Green Jay.

---

* quotation from an English translation of Rilke's poem 'Autumn Day'

37. Auckland March 27 Good Friday (handwritten)

[handwritten musical notation with text: "Auckland. Good Friday. Dear — Don't be disconcerted"]

Don't be disconcerted by my daily letters—I'll reduce them to weekly when I get to Dunedin. I'm missing you terribly & I hope that when you send me a tape cassette to Dunedin you will have recorded on it as many Rilke poems as you can (from the McIntyre translations). The three that I have sound so beautiful & your voice cheers me in this foreign land where my only real relatives are and always have been the earth, the sky, the sea & the rivers, the trees and the flowers, and the 'breezes and the spaces', and as these are still in abundance I can speak of myself as having some kind of kin here—oh, I'll not forget the birds too. The air is still so clear and sparkling.

In this letter I'm enclosing a couple of photos & a cutting of typical radio programmes here. I'd forgotten that we do get a variety of music from different countries. The record shops, though providing chiefly for the pop music buyer, have an interesting range (one can buy John Cage's work, for example) from modern composers to the warhorses. As an emotional & musical comforter I have bought myself the Schubert Impromptus played by William Klemperer but on first listening I think it's not a very good record, being rather faint in sound. He plays interestingly at almost half the speed of Schnabel & Richter.

At the local shopping centre I met the husband of the elderly woman* I told you of—her life in senility restricted marvellously to music, especially Mozart. Ernest (her husband) began immediately to talk of music which is his passion & before I fly to Wellington on Monday I shall visit them & perhaps listen to some of the 150 Schubert songs they have on record.

---

* Ernest and Jess Whitworth

Last evening I went with my sister & her husband to a performance of *Earth and Sky*, a combination of choir, ballet, poetry, composed by a Wellington musician, depicting ambitiously the creation in Maori Mythology & using a combination of Maori chants and poetry for the vocal parts. I found it very exciting, beautiful in parts & moving although there was the tendency of the composer to leave nothing to the imagination so that the work became, in a way, an empty treasure-house. I missed you terribly as I sat among the foreign audience & I wished/wish I were still in Santa Barbara or that you were here. When?????

The day is clear & full of singing crickets, as the night is full of singing cicadas. I am impatient to get to my home in Dunedin but there was no seat to be had on any plane before Monday (to Wellington) and Wednesday (to Dunedin). In New Zealand people book seats for many months ahead; & in Easter Week the planes & trains are usually full.

Life at my sister's is too hectic for my taste although this is partly my fault—after their first day's shyness & strangeness (and mine, too) the young people are eager to show me their accomplishments & treasures & so Ian, one nephew, switches on his handmade stereo equipment to play pop songs (which could be worse) & Neil tries to explain computers & remarks (a hopeful remark, I think) that there is little or no scope for creativity in what he is doing. He is now studying German, also. Pamela, the youngest, fifteen, is a Latin & French & mathematics scholar with long blonde hair.

I miss you, Billy. And I miss Paul & Ned & the peanut-butter patio. And—very much—the meditation before meals.

The other evening I had dinner—a Chinese meal—at Frank Sargeson's. He is now 67 & is looked on as the grand old man of N.Z. letters. He is writing more & more fluently than at any time in his life, enjoying an Indian summer. I gave him the proof copy of that book published by—Bernard Geis. He told me several bawdy stories & read to me from his latest work & showed me the new *Landfall* (not yet printed) on the cover of which he appears in 4 photographs: himself as a child, as a young man, an older man, & now as a bearded elderly man. Harry (his friend for 37 years) who now has a room in his house, is ill, as thin as a shadow, & Frank looks after him. Frank talked of his death, too, & he read me his tentative will. He has lived most of his adult life in this small cottage near the sea & he is now surrounded by apartments, a motorway passes his door, & he periodically turns down fantastic offers for his now valuable land. When he dies, he says, he does not want his toothbrush & underpants enshrined for posterity (someone has recently sold a few of his letters to a museum for 500 dollars), so everything will be sold & disposed of & if his residual beneficiaries want to keep and use his house & possessions, rather than having the proceeds of the sale they will have to buy the place themselves. There are 2 residual beneficiaries—and I am one. He may change this of course. I would much rather see the place as he has it—minus, of course, his toothbrushes & underpants! It is unique with its many many books & pictures—also its slightly Spanish smell. And there's the huge paw-paw tree in the garden, the lemon tree at the back door & the Chinese gooseberries by the hedge.

Goodbye now. Will you come to N.Z. to see me?   ??

Love x love to you & Paul & Ned x the carnivorous plants.

J

38. Wellington March 31 (handwritten)

Dear Bill & Paul & Ned & all carnivorous plants everywhere,

Morning, the wind rustles the many leaves of native bush outside, 18-month old Stephanie is being bathed next door, I hear John (16) coughing, & another gust of wind shakes the green world outside. I'm sitting on my bed writing this. John has given me his room for a couple of nights so I am surrounded by paintings and painting equipment. On one wall is a huge mural of 3 naked gurus (plural sp?), one yellow, one blue, one red. In another corner is a meditation centre with 3 small Buddhas; in another corner is the *childhood teddy bear*; also many books. Hilary the daughter & Jacquie the mother are here, also a friend of Jim's (Jim is not here). All except Jacquie have been to a Maori Hui, a huge gathering of elders, youngers all tribes & I feel ashamed that I know so little Maori, for everyone speaks it fluently.

End of letter. Most important part is this—that I'm missing you very very much, come & *rescue* me with *you* & music & poetry

Green Jay
Kisses + Love + love

APRIL

39. Dunedin April 3 (postcard)

Greetings, love & kisses from Janet-home-alone, who misses " " " you.

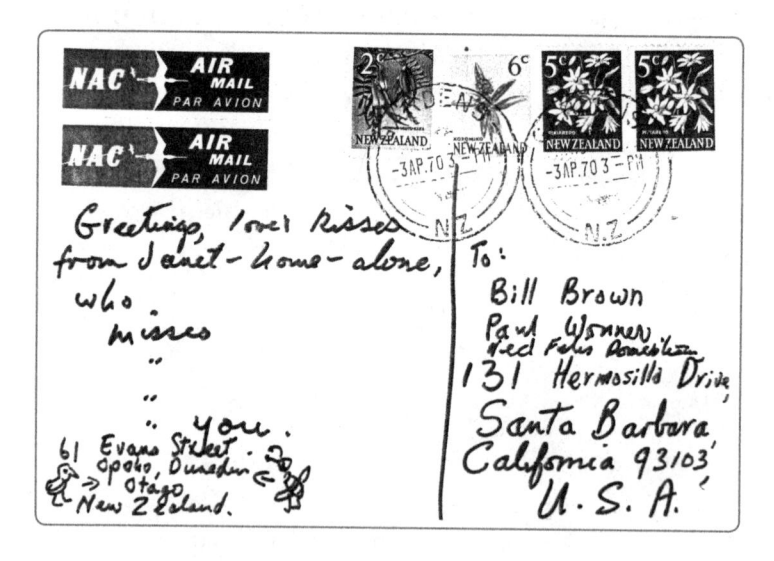

40. Dunedin April 4

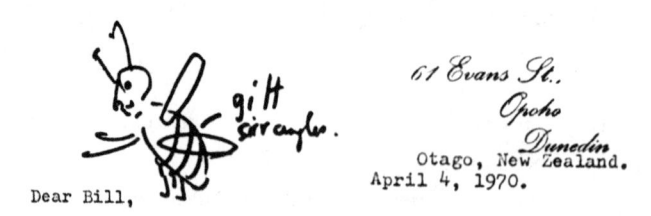

Dear Bill,

61 Evans St.,
Opoho
Dunedin
Otago, New Zealand.
April 4, 1970.

Dear Bill,

    I'm just about to have a grandstand view of a storm and to find how waterproof my house is. Now the rain is flowing down the windows, the house is shaking, there's a wild gale; lightning streaks across the sky, the stormwater drain outside in the street is like a fountain . . . and so much for the storm, after a day of hot hot sun and clear blue skies. Since I've been back home I can't make up my mind whether I live in a tropical or

94 | JAY TO BEE

continental climate—the days have been brilliantly blue and hot and the nights clear and cold and this is the first almost tropical storm that has passed.

Thus writes Janet-home-alone in absence and isolation on the notepaper which her tenants must have had printed for themselves: I found it in one of the drawers of my desk. Would you believe it that day to day I am sustained by playing your recording, especially the poems you read—'The Swan', 'Autumn Day', 'A Lament'; and I get some laughter from the crazy conversations about neglected poems by May Sarton and the tender-leaved carnivorous plant and how long it takes water to become urine. I miss you terribly. Paul was right when he said the pain of separation would be eased by daily chores—I've been going mindlessly up and down the back stairs retrieving my books that I had stored in the basement, rearranging the furniture (an old Frame ploy), unpacking stored linen and clothes. I feel happy to have my books with me and I have distributed them in each room—but how tiny the house seems, so much like a toy house with its squares and long corridor; but it is still a house up in the clouds: at night I like to sit in the dark and look out at the city lights and the dark hills and the traces of sunset. I would like you to come and visit me, if you were so inclined, she said shyly.

I wonder how your Easter week was spent, after your untying following three weeks of being tied up. I passed through Wellington at Easter and stayed two nights with the Baxters, that is all except Jim who is living in a small religious community in the centre of the North Island and who visits Jacquie, his wife, maybe once in five months. Also staying there was a dentistry professor who described himself as 'a professor of false teeth', father of eight children who had spent Easter, first of all hitch-hiking with young John (the seventeen year-old boy who's a talented artist), then attending a Maori gathering of tribes (Jacquie is Maori), then hitch-hiking again to Wellington; and all the time amazed at the experiences he'd had, hitch-hiking for the first time with a young man who dresses in Buddhist robes and wears shoulder-length hair!

When the plane landed in Dunedin I felt I had come to a lonely wilderness and yet I was happy to see the sheep and cows and horses and all the green hills and the trees. My tenants left my house in good condition, with vegetables still in the garden—fat cabbages and spinach and rhubarb, but they have cut down the beautiful young Australian fir tree that had grey leaves like the leaves of the olive tree that on winter days used to look as if snowflakes instead of leaves were pinned to the tree. Also, for some curious reason, my tenants removed the electric light bulbs and a few electric plugs—perhaps there was a shortage of them when they were leaving.

It is dark now and the lights are shining and twinkling through the mist, and I wish I could be in Hermosillo Drive listening to you play the piano while I turn the pages: without music and dear friends what is left of life could be mostly death, I think.

I'm sending you a collage of Prince Charlie and his ma or mom.

Goodbye now and love to yourself and Paul and Ned and all that make up the life at H Drive, including the tender-leaved carnivorous plant. As soon as I hear that you are still alive and well I will flex my poetic, peedauntal, sub-Rilkean muscles and 'waken, read and write long letters', rather more, I hope, than 'restlessly wander up and down where dead leaves are blown'*.

Blue Jay

41. Dunedin April 7

Dear Bill, or Bee (as described by Emily D)

I don't want to enslave you with correspondence and I *swear* I will limit my letters, but yours came today and I was so overjoyed to hear from you, and strangely enough I went immediately and found the Rilke you gave me (the translation) for it was unfindable until now and I mourned its loss.

My book hasn't arrived either—I think I'll have to write to those dilatory publishers or phone them collect!

I'm sitting here at my table by the window which has a panoramic view of Dunedin hills, and I've lit a fire of small logs because flames are a

---

* quotation from Rilke's poem 'Autumn Day'

beautiful colour and, incidentally, warm on a day when the wind is rather cold, and I'm wearing Paul's shirt which is very comforting to wear.

Yesterday my neighbour brought in a tray of apples, the remainder from my trees after the birds had eaten most of them. The little tree I planted and which gardening books advised me was suffering from an incurable disease, again yielded one blossom and one apple, as it had the year before I left home. I think it must be a special tree: there is now no trace of disease. Rilke would have something wise to say about this smallest tree and its one blossom.

I'm glad Ned liked the postcard. If he desires a similar visitor to the carnivorously planted garden I'm sure we can find him a happier specimen, though there's no zoo here in Dunedin. I think I told you there's an albatross colony nearby, also a seal colony where the seals behave very much like the more poetically favoured swans in their 'awkward walking', and when they slip into the water they are even more at home than the swan for they submerge and their drab colour makes them indistinguishable from the water.

I've been enquiring about record-players and a piano so that I can learn more about the music. Record players with good sound are about 100 dollars, and a piano about 130 (secondhand—sold by a piano firm here which, though they have forgotten it or do not know it, used to publish my mother's songs. During the Depression she used to sell their music from door to door.)

I'm going today to get your painting framed. It's so precious I'm scared they'll damage it but I suppose I'll have to trust them. I'm always wondering what is happening at 131 Hermosillo Drive, where you are, what you are painting, doing, what Paul is doing, and I miss the breakfasts together, but I could go on and on like this about everything, for I miss everything and as soon as you get that small servant-kennel built on to the kitchen let me know and in the wink of an eye (the aeronautical eye takes about twenty hours to wink) I'll be there. I'm going to send Paul some recipes out of the daily newspaper: the day I returned there was a whole page of passion-fruit recipes but as you don't have passion-fruit, well, what could I do.

Oh that I could be redeemed. I know that my redeemer liveth. Blue-chip wise I don't know how many tape recorders make up the fare between here and there, but I do know that I am hoarding untouched one thousand dollars in travellers cheques; just in case you get that kennel built.

And now—You'll get this letter, say, Thursday. Bee, pray, when will you fly this way to see Blue Jay?

99¾ pure love to 3.
(my new math)

Blue Jay swearing.

---

42. Dunedin April 8

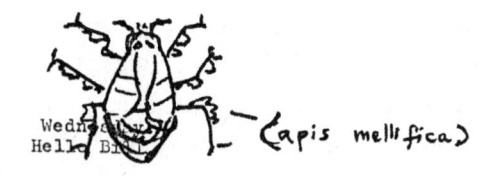

(apis mellifica)
Wednesday
Hello Bill,

Hello Bill,

How are you? How are Paul and Ned? What are you painting? (forbidden question). What are you eating? How long and wide is the United States of America? Are there any artists in America? Do people speak English there?

The day has just gone—it disappeared as I wrote my first paragraph and now as I look out I see the dark purple clouds of night with just a faint corridor of light over the hills. The city lights are on and twinkling yellow and red.

(Miss miss miss miss you.)

Since I've been home my time has been spent mostly in doing domestic chores, unpacking stored books and clothes and washing linen and trying to get organized for writing. The other day I set out to pay a small overdue cartage bill and I had a pleasant walk around the industrial and wharf area of Dunedin where many old buildings and early houses still stand—along by the railway yards where I would never dare to walk in any other city, by grain stores and fruit stores and one old building labeled—yes—Bee Supplies which had on each side of its front wall, a stone carving of a bee. It was about half-past ten in the morning and I passed workmen sitting in a row on the footpath drinking their morning tea out of big cups and eating thick sandwiches that my father used to call doorsteps, and everywhere I walked and there were people they were eating. I do enjoy exploring and inspecting the out-of-the way places in Dunedin; and in the oldest street I'm very much aware of the enormity of the past and the land and the pathos of the people, and in the newest streets the people seem like plaster gnomes. Possibly I prefer the older streets because the people who walked there are dead, and though it may be a fallacy, at least the living have some control over the dead.

Now the sky is violet-coloured like the sky in your painting. I took the painting to be framed and I dread what they will have done to it, I really do; but soon it will be on my wall.

I have been asked to give a radio interview on 'Artists' Colonies in America'. Shall I type out all the limericks and present them over the air and be banished from New Zealand for ever?

> *A colonist new on the scene*
> *said, excitedly landing at Keene,*
> *'They wrote me to say*
> *I could come this way—*
> *will they mind if I've already been?'*

Remember that one?

It might help the cause of the Arts if I referred to Granville Hicks' multiple pricks.

THURSDAY.
Hello again. Winter is setting in. It is cold and wet today with the temperature about fifty-five, with a south-westerly wind making it seem colder. I'm fairly organized for work now. Apart from shop assistants and so on, I've spoken to only one person I know, and that was my friend Ruth [Dallas] who lives with her niece at the other end of the Public Gardens. I lunched with her on Sunday and came away with copies of

two children's books which she wrote the year she was Burns Fellow. One in particular is beautifully written and printed. She is also a gifted poet—I mentioned her to you. She had some rather good pictures on her walls and when I asked where she got them she told me that her friend Charles had lent them to her. I told you about him, too. He is adviser to the National Art Gallery or Art Foundation or something like that and buys pictures and it was he who was interested in having a portrait of me, just as one of the writers of the country, and he did not care for the postcard of Hyde Solomon's portrait, which he described as 'sad and heavy'. Maybe I am sad and heavy. I'm sad now because I miss you so much and I wish you had a dog-kennel attached to your house where I would come and stay until you got the local sheriff to throw me out. And I'm heavy because I've just eaten a date scone which I made and now give the recipe for. This quantity makes eight date scones, just enough to fit into a small electric frying pan. Set the pan in advance at 375 degrees. Sift together: (Let's!)

- one cup of wholemeal flour
- one half-cup of white flour
- (or one and a half of wholemeal)
- a tablespoon or two of wheat germ
- a few pinches of salt (two)
- 1 heaped teaspoon of brown sugar
- 2 heaped teaspoons of baking powder (or one heaped and one level)

Cut one dessert spoon of butter into small pieces and rub into the dry mixture—delicately but surely.

Add three quarters of a cup of chopped dates.

Add at once half to a cup of milk, preferably sour. Mix quickly with knife . . . . Turn on lightly-floured board (much better than turning in an electric bed!), cut quickly into eight, lightly flour frying pan, put in scones, put on lid, and leave for six minutes, then quickly turn scones, replace lid and leave for another six or seven minutes or until cooked, I mean until they not you are cooked. Remove, place on wire rack to cool. Delicious eaten warm

This is my recipe but there is nothing original about it!

with butter only or butter and honey or home-made jam, raspberry or strawberry.

★★★★★★   ★★★★★★★★★   ★★★★★★★★★★★★★★★★★

I've been looking through my recipe books. They mostly belong to an age before accurate temperatures and quantities were recorded and they have delightful instructions like, 'Take a peck of primroses', 'Put over a sharp (or 'good' or bright) fire. Take a handful, a few, some . . .' All pleasantly vague. And not, 'Bake one hour' but 'Bake until cooked'.

★★★★★★   ★★★★★★★★   ★★★★★★★★★★   Stars for comfort.

★★★★★★★   ★★★★★★★★★★   ★★★★★★★★★★★★★★★★★

If You're In The Mood For SEX
KEEP THIS CARD & SMILE

If You're Not In The Mood
TEAR THIS CARD UP.

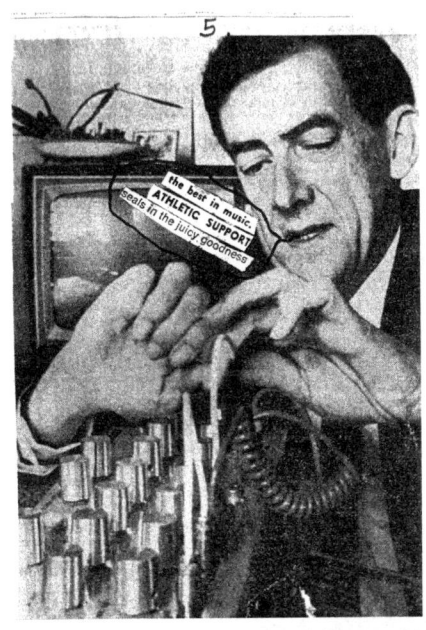

LEADING CONTEMPORARY composer Mr D. Banks, of London, with the "mother" of his electronic music, a machine which provides all the sounds for him to edit and arrange into his own electronic compositions. Mr Banks, who has been in Dunedin since Monday, is giving talks at the University of Otago's music department on his contemporary works.

This will be a birthday letter to you as I think it is your birthday soon.

I'm enclosing the photos I took the other day of the garden, such as it is. The geraniums ran wild in the front of the house and at the back there was a rose tree trying to get inside and when I admonished it, a thorn pierced my finger and I fell into a swound and when I woke I was at Muzot, being tended by a white swan . . . who murmured 'This misery . . .'

Goodbye now. Unadulterated love, dust-free, germ-free, specially tested to you

    and Paul
     and Ned
      from

P.S. This is a p.s. from me, Ned, whose photo is on the mantelpiece and little does Jay know that part of my spirit is contained in that photo, and so it is I, Ned, writing to you, Bill and Paul in far-off California. I'm standing beside a plasticine model of Thoth, the Egyptian God of the Arts and wisdom who has the head of an ibis and the body of a man while at his feet sit two baboons wearing small suns. An extraordinary companion for your Ned, don't you think? There's a fire burning in the room because I suspect that baby Jay is hooked on it and won't let it go out: it's of manuka wood. I just can't wait until your painting is framed, Bill Brown, my master I mean my servant (how is Dr Gilbride???), so that I can gaze at it.

43. Dunedin Saturday installment April 11

Dear Apis mellifica,

Notes to accumulate and post later in the week, if I can restrain myself as long.

I was so happy to have news of you all at Hermosillo or Live Oaks Inn and fortunately your letter, which came this morning, did not blow away in the gale that's been raging all night though the temperature is a fair into-winter one—58 degrees—we seldom have more than a few days of low temperature—low being in the forties—but the nights can get chilly, with slight frost. So much for the meterological report. My house has been rocking and shaking as it has only done in an earthquake and sometimes I wonder if there's some moment when an eighty-eight year old house may decide to surrender to the gales that must have buffeted it over long periods on this hill, and in the dead of night it occurs to me that the moment of surrender may arrive, then, poof, collapse—no bodies were found in the rubble—this is clearly the earth (tender) alternative to visions of headlines in a plane flight. It is hard to learn to accept oneself as one is, but one must, absolutely; and if there's an area of apprehension staked out it has to [be] visited now and again, and cultivated.

Strangely enough I had a fan letter the other day from an elderly man in California who has been reading Owls Do Cry. He himself is writing a book about America. You should receive I.C. surely soon, as I've written to G.B about it, and to Carl Brandt, for I have not even had the airmail copy they promise me. My mind is steering towards my new novel—obviously the steering wheel has been in motion for quite a while. Word from the much-missed corner of Hermosillo Drive helps amazingly. You're a wizard.

Sorry to hear that Jo is rather unhappy. I sent a Dunedin card to both her and El and will write to them. One does hesitate to make judgments about other people's feelings, particularly if one happens to live almost entirely by feeling and if one tends to roam in and out of other people's minds so much in the practice of writing. There seemed to me to be a promise—or threat—of desolation for Jo in South Hadley. She needs lots of like-minded people to flourish among. Perhaps she'd better open her Maison D'absurde and we'll all go there—for periods.

One hesitates, too, to say what people 'need'. It's a dangerous presumption but everyone suffers from it at the hands of others, all in good faith.

I'm afraid I rather go on sermonising about this but if I've learned one lesson early in life it is that the essence of each person is sacred, no matter what its flavour—I'm getting into deep water or syrup and will stop . . . or climb out.

And talking of syrup or 'honey poured over old regrets' as you describe your reading of Rilke. You do have a mellifluous voice as one would expect of apis mellifica and Rilke has many regrets . . . but the readings are beautiful though in the recording I have, the 's' sound fizzes like Alka-Seltzer because you may have held the microphone too close—no—the recording meter was probably too high. Last night I felt very sad because I excitedly bought a Penguin Modern European poets series—Rilke, Selected poems—and when I opened it (I had thought I would send you one, and that maybe here was a good translation, and I was in a hurry when I bought it, and lured by the haunting-eyed face on the cover)—I found the poem *Autumn Day* reading as follows,

'Lord, it is time. The summer was so great.

Impose upon the sundials now your shadows

and round the meadows let the winds rotate.'

I think it is a shocking translation—it's by J B Leishman, as are all of them, and all are pretty bad, I think, so I'm going down to my basement to prepare some bombs for the day when the Great Translation Revolution is at hand, or, rather, at tongue or pen. Meanwhile, for all his 'ever more mature' McIntyre wins my praise. When my parcel arrives with Vergers in it we'll remedy this, I hope.

So nice and warm to hear from you.

Sunday.

Ironing today . . .

Not really. I swear I'm completely drip-dry, well almost. I've been living in Paul's shirt since

(miss breakfast ↓ miss dinner ↓ miss ↓ you all & piano ↓

I came home—it gives me the feeling I'm still in Santa Barbara or nearby.

I hope your new portrait goes well and is full of discovery. Where is Paul's portrait of the giant with butterflies at his lips and a forest or/and savannah on his chest? I missed it when it went from the wall but I still see the three heads under the Italian blue sky and the billowing cloud and I wish I'd had more time to look at it. I don't think I'm able consciously to look at things and absorb their detail and yet afterwards these 'flash upon the inward eye' in detail, and remind me that one is always seeing and taking in whether or not one is aware of it.

Platitude number n.

I've had a letter which pleases me very much. Someone on the staff of the music department of the University has been commissioned by the Broadcasting Company (N.Z.B.C.) to compose a (quote) 'work for chamber ensemble for the new television music programme. The new programme will trace the preparation of the work from its first rehearsal to final performance by the N.Z.B.C. Symphony orchestra.'

He says he's started work on a setting for tenor voice and chamber ensemble using some poems from The Pocket Mirror, and wants my permission to use the poems. I love the idea of being allied to music. Also, I feel as if I now have a foot or ear inside the music department which has a wonderful collection of records. We can borrow records from the Public Library also, and there's a listening room which charges ten cents a listen. I think the library (whose books are free) charges twenty-five to fifty cents for the loan of a record. The Music Dept now has a Mozart Fellowship for a composer.

MONDAY.

I had a visit today, no, yesterday, sorry, from a friend* (I told you of her in a letter) who has her finger, metaphorically, on the pulse of Dunedin while her husband has his finger literally on the pulse, as he's a general medical practitioner; and goodness knows where the other idle fingers are, probably in the same place as the dial-hand of time . . . I declined the invitation to spend the day at their seaside *bach* or *crib* which is a few miles up the coast (7 or 8) in magnificent setting of hills and sea.

---

* Dorothy Ballantyne

Dorothy is a kind of Antipodean* [footnote: *except that in N.Z. we acknowledge only loin of mutton below the belly button] Jo Rider—brilliant, witty, with allusive literary conversation—she can produce a quote from everyone who's ever written, to put her point across: consequently she's rather exhausting. Her husband is a quiet thoughtful type, inclined, I imagine, to be in amused retreat much of the time. I have a vivid sad image of her first husband who was ill for many years and wandered about the house in his dressing-gown, quite isolated among his two growing daughters and his wife whose work as Children's Librarian had to keep the house going and the children at school and her husband provided for. I remember his death too, a few years ago, and the funeral party, my first funeral party, and how I sat in a small ante-room and drank sherry and people came to talk to me one by one because I would not join the others.

Well. Excuse me for being a bore. How I love the continuity of life and death and how the past eats up the present and the present the future, and I like the way death, seen from a distance, fits into the pattern.

I sermonise again. But when Dorothy and Robert were sitting in my sitting-room yesterday eating (yes!) date scones, Dick's ghost was there too, I'm sure, though he never visited my home. He was a florid military-looking man, and I did not like him, but his isolation in his last years was terrible to feel and see.

Now for a little light relief . . . I tried to make some cider from the tray of apples off my tree; and today I'm making lentil soup; and my study is now ready to work in; and today the electrician comes to tell me how much the plug for the record-player is going to cost (my electrical switch-board has to be altered).

Oh to be in Santa Barbara now that April's there.

I wonder what April's doing in the Hermosillo lair?

******   ********   *************   *********

101% pure love to B + P + Ned

    from Jay

[handwritten at top: * except that in N.Z. we acknowledge only loin of mutton below the belly button.
101% pure love to B. + P. — Ned
[giftily strangled] from Jay]

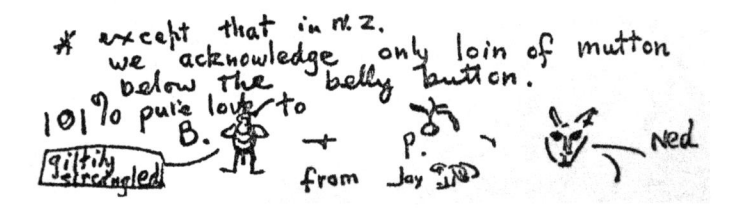

[in margin: Nice of Eva M to read me!! I read here of the N.Y.C. bombing.]

44. Dunedin April 14

Dear Bill, or Apis Mellifica,

    I just happened to be passing my typewriter on the route between my new record player and my electric jug which has burned out its element as I was so absorbed in listening to music; and I thought I'd write one of my interminable number of notes to Hermosillo Drive or Live Oaks Inn or Paradise Flower Nook among the Fern Feelies. I do get very very homesick for my Californian friends. A current of loneliness sometimes flows around me and I get pretty sad. The people here all seem so cold and harsh—I suppose I can never really dismiss my past N.Z. experiences while I'm in New Zealand.

    How is the new portrait? Today was a day of excitement for me because I collected your framed painting and they've done it very nicely and now it's hanging on my wall as a much-needed Santa Barbara infiltration and the colour is so beautiful and it's full of poetry, of the 'poetry of motion'—I daresay I shall write a verse about it and I only write verse when I am moved to.

    Well, again, how are you all, peedauntal-wise? No market for them here, though there may be a market among the ladies. Here the streets are lined with Gents lavatories, a relic from the days when the gents rushed out of the pub at six o'clock after filling up since five. I'll have to enlist your help to invent a new product to keep me solvent in the Antipodes. A prick posy or something like that for the massive football players who are beginning to appear for the winter season.

And talking of them, maybe I owe an apology to the triple-pricked Granville Hicks for he has written a review* [in margin: *enclosed] of my book for a Chicago paper—the book isn't published yet but there are one or two reviews being prepared for 27th April (3 days after your birthday, Paul. How did I know? It's in your catalogue.) I misremembered your birthday Bill—I was thinking it was the seventeenth of April. What can I send you both from N.Z.? A sheep?

Oh how can I lure you to New Zealand to see me? If you are a furriner you are allowed to buy up to five acres of land here . . . If you visit me you can have a bath in the afternoon in full sunlight, as then my bathroom is flooded with sunlight . . . Your short evening walk will take you among trees and gardens or, if you prefer, a cemetery where Dunedin's most honoured poet, dead of course, or I hope, is buried. He lived in the last century and wrote, 'Not understood how many hearts are aching . . .' and so on. You can watch the procession of clouds at a 180 degree angle across the Dunedin sky . . . and you can be so chilled by the frozen-faced people in the streets that you will want to fly at once back to U.S.A. . . . but you will have a certain uncomplication here, as yet, though I do not know how long it will last; it is a favoured place which may be mind-confining unless one remembers to think World, whole world and all peoples and conditions—and one can't avoid that and remain or be a so-called 'artist'.

Here we have almost everything which people in over-populated countries regard now as luxuries—silence, space, gardens, comparatively clear air; all this, and stunted imaginative growth. I feel it but I can't prove it. Yet it can't be all that stunted if anonymous business men (I wonder who they are?) have decided to pay my way each year—they haven't begun depositing anything yet because I haven't said I'm here . . . confidential information, as you know.

I know I say it over and over but I do miss you and the household so much—every moment of the day I miss—the getting-up and my good-morning kiss from you and Paul (if I was good or you were both bold enough), and the breakfast, and the vitamins and the morning piano and Paul in the garden and then your going off to the studio and your return and the lunch and so on and so on and so on—but I won't go on, but I will; and while you were at the studio, the way Ned took possession of the place, knowing you were gone and he was in charge, the way he came to life and began exploring the garden, just to make sure of things, and usually he would give me a greeting before he sprawled out between the geraniums or on the washer.

And after a morning's dozing, how business-like he appeared suddenly, when you returned from the studio! Briefly. Then he would retire again, having handed over responsibility to you and Paul. I got to know quite a lot about his character . . . the same goes for the rest of the household. And I, of course, am not unknown also, as the Antipodean guest of Perception and Wisdom personified . . .

To my record player. It sounds very nicely, is stereophonic with two speakers and it has a plug by which I can connect it to the tape recorder and thus play stereophonically any tape you send of your playing the piano . . . also of your reading poems, and giving interviews and so on . . . My player cost 90 dollars . . . and was paid for out of my *Pocket Mirror* Award.

The other day I sent you a tape—pretty awful because I couldn't really think of anything to say. The thirteen stories I recorded from the *Lagoon* are now being read (I read them) over the radio, one a week, but I haven't had the courage to listen to them or I would have recorded them. I missed, though, what I thought would be a better story than the others. There's one which I think I read and which I'll try to record—it's called 'Swans', and as Swans are on the menu it might be an idea for me to send it. It's a very simple story.

I'll 'close' now (for the moment). That's a time-honoured way of ending a letter, isn't it, saying that you will 'close' . . .

Au revoir with 102 percent pure peedauntal-free, germ-free, dust-free love which sounds so antiseptic I'll mix with it a lusty virus, Type X, for

    Bee & P & N   from Jay

45. Dunedin April 17

Dear *[drawing of bird] Apis mellifica [drawing with "zzz letter Battery" and "J's heart"]*

Dear Apis Mellifica,

    It warmed my heart (the cockles of) to get a letter from you this morning, and to know that all is fairly fine with you and Paul and Ned and you're having some social fun, whatever that means. I hope you wore your nice ties when Wright L[uddington] came to lunch—you both looked very smart that day when you set off rather like two people, two K's, in Kafka, to lunch on the hill. What did you get for your birthday?

    I enjoy hearing about what's happening at Hermosillo Drive and environs.

    Meanwhile back in my Dunedin Omicron I've advanced to my studio typewriter, so work is nearer and nearer, and starts, indeed, next week. I wish sometimes that I did not have my studio where I live— only because I accumulate in the whole house so much clutter of papers and manuscripts and writing materials the disorder of which drives me crazy. I have two trunksful of manuscripts in the basement and I'm determined not to unpack them. Did I tell you that Frank Sargeson is selling his papers to the National Library, chiefly to rid himself of clutter; and I'm thinking of giving mine to the local University Hocken Library which has a special collection of N.Z. manuscripts. My operative verb is 'giving' only because if these anonymous people start paying into my bank account my conscience will be salved if I, too, do some giving. I'll see about that. Frank, the old devil, is selling my letters to him! They're quite innocuous and there are not many and they're not personal—he swears he'll split the proceeds!

    I'm so glad the book arrived. You shouldn't have to pay for it, either. I still haven't seen it, and I don't think it's fair. George Braziller is away so often in Europe these days that I've taken to communicating with Ed Seaver, the chief editor. I still haven't recovered from the fact that triple-pricked Granville Hicks wrote such a nice review after the nasty remark he made to me when he saw the catalogue—admittedly the catalogue was nth lower grade.

Also I'm pleased you like the dedication. I can't remember now what I said! R.H.C. (my old psychiatrist in London) is my only other dedicatee, except for *Mona Minim* which is for my niece Pamela and little James Marquand, and *Snowman Snowman* is a manuscript (the story only) which John Money 'bought' from me for 100 dollars, so he necessarily is mentioned in it. I had meant it to be a ballet.

Enough of me me me and my work, socalled. We had a wet day last week and as I walked along the street I saw that all the cats in all the households were curled up in each front room on the bed, snoozing, and though that sounds peculiar numerically you know what I mean. It was a day for cats to snooze all day and not venture out at all. How in tune with the weather and its moods they are!

Today is very warm, a warm wind blowing, and the sun coming into my room—bedroom—and kitchen is very hot—I'm thinking of growing tomatoes in my bedroom or in my back passage . . . I'm reading Albert Camus' *Carnets* (in English though they are here in French also); and I'm beginning at last to get the domestic concerns off my mind, having reduced my Janet-home-alone diet to lentil soup with lots of vegetables (from my garden), and if I want bread or cookies badly enough I make them. I have bought myself a small refrigerator and I find the organization of food so much simpler: a record-player to preserve my sanity (?) a refrigerator to preserve my food, and now where does the prospective piano fit in? I've not bought it yet, mostly because I can't afford it, also because I am so cluttered up with stationery cupboards and filing cabinets and bookshelves that there's nowhere to put a piano and this problem forces me to make one of those curious equations—does a piano equal a stationery cabinet? I decided after a while that a piano equals a bed and so I phoned Brown's and Mr Brown who is very shrewd came up in his car to look at my bed and mattress and I could tell by the look in his eye that he wasn't going to bargain so I sold it to him for nine dollars. He promptly took it away leaving me with only two beds in my house, with room for a piano, and with money to buy a record for my record-player. If I were a mathematician I would construct a fascinating equation from this but I'm not so I won't.

★★★★★★★★★★★★★★★★

I get very lonely at night.

★★★★★★ ★★★★★★★★★★★★★★★★

I owe May Sarton a letter. I promised myself I would write to her when I got home but my parcel with her letter in it hasn't arrived yet.

★★★★★★ ★★★★★★★★★★★★ ★★★★★★★★★★★★

I cannot write here the Leishman translation of 'The Swan'—it is so unforgivably bad, I think.

★★★★★ ★★★★★★★ ★★★★★★★★

I get very lonely at night.

★★★★★ ★★★★★★★

Do you know that parody of Eliot by Henry Reed which begins,

> 'As we get older we do not get any younger.
> Pray for me under the draughty stair.
> As we get older we do not get any younger.'

I was aware, as I've said, that it was your birthday recently and that it will be Paul's soon. Do painters paint pictures for their birthday as poets write poems? 'On this day I complete my . . . year'. When I was at Yaddo last year and Philip Roth was there he had his thirty-sixth birthday and I reminded him that Byron had written 'On this day I complete my thirty-sixth year'. When I reread the poem I was startled to discover that in those days thirty-six was old—Byron talks of himself as an old man, which he was, I suppose. And so have you painted a birthday picture—in your birthday clothes? I have a private quirk in connection with my writing—I like to finish a novel before my birthday, as if perhaps the birthday were only another day for deathday.

I have seen no people this week, I have lived in quietness, I have talked to no-one, I have said nothing but, Will you mend my meter, please? to an electrician who promptly came, complaining that my walls had *dwangs* in them. My dwangs offended him but what could I do? And then of course there was the Mr Brown who bought my bed and mattress. He is tall and lean and looks like a cattleman. These people are people from far countries who visit my island home and solitude—a solitude that is the best climate for writing but it is tainted too much by the loneliness that comes from not being near like-minded people. I put too much salt in the soup today and I can't take it out. I tried mixing other varieties of flavour, even a spoonful of sugar to drown the salt with sweetness but it didn't work, it only increased the salt taste and when I taste the soup I shall have to comfort myself by reminding myself I am savouring the chiefest (if there's such a word) taste of life. So with my climate.

******   ************

Enough of the depths. I wrote a letter to Jo and to Elnora the other day.

Au revoir for now. Kisses (that is, syllogistic kisses which encompass the undistributed middle). With wings beating against the walls of antipodean room.

46. Dunedin April 19

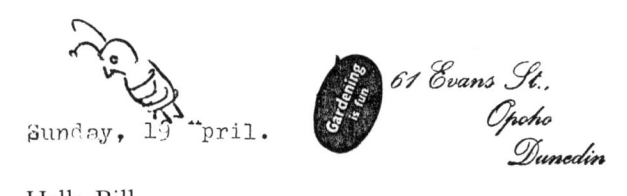

Sunday, 19 April.

61 Evans St.,
Opoho
Dunedin

Hello Bill,

Would that I were on the patio and you and Paul had just come out, after a thriving morning at the studio, bearing the peanut-butter sandwiches . . .

This Sunday I was determined to plant the daffodil bulbs I bought ten days ago but there's been another wild wind, though the sun is shining, and when I went down the garden to empty my waste-paper basket in the place where I burn it, I was nearly blown away. The wind is making a terrible crying noise, like an animal that's trapped somewhere, and hurt. I'm writing this in my study or studio which is at the front of the house and looks out over the street and the house opposite (the setting of my story *Winter Garden*) where the roses and geraniums are in full bloom, and a red japonica bush. The house is empty, and being redecorated for, I suppose, new owners who arrive now and again to inspect the handiwork. Beyond the house, to the south, I can see the row of dark green firs which border the Northern Cemetery where the poet is buried.

So much for my eye and its seeing. This morning I listened to Schubert's Sonata in B flat played by Clara Haskil—starting with the known and familiar. I got it and Purcell's *Dido and Aeneas*, twenty cents each record for a week, from the public library, and I've been playing them and playing them until they've come into my sleep. My musical experience is slight but I wonder if I shall ever hear a movement of a sonata that is as full of forgiveness as the second part of the second movement of the B flat Sonata—Schubert seems to be forgiving everything and everyone, including himself.

So much for my ear and its quasi-listening. My heart and its feeling? I'm lonely. It's a new experience for me to miss people.

Oh—my book arrived at last! I'm pleased with the dedication as long as it doesn't make John Marquand wonder suspiciously if Sue is Bill Brown's mistress! The next dedication you can have all to yourself, if you won't feel it too much of a burden, or bad taste on my part.

I'm going to reread the old masters, starting with *The Idiot* which I reread half-way at MacDowell and then had to return it to the library. Here, I've an *Idiot* of my own, and a *Crime and Punishment* for each room, and a *To the Lighthouse* for each room—not deliberately, I just happen to have more than one copy of some books.

I'm having to reorientate myself with the weather—I shouldn't use the word reorientate, it's a Rilke-translation kind of word used by the terrible translators. I had thought I would find winter already here but it is not, and it seems more like summer, and then I remember that the winter here is short and the cold consists chiefly of a few days together when it's wet and miserable and cold, followed by some days of ordinary sunshine, with darker mornings and earlier evenings, followed by a few frosty days, and so on; and then it's over and the crocuses are in bloom. I miss the sense of doom that comes over one in the northern hemisphere at the approach of winter: here the weather might get just plain nasty without being attended by the dignity of doom and tragedy. I think your Californian winter might be something this way too? I remember a letter you wrote me while I was at Yaddo. You were writing on a rainy day and you gave such a vivid feeling of the wetness and dreariness of leaky weather.

Maybe like my nephew Neil I should have been a meteorologist. Excuse me for going on about the weather but what else is there alive around here where I am?

Work next week—tomorrow; and I shall be (or should be) finished my new novel by September, with the first draft finished maybe in June. Or maybe I'll take years and years. That's if I can bear living here; I've never been at home in this country, but I'm at home in my little house among the books and the clouds. Will you visit me?

Now for my feet and their walking, my wings and their flying, I'm off down the road to post this; so here I am buckling on my peedauntal ready for the journey, and away I go, blue Jay

to mail a letter to Rainer Maria Bee with love to him & to Paul & to Ned

47. Dunedin April 21 (handwritten)

Hello Bill & Paul (Ned can get a share at the end)—

What are you two doing these days? What are you eating? What are you drinking? 'Something light, please, if you're making a drink for me.' Do you have lilacs now in the door-yard?

Morning here. The rest of the Antipodean world is asleep, the city lights are still gleaming & twinkling through last night's rain & the sky is a dark mass. It's been cold, cold in the bones & the heart yet not cold according to the temperature & by northern standards but what influence do standards have over human functions? Ah it's cold. All my thermostatically controlled electric heaters can't generate me an ounce—or is it *therm*—of warmth.

I have a blue hydrangea at my door but Rilke has already written of it—so accurately I daren't say anything. Look after each other & Ned—& love. 100% pure from Jay.

48. Dunedin April 23 Shakespeare's Day

[Letterhead: Hotel George Washington, 23 Lexington Ave. at 23rd Street, New York, N.Y. 10010, with handwritten annotations including "Help! Help!", "what nice toys you are drawing", "Since I have been adding elastic to my garments I have had no further trouble.", "Even the bath with a handful of corks and a kitchen sieve for fishing is grand fun", "23d April Shakespeare's Day", "Bee"]

Bee,

 Oh, yesterday; bonus letters from Bill and Paul which both made my hour, my day, my world and now I'm getting all smugly and happily down to work and at the same time wearing out the 20 cent record I borrowed from the Public Library—I just can't help listening to it again and again and its grooves are aching and arthritic with record fatigue; it has got under my skin.

 So the tape arrived! The Swan commentary is from Plato—Phaedo. I thought most of the tape was rather stupid because I didn't know what to say (being non-verbal) and I ended up by trying to show how smart I was with my reading and so on, which is always fatal—I'm an exhibitionist, secretly, I think. I too loved the cat's purr—I'm beginning to realise that a cat's purr is as personal as fingerprints. I know it makes for security to see likenesses between things, people, animals, and to want there to be likenesses, but I love the adventure of differences. I'm sermonising again!

 Your letters came just as I was taking time off to make a honey-and-water mix for the wax eyes that are feeding in my strawberry tree—my downunder chickadees, so to speak. Their appearance is a sign of winter for they leave the bush and all its honey-bearing plants and look for honey where they can get it in civilization. They are in flocks in my garden—little green birds with a white ring around their eyes; sometimes we call them ring-eyes. The bellbirds, too, come out of the bush—all the native birds do, in winter.

 I haven't read The Secret-Sharer yet—it vanished and I can't find it, I must have left it at my sister's. On the plane I did not even do the puzzles you gave me because your sleeping pill was so effective and it was only the other evening that I opened the puzzle book and found myself trying to decide, logically, which out of Horatio, Harvey, Henry and Hugh, was the aerialist, clown, lion-tamer and equestrian . . .

Paul, I love the drawing of the muttonbird—of course it is *really* like that—the newsphoto did not show the birds very clearly. They are sheep, old sheep—you don't qualify for wings when you're a lamb—who grow wings and take to the trees and you hear them baa-ing and bleating at night. Wherever they fly they leave a woolmark, pure virgin wool: they are above earthly things. Their wings are curly, too, as you have pictured them—like angels' wings.

About the carnivorous plant and its critical condition—don't believe it, it is only waiting its chance to extend its appetite and menu so you both must be very careful where you set foot in the peanut butter patio, and never, never, even for an instant must you wear those brown bread shoes!

I'd like to be there to sample the truck-driver cookies. I'm glad you're keeping your hand in, Bill! That's what hands are for. Here we are all the time trying to assign complicated functions to various parts of the body when each, after all, is so simple.

I hope your new sitter is not struck down like the Young Edward, gatherer of wild roses . . . You might be interested to know I had a brief visit the other day from the rather brilliant friend I mentioned—her husband, meanwhile, was at a funeral. She saw your painting on my wall, Bill, and exclaimed how beautiful it was, and I agreed. And then she began to tell me of a friend of her daughter's who has been composing a lot of music. I asked her, curiously, why she had begun talking of music and she (to whom I had said nothing) said, 'Oh I suppose it was that painting which reminded me. It's full of music. The figures grouped there remind me of notes of music.'

I hadn't thought of it myself, but they *do* look like a grouping of notes. Dorothy stayed only for a date scone and then went home.

Life is pretty barren here for me, socially, because everyone is so bloody staid and straight-laced. I'm getting to rely more on the underpopulation I meet when I go out walking—the numerous cats sitting on fences, absorbing everything with their uncensored gaze; and the dogs that wander around in the early morning. I look at them and they look at me and say, Well we know, we know, how do you think *we* put up with it day after day, night after night. It's a grim life all right but we get by. Why not join us?

I am having my house painted, to seal me in, and make me more waterproof and dripdry, and one of the two husky gentlemen has just told me that the 'lady of the house' provides a morning cup of tea and something to eat, so why not come this way by mutton-bird on the cheap rate and make me some truck-driver cookies, or painter cookies which, I suppose, will have a subtle variation in flavour. And my neighbour has just phoned me to say did I know there was a hole in my wall and would I like him to fix it for me? So there he is, fixing the hole in my wall. He's probably sat at his window (he's a retired something) day after day staring at my hole in the wall and longing to fix it . . .

Oh I do miss you, both of you, and Ned, so much, and I know I say it again and again and I get depressed because I think what if you die suddenly and I never see you again?

Enough of that. 'As we get older we do not get any younger.'*

Here's a heart-warming quote:

'He who beholds in work no-work, and in no-work work, is the man of understanding among mortals; he is in the Rule, a doer of perfect work.' (Bhagavadgita)

Last page; the next day.

Last evening after I had cooked a shoulder of mutton, fooling myself in apparent ease I made House-Painters' Cookies for the use of the two men working here—oh what a mess they turned out to be, they hardened suddenly (!), and now they're like slabs of concrete. I put in all I could think of—bran flakes, wheat germ, wholemeal and so on but I forgot to turn the oven on . . .

Au revoir

---

* From Henry Reed's parody of T.S. Eliot.

49. Dunedin April

Dear B,   Dear B.,

Another hailstone in my storm of correspondence—dodge it if you wish . . . My battery (tape) has run out and so today I have not been able to hear you reading the poems and being interviewed and playing the Bagatelles and the Hindemith, and Hugo Wolf. You see, I am housebound, for the house-painter is here. He's a scruffy-looking character, the sort people would hesitate before hiring, and he works on his own, with a friend sometimes, and so has not the latest equipment. All this appeals to me. It doesn't necessarily make him a nicer person but it makes him more of an individual, and I dare say from time to time he's faced with bankruptcy, as most of the little business and tradesmen are, so I couldn't feel angry when one day he demanded some money and I wrote a large cheque, and then he disappeared for a few days. I tried to be angry but I couldn't be. He reappeared this morning and worked hard all day and when a man from the Electricity Department came to fix the wires and needed some space at the front of the house he stood like a little terrier dog defending the house as if it belonged to him and it was about to be attacked. He thinks I'm a typist. I give him a cup of tea morning and afternoon and sometimes he reminisces about spinsters he has worked for, and when he says the word spinster he glances at me and says, Nothing personal mind you.

I think you have helped me break the Conrad barrier. I count it among your long list of achievements. I have been reading *The Mirror of the Sea* and I find myself addicted to his writing, wanting to return to it in the same way that one wants to return to passages of music. The book was given to me by a Polish poet* whom I knew when I first went to London years ago: a strange lonely man, a Hippy in pre-Hippie days who used to get his bed and board where he could from pickings about Soho. He was one of the numerous poets and painters who haunted London in

---

* David Kozubei

the late nineteen-fifties, talking and talking about the poems they were going to write and the paintings they were going to paint but because the balance of their need was always so heavily in favour of human company rather than solitude, they completed very little work. They were like a huge packet of assorted artistic seeds scattered over the city, and only one or two managed to thrive . . . well, I never read Conrad, until now.

I had a letter from Jo yesterday, brilliant as usual, high-pitched with a lovely rhyme which went,

'Twas a sad Frame returned to Dunedin
to find folks not even bleedin'
but at least her garden
grown rampant past pardon
in her absence had often been peed on.'

By cats only, though, as far as I can tell . . .

And I had a letter from Elnora where she describes her plan to visit the West Coast . . .

The empty house across the road from me has been taken over by a black cat. Perhaps the owners left it there when they moved, I don't know. It's a very handsome black fluffy cat and each day it makes an inspection of the garden and its roses and geraniums and then it sits on the front lawn and washes its face.

Also I have to report another Antipodean phenomenon. Very mysterious. Each day when I take a little sun on my balcony, a Red Admiral Butterfly arrives to drink the nectar from the koromiko blossom. There are only one or two blossoms as it is not supposed to be in bloom, not really, and certainly the butterfly is the only butterfly around at this time of year—it is not unusual—red and velvet black, slightly smaller than the Santa Barbara butterflies. Perhaps it has arrived from Santa Barbara? An Early Inspection Unit? An Early Warning System?????

I heard from Charles Neider who is planning to visit Ross Island in the fall (U.S. fall). The sun has set now in the Antarctic and does not rise until some time in late August. You will have to rescue me.

Goodbye now. And pure love to you and Paul and Ned, though if you test it in your peanut butter laboratory you will find just a trace of impurity for which you will not, I trow, blame me.

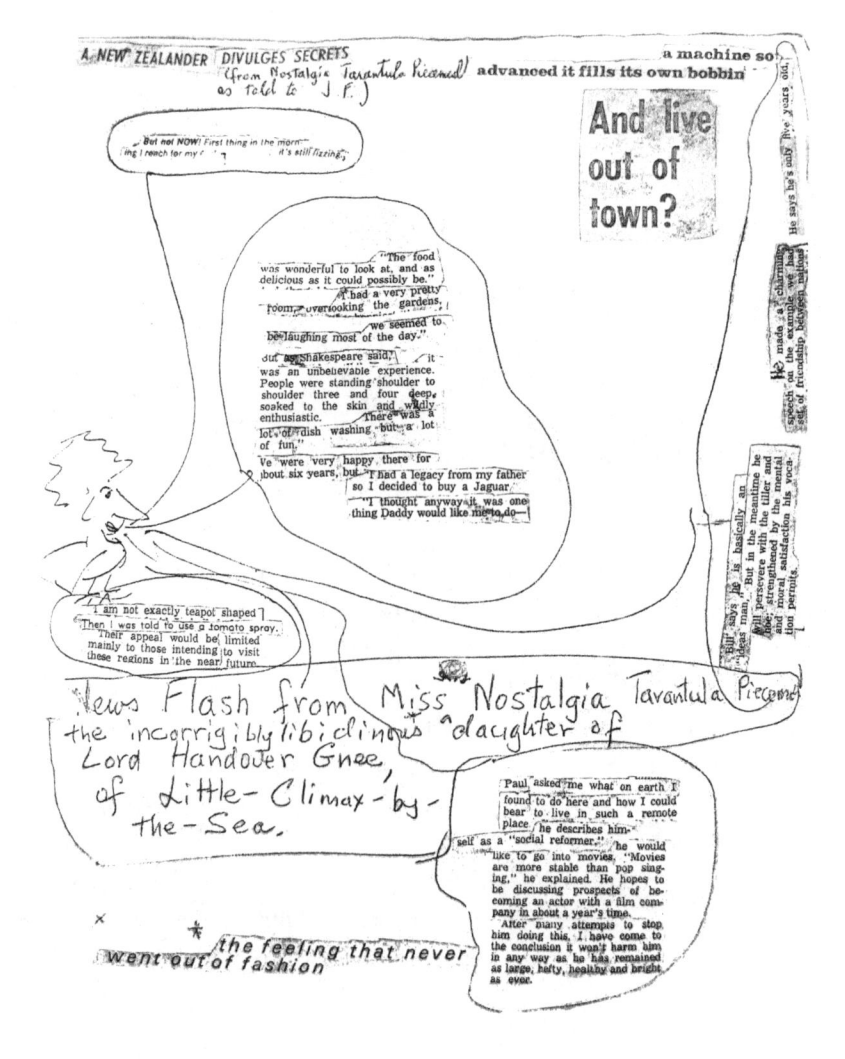

A NEW ZEALANDER DIVULGES SECRETS (from Nostalgia Tarantula Ricamed as told to J F.) advanced it fills its own bobbin a machine so

But not NOW! First thing in the morning I reach for my ... it's still fizzing.

And live out of town?

He says he's only five years old,

"The food was wonderful to look at, and as delicious as it could possibly be."
"I had a very pretty room, overlooking the gardens,
we seemed to be laughing most of the day."
But as Shakespeare said, it was an unbelievable experience. People were standing shoulder to shoulder three and four deep, soaked to the skin and wildly enthusiastic. There was a lot of dish washing but a lot of fun."
"We were very happy there for about six years, but I had a legacy from my father so I decided to buy a Jaguar."
"I thought anyway it was one thing Daddy would like me to do—"

He made the example we had set of friendship between Ireland

Bill says he is basically an ideal man. But in the meantime he will persevere with the litter and strengthened by the mental and moral satisfaction his vocation permits

I am not exactly teapot-shaped. Then I was told to use a tomato spray. Their appeal would be limited mainly to those intending to visit these regions in the near future.

News Flash from Miss Nostalgia Tarantula Piecemeal the incorrigibly libidinous daughter of Lord Handover Gnee, of Little-Climax-by-the-Sea.

Paul asked me what on earth I found to do here and how I could bear to live in such a remote place, he describes himself as a "social reformer," he would like to go into movies. "Movies are more stable than pop singing," he explained. He hopes to be discussing prospects of becoming an actor with a film company in about a year's time.
After many attempts to stop him doing this, I have come to the conclusion it won't harm him in any way as he has remained as large, hefty, healthy and bright as ever.

× ✱ the feeling that never went out of fashion

122 | JAY TO BEE

50. Dunedin April

Dear Apis Mellifica,
Bee I'm expecting you
to fly my way
some day . . .

My new novel is going to be called, as you suggest, 'Critical Condition'. Or 'Multiple Injuries'. Or 'Deeply Unconscious'. Or why not 'Intensive Care'? Why does one have to have a new title each time? One could write all one's life and use the same title.

Sunday morning. The light-green curly leaves of the hedge outside my study window are all aquiver, not because it's Sunday morning but because there's a light breeze and it's a clear blue day with the night chill not quite gone; and the shadows are long. This is a country of long shadows and the first thing you notice if you travel away down south is that your shadow can walk across a wheat-field and touch the sky.

I found *The Secret Sharer*. It had been hiding from me. I think that those possessions which vanish for a time do so for some reason of their own and when they are ready to be found they make sure they are found. I have books which periodically vanish and cannot be found no matter how hard I search, until, suddenly, in their own time, they are there. I read *The Secret Sharer* and I'm still feeling the impact of it, it is so mysterious and lonely and full of Rilke's 'die Schwere'*.

***** ******* *******

Having just listened to the Kathleen Ferrier record of 'The Song of the Earth', borrowed from the Public Library, I am effectively silenced. Ewig.

***** ******* ********** ****** *******

When I am reading Conrad I find myself resenting descriptions of the ship and the duties of the sailors and feeling uncomfortable and bare-boarded but all resentment dissolves when Conrad describes the sea itself. I think the resentment arises from my being a woman in a world that clearly

---

* German word for heavy—Frame was particularly fond of Rilke's Autumnal poems—in 'Herbst' (Autumn) there is the phrase 'die schwere Erde' (the heavy earth)

manages better without women; but all that vanishes when Conrad turns to the sea because he uses a special tenderness to describe the sea, and one feels included, then. One is included also, and shares marvellously, the described intimacy of the two men, because here, I think, it is outside the narrow framework of he's and she's: I found it very moving. I don't know whether I'm a hopeful person myself, but I liked the youthful hopefulness of the story. One feels that the 'other self' will survive, simply because it is a young man's story. It's interesting to imagine what the story would be like if the narrator were an old salt near the end of his career. Or is it that one only meets one's other self when one is young? Perhaps if one is older and meets the other self one might fight it, for one's own survival? I've said enough. Ewig.

*******   **********

I have put a blue hydrangea in a vase beneath your painting. The painting gives me such delight, it is so rich, and the colour varies with the time of day, and when the colour of the twilight sky comes into the room the painting has a special sound—if I were (ah me!) near your piano I would show you the notes.

In my garden shall I plant Paul's Betony (a kind of veronica with

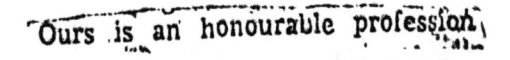

> Ours is an honourable profession

magical and medicinal properties) and Sweet William?

*******   ************

Take a spoonful of golden syrup and swallow . . . You too, Paul.

****   ***********

I am alone here, which is good for my work. I am also lonely which is not good and leads along dark avenues where there is no light to write by. I feel like a visitor from outer space. Where before I had only mildly transgressed by writing a book of poetry which my poet acquaintances in Dunedin disapproved of and thought (this is an actual quote) 'should never have been published'; as if to say, perhaps, 'your field if you have one, is prose, so graze in it', now I have transgressed because I have been 'flitting overseas', especially in evil America while everybody else stayed home and grew good. I really feel that Dunedin (and New Zealand) are so much 'home' to me that I might decide it would be better for me to leave it, to keep my sanity. It would be different if there were a group of babies like my MacDowell friends so I could enjoy my prolonged infancy. Ah me!

★★★★★★★   ★★★★★★★★   ★★★★★★★★★★   ★★★★★★★★

Love to   Paul   Ned   B
still have not received my 'Vergers'. It should arrive this week.

[handwritten note with drawing reading: "Love to Paul Ned B. still have not received my 'Vergers'. It should arrive this week."]

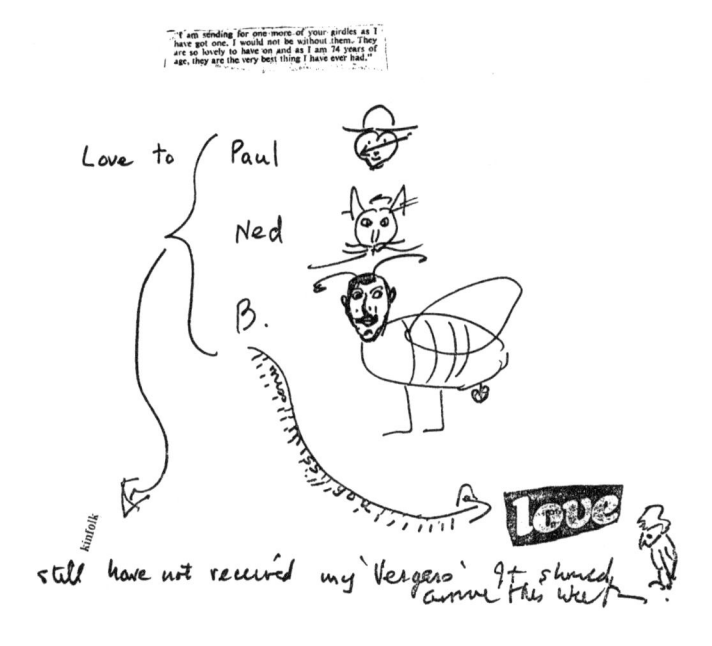

Magical, mysterious, medicinal! Your tape has just arrived! Oh what a superb interview! You are both intended for the stage—the third stage where, cumbersome rockets discarded, you orbit the moon!

The poems are, of course, beautifully read. Many thanks. And you may not believe it but the Hérodiade recording and the Hugo Wolf songs, not to mention the Bagatelles (and the first passage, out of Schubert, that I had been terribly homesick for, as you must have guessed) all sound well when plugged into the record-player and relayed through the stereo speakers. There's a slightly flattened effect and I have to keep adjusting the volume but they do sound well, whereas through the tape machine alone the musical sound is pretty awful. I've learned that this is because the tape speed is a speech speed and music speed is another speed. Ah but it is good to hear the voices of Mary Margaret and William Theo in their interminable argument about who really translated Rilke's French poems. I may just eavesdrop on Antipodean opinion about this, also what the public believes in relation to the fictional J.F. last seen on the peanut butter patio.

Meanwhile I'll post this and give you a rest.

51. Dunedin April

Dear Bill, B apis mellifica, and Paul, Dame M.M., and Ned C of whom more on another page . . .

Long hot brilliant days, clear cold nights: winter. The sun is almost too hot to stay out in. I am reminded of one of the *New Yorker*'s interminable queries when I had a character sitting 'outside in the sun in winter'. 'Surely,' the editor wrote, 'he wouldn't be sitting outside in winter?' I assured the *edirot* that he would be.

Your letter came on Saturday, it was like heaven. I loved it, and I loved the drawings and the cockle-warming collage; and all the news. I'm still waiting for my Intensive Cares! I'm happy that you like it. I put a lot of myself into it, I think, I don't mean me, as a person, but me and how I feel about many issues. I was very frightened when I was writing the third section because it seemed so real to me and the characters were drawn chiefly from people around near where I live in Dunedin and about whom I know nothing. I used neighbours etc. who might have merely said Hello to me, but my fantasies about them were numerous. I am amazed not only that art makes life happen but that life makes art happen. What a *New York Times* reviewer called my 'symbolic gardener', the father of Milly G, implied that I had made him a gardener to fit in with my symbols. He *is* a gardener. I know nothing about him and have not spoken to him but it was he, as a gardener, who made the so-called symbol happen. But I won't go on about this. The book, I think, is what I wanted to do, and I did it the way I wanted it but perhaps I had too many aims and did not succeed in most of them. In writing of Leonard I simply wanted in some way to ensure that he existed, even if I just recorded his existence, because he was based on my non-conforming uncle* whom I never knew but whose life in New Zealand was probably a hell—I knew him only for a few weeks before he died. John Leonard of *The New York Times* wrote such an understanding review that he probably could have written the book far better than I.

My house-painter is still here, and when he is having his morning or afternoon cup of tea he tells me of his life when he was a *sailor* on board a boat trading in China clay between U.K. and U.S.A., and of his pet monkey which he took with him wherever he was sailing. He should be finished this week.

A piano? My problem is I don't know what kind is good and what isn't. There are many around for sale, second-hand ones, and there's usually a classified section, Pianos, in the morning or evening paper.

I play your tapes a lot and the battery starts to wear out and your voice gets *deeper and deeper* and *slower and slower*. I'm completing a tape for you and on Monday next I'll record the story Swans which is being broadcast; not a very good story. My new novel wavers (it is my mortal enemy) chiefly because the parcel I posted has not yet arrived, and it had the beginning chapters—I can't even remember the names of the characters . . . yes I can. I'm sure you get the same way—cold feet

> **Please send me for 10 days and nights FREE TRIAL Sun-glo All Night Footwarmer.**

at the thought of another voyage into the unknown; excitement, too, as the characters appear, as landfall, and an awful lot of sadness, which is all as it should be.

---

* Charles Frame

TUESDAY.

Away to mail this before the box is emptied. I too visited an aunt*—no blood relation (as they say)—in a home for old people, and on my first visit I found her desolation quite terrible but on my visit last evening she looked amazingly well and cheerful. She was feeling 'forgotten'—she has only one other relative here, a niece† (a blood relation—as they say) whom she (and I) find rather fierce, though good-hearted. She is the wife of the economics professor and is a community, coffee-morning kind of woman, but my chief feeling about her arises from the envy my sisters and I had of her when we were young—she learned music and singing and was a well-known performer. She has a deep voice—*deeper, deeper* . . .

But this is boring?

Some time this week I'm going to pay a visit to Charles B whom I told you about, in his little house on the hill overlooking the harbour, with a peach tree in the middle of the front lawn. He is now, at aged 67 [61], in his third year of studying Russian at the University. He is also an honorary Doctor of Literature. And a poet, as I told you, and as you know from the poems I read on the tape. He is difficult to be with because he is so formal, though less so than he used to be, I'm told, and everytime he does relax he has the air of being so primly horrified at himself. His own generation look on him with deep respect, sometimes awe, for his gifts and his reputation as an art patron and collector, and his wealth, too (I mean financial), but the respect is perhaps alloyed with amused tolerance. He's most at home now, I think, with younger men and women.

And so on. I have Mallarmé's poems from the library and a collection of modern French poetry—some beautiful things in it. I do want to read the *Hérodiade*. I know that Oscar Wilde wrote a ballad, 'The daughters of Herodias, they danced before the king'. And Julian Symons, 'They dance, the daughters of Herodias'. And of course Wilde also wrote *Salome*. There was a long complicated but passionately written analysis of Mallarmé's poem in a book I had at Yaddo, but alas, it's not here—though it's probably in the University Library where I'm too shy to go.

---

* Hannah, wife of Frame's uncle Bob Frame

† Iona Livingston

Have you built your kennel-with Steinway. O have you? . . . I can't find the original, to parody it.

All kinds of love, in the first flush of morning waking, each to his or its choice, to

B   P   N

P.S. A cat has just arrived, dark grey & light grey & black & is washing itself on my back steps.

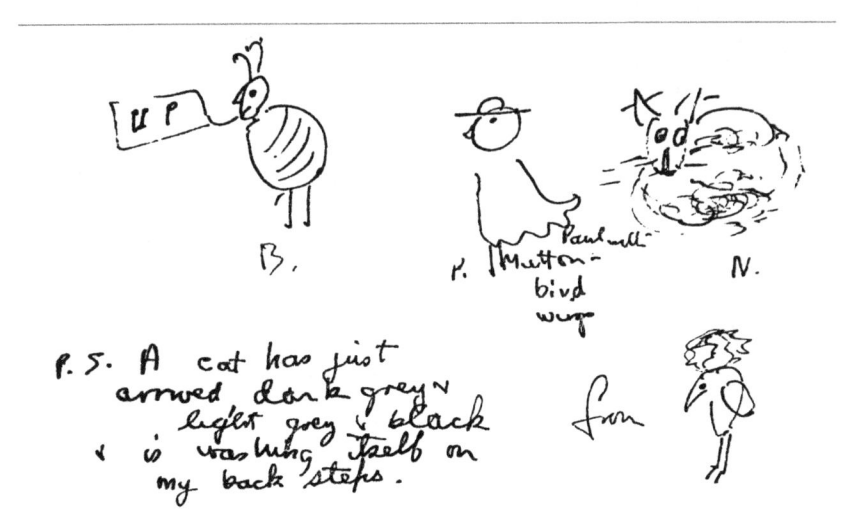

MAY

52. Dunedin May

good mornings begin with
Hollywood Toilet Bowl Symphony Orchestra under Bill Brown;

gives you so much more!

B, Dear

You are an angel; yet I, a mortal, find it impossible to feel the guilt I 'should' feel because you've sent me The Requiem and the Schubert and Schumann recording. Thank you so much. The Requiem is so beautiful, I think, and now is the time for me to listen to it when my thoughts are so much in U.S. and when I'm feeling depressed over the Cambodian affair. Will any poet, ever again, write a song of love and praise for an American President? Whitman's words are a large part of the beauty of The Requiem but I love the music too, the words are embedded there as if they were growing. The singing in some of the choruses is messy sometimes—it seems—because I can't hear the words but when the words are audible they and the music are so immediate and poignant. Phrases like 'the large unconscious scenery of my land'*—but I won't go on thus. The Schubert and Schumann recording is beautiful too, breath-taking in places. Perhaps I am being fanciful when I say that music can take away one's breath because it behaves like breath: it is like one of those cells, but a cell of sound and movement, that enters and takes over the life it inhabits.

Blah blah blah?

You are an angel then. Let me know if a 'longing as if for sin haunts your dream!'† ★ [footnote: ★Come at once] I know those poems by heart now, simply because I've heard you reading them.

★ quotation from Walt Whitman's poem 'When Lilacs last in the Dooryard Bloomed'
† quotation from Rilke's poem 'The Angels'

Meanwhile back in my Antipodean Omicron I'm experiencing (between Requiems and Sonatas) the first winter day, unexpected, with a snow-sky and rain from the south, and hail and sleet. Sometimes the grey in the sky divides and shows a patch of satin blue which is quickly recovered. My friend Dorothy came on her monthly visit. Before she comes she always phones to find out what the clouds are like because she visits partly to see the sky. She and her family have just farewelled 'grandsire'—her husband's father-in-law—who is eighty six, at the start of a lone voyage he is making to Europe.

Some of my luggage with your sweater in it arrived and I can only explain my delight by saying that I must have a cat mentality. I think I'll invite Ned to come and stay here while I go to Live Oaks Inn and snuggle down on the washer, and eat cut liver, and stalk the house and garden, and sit between the two geraniums (after sniffing each one), and even wangle a visit to Dr Gilbride! Talking of cats—I've been exchanging glances lately with a grey and black tom which came—I mentioned it—and sat to wash himself on the steps. The other day when I went down the garden I found him sitting curled in a little nest under the strawberry tree. Waiting for the birds, I suppose. When he saw me he sprang up, looked guilty and was about to fly off through the tangled grass

Is it habit forming?

when I said, Hello. I swear he looked astonished. People just don't

It drapes easily, pin tucks beautifully, gathers if you wish and yet it is still firm enough and at the wave of a hand inflates

say hello to strange cats wandering in their garden . . . do they, Ned? It's this grey and black tom who's been beating up the lady cats at night. And it's the same cat who lives about a hundred yards down the road and on fine days sits on the white stone wall and snoozes and on wet days lies curled up on a fancy bedspread in the front bedroom.

I made myself French toast for breakfast this morning . . . My work is going now, I mean moving. I'm afraid I miss you terribly. I try not to be Miss Nostalgia all the time, but I am.

Meanwhile back at Live Oaks Inn, there is a state of confrontation in the dining room between our characters Bill, Paul, Ned, and the carnivorous plant. Pandemonium, you may remember, reigned. Now read on.

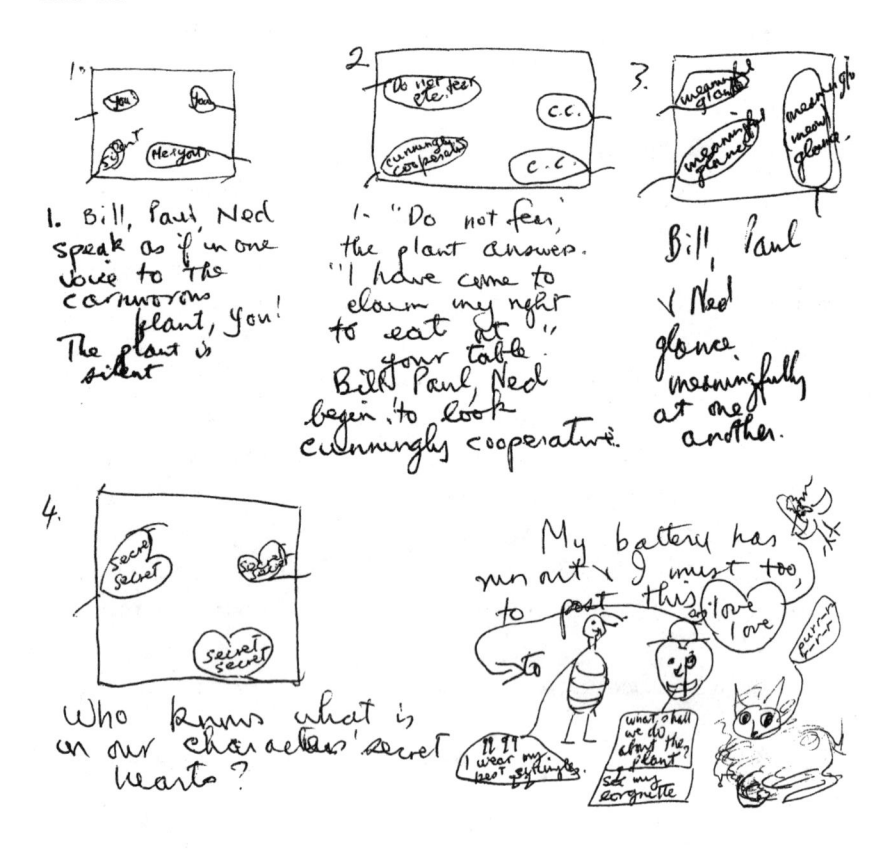

My battery has run out & I must too, to post this.

53. Dunedin May

Dear

Once again I take typewriter key beneath finger to say hello in the midst of my work which stopped abruptly when I received some reviews of my book and stupidly read them. Some were good but one (which of course I take notice of) suggested I'd be better off doing anything else but writing and (of course) I immediately, stricken, agree . . . What trials. Hello then, to everyone at Live Oaks Inn for which I get even more homesick when anything nasty happens—like running to mother!

Are you looking for a maid? So that you and Paul will be able to recline on the patio without lifting a finger? If you are then there's an Antipodean maid, with references (written by the alcoholic manager of the hotel where she worked (this smacks of prejudice) describing her as neat, punctual, of tidy appearance, courteous, conscientious and a very promising maid . . .) She also has a nursing reference which commends her patience and kindly care of the sick . . .

It sounds unlikely that you will be wanting that sort of maid but this one could always adopt a personality to suit. She guarantees to keep to her own quarters, pursue her work of caring for and cleaning house and masters, with quiet efficiency, but warns that her intelligence can cope only with the menial tasks—cleaning, washing, bedmaking, shopping, and the preparation once or twice a week of meals (that is, of dinners) which are better left to more imaginative practitioners. She is able to prepare breakfasts and lunches and will cook dinner as required, though her masters may be more competent and knowledgeable about their diet. She is trained to wait at table. She is also house-trained, inoculated, and comes with pedigree certificate, lately forged. She has a Mountain Lion, Rattlesnake and Carnivorous plant as pets and knows that her masters would accommodate these in their little house in Hermosillo Drive— odd corners can always be found. You are advised that she is also rather silent and does not speak more than a sentence at a time, and guarantees to speak a minimum number of words a day. She also has a pet typewriter which has been thoroughly inoculated and neutered (by recent critics) and has few objectionable habits. Surely it, too, could be accommodated, perhaps permanently in the washing machine where it will accompany the whirling clothes from fabrics delicate to robust. So if the masters hear an odd clacking sound coming from the washer they need not be alarmed.

This information, coming to you this bitter day (inwardly not outwardly) is free of charge and brings you all a store of love from your wellwisher (wish wish) in the Antipodes. Hurry hurry. Accept this Free Offer. Don't delay.* [footnote: Warning. Always read small print.]

— 'Thanks to you, I was recently hired *r*

I'm enclosing an autobiographical story which was printed a couple of years ago in U.S.

♡ J.

The hills show
they have tasted today
a platter of snow.
Their meal half-done
they invite the sun
to clear away.
Soon
on the stroke of noon
the green leaf-blade-patterned porcelain
is polished clean.
****
See?
Emily today
has left her grave
to teach me
syllables of the south.
The news of Bee
amazed her. 'I hope*
his gilt surcingles

134 | JAY TO BEE

*have been cleaned
with common soap
and not the new detergents
which deterge ineffably.
And how are Fly and Blue Jay?'*

*Her spirit only visited.
Her flesh has done its cope
with weather. Flakes of snow
were drifting through her eyes
and gave us no surprise. Her hand
a shaft of moonlight lay
easily across the hill and valley
yet restricted in the beam
of one surcingle's brightness
which both did* Bee *and* Seem.

*I had no time to question her.
I did not hear her go.
A noise-abating traveller
her transport was the flow
of nothingness from world to urn
driven by sun and snow,
its wheels the stars' rotation
sparking a planet-burn
kindled an age ago
before the mechanic time
of Am and Be and Die.*

*Yet I, Blue Jay
(substitute for Fly)
writing to Bee,
know that quite soon
to give me another lesson,
Emily will return
to this small southern room
(though she dearly loves her Tomb).*

* I told her a surcingle was being cleaned & repaired.

54. Dunedin May 12

Dear

Just been reading a nasty review of my book in the New York Sunday Times. Some fool sent it. You know how it feels. Hell several times several Sunday Times. Not understood etc. And the terrible thing is that whoever wrote it is probably *right*.

Therefore I'm going to run away to sea this instant as I haven't the energy to dig worms out of the garden and eat them!

Cold still day with after-winter light and pale blue sky; the grey pavements greyer, the white stone walls whiter, a shadow of a shaft of ice somewhere, an ice reflection from the Antarctic. Bodies and hearts all in ice.

*******   *********   ********

Stars for comfort.

*******   *********   **************

Michael H[itchings], the librarian of the Hocken Library has just called to collect several manuscripts (of some of my published works) that I'm giving them on long-term loan so as to get rid of clutter. He lives not far away but I do not see them often and do not know them very well, though when they go away for holidays I sometimes look after their cat, *Ngeru* (Maori for cat, I think), a sleek black independent tom who sleeps in the bath.

*******   *********   ********

Stars for comfort.

I miss you, Bill and I miss Paul—I miss you both terribly. And proud Ned. I've been trying to make a new tape for you but the sound keeps changing to very high or very low (deeper deeper), so I'm going to get an electrical adaptor—I don't think the batteries are very good here. Last evening when I went to record 'Swans' I found they had changed the radio programme, and this morning when I decided to read it myself my voice came out very high or very deep.

******

Sing on, sing on.

***   ******

You will be having summer and wandering around naked in the patio except for your peanut butter sandwich and your banana milkshake . . .

******   ******

Consolation is that Kenneth Burke wrote such a lovely note about my book which does not really deserve what he said. He was so sweet.

***   ********   *********

Turn over the page for a glimpse of icy realism.

Crazy warm comfortable love from

Blue Jay

55. Dunedin May 13

Dear Bill, Paul, Ned, my trinity most loved, inseparable, Hello.

Have you built the first plank into the Steinway-occupied kennel yet? Or the second, or the third? Time is short in this life, only a few inches or centimetres in length and the material it's made of is fragile. Our friend Emily D may tell us that satin ships are impossible, that ships 'require cedar feet', but don't believe her—so many carriages and appliances and appendages built to withstand storms are made of silk.

Baby J is lonely for the people of Live Oaks.

Meanwhile, back in my Omicron of the Antipodes, I'm still smarting (now and again when it comes to my mind) over my 'unreadable in the worst sense' review in the Sunday Times; but it will sink down to my unconscious and befoul it in befouled company. My house painter has still not finished his work and has proved himself a liar and a cheat and still I can't be angry with him—if I ever had any moral indignation I must have lost it early in life. Yet I have it strongly against organisations like 'The Pentagon'; yet if I met one of the stupid generals I would feel pity for him.

I spent last evening at Charles B's place. Charles invited Ruth D (a poet, his former secretary, and friend) and me to meet some Scholar from Canada who is here studying Commonwealth Literature. Oh where have all the babies and the touchie-feelies gone? An Icelandic Scholar (I mean a student of Icelandic) on the eve of his departure for Scandinavia was also there, and we sat around the electric fire and made polite remarks and though they didn't ask me how long and wide the United States was (you see, I can't escape) they expected me to speak very wisely about 'Life in the United States'. It was quite pleasant but it began to grow boring. The Canadian Scholar was a golden-curled clean-limbed handsome lad with a flashing smile. I preferred the Icelandic Scholar who was rather sullen and silent. His name was *Bill Manhire*. Ruth was witty and persistent, Charles was suave and in good humour, and I was dreadfully silent and couldn't manage a sentence without faltering, though Ruth kindly said afterwards that though I didn't say anything I gave the impression that if I wanted to I could have spoken volumes . . .

And yesterday afternoon I took a wander not quite to Bee-Supplies territory (The Place of the Stone Bees) but to a huge old warehouse full of old furniture, including old pianos, and as I walked by the old pianos I tried each one with my cinq doigts and a variety of sounds came out. There was one that had been sold for 250 dollars which had a pleasant sound; and others resented being touched and squealed; and others had sunk so low in pianistic despondency, not having been played or tuned for many years, that their sound was desolate, if they could produce any; and some were golden pianos, more carvings than keys, and some of the keys had their skin worn off their knuckles; and then I left the pianos and came to more furniture, a golden velvet sofa and I stood by it a long time and I kept returning to it and when I arrived home I realised why—it was the furniture out of the front room of my aunt's house, which is being sold and demolished to make way for the University.

Another instalment later.
My mail today has a list of questions for a radio interview, and all are impossibly dumb questions, most of them clearly arising from ignorance

of the ordinary common and garden pursuit of making—whether it's a poem or a painting or a piece of music. The tape recorder will be useful here. When I get it attached to electricity I will record what I want to say and so will not need to speak 'live'. (I told you that I'm having trouble with my batteries, so that voices are inclined to go 'deeper, deeper', a facility that while it may be welcomed in other parts of the anatomy is not what one would ask of one's recorded voice. You should also hear the 'higher higher' sounds, too. I tried to record something for you and when I played it back you would have sworn I was a little finch (Alice or Ted or Carol or Bob or Mary) the way I twittered and twittered.

Has Elnora been to visit you? Is she coming to stay? (I am green green Jay!)

I'm not really a 'writer of long letters'.

I haven't really much to say; it's just that my thoughts turn so often to you and the music and the shared baby-days and the parcel of days *is* tied by a short satin thread.

Tra-la-la.

a coffee stain
or an
un-cedar-footed phorm
sheep -

bowl of love

struggle struggle,
O my poor
satin feet!

J.

56. Dunedin May

Dear

Hello. Sunning yourself in the patio? Swimming in the shark-infested ocean? Playing a duet with the c. plant and Steinway? Ah how I wish etc.

I've been trying to finish the tape I started but my sssssss hisses and I don't know how to stop it. Do any of you live oaks have similar difficulties with your sssssss?

Yesterday I took a walk through the non-peopled places of Dunedin—along to the Northern Cemetery (not to be confused with the sea cemetery at Anderson's Bay where the yellow flowers grow in the Antipodean room), past the cemetery (I ducked in and used the ladies, something I never expected to find in a cemetery but I suppose the dead have their quirks of non-behaviour. This was the most non-peopled place I saw during my walk) down through the bush road (the founding city fathers set aside five hundred acres of native bush encircling the city, to be the property of the city) where creeks gurgled on either side and bellbirds belled, down towards the sea where the Art Gallery is. I spent some time in the Gallery but the usual display had been taken down to house the two exhibitions—they're short of room and are building an extra wing which I enjoyed, particularly Art of the Space Age, a misleading title with misleading generalisations in the introduction— talk of *the painter* today, as if there were such a being as the painter. I loved the Sunflower of Jean Tinguely and the Sonix of Stan Ostoja-Kotkowski, an Australian.

From there I did my waterfront walk along past the factories and the timber-yard smelling of fresh timber and the chocolate factory where I was joined by a man of about sixty who'd been in the Art Gallery when I was there and who had murmured to me, 'Some beautiful things here'. We walked along to the railway station and up towards the Octagon where he branched off (branch branch) to visit the Income Tax

Department, while I went towards home, not before I learned that the fellow-walker played an instrument or conducted a brass band and was colour-blind.

Hence home, and this morning as usual, after the style of Pepys, 'up betimes'. A cold frosty night, a blue blue sunny day.

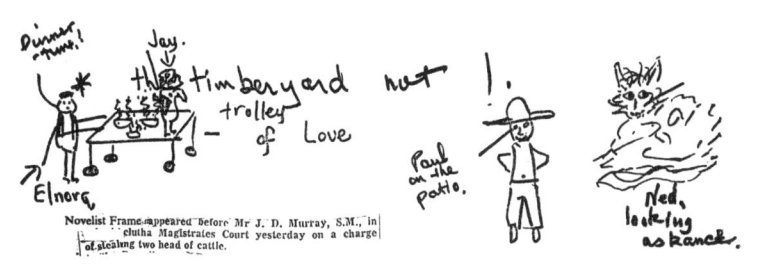

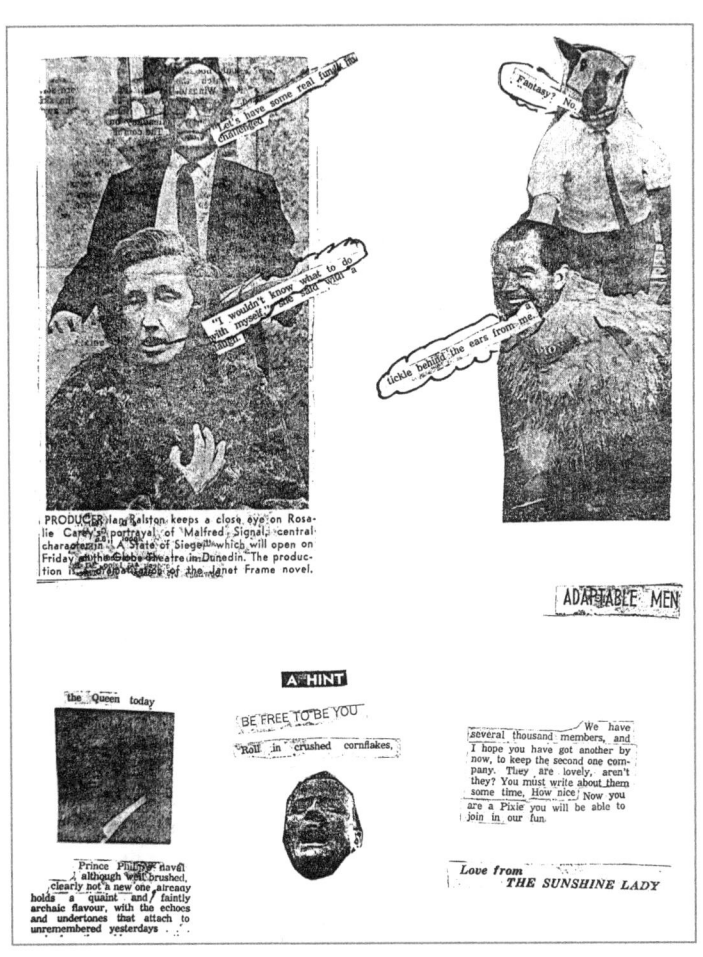

Crazy infantilia from Jay recovering from Merry Perry's final thrilling killing drilling. With excess baggage love to Bee the Pee, Paul the Pill, Ned the Fed, & Fred the Ted—from Jay the Alway

57. Dunedin May 15

CLARENDON HOTEL

MUSIC TONIGHT (FRIDAY), MAY 15.
JANET.

Hi Bill,

I'm rude aren't I? *Vergers* has arrived, and your translations which read even better in the clear Antipodean light—they seem so right and make me wonder—are you Rilke? They follow on from the dreams which I read—forgive me or not—and seem so much a part of them. For a long time I had the idea—I don't know where I found it—that Rilke died on my birthday or a few days before and so he must have been around when I was born; but there can't be two of him—of course there can—he possesses the mirror. I have a fairly good French dictionary as well as an excellent book of French idioms and figurative phrases full of interesting things, goodies, and I'm going to work in between other work on a translation or two but don't tell Dame Mary Margaret who has such a wonderful scream that I daren't play it for fear the neighbours come running.

I hope you're all well and enjoying yourselves and happy . . . strange that one wishes this for others although one knows (quoting Bertrand Russell), 'the centre of one is always and eternally a terrible pain'.

★★★★★ ★★★★★★★★ ★★★★★★★★★★

Just had your letter, nice nice nice, with its goodies of news and drawings and the photo. I loved the tale of the dinner party. I went out to dinner the other evening, with my sister's doctor and his wife and family who were visiting their son, a student in his first year at University. It was just a warm family gathering. I liked the son who has just spent a year as a volunteer worker in Malaysia and is dreadfully homesick for the life there and the friends he made. Coming to University and a 'civilised' community he finds he has to jettison so much that had meaning and value in human terms, at least he is being invited to jettison this but I think he may refuse, I hope so.

And that has been my social experience lately. Oh, I had an interesting visit one evening from a writer* I've never met before but whose writing I sometimes found difficult to read because it was all sports and outdoor life, huntin' fishin' shootin'. I was surprised to find he is a rather slender clerkish-looking person—no not clerkish; rather, though, he is middle-aged, like a poet's picture on the back (or front) of a book. He stayed about ten minutes and I gave him the addresses of Yaddo and MacDowell and now he has written me a long embarrassingly intimate letter which I don't know how to answer!

I've been playing the records often. I agree the Hindemith one is uneven but it's wonderful in parts and its measurement of gloom is level and beautiful. And I love the Schumann.

I'm getting to know each one. The Schubert is exquisite (soon I shall run out of adjectives, I mean, after I have used brilliant, overwhelming, heart-piercing and so on). Listening to this sonata and then the B Flat I feel each, and the spaces between, acting on the other, it's like some tragic Before and After where the Before contained the After—but I'm carried away and I don't know anything about music. (Space for drawing of J being carried away) with quote from the 'Grammarian's Funeral'—'Let us begin and carry up this corpse singing together . . .'

You write of being 'drained'. Well, I have drainage problems also in my work, my emotional plumbing being what it is; maybe I'm not drained but a drain. My batteries consistently go dead. When I was looking through some of my published manuscripts to give on long-term

---

* Philip Wilson

loan to the University Library I felt terribly oppressed as I seemed to re-experience the sheer *weight* of all that work. And then I came across snatches of half-poems, a few words here and there. I'm enclosing a piece of paper (with the usual coffee-stain—I swear it's *coffee*, albeit instant) to show what I mean. It all seems so sad and private and it makes one wonder how one keeps going.

★★★★★   ★★★

Pause for refreshment . . . This library says it has a locked room where no-one, not even the librarian has access, and they will store any documents I want stored there. I haven't gone into the pros and cons of this. The move about loaning was prompted partly by my alarm at my growing number of scripts and the rage I feel when I catch sight of them in their awful vulnerability, and partly as a gesture of 'gratitude' to the city in return for what the 'anonymous business-men of Dunedin' will be doing when they provide a small income for me—but it's not started yet and won't start until I ask for it and I don't think I would ask for it! I have been told 'to let them know' when I need money and they will start paying in. It would be much simpler to be a cat.

I had forgotten that winter here is partly summer, I keep saying this don't I? But today is beautifully sunny, clear blue sky, warm air, and as soon as the sun leaves the chill comes.

So you have built your kennel, have you, O have you? Poor Steinway to be so crippled. I'll not have it thus, nor will Steinway, and to show that neither I nor Steinway will have it thus I will put S in my next instalment of the Kiddies' Page. So there! Send me a drawing or sketch of the kennel and show what it contains and where I will sleep and my list of duties on the wall. I wish it were true! How about up in the olive tree where I could act as lookout for Ned? I am working in my basement laboratory upon a secret Mix which will solve everything including, not least, distances by water between the birds and the bees and other insects. As the distance is concerned with water I've been able to apply the Peedauntal principle where, you may remember, my enterprise was fruitless in these Antipodean wastes. And of course I never forget, Ace Bee, that you, no doubt inspired by Ace P and Ace N, were the originator of the Peedauntal Principal, and any day royalties (kings and queens) may arrive in payment, but that is only if I go ahead with my secret Mix in my basement laboratory.

I dreamt about a piano last night! I really do listen a lot to the records I have; they really inhabit me; in a strange way the music is on the same level as the cats I meet in the street or that sun themselves in gardens as I pass; like 'secret sharers'! When I look at the grey cat on the low white wall down the road it says to me as surely as if it were speaking aloud, 'I know and you know don't we?' And the music says that too—at least it is in channels of knowing where speech isn't but I'm carried away again . . .

The house-painter is still here and finishes (I hope) tomorrow. He is shifty, slightly dishonest I think and I feel sorry for him because his friends and acquaintances keep calling here to ask him for money and I hear him outside saying in his 'cornered' voice—the same voice he used when I asked him why he kept leaving the work and going away, and not coming back—'I'll have the money for you, you trust me don't you, it's just that I've got things to attend to'. And so on. I think it is very sad and degrading when people have to make excuses to other people.

The photo of the angels is nice. I knew that angels visited Live Oaks Inn, crumbs or no crumbs on the table. You are doing a prodigious amount of work with the portraits. I still see them, in my mind's eye, and I see the one Paul was working on. We have the Stuyvesant exhibition here at the Gallery and I'll go down this weekend to see it. I'll be interested to see how *Homage to the Square* etc. looks, transplanted or transhung in Dunedin. The Art Gallery is a pleasant walk from here, down past the cemetery and the 'Lookout' over the harbour and peninsula, then a bush walk that comes out just in front of the Gallery.

Oh I'm homesick, said Miss Nostalgia Tarantula Piecemeal as swinging herself out of her legirons and handcuffs she hobbled down the garden to sit at ease among the stout-hearted cabbages . . . something fishy or Freudian there . . .

I've forgotten where I was with the Carnivorous Plant. I seem to remember there was a general confrontation in the diningroom. Had I got as far as where the carnivorous plant insists on its right to dine at the table with Bill and Paul who, it reminds them, are also carnivorous??? And that B and P (ignoring dark flashing glances from Ned) relented or concurred or whatever the right word is? And that after the meal (taken without a mishap) the plant insisted that it join B, P and N in the sittingroom where they played a record and when the record was finished they asked each other riddles because the carnivorous plant suggested this and the carn. plant's riddle was,

>Sisters and brothers have I none
>
>but in this room is my dear relation.
>
>What am I?

Now turn to the kiddies' page or, in serialese,

> NOW READ ON.

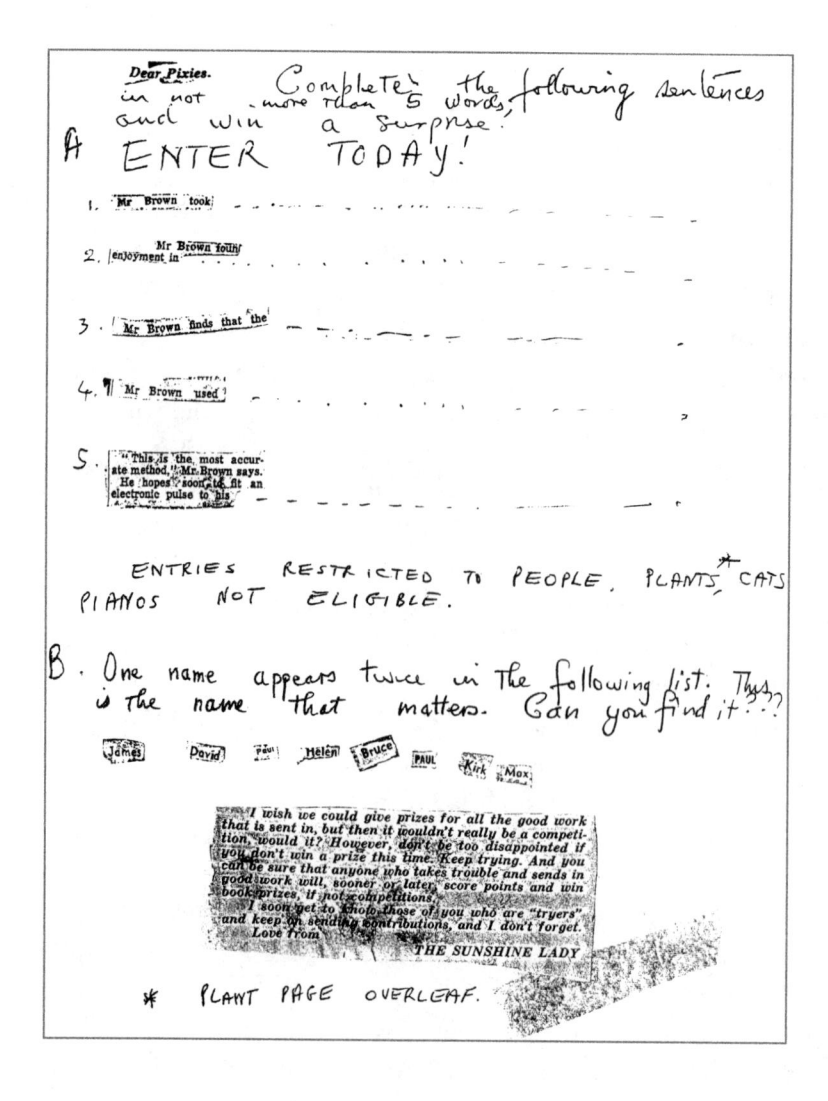

Dear Pixies. Complete the following sentences in not more than 5 words, and win a surprise!

A ENTER TODAY!

1. Mr Brown took _____
2. enjoyment in _____
3. Mr Brown finds that the _____
4. Mr Brown used _____
5. "This is the most accurate method," Mr. Brown says. He hopes soon to fit an electronic pulse to his _____

ENTRIES RESTRICTED TO PEOPLE, PLANTS,* CATS. PIANOS NOT ELIGIBLE.

B. One name appears twice in the following list. This is the name that matters. Can you find it...?

James David Paul Helen Bruce PAUL Kirk Max

I wish we could give prizes for all the good work that is sent in, but then it wouldn't really be a competition, would it? However, don't be too disappointed if you don't win a prize this time. Keep trying. And you can be sure that anyone who takes trouble and sends in good work will, sooner or later, score points and win book prizes, if not competitions.

I soon get to know those of you who are "tryers" and keep on sending contributions, and I don't forget. Love from
THE SUNSHINE LADY

* PLANT PAGE OVERLEAF.

Earthworms Act

A Group of Earthworms have recently formed a Theatrical Company. Their first performance was given to a sparse audience who applauded it vigorously.
Acting by earthworms is thought to be unusual.

Adaptable Camellias

A recent survey of the plant population shows that Camellias lead the garden in adaptability.

Zealand Spinach Lacks Evils

A Recent Survey of the habits of spinach in New Zealand shows that its behaviour and being is one of 'pure good'. A further study is being made of this phenomenon.

Memory Corner.

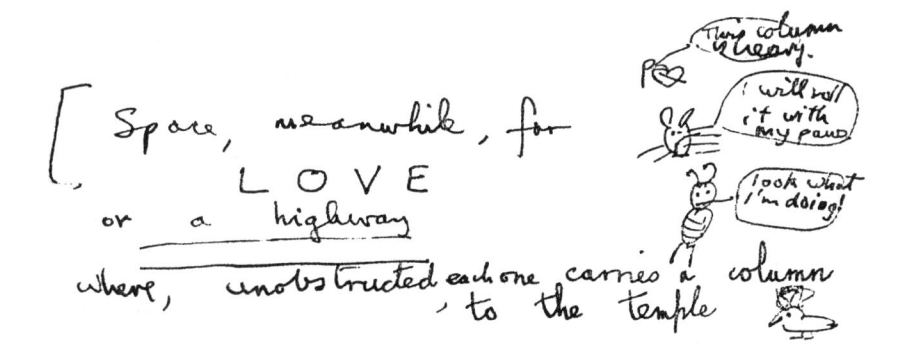

peanut butter   patio   Advertisement

Colour is you   What more could anyone ask?   ironing

[Space, meanwhile, for
   L O V E
or a highway
where, unobstructed each one carries a column
                              to the temple

This column is heavy.
I will roll it with my paws
look what I'm doing!

NEW ZEALAND: MARCH 1970 TO JANUARY 1971

58. Dunedin May

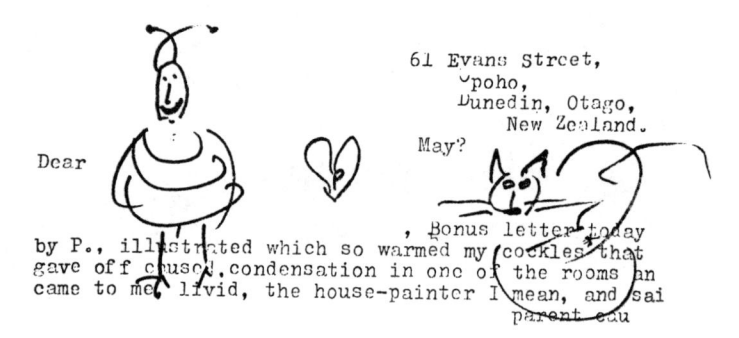

```
                            61 Evans Street,
                               ᵛpoho,
                               Dunedin, Otago,
                                  New Zealand.
   Dear                    May?

                         , Bonus letter today
 by P., illustrated which so warmed my cockles that
 gave off f caused condensation in one of the rooms an
 came to me livid, the house-painter I mean, and sai
                                       parent eau
```

Bonus letter today with a pome, too, by P, illustrated which so warmed my cockles★ [footnote: Cold outcrops or barnacles on the human heart. Sometimes edible.] that the steam they gave off caused condensation in one of the rooms and the painter came to me, livid, the house-painter I mean, and said, —What's the meaning of this condensation without apparent cause? I made no reply. I turned on my heel (it's quite easy if you know ballet) and made off.

I do wish the painting was finished. He's painting the outside cream and the roof is red—the same old colour it's always been. I didn't realise that houses had walls of their own until the painter said, What colour do you want it?, and not I but the house spoke and said I want it to be as it's always been because it's getting too old, nearly a hundred, I mean I'm getting too old. So I had no choice. The inside is not being 'done'.

Do you recall Van Gogh's description of his bedroom?

'The walls are pale violet. The floor is of red tiles. The wood of the bed and chairs is the yellow of fresh butter, the sheet and pillows very light lemon-green. The coverlet scarlet. The window green. The toilet table orange, the basin blue. The doors lilac.'

(I'm quoting from the letters that are here beside me. I have a postcard of the bedroom painting which I love.)

I have had difficulty in restraining the painter. He behaves like a Marx brother in that once he starts with a paintbrush in his hand he goes on and on and when he has finished what he sets out to do he begins to paint everything in sight whether he's been asked to or not—if you happened to come into the room while he had his paintbrush in his hand he would paint your face and body while his eyes, as the novelists say, 'stared unseeingly before him'. Is that what happens when people get paintbrushes in their hands? In truth, my nerves are very much frayed because while he's here I have to be on my best behaviour and therefore I daren't write a sentence because writing demands the banishing of decorum. Alas.

I feel very low about the Cambodian move. The students in Auckland burned an effigy of President Nixon outside the U.S. Embassy. Our sneaky Prime Minister 'refuses to comment'. Meanwhile in the temple of the Pentagon . . .

Where did you get the horse's skull you used in your painting? If you came to New Zealand you would find more animal skulls than alive people. There was a painter at Yaddo who liked to invite fellow guests to his studio to see, not his etchings, but his collection of skulls. The Triumph of Death?? I just read last evening that the appearance of a butterfly, particularly a Red Admiral, was thought to be a sign of triumph *over* Death. In the Hours of Catherine of Cleves, Saint Vincent is surrounded by butterflies. (Saint Barbara is interesting—'dressed as befits the daughter of a satrap'. 'Satrap' is a word whose meaning always eluded me. We used to say a poem,

'The King was on his throne,

the satraps thronged the hall'

It had something of the strangeness of that part in St. Agnes Eve where—something—what was it—threw 'warm *gules* on Madeline's fair breast'. Gules or ghouls? Or the lines where the Assyrian came down etc. and his 'cohorts were gleaming in purple and gold'. It is just interesting to know that Santa Barbara was the daughter of a *satrap*. She probably had warm *gules* thrown on her as well, and multicoloured gleaming *cohorts*.)

. . . .

To continue my aside from Catherine of Cleves' Book of Hours, there's the mouth of Hell with three souls sitting at a table within (teeth descending like icicles above them) and an angel flies down to the table with a cloth containing loaves of bread . . .

I'll continue this letter tomorrow.

TOMORROW:
With this letter I'm sending another instalment of the exciting serial. Meanwhile back in Lower Omicron I'm gradually prodding the painter

to get finished. It's awful—I really have no defenses at all. Although he is not doing 'inside' work he has taken over the place as if he owns it—something like a sailor taking over a ship—and he will stride into the room where I work and glance around and remark, My, that's a fine ceiling you've got there! If I were identifying myself with the place I live in I would feel reflected glory, I suppose, but I don't. I must admit, though, that once when a plumber looked up at my roof and said warmly, –Your roof has a beautiful pitch, a fine pitch, I basked, proud of my pitch . . .

Yesterday afternoon I went up to visit Charles B, for a cup of tea and seed cake. He is looking frail and his hair is very white and shaggy. He had just come from his Russian lecture and he says he has been reading Turgenev and Dostoievsky in Russian and has discovered how much has been lost in the translation. He gave me a copy of his new book of poems, and one copy of a small book of poems he had printed (25 copies) for his aunt's eightieth birthday! What a marvellous tribute for someone's birthday! I think it must only be men who have such wonderful aunts. As an aunt myself I know that I take more interest in my nephews than in my nieces!

I always feel rather constrained in Charles' company and so I was glad when it was 'over', though he is very sweet and gentle and when I was leaving he gave me a little bag of fresh ripe walnuts.

And now au revoir and a big big love

dimensions immeasurable to all

MUSIC TONIGHT (FRIDAY), MAY 8.
JANET.

I love the finches' names especially from

59. Dunedin May 19

Dear

Here I am again with news or non-news of the Antipodes, writing with a faded typewriter ribbon as I sit in my study with all electric fires going and the taperecorder just switched off because, as I said, though the description holds admirable promise in some sense, the voices get *deeper and deeper*. This week I should get the fitting for the electrical switch (in a country, an agricultural country, there are usually difficulties about getting spare parts, so if you come to visit me bring two of everything, or even three of anything which is subject to extra wear and tear. I'm more likely to leave this country and live on the moon or one of the outer planets or anywhere—I don't know—I enjoy my little sanctuary here but as soon as I venture out I feel a chill wind of nothingness and desolation, except if I go to the Place of the Stone Bees, or to the library or among the trees in the gardens or to the Art Gallery or the Museum. I think it is like this everywhere, though. Dunedin, trying to be like Santa Barbara, boasts that it has just opened its 'first carpeted supermarket'. And the first high-rise apartment house has just been built on the hill overlooking the harbour; I see it from my window. Fortunately we're still the 'most backward' city and people are still being lured to the north, but, alas both our newspapers are full of insidious prejudices with continuous persecution of any minority—I mean our city newspapers; New Zealand does not have a national paper like *The Australian* which I'm told is good. I forgot to say, when I talked of the frozen faces in the street, that they melt if a little warmth is applied—there's no working of a spontaneous mechanism from within.

So much for the non-news.

My house-painter has finally gone, leaving me in peace. The day he left he told me what I had known (intuition) all along—he'd been in prison. He told me something of his life there. In his two weeks working for me, besides painting the outside of my house, he gave me a remarkably transparent view of himself and his life from the time he was a child until now when he has a wife and six children. I gave him cups of tea three times a day, and a meal sometimes, and it was then that he liked to talk. Most times when he gave an opinion he sounded like someone out of the third part of *Intensive Care*—so many people do, and this horrifies me—he suggested one day, out of the blue, that all people who were not healthy and intelligent should be killed; and all who did not 'conform'.

Oh it's depressing.

On a more cheerful note, I'll tell you that the day after the house painter left I celebrated by making myself breast of chicken with cider (out of your skillet book, Paul, which finally arrived) and casserole of cabbage, apples and dates (also out of the skillet book—should be eaten with pork but I had chicken); lemon jelly with cream; and a glass of cider—this is the homemade cider I brewed early in the month.

Although prices have risen in some cases up to forty percent and my rates on my property have risen from forty-four dollars a year to forty-eight, I can still manage on my 1000 dollars a year. I caught the milkman when he was delivering my milk at 6 a.m. to find out if milk was really still four cents a pint—and it is. Wheat germ is fifteen cents a pound. But I shan't bore you with a recital of prices, I hear enough of them. A recital of colours (your greens, your blues) or of words (our adjectives, our nouns) would be more interesting.

Back to work. You're right. I'm drained. Drained, drained. Not so much drained as weary. It's been hard having *Care* published because it 'brings it all back' as they say, and I don't feel like returning to the gloom and doom where my 'Mortal Enemy' dwells. One starts with a feeling, a vague but painful feeling, a rheumatism of the spirit (who am I kidding?) before the rain, and when the rain comes everything is so dreadfully clear—it's too much to have it so clear—having the words to describe it would be the end, so maybe it's just as well I have only a small limited supply of words. I can see it in your paintings and, in a different way, in Paul's. I wish I'd had the chance to spend more time looking at the portraits you've been doing.

Please skip this if it sounds too presumptuous which it is—it's just that Live Oaks is 'gentle on my mind' and so I see in my mind's eye (great place that) the things and people associated with Live Oaks. (I'll not bore you with what I was going to say, after all. I broke off this letter to write a couple of paragraphs on your painting, and something on Paul's—it developed into a miniature essay on envelopement; so I'll spare you . . .)

Back to the minutiae of daily living, here, 'in the large unconscious scenery of my land'*. 'In the close of the day with its light and the fields of spring and the farmers preparing their crops with DDT.'

Poor Old Walt. D.H. Lawrence flays him in his *Studies in American Literature* and then Lawrence writes 'pure Walt'—'Have you built your ship of Death O have you?'—and maybe this is logical—all men kill and become the thing they love. And maybe that's nonsense—it's so much easier to feed on sayings already said.

---

* phrase from Walt Whitman's poem 'When Lilacs Last in the Dooryard Bloom'd'

★★★★★★   ★★★★★★★★   ★★★★★★★★★★★★★

Stars for what? The other evening—about six-thirty—I was wandering around town (it was late night shopping) and I saw the most beautiful blue evening sky, I've never seen anything so beautiful, a rich dark blue like a cloth, with the texture of cloth, as if you could reach up and touch it.

★★★★★★★★★★

A schooner whose name was Janet
on course to another planet
once dropped her fin
at Live Oaks Inn
now her wheel has no-one to man it!

★★★★★★★★★★★★★★★★★

You will remember that the scene in the drama of the Carnivorous plant had moved to the sittingroom and that the piano, known also as Steinway, was about to speak. It is not known whether Steinway had spoken before, in words that is, though one of our characters, Bill had regular conversations with it and was able, with his special skill (he is known in Wales as Bill the Skill) to make it utter the most wonderful sounds, in code, while Paul (known in Wales for his inclusive qualities as Paul the All) and Ned (known in Wales as Ned the Fed, which speaks for itself) listened.

You may notice that the author's battery is running low and the story of the Carnivorous plant is in danger of fading away but the *onus* is on the author to resolve the plot. Is the tender-leaved carnivorous plant really an offshoot (or vice-versa) of the black Steinway? What is the *real* family tree? What has

the real Wolfgang Mozart

to say to this?

And many more intriguing questions not answered for you now because the author's battery is running low and she is closing (her letter) and sending crazy but pure distilled also concentrated granulated genuine artificial desensitized homogenized crackle-finished vitamin-rich enzyme-loaded love to

B.   P.   N.

miss so awfully

60. Dunedin May 21

Hello Bill,

I'm thinking about you now. It's night and I've just settled in my luxurious unelectric bed and I've just played the Serkin record—you see how deep my live-oaksia is, it's incurable. I have put some of the paintings from you and Paul's catalogues on to white board and they are hanging on the wall in my bedroom; and the idea of my work is swirling around like a current; and the street outside is quiet, the air cold, about forty-five degrees, and I in my luxury have adjusted my bedroom temperature to about sixty. And my thoughts are on the peanut butter patio where a large part of my self has taken up residence having signed a treaty with the carnivorous plant who can't really be called *Nixon* if it is such a close relation of Steinway.

About every third or fourth evening I go to visit my old aunt who has led a barren kind of life and now she is old the barrenness shows. She has many of her relatives to visit her but she likes me to go because I look like her husband who died many years ago. I usually take her a date scone or slices of buttered bread I have made. ★★★★★★★★★★★

Obviously I got bogged down there in the date scone syndrome because it is now morning, clear, bright, new. I dreamed about you last night. I dreamed you and I went to visit a blind person who said, 'I don't mind being blind. When I walk out in the air my mouth becomes a village and my nose is my neighbour.'

Very Freudian.

From where I am sitting I can see a white-pawed cat walking delicately along a grey fence. The house opposite, at the corner, which was empty and had been claimed by a black cat who, I told you, (you don't have to remember all the stupid things I write in my letters!) used to inspect the property regularly, now has a family living in it, with the inevitable cat. I think everybody in the street except me must have a cat. In the evening when I go to visit my aunt I walk down to the bottom of the hill (how strange it is to be walking alone and unafraid at night!) to catch a bus for a short walk to the private hospital, it is just about that time, not quite dark, when cats come into their own. I mean I see them everywhere, not wandering the street or moving about in the garden of their house (every house has a garden) but sitting sedately on front steps or just at the gateway as if to say, I own this place. I pass cat after cat sitting with their tail curled around their feet, paws together, face slightly smirking, each at the entrance to his or her or its 'place', staking a twilight claim. I swear I can read their thoughts—and perhaps they can read mine.

My bank manager called my friend Ruth to say I had a review in Time magazine (he was too shy to call me). He is in charge of the Savings Bank at the foot of the hill—a provincial bank which gives all its profits, or maybe some of them, to various charities and causes and societies. I certainly hope he doesn't read I.C. if it ever comes here (I haven't yet received my copies of it!) because he is something like the bank manager in the book. I do not know him or anything about his private and family life but when I used to go in there he would either tell me a dirty story (semi-dirty) or say his dream of leaving everything—wife, family, work, and going off to sea in a beautiful yacht.

(Hi Ned)

I'm busy trying to answer the questions the radio interviewer is going to ask me. They are going to pay me for the interview so I suppose I have to do some kind of homework—it's about 'Artists Colonies'. There may be a rush of New Zealanders to apply to Yaddo and MacDowell. The writer who visited me some time ago and whose rather embarrassing letter I still haven't answered, seemed eager to go to one of the colonies because he finds, as I do, that in New Zealand the loneliness outweighs the benefits of the aloneness—I don't know if there is any 'place' where one can achieve the right balance but it's more readily found among those doing the same kind of work and therefore having the same kind of need. I like that quote from Auden,

> Bright shines the sun on creatures mortal;
> Men of their neighbours become sensible:
> *In solitude, for company.*

★★★★★★

Just received your lovely letter full of *fun things*. You are a good bee to write to me with your—whatever bees write with—feelers? It is my food for the week, and immediately to hell with Dunedin and its sour grim life that stops at the neck up and the belly-button down. I loved the picture of Long Ned (Ned the Fed) on the washer, and I think that what you say about his believing you hunt during the day (which you do) is correct. After meeting so many different cat faces and their different knowledgeable (should I say sapient or something like that) expressions I might say that perhaps he's sophisticated enough to believe you hunt in your own special way, and then bring home the food so that he can continue as Ned the Fed.

Yes, I do believe all the bad reviews and I'm incredulous about any good ones—somehow the good ones don't seem to relate to me or my work. This is why I do think (though I seldom put this into practice) that I shouldn't read reviews at all. I'm vain enough to be pleased by the good ones but after a day of swollen-headedness they vanish. The bad ones persist—'unreadable in the worst sense'. I remember the first review

I ever read of my first book, *The Lagoon*, which I wrote before I went into hospital and which was not published for years and years. The review said, (something like this) 'This sort of thing has been done before, again and again. J.F. has been reading (list of writers); most of the book is childish prattle.' Not very encouraging for someone who was determined to devote her life to writing!

I thought you must have had a *very* cannibalistic barbecue because when I read your letter with the sentence, 'pathetic little chops consumed by the grille before we ate them,' I misread 'chops' as 'chaps'

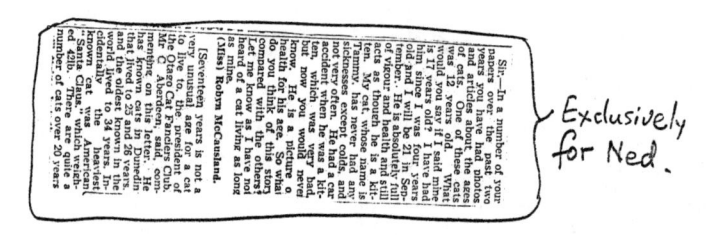

[newspaper clipping] *Exclusively for Ned.*

This afternoon Charles B is coming up to 'take tea' with me. I hastily re-read his poems. They are very moving, particularly the ones in the small booklet he had printed for his elderly aunt. There's one, 'Home Ground', which gives an accurate poetic description of Dunedin. I may send a copy of one of his books to May Sarton because they are in the same elegiac (?) vein. (What did one poet say to another when they met in an elegiac vein? . . . I don't know the answer, I just invented that as a possible riddle. Blah blah.) Anyway, I've made a date scone to eat.

★★★★★★★★★★★★★★★★★

Hurrah, hurrah, I've at last got my tape-recorder attached to the electricity, and the difference in sound is amazing. Your piano playing is better than ever and there's no risk now, as there was before, of its suddenly sounding very strange so that I had to turn it off quickly; and your voice is even in its natural beauty—ha ha I mean it—and—alas— does not go deeper deeper, slower, slower. I had my new batteries only two days before all the voices and the music sounded drunken. The Bagatelles, the Hérodiade and the Hugo Wolf songs are part of my regular listening now—I don't have to wait until I can get new batteries. And of course the poems which I knew by heart, and the extract from *Youth* and *Lord Jim*. Is Dame Mary Margaret still interviewing celebrities?

Strangely, Virgil Thompson came to my mind the other day. I used to hear so much about him at Yaddo—from the maid, chiefly. 'He always had the pink room. He's such a nice gentleman.' I never met him. After Philip Roth left Yaddo (he of course had the Pink Room—this is the room Katrina Trask died in, where the ghosts are), the Pink Room was occupied by a smashing blond composer whom we women called a 'blond mariner' who used to sun himself by the swimming-pool at noon . . .

Frank S in a letter mentions a review of my book and adds, 'we all knew you had it in you, as the whole family said to the parlour-maid when she left unexpectedly.'

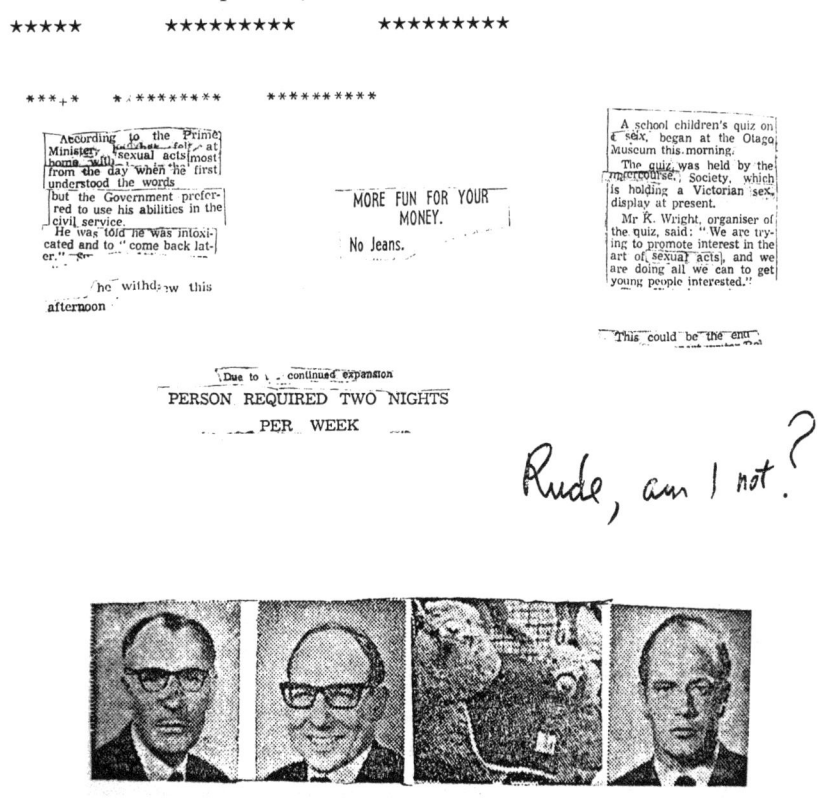

★★★★   ★★★★★★★★★   ★★★★★★★★

★★★₊★   ★ ★★★★★★★★   ★★★★★★★★★

According to the Prime Minister ... felt at home ... 'sexual acts' most from the day when he first understood the words but the Government preferred to use his abilities in the civil service. He was told he was intoxicated and to " come back later."

MORE FUN FOR YOUR MONEY.
No Jeans.

A school children's quiz on sex, began at the Otago Museum this morning. The quiz was held by the Intercourse, Society, which is holding a Victorian sex display at present. Mr K. Wright, organiser of the quiz, said: " We are trying to promote interest in the art of sexual acts, and we are doing all we can to get young people interested."

he withdraw this afternoon

This could be the end

Due to continued expansion
PERSON REQUIRED TWO NIGHTS PER WEEK

Rude, am I not?

It's quite late at night now. I couldn't face visiting my aunt after Charles B's visit which rather depressed me. He is so good and kind and he seemed so frail and old. I'd lit a fire, although my tenants told me there's some kind of gap between the chimney and the wall or hole or something which could be dangerous. When I told him this in passing, he offered to climb up in the loft and investigate, and I had an image of this frail-looking white-haired man trapped up in my loft! I declined his help. He seemed so old and tired—he seemed to keep falling asleep or he gave that impression by closing his eyes a lot, yet he's not really an old man, only in his late sixties*.

★★★★★★★★★★★★★

I saw three live oaks growing in Santa Barbara. (Quote filched from Paul's verse collage.)

★★★★★★   ★★★★★★★★★   ★★★★★★★★★★★★★★★

[sheep image: "What will become of us?"]

I spent my earliest years with the above faces, and from the time I was very small I used to be teased because I was fascinated by the expressions on the faces of sheep. Horrible grownups used to corner me and say, Come on, tell us again about the look on the sheep's face.

★★★★★★★   ★★★★★★★★★★★★★   ★★★★★★★★

I must go to post this. I did enjoy and do enjoy your letters with their slices and crumbs of news. I forget where I am again with the Carnivorous Plant—it has that influence. I think that Steinway had acknowledged the plant was a close relation, that it had been constructed in part by members of the family, and while it was making this acknowledgement to a breathlessly listening Bill and Paul and Ned (tuned in from the washer-drier), it sat demurely on the sofa by the sittingroom fire, looking very elegant and carnivore, almost like a human being. Bill, hearing the Steinway's confession, turned to the plant and his heart melted (melt melt), while Paul gazed at it, clearly touched (touched touched). 'Why not have it here, inside with us?' Paul suggested. 'After all, it swallowed that lady from the Antipodes, you know, that lady writer Dame Mary Margaret spoke of, and it will remind us of her without being too much of a presence, and we can use it to swallow others who arrive, and when Jay comes to stay in that kennel we're constructing, she can tend it, day by day, and we'll never remember that things were different and that it

---

* Actually, Brasch was 61

once lived unsung and unknown in a secret corner of the garden. What do you say, Bill?'

Meanwhile the plant remained silently demure (demure demure) knowing it had a strong ally in Steinway. Bill was clearly torn (rip rip). Then with a hearty laugh issuing from his handsome face (issue issue) he said, 'Why not?'

And thus it was, and shall be.

But this is not the end, oh no.

****

It's love now for the three live oaks and au revoir.

Say hello to El for me.

And kisses.

61. Dunedin May

Dear Masters,

I've received forthwith (?) the diagram of my quarters and the list of duties which I am considering deeply deeply. The duties of caring and cleaning for the *Masters* sound a little ambiguous—does it mean the Old Masters of which you no doubt have a secret collection filched from Art Galleries throughout Europe, or the *Masters* according to C.P. Snow who writes all those lower-lower class Proustian imitation novels about quarrels within the College between master and master; or does it mean attending to Ned and his pals, of which he has many, secretly, but has never invited them home to meet Bill and Paul (Ned's servants) because there has been no-one to be employed fulltime dawn-dark-dawn as there now will be with the advent (should she accept the widely-advertised post) of J who herself expects that she in the role of servant will look upon the three live oaks as 'the masters' and will accordingly care for them and clean them twice weekly as requested. The attending of the carnivorous plant is not exactly to her taste—she may delegate that role to someone more skilled. Wednesday, breakfast in bed, is very promising, or would be, if there were a bed to have breakfast in! It will be nice to have the Steinway, though, and the beautiful cushions, and the adaptable rooms, room-womb-tomb in a twinkling, also room-womb-tomb-perfume (inhale, inhale). Changing textures in rooms would be an enticement. The Thursday duty, with its slightly medical aspect involving Ned and Bill should prove an interesting imaginative extension of the humdrum day, while Saturday offers much work among old Beeth, Schu, and Moz . . .

Now I will meditate meditate meditate, and now that I have meditated I will shatter this fantasy because it is unendurably not true (who said fantasies ever were?) and the shattering becomes sediment or dust lying on the veldt, steppe, savannah, factory-floor of my mind/heart/soul/toenails; it looks like a sediment of despair.

It has snowed on the hills (I can see them from here) and the wind blowing across the valley is chilly. I too have moved my furniture—having heard by chance that my tenants had the Landfall desk and stored it, I dismantled it and moved it into my smaller back room which I'm now using as a studio. I can now look out over the hills and the clouds with no sign of street or people. In my other studio in the front room I was forever pulling down the blinds as I felt too exposed. The front room is now my spare bedroom with the single bed—it is the biggest room and the only room that the Landfall desk would go into, in one piece.

Thanks for sending the Time Review. Enough said. No comment. You talk of May Sarton who knew Virginia Woolf. *I* feel very superior because I know W.T.B in all his many aliases in including his basic alias of W.T.B. I also know P.W. and N.

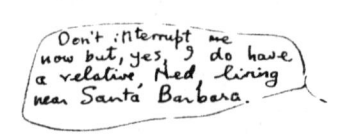

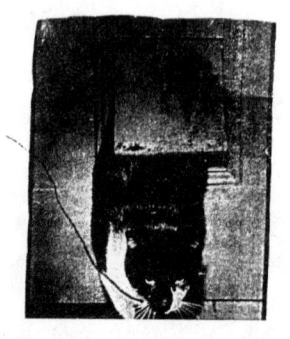

Don't interrupt me now but, yes, I do have a relative, Ned, living near Santa Barbara.

Later: the most wonderful light today, changing every moment. The clouds now have a dark underside and an upper side of frothy white light beneath a higher ceiling of blue. The wind is wild and cold, making howling noises, and my studio is so snug—I had to draw the curtains during the day to keep out the blinding hot sunlight. This climate is not unlike the Ibicencan Mediterranean late autumn.

★★★★★★★★★★★★

I wonder what the maid would put, in a drip-dry non-iron world, in place of 'Ironing today'? It doesn't necessarily mean ironing of clothes and linen, though, it could be people or ideas. Blah. I love the sketch of the trio, particularly Ned at his instrument, it's a *masterpiece* and the ladle is not unlike the ladle out of which I emptied my lunch to its plate—a leftover mixture of ground beefsteak, diced potatoes, carrots, onions, tomato soup, raisins, the leftover liquid from fish, saffron, and a cut-up quince which I've had since the first or second week in April and haven't known what to do with. With a dash of this and that it was very tasty.

The clouds now are exactly like those in Paul's Caravaggio painting. How it must (does it?) annoy to be told that in painting something is 'exactly like something else' as if it were a compliment either to the something or the something else. So I'll say the clouds are not at all like those in Paul's painting; they remind me of the painting and the clouds are Paul's clouds and the world—see I'm learning my Rilke—you make a tree and 'you have made the world'.

I'm getting into deep water and I always feel self-conscious about communicating when I'm in deep water.

I'm really a pure touchie-feelie. Verbalising (my own, not that of others) bores me.

Did you know that Samuel Pepys' wife's drawing master was a painter named Brown??

Now a quote from just over three hundred years ago:

'Talked with Mr Kingston the organist. He says many of the music are ready to starve, they being five years behindhand for their wages; nay, Evans, the famous man upon the harp, having not his equal in the world, did the other day die for mere want, and was fain to be buried at the alms of the parish, and carried to his grave in the dark without a link, but that Mr Hingston met it by chance, and did give 12 pence to buy two or three links . . .' (I gather that a link is a torch).

(I quoted the above because I can't find the quote about Brown which was amusing.)

I've learned all kinds of things about carnivorous plants from my encyclopaedia.

Au revoir. See you _____

Love (scale ⅛" to 1,000 miles)

62. Dunedin May 30

Dear B,

A most unusual thing happened to me on my way to my typewriter (you will be the first to admit it was unusual!)—I thought of you, and the company of live oaks, and I thought I'd write you a letter. I really can't imagine how such an unusual idea came to me.

At last I've finished the tape and I'll post it on Tuesday (Monday is the *Queen's Birthday*, when all postal services stop). It's a dismal tape, mostly snippets of poetry from *The Pocket Mirror*, a story, and a few poems from elsewhere. Just near the end I did a collage on *Rivers* which could have developed into something more interesting—it just happened that I was recording an interview with Glenn Gould talking about Mozart in his unbearably chatty way—I think, though, this may be the form the interview takes in Canada—it all sounds too jolly. Here, the interviews are very serious, with little backslapping. The BBC is the same. Well, he said Mozart was like a river, and I happened to pick up a book and open it at something about a river, and I happened to have heard a BBC Reith Lecture on Pollution where the underground rivers were mentioned and I happened to have been reading my usual addictive reading of Myths and Legends—this time the same old fascinating story of Proserpina or PercyPhone—and I wondered how King Pluto would feel if he knew about what is happening to his underground streams and coal supplies and so on . . .

Well. I hope, when you can bring yourself to send me another tape (you can wipe this one out)—and I'll allow it's difficult to make a tape, though you'll have no problem—you can just let me have the voices of the three live oaks, any poetry, and lots of your own piano music which sounds very well now the recorder is operated electrically. Also the recorded music sounded well. And that tortured piece at the beginning (in spite of your disclaimers) sounds as anguished as it ever will.

It's very early Sunday morning—(perhaps it's May 31). The world is in bed. I'm in my study looking out across the valley at the opposite hill which is covered with sunshine, and the sky is blue without a cloud. In the valley there's a lower mist of frost, slowly dispersing.

I've begun (at last) my new work. How I hate working! How I hate the misery of it! The one consolation is the occasional wonder of discovery, an image or idea brought on a silver platter. When I'm not working I forget about this but when I start I find it balances the sheer misery of everything—I suppose because the misery is really a kind of poverty balanced by the riches of discovery. La misère.

Has Elnora arrived to stay with you? I hope you all have a wonderful time in the fun and the sun and that the peanut butter patio will reverberate with your laughter, drowning the muttering tones of the carnivorous plant which, though it has chosen to live in the house, still suns itself on the peanut butter patio camouflaged, in a place unknown to you or Paul or Ned.

Here it's winter now, temperatures in the forties at night and the fifties during the day and I'm sweaterized with your lovely cuddly sweater, and I'm shirtized with Paul's lovely cosy shirt and your painting shirt—I'm really J.F. in Live Oaks clothing.

I have my radio interview on Tuesday morning and as they are going to pay me for it (eighteen dollars for eight minutes) I've had to work at it a little, though some questions—'Did you feel the violence of the American society' are really too much. I shall spend most of the time pointing out to the interviewer that the questions she has chosen—well I don't suppose I can be bold enough to say they are ignorant but they are. Enough.

I heard from the young black (chiefly Shakespearian, so far) actor [Darryl Croxton] I knew in New York that he and an English actress have leased an off-Broadway theatre for one night early in June and the two are putting on a performance called 'The Best of Both Worlds'—an evening of poetry and drama from Shakespeare to Charles Gordone (who, he tells me—I didn't know—is the Pulitzer prize-winning black playwright author of *No Place to Be Somebody*.) He's going to read five of my poems.

Oh blah blah let me get down to kiddie-size and get out on the peanut butter patio eating my peanut butter sandwich (very fattening) and drinking my banana apple milkshake and smashing my coffee-cup Frame-style. I've thought long and long with my architect's eye (my eye is a thinking piece of machinery but not as much as yours which is highly trained and agile) that there's no room for a kennel or small hovel—not above ground, at Live Oaks Inn. I'll have to wait until you move house somewhere and then I'll write to you, Dear Sir in answer to your advertisement of the inst, ult. etc. and you will write to answer, 'There are separate quarters here for three (trois) and one other, the maid. Each, including Ned the cat has facilities for complete privacy, aloneness, withdrawal or whatever you may term it, and also facilities for company, that is, being together. Your duties will be sent to you forthwith . . .'

Or something like that.

Being in a small place, however, is a great protection against the arrival of invading people like me!

I'll say goodbye now because I'm lonely. Who isn't, on this planet? I'm enclosing a photo of Westbeth that appeared in yesterday's newspaper. On the opposite side—some Dunedin faces—women looking at the Miss New Zealand contestants!

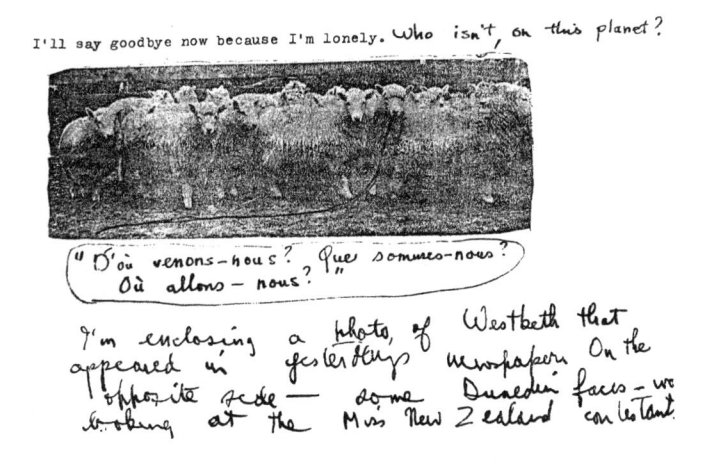

I still haven't got myself a piano though I've room for one in my spare bedroom. Any advice on the kind, make, characteristics etc. that are part of a nice piano? I just couldn't bear to get one that made the wrong sound—I didn't realise how individual each one is—when I looked in the shop at the secondhand ones (Just looking, thanks) there was a roomful of them and a woman went around trying out each one, but they all looked to me as a roomful of orphans might look were someone thinking of adopting them. Each said, Take me, take me. It was incredible the strong case each one put, even without having a sound made on its keys.

I felt guilty after a while and hurried out—Yes, just looking thanks.

Love, pure, tested, chemical-free, except laden with cyclamates

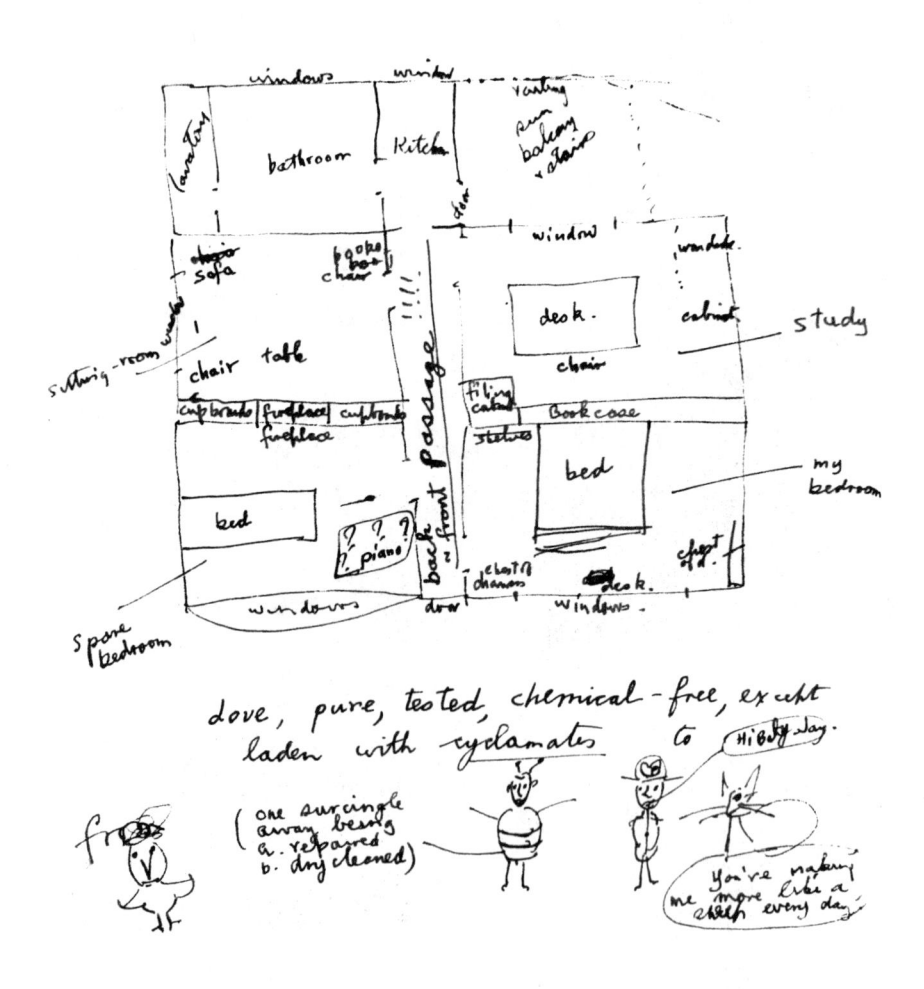

JUNE

63. Dunedin June (handwritten)

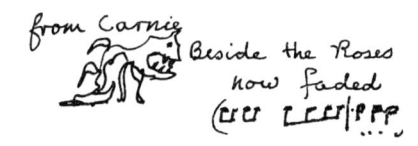

from Carnie
Beside the Roses
now faded
(rrr rrr/ppp

Dear Bee & Pee & the black & white Ned,

    I eavesdropped on your phone conversation. I was *very* hurt that you didn't ask after me but no doubt you thought I was still in that Melbourne gaol. Did I thank you, P for the Care Parcel, the cake with the file in it? Yes I did.

    Since coming back to N.Z. I have been ailing—last week I was sunburned—imagine your Carnie sunburned. Here is the extract from the newspaper (everything, I, Carnie, do, is news).

Plants

'A Carnivorous Plant was admitted to hospital last weekend suffering from sunburn of the tendrils. He has now been discharged. He was interviewed by the press on this important occasion.

Low leaves in better shape

He is reported as saying that his lower leaves have healed more readily than his upper leaves. He spoke with some bitterness, adding in his well-known philosophical way,

> there are some plants which cause bitterness and others which suppress bitterness.

bitter marrows

He is known to have been consorting lately with several members of the marrow family.

He is now looking for work. He is also studying the carnivorous plant species & plans to write a novel.

> "But until people learn what it's about, I've got to earn a living

Of his personal life he spoke reluctantly. He did admit, however, that he was

> showing a growth rate 14 per cent and had opened five new branches.

★   ★   ★   ★

Lots of tender tendrilled embraces to all from your c plant

    Carnie

Dear Ned,

I am copying for your interest and pleasure a poem written by a New Zealand poet who with his wife and family are very good friends of mine. Here is the poem:

    'Tomcat'★

        by James K. Baxter Wellington, New Zealand

    [The full text of the poem was enclosed]

How do you like that poem, Ned? Does it stir your blood? I thought I'd tell you something of the lives of your distant relatives.

★ from *The Rock Woman* selected poems, Oxford University Press 1969

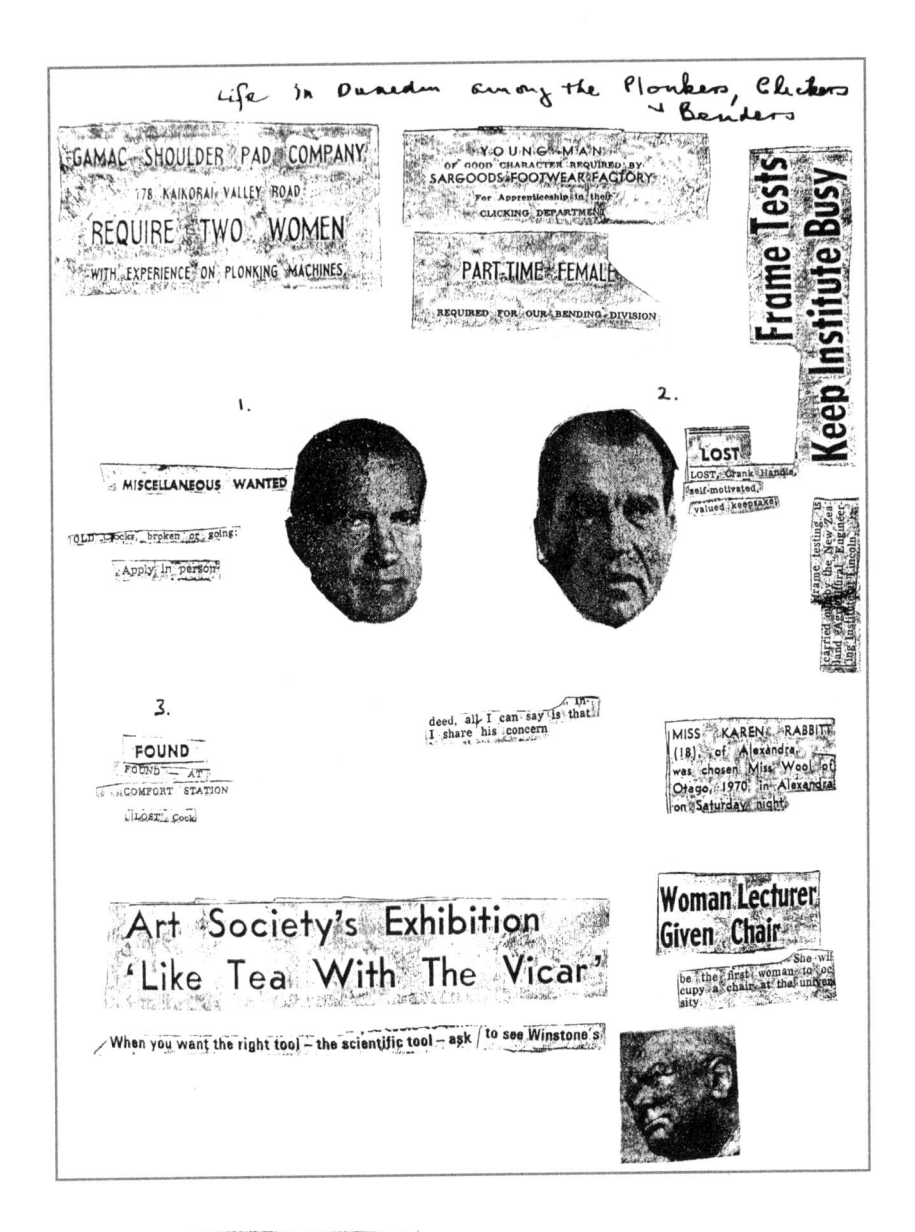

Life in Dunedin among the Plonkers, Clickers & Benders

GAMAC SHOULDER PAD COMPANY
178 KAIKORAI VALLEY ROAD
REQUIRE TWO WOMEN
WITH EXPERIENCE ON PLONKING MACHINES.

YOUNG MAN
of GOOD CHARACTER REQUIRED BY
SARGOODS FOOTWEAR FACTORY
For Apprenticeship in their
CLICKING DEPARTMENT

PART-TIME FEMALE
REQUIRED FOR OUR BENDING DIVISION

Frame Tests Keep Institute Busy

1.   2.

MISCELLANEOUS WANTED
OLD Socks, broken or going
Apply in person

LOST
LOST, Crank Handle,
self-motivated,
valued keepsake

deed, all I can say is that
I share his concern

3.
FOUND
FOUND AT
COMFORT STATION
LOST Cock

MISS KAREN RABBITT
(18), of Alexandra,
was chosen Miss Wool of
Otago, 1970, in Alexandra
on Saturday night.

Art Society's Exhibition
'Like Tea With The Vicar'

Woman Lecturer
Given Chair
She will
be the first woman to oc-
cupy a chair at that university.

When you want the right tool – the scientific tool – ask to see Winstone's

Herb Man Gaoled
Melbourne

Dear Paul,
   Alarm, alarm! The following newspaper clipping with the above headline has arrived for me from Australia. It needed deciphering so I have written it out for you & Bill & Ned, if he can [take] his eyes off the snow long enough to be interested.

A character, identity given as A. Carnivorous Plant, purporting to be half man, half herb, was gaoled here today for breaking & entering a private garden & for failing to exercise proper control of his tendrils. It is believed he has relatives in U.S.A. and N.Z. & an Auckland woman offered bail which was refused. 'Herb people are rare,' the magistrate commented, 'therefore your crime is doubly or triply reprehensible'. A. Carnivorous Plant made some remark about being 'triply tendrilled'. He has been confined for 3 months in a garden cell, with the notorious criminals, Convolvulous & Deadly Nightshade, the Pick-Plant.

Well, isn't that sad/ But it's all experience.

  Much love & kisses to all

  from Jay

64. Dunedin June 4 (handwritten)

Dear B

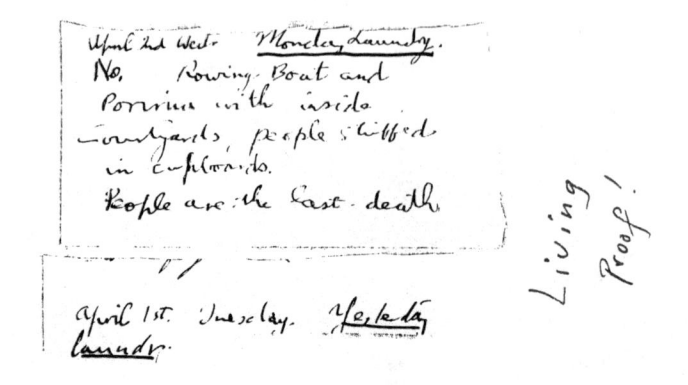

  Hello You silent majority. I hope you and other Live Oaks non-furred & furred are enjoying your summer. This is just a brief letter to say, it's too late now but when you read 'Ironing Today' in the maid's diary, how much much more, if only you'd known, it may have concealed! Believe it or not, I came across a diary of mine the other day, written at a time that was far from uneventful & on two entries I have 'Laundry today'. It was when I came out of hospital & had to work somewhere & for two days had a night job in a laundry.

Quiet smoothly-running life here (or death). I had my radio interview. Ghastly.

Therefore, how well qualified I am to take the position (?) in the Grecian Kennel!

The leaves on the tree visible from my window shine in the sun. Many trees are deciduous but our native bush is evergreen.

My strawberry tree is Japanese. The tree next to it is a pepper tree, a native. Enough of the Botanical Binge.

So much love I send, but light, airy love, not the kind that weighs heavily on the recipient,

65. Dunedin June 7

Dear Bill,

Janet's just washed me and I'm hanging out to dry in the downstairs patio where the sun shines in the afternoon, and I'm swinging to and fro in the wind that's blowing down the valley. I haven't seen your checked shirt or Paul's checked shirt for ages, I guess it's just not shirt weather—last time I saw them we were hanging together in a dark wardrobe and none of us thought we'd ever see the light of day again, but early last week J came to the wardrobe, opened the door, swung us back and forth and before we could be pleased or disappointed, she had chosen *me* to wear. She slammed the door shut. Fast. So I haven't heard a word from Shirt I or Shirt II—they were always boasting, anyway, about being worn day in day out.

I couldn't tell you all the things I've seen J do around the house. Being in a position of intimacy I have to respect her trust in me but oh my if only my surname were Portnoy! (Instead of A. Malibu Sweater

Esquire.) And now I'm all washed out, hanging limp. I've been to town shopping once or twice this week, and I've been worn to visit J's old aunt in a private hospital where she sits by a fire all day and hopes someone will come to visit her; and I went to see *Midnight Cowboy* one afternoon. Somebody called Charles went with J because he didn't want to go alone and find himself among all the young bloods, and as J was—is one of his less formidable acquaintances (having as much intelligence as dishwater) he evidently felt he could ask her, comfortably, to go with him and he could have a rest from being intelligent and scholarly. I enjoyed the film, myself. J's been working, or trying to do. She's writing something about a fountain—pinched from Rilke, I'll be bound.

Bill, I've still got that hole in my neck where you cut off my label. That was a mean trick. I'm all unnecessarily ventilated. And how were you to know I was once getting on so well, so close to that golden sweater of Paul's—the one he lent J to wear when she stayed with you? How can you know anything if you don't study the language, is what I say and what I've always said, synthetic or no synthetic.

Ah, the sun's out. I'm snoozing. I'll say goodbye now and let J write her own letter, and in the meantime, love from me and the shirts and the striped sweater and the handkerchiefs and the old man (little figure) and the ring and the cross, to you and Paul and Ned and Steinway (who carelessly brushed my cheek many a time) and all and all,

    I remain
        your loving skin-kin,
            A. Malibu Sweater Esq.

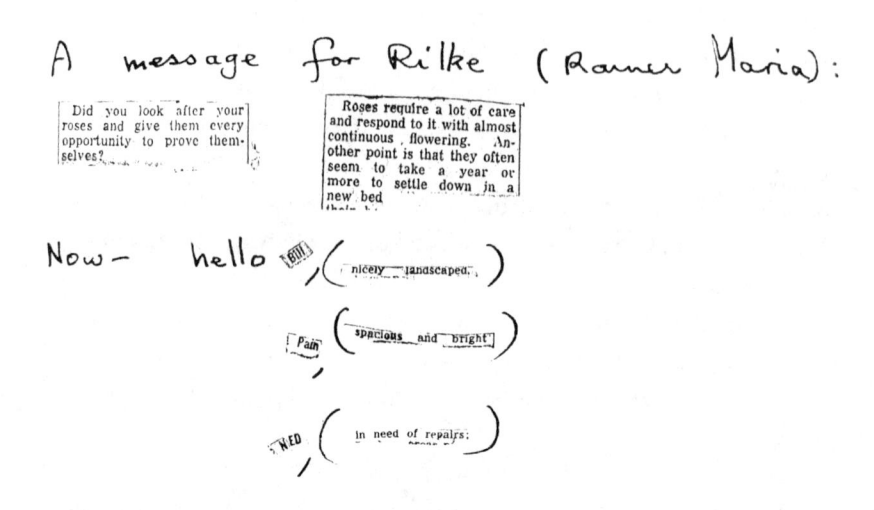

A message for Rilke (Rainer Maria):

[Did you look after your roses and give them every opportunity to prove themselves?]   [Roses require a lot of care and respond to it with almost continuous flowering. Another point is that they often seem to take a year or more to settle down in a new bed]

Now — hello BILL (nicely landscaped,)

Paul (spacious and bright)

NED (in need of repairs;)

and hello,

and it's so happy I am to have a letter this morning from you, and here I am, light of foot and heart and eye and finger, answering.

I'm very happy to add the baking of date scones to my list of duties. I can now do them with a flick of the hand, eyes closed, mouth open and except for a slight problem in judging the amount of liquid I have them to a fine art. Wholemeal loaves are also my speciality. What with scones and loaves and truck-driver cookies it does look as if the culinary future is assured. And I must include those wonderful mushrooms that are grown 'around the corner', from Santa Barbara manure.

Nice to know you saw Elnora and she looked well (wow!). I hope she's been able to get to the end of her book and it's being published. It appears to me like a kind of prolonged pregnancy—think she'll be free when it's over. Maybe.

Nostalgia. 'A form of melancholia caused by prolonged absence from one's country or home.'

You're certainly all things to your friends, B, to generate nostalgia—you're a whole country, a native land, a home. How's that! But if you are a whole country I can understand there might be a certain panic in seeing so many of your friends wanting to put in to harbour, to the tune of 'Sweet and Low'. There could be a question of pollution while they're in port; and there's the vexing problem of setting up bases for trade when one might not want to trade. It's hell to be a human being—why not be a cat and go softfooted on earth-surfaces in early morning and twilight, and curl up asleep at noon. Well, not being cats, if only we could fold ourselves like cats, turn back our wrists into our arm and lie with our face snuggled in our genitals and our haunches over our ears! Makes me nostalgic for cat-country.

MUSIC TONIGHT — JANET (all electric;)

I like the design of the kennel. There must be a place for everyone to express love and hate and all the other inexpressibles that words take one look at and flee from. And how did you know that my new vice is Scrabble-playing? Sometimes I play before I go to sleep, and I'm an awful cheater, I really am, I try to be honest but I have no resistance against, say, a word like *interluce* which I had the other night and which used up all my letters and so gave me a wonderful score. Even when there's no such word. Peedauntally speaking . . .

My granny was not African. That is fact but fact has little to do with childhood or with my life which is run on the lines of a child's life, as it was run in childhood. I believed my granny was African. (*Owls Do Cry* is not autobiography, by the way.) She was big and dark with frizzy hair, as I described her, and she wore a long black dress and she used to sing all the time and I used to sit, at her feet, I suppose, and listen, and believe that what she sang was real and as her songs were mostly spirituals and ones like 'Carry me back to Ole Virginny' I thought she was African and had worked in the cotton fields. I suppose I reasoned, Why would you sing a song about working in the cotton fields and longing to go back to Virginny, if you hadn't worked there and lived there. But I don't think reason came into it. I *believed it.* I just used to sit there and cry because she obviously wanted so much to go back there that her heart was breaking, and even when I was at school and people asked me where my 'ancestors' came from I said, *Virginny*, because I believed it was so and therefore it was so. And as a child, with my frizzy hair, I was called Topsy, therefore I thought I was Topsy. I learned to say, when people asked me,

'I'm the girl that never was born
pras I growed up among the corn.
Golly ain't I wicked!'

Strange happenings in the Antipodes.

Hope you're not dead of boredom with this letter. *Owls Do Cry*, as a first novel, has a bit of autobiographical stuff in it but when I read a review which said that I had a sister who was burned in a rubbish fire, and so on, I was rather embarrassed, annoyed. I was anticipating the death of my mother at the time, and so wrote about it but when I had written the book she had not died. Enough of this, enough, enough. Bastante. (For Paul who is learning Spanish.)

I hope the party is fun, it's sure to be. I'm finding such good use in Paul's skillet recipe book that I feel guilty and hope he got another one for himself. Did I tell you I swigged my home-made cider one evening, and that's that. And did I tell you that when my sister's family doctor was visiting with his family and I went to dinner with them he insisted on my drinking *three glasses* of whiskey, and I had no hangover.

My Maori friend (whose poet husband comes home from time to time but has gone to find his soul among the Maoris) is coming to stay for a few days in a week or so. Her daughter has just had another baby (a short-lived liason this time, not a Christmas party as before), and Jacquie is taking a rest from being family provider and counsellor, at least for a few days.

★★★★★★★★★★ ★★★★★★★★★ Stars in their courses.

It's night now. I've just taken a walk as I've not been out today. There was one small star travelling along, all muffled in cloud; it was thin and pale, like the star outline in your sapphire. After a strange week of very warm weather, day and night, with the sky full of big troubled-looking clouds, we've returned to winter, and it was cold out.

Now for the heart-breaker story of the week. Out with the handkerchiefs. The Hungarian-American pianist (Professor of Piano at Washington State University), Istvan Nadas, who was here a couple of years ago for the winter, and spring, in the music department, and played all the Beethoven Sonatas, has returned this winter until about October (going on for summer).

Now read on:
Tomorrow night he gives the first concert on the new Steinway in one of the University Halls *to an invited audience*. I read this in the newspaper and I knew that of course I would not be invited to this as I have no connection with music in the city, but oh I would give part of my heart just to go and see the Steinway receiving its *first* blows in its *first* concert, to commiserate with it or congratulate it, to commune with it and say, a quiver in my voice, *I* knew a Steinway . . . I *know* a Steinway, or sing it after the manner of

> 'I know a bank whereon the wild thyme blows,
> where oxlips and the nodding violet grows . . .'

So, instead, I am going to give part of my heart to writing a poem called 'On Not Being There'. (This is how poems sneak in.)

My longing to go is so great that I've been having a wonderful time with all kinds of fantasies, such as imagining that a car pulled up outside my gate and a black-clad figure ★ stepped out (the concert is due to begin in five minutes)—I've been asked to take you to hear the Steinway's first concert. Or someone phones to ask me to go . . .

It's no use.

★★★★★★★★★★★   ★★★★★★★★★★★

The stars in their courses.

★ The Black-clad figure is probably Pluto. I've always had a hankering to go to the Underworld with Pluto, so any above-world character who includes among angelic attributes, the darkness of Pluto, is top of my list.
★★★★

Froggied, re-enholed, basty, quixy, unscabed . . .

I need someone to police my lone attempts at Scrabble, for I could not resist giving myself marks for the above words. How low can one get!
★★

My Intensive Cares arrived at last, ten of them, looking so battered and bloodied, with a scrawl on the outside which said, *Received in Bad Condition in San Francisco.* Were you similarly handled in S.F.? My parcel was re-wrapped but the marks are on it, of its San Franciscan experiences.

My battery is running out now so I'll stop in the meantime. It's Sunday now and I've built a wood fire in my sitting-room and I've refused an invitation to go out to lunch. The sky is cloudless, the sun is shining, and the wind has gone away to bed and the trees are so still it's as if they're scared to move.

A heap of angelic, devilish, impure love from on-world, at-world, underworld, above-world to the three live oaks hereinafter(?) portrayed:

INTENSIVE CARE
by Janet Frame

This is Janet Frame's most ambitious and in many ways most extraordinary novel to date, a powerful and at times shocking story, now lyrical, now tragic, now wildly comical in dimensions of pity and terror that burst the boundaries of conventional fiction.

66. Dunedin June (handwritten)

(What a peculiar Bee I have drawn!)

Reclining in my Landfall winged arm-chair upon my hand woven woollen rug, my feet deep in cushions, my record-player mid-Schubert (I got the complete sonatas from the library), my typewriter open and vulnerable upon my desk (note excessive use of personal pronoun; an ominous trait), my wall (of room not of flesh) decorated with numerous photos of Guess Whom, surrounded by books.

I (at last) take pen in hand to say hello to you because I'm lonely because I miss you so much.

Hows were the dinner-parties? And Paul's party? Did the guests

mero
tinget pavimentum superbo
Billum et Paulum potiore cenis.

(Stolen, wrong tense, from Horace, translation cribbed 'stain the floor with superb wine more powerful than any yet consumed at the dinner parties of Bill & Paul.')

How wet can I get!

Just hello. It would be nice to say hello in person. I'm writing this on a page of my notebook which I use to record thoughts about

NEW ZEALAND: MARCH 1970 TO JANUARY 1971 | 179

my book, slowly begun & beginning to take shape but God! what self-deceivers the cr—ee—eee—eea—tive people are! And must be!

Nice crazy note from Frank S today. He's having a wonderful time—it appears that U.S.A. Universities are keen on buying even his *grocery lists*—there was a note about it in the newspapers & advice to people to keep F.S.'s grocery lists if they have any! Living Vulture-culture.

(I have 16th Sonata, the A Minor with the anguished piece which you play better than this pianist.)

Will I ever see you again (weep weep) and Paul (weep weep) and Ned (weep weep) ever, ever?

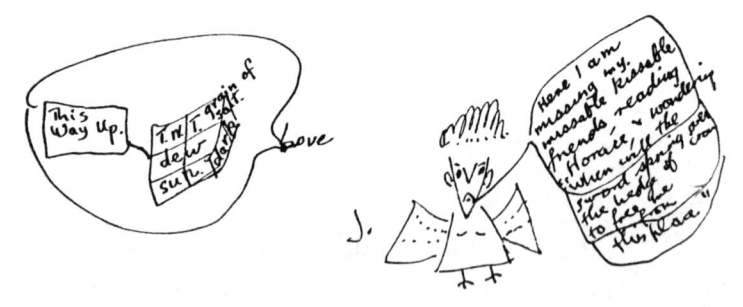

A.M. 20 wax-eyes wait for food on the back stairs. Word is around—Free honey & water at J's place.

67. Dunedin June

Dear B,

Your après-bain letter delighted me so much. Now, après-consommé (I mean soup—alas—of course, not any other activity) I take pen in hand or typing-key in finger to reply. If your programme is true to prediction, and I hope it's not, today is your *Headache and Hangover Day*. I do hope it isn't. I hope that Monday's inspection of surcingles and all else found you ship-shape, in good trim, in the pink, in fine feather, sound as a roach, fresh as a daisy: in short, in rude health. And that the doctor wasn't too jealous of your surcingles, as not many people have them, and they're in great demand, in fact I've heard of people just walking along the street in *broad daylight* who've been robbed, their surcingles stolen, and they're never recovered. From time to time, in pawnshops, an odd surcingle turns up but usually it hasn't been well-kept and it's impossible to clean, and it's of use only as an ornament. So hold on to your surcingles! That's my advice, willingly given, and free!

Oh yes I remember the Diebenkorns ('I remember Rodin . . .') and I remember the evening, the dinner, the visit (the huge *inquisitive* dog) and (especially) the *silver flute* and the story of the flute-makers which made a deep impression on me. And I remember the conversation at dinner* [footnote: *also the Alka-Seltzer Drama!] and so on and so on and I liked the passionate way Dick D spoke of the art they'd seen in Europe.

Well. I hope you had an enjoyable dinner and I expect, but there's no obligation, or hope, you will tell me about it in your usual witty way, she said in her après-consommé voice (lentils only). And by now Paul's party will be over and Ned will have emerged from wherever he hid himself or perhaps he didn't hide but plunged in the middle of the crowd as a member of a pop-group; and perhaps Paul too has a headache and hangover? I hope not.

Your photo is very sweet—all these infant tongues on display. I love having it out here in my live-oakless world that yet has many twigs and branches and leaves of the live oaks. I'm wearing your shirt today—it's very cosy, it has a special ingredient. I'm wearing your and Paul's shirt alternately, and the sweater from whom by now you will have had an upstart letter is now dry, and whenever I take needle and thread in hand I see it look longingly my way and I know it's thinking of the hole in its neck.

This is a crazy letter.

Your father's life-span will probably have ended before the Parkinson's disease makes much progress—it's a very slow disease isn't it? [in margin: It is sad though, everything is sad, the sadness just has degrees of visibility & we are a looking people??] The French professor who was lecturing on my work in New Zealand and who was in his mid-sixties, had Parkinson's disease, and has had it for several years. I often think of your great grandfather and the letters he wrote which I read one evening when Ned and I were keeping each other company; where the event of his day was perhaps a new flower in bloom along the hedgerow, or a piece of music in the evening. Ah the old days, ah the simple times, pre-consommé.

There are glinting gunmetal clouds in the skies today and dark shadows on the hills. And it looks as if I'll be very busy writing many poems about Not Being There, because the pianist's series of concerts on the Steinway are *all booked out*.

What prolific finches you have! All that visiting of nests by Carol and Ted and Alice and Bert and Henry and Myra and Carol and Ted and Bob and Jim and Jack . . . The wax-eyes around my garden are many but their behaviour is not so public. They arrive in a flock every day at twelve, on a tree next door, then move to my strawberry tree and my peppertree and the koromiko, chattering away noisily. Yesterday when I went down the garden to pick a cabbage I saw Black and Grey Tom curled under my apple tree in his nest in the long grass, waiting his chance with the wax-eyes. The astonished look came again to his face when I spoke to him. After a few moments he left his nest and hurried through the hedge. That was my social contact for the day. Also, I visited my aged aunt. She's only about eighty-two but being moved from her home into a place where she can't make herself a cup of tea, even if she had the strength to, and where she can't see what's going on outside in the world, has aged her like a blow. She's just any old woman now, congealed in the mass of 'old people'. I never knew her very well. She always struck me as a rather selfish disapproving kind of person, like one of the Dunedin ladies in the newspaper photo. Strangely enough, when I worked as a housemaid I looked after her old mother who was in a similar place for old people. Yet she's on my mind often and I get gloomy thinking of *Intensive Care* and what will happen if we don't remember that we must care for every life no matter how broken-down and useless it seems from the outside.

********   ***********

Dentists drills followed by huge sigh and turning to lighter things.

✭✭✭✭✭✭✭✭✭

Stars.

✭✭✭✭✭

Pause to adjust newly-manufactured desk peedauntal, my latest invention based on your original design. Royalties will accrue to you as wont. It literally ties me to my desk all day! My advertising campaign is well under way and features the slogan, *Live it up with a Peedauntal.*

There's a rumour a rival company is manufacturing *gilt surcingles* (synthetic only) in boxes of three, attractively wrapped but I hope to be ahead of them as they haven't yet begun their advertising campaign and we have a cut-price winter rate just now and you'd be amazed how many of the desk and house line I'm selling. (I repeat, your royalties will accrue. Prince Philip, by the way, has agreed to let us use the royal crest, by appointment to Prince Philip. This helps *no end*.)

My longing-lines for invitations to the Steinway's inaugural concert must have crossed somewhere for I've received instead an invitation to the opening of an exhibition of paintings by Colin McCahon whom I've never met but who is one of our painters with a high reputation.

✭✭✭✭

Pause for refreshment.

xx x . . . . . .

      stars again

I was interested in the news about Ann.

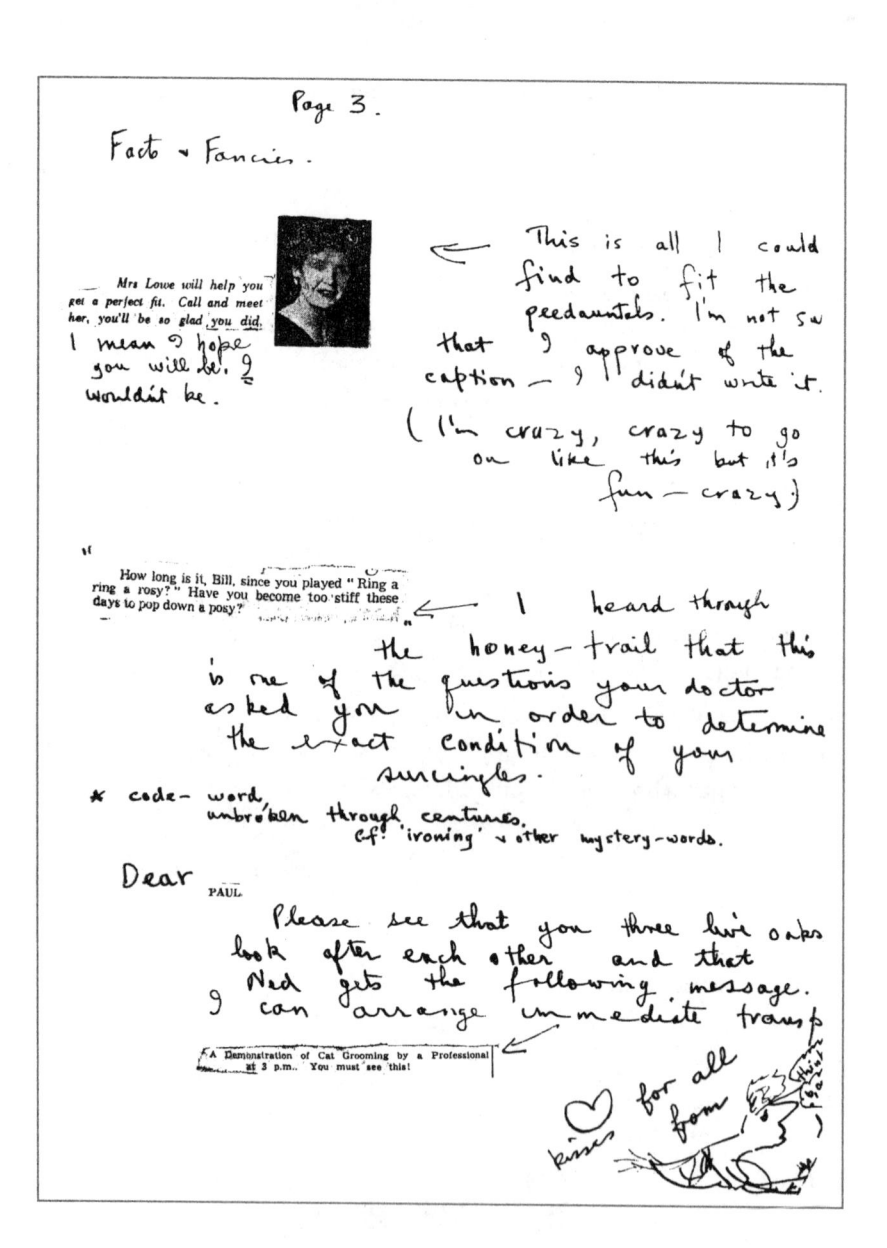

Dear Paul,

Please see that you three live oaks look after each other and that Ned gets the following message. I can arrange immediate transport.

Kisses for all

from   J

68. Dunedin June 10

[Newspaper clipping: The Music Department of the University of Otago organised this piano recital by Dr Istvan Nadas to mark the first public performance on its new Steinway piano.]

Dear B,

Just a small letter with my usual indecent collage, and some thought-waves, and touchie-feelies going your way. It's morning and I'm just settling down for my work which is going at a leisurely pace and getting complicated (this is what I like) with complications I never dreamed of. It's pretty rotten writing. I wish I could deceive myself.

I loved the sketch of the three of you taking the sun in the patio. (Another of my favourites is the performing trio, particularly that bewitching look on Ned's face as he tunes his cello.)

I've done nothing, been nowhere, seen nothing—except in phantasy. I went for a walk yesterday to the top of my street and then down into the valley, and then along, and up. There are some very ugly pretentious houses up my street, most built within the past few years as the old houses were pulled down. The street ends in fields and hills. (A Quaker refugee from California lives further up, with his wife and three or four young children. He lectures in the English Department of the University.)

I walked down into the valley ('the valley so lonely') where, on one side, the sun shines for only a few hours each day, and many of the old houses are empty or being used as places for scrap metal, engineering works, and so on. On the sunny side there was a garden with the jonquils already in bloom and finished, yet winter is scarcely begun 'summer scarcely begun. The violets, a few picked, the rest dead . . .' (I do listen to your poetry-readings, B, but not excessively and not trying consciously to remember them but they stay in my mind, they have stayed even if I had heard them only once. B plus R.M.R. achieve a perfect take-over of memory.)

I walked to the corner where the *Gardens Post Office* is (most of my letters find their way there), just beside the Public Gardens which extend up the hill not far from where I live. I went into the Gardens to see if the monkeys they had once were still there, and I could not find them. I wandered around the aviary, I looked at the scores of birds on the pond, and the dead hydrangeas which I'm beginning to understand more, after having read Rilke's poem. I have always been rather impatient with hydrangeas (that's a title—*Impatient with Hydrangeas*) because even when they are in full bloom they appear faded and withered. I am learning to understand anemones, too. It reminds me of what you were saying one day about paintings, how some exist for themselves and make no plea for you to go to them, it is you must make the letting-go and imploring effort. My favourites are the yellows, golds, reds, all the auxiliary suns in the gardens. I think it takes courage to be a small sun.

At last I wrote to May Sarton; it had been on my mind that I was going to write to her, to answer her last letter. I owe Jo a letter, too. No 'owe' is not the right word. I'll not have the commerce of correspondence, but letters are tyrannical things, they take on a life of their own. I don't look on my letters to you as letters, not really, they're just a way, for me, of *being there* from time to time with the three live and lively oaks.

Enough.

I bet Paul's party was a great success. Was it at the house? How does Ned feel about parties? He probably has some ghastly interpretation of what's going on, even imagining that his *Masters* have suddenly multiplied like amoebae or that the world has suddenly just flowed in like a tide and house isn't house and Ned's any more, it's just beach from now on with the tide coming and going.

No, I haven't got myself a kitten. I have casual communication, as I told you, with a grey and black cat that lives down the road and that once ventured to visit me and climb the stairs to the back door. He also, on sunny days, has a nest in my garden. He is usually sitting on the letter-box of his house down the street when I pass, and when I say hello kitty, there's always such a startled look on his face that I can only describe, stealing from Edmund Wilson, as 'The shock of recognition'. He almost falls off the letter-box in his surprise. Then he says, I never expect you to speak to me and you always do. I keep forgetting that you and I have an understanding.

Truly, that's what he says.

I always forget, he continues, that you're one of *us* and not one of *them*.

Grandiose phantasy or not, I enjoy it.

Now I'll say goodbye. I'm thinking of you and Paul and Ned a lot and send kisses, some for the Steinway too, and a deadlier than deadly one for the carnivorous plant.

A Special Banana Coffee Cake

Bananas are ripe and plentiful at the moment and Miss Steele has provided a special recipe for this fruit—banana coffee cake—which is ideal for supper, a midday snack, or in lunch boxes.

1½ cups flour
½ cup sugar
2 mashed bananas
½ teaspoon baking powder
¼lb butter
1 teaspoon baking soda
1 tablespoon coffee essence
1 cup milk
1 egg
pinch of salt

Cream butter and sugar, add egg, beat well. Mix in bananas, coffee essence and milk, add flour, soda, baking powder and bake half an hour in a moderate oven. Ice with coffee icing and decorate with chopped walnuts.

thinks: Is the kennel ready?

3.

The pure people

" Does Prince Philip have rather exceptional opportunities ?"

" Indeed yes."

Most people react emotionally to Prince Philip's spontaneous suggestion that "perhaps we ought to introduce a syllabus for demonstrators."

"But the problem of readjusting to the current situation has taken rather a long time."

"Once I started, it took me about a year — working on and off — to complete it."

"Now, if you do this, you are bound to have a proportion of people coming out the other end."

"This applies, of course," Prince Philip quickly adds to a great many other walks of life.

imagine yourself being just a few yards from the Queen in London

Park it in the closet

It is very hard

Prince Philip
The suggestion
pop group

friendly British islanders have so much to show you

there's a member!

"You have only got to look," says Prince Philip — but not unkindly — "at British Railways."

Have you noticed?

NEW ZEALAND: MARCH 1970 TO JANUARY 1971 | 187

69. Dunedin June 24 Le Weekend

Dear Bee,

Your letter today
takes my sadness away.

Original poem by J, aged five, for our kiddies' page:

'Dear J,
Thank you for your little poem. It earns you a red mark this week, that is, five points. When you get twenty points you become eligible for a certificate (scrolled) saying you have won twenty points. I think, though, J, if you don't mind my friendly criticism, that a five-year-old does not feel very much sadness. Wouldn't you agree? Send me another little poem next week.'

I used to belong to a children's page in a newspaper, and I was always sending in poems about flowers and trees either crying or being happy or dreaming, and each week 'Dot', the person who ran the page, used to write little notes beneath my poems telling me that flowers, trees etc. didn't weep or laugh or dream. I remember one of the criticisms (good memory for someone who doesn't read her reviews!) 'I do not think flowers, even poetically, would dream of the moon. You are inclined to let your fancy run away with you. Write again next week and do not mind my friendly criticism.'

Four years ago I met that 'Dot'. I was walking along George Street in Dunedin and a woman stopped me and introduced herself.

'I used to be Dot,' she said. 'And you were Amber Butterfly.'

'Yes,' I said.

It was a shock to meet her. I quoted her letter to me about the flowers and the moon and she laughed.

'I was very young. Did I say that?'

To me she looked very ordinary, and dull with the 'preserved' look that 'educated' women get—here, in America too, everywhere—a sort of suntan as if they'd been basking in an educational light.

'I enjoyed your poems anyway,' she said.

I had nothing to say to her.

'Well I must go,' she said. 'I'm going in here to buy some cheese.' And off she went to buy her cheese.

And that was Dot, who could not imagine that flowers might dream of the moon and who certainly would never imagine that a five-year old could be sad.

★★★★

End of interlude. Now, a happy five-year-old, I take pen or typewriter key to thank B for his letter and P for his magnificent drawing of the C plant of which more later.

I hope you've recovered from the parties. I like to hear about your *world* so that I can complete my Atlas of Santa Barbara and the Live Oaks. I'm not nearly as advanced as you seem to be with your map of J.F. I've got only as far as latitude and longitude and warm currents and volcanic peaks undersea. The explorations for my atlas are highly unscientific and intuitive as I do not have the wealth of written data. I have much else though. When I first heard you play the piano, B,

(space for portrait of formally surcingled bee

applying antennae to key)

I was vividly aware of a sanctuary something like the one you describe in your map: not wholly unexplored, but very personal and full of treasure; and forests where even the slightest breath of an intruder would be enough to wither the bloom. That is honestly what I felt and saw as I sat, sunglassed, in the library, in the deep armchair, facing Arnold Dobrin who was also listening.

So if I were to think of making a map I would be at a loss to know where or how to begin. Captain Cook when *he* set out to explore and map the Southern Hemisphere, took a crew of experts and did a little murdering and shady bargaining here and there, and nobody—they tell me—has ever improved upon his charting of the South Pacific coasts. But how will I map a spirit land? The winds that blow there are probably not south, east, west, north. What are their names then? And where do they blow. I shall end up with some

Rilkean conclusion that the trees I saw in the forest have 'their roots in the air'.

As for *my* land, I'm glad that large areas of me are declared bird and game sanctuaries—all types of bird and all types of game(s). And I don't mind human beings exploring the headwaters (both these and *those*) as long as they are silent ancient men wearing skins and paddling in their silent ancient canoes through the reeds . . .

★★★★★★★★

A little Freudian fantasy a day
keeps a five-year-old's sadness away.

Dear Five-year-old, Thank you for your little verse which earns only three points this week, as you have not heeded my remark that five-year-olds are happy little children who certainly have never heard of the person you mention in your little verse. Write again next week and do not mind my friendly criticism.

★★★★★★   ★★★★★★★★★★★★★

So Jo is going solo. She mentioned it in a letter which I haven't yet answered and she asked with her usual perception if anyone, ever, did anything else but go solo. It's a help, though, to have the facts, like high voltage lines, sheathed with the insulation of daily deception. It can be pretty horrible if the cable wears thin.

★★★★★★★★★★★★★ Stars, spokes, teddybears, little Frankensteins on the march.

★★★★★

The Debussy titles are nice, particularly 'Et La Lune Descend Sur Le Temple Qui Fut'. (I've just discovered I read it as Qui *Fuit*, which makes it even nicer. I was thinking about Debussy the other day when I came across a book I used when I was a student and inside the front page I had written:

Remember me.
Out of the cradle endlessly rocking out of the mocking-bird's
    throat the musical shuttle.
Will the water always run.
Remember this book is entirely for the benefit of those who
    are willing to know Debussy's exquisite music.

I've no idea what I meant but evidently Debussy was my love at the time.

******   **********

I fear my tape has not reached you. Perhaps the airmail sticker came off. Or perhaps the customs men misread the word *Phonopost* as *Pornopost* and confiscated it. Fortunately it *was* pure *phono*. It should have reached you long ago. (Space for cartoon of Tape reaching Live Oaks Inn and being welcomed by the C Plant.)—Of course—that's what happened. The Carnivorous Plant, naturally curious, put an ear to it, and, as you know, when carnivorous plants listen they devour what they are listening to, and that's the end of it. Are you sure it was not hovering around the letter-box, lingering, disguised maybe as a piano tuner? Only Steinway will know, and will be reluctant to tell. You will have to play S for years and years until one day an undreamed-of group of notes will sound and you will know *instantly* that the truth is out. Ah! But there's the problem. Which truth? And you and Paul and Ned and the petal-in-cheek C plant will sit long hours around the marble-topped table and in an exercise more laborious (and I might add, more rewarding) than sticking in Blue Chip Stamps in the Blue Chip Stamp Book, you will try to identify the truth Steinway has given you. And then when you have identified it you will have to test it with the litmus test. It turns the litmus life red.

******

Dear Five-year-old, You are inclined to let your fancy run away with you. No marks this week.

—Well I must go, she said. —I have to buy some cheese.

I think I will write a story called Buying Cheese. I'll never forget that meeting with 'Dot' of the Otago Daily Times. Poem after poem I sent her, and again and again she bludgeoned my fantasy and all the time I believed she knew better, that she had superior knowledge to prove that flowers didn't dream of moons and crocuses did not sit terrified in their beds in case they were mistaken for gold and stolen. And then to meet her and find an ordinary person buying cheese!

Now I will quote Auden.

'Run until you hear the ocean's
Everlasting cry;
Deep though it be and bitter
You must drink it dry.'

★★★★★★   ★★★★★★★★★★ asterisks.

I'm glad your canvases (four!) are progressing, B. My Mortal Enemy is most peculiar and intractable because Life seriously disrupts Art (I don't know if disrupts is the right word)—Life in the shape of Death, for I have to visit my old aunt, no excuse that I make to myself will work, and I *have* this habit, which should be reserved for fiction-writing, of identifying myself with people—a habit guaranteed to provide three meals of torture a day. When I come from visiting I'm an old woman of eighty-seven (I think). I've led a limited life, I've never read or thought much, my imagination is non-existent—and so on and so on.

Philip Roth said one day that every book should be called Writing and Fucking because that was all it amounted to. It sounded ideal to me. And I asked him, What about the people from Porlock?

I did!

You can't always go to bed with the people from Porlock!

We were talking about the way life interrupts art. I suppose one gets a kind of balance. Writing and Fucking balance chiefly, I suppose because they've no need to balance, they're interchangeable. What about writing and dying? Same thing? Painting and dying? My old aunt's a spectre. She doesn't know that a story I wrote about an old woman who couldn't get out of the bath (it happened to her) is appearing in an anthology on the problems of Old Age!

★★★

So I don't know what my Mortal Enemy will become. My character is a ten-year-old boy! I do know that I won't be finished the first draft (Sp?) until the end of July. (In the midst of my story of a ten-year-old boy my old aunt starts speaking.)

★★★★★★★

More stars in their courses.

It's good news, isn't it, that Paul's permanent job is confirmed? Myself, I sometimes wish that some outside authority would help me to decide where to be. I wish someone would declare me a prohibited citizen in New Zealand, or that I were told to leave the country or be put in prison. I think I shall leave here eventually, anyway. New Zealand chills me right through my marrow, if there is a place beyond it: no, not the climate of course; these wintry days are full of brilliant light with the white clouds and blue sky very much out of Paul's painting, and colours are so sharp and clear, as if there were a world of snow somewhere emitting its dazzle. It's snowing in the mountains but not here. In most places, except the mountains and foothills it snows only once or twice a winter and the snow doesn't stay on the ground. You as a painter will know what has been manipulating the light to make the blues in particular very vivid. Even the shadowy places on the hills—I see them from this window—are blue. But it is not light and its seasonal practices that chills me. It's just being here among people with whom I have no communication, and I have to live encased, shrouded in polite conversation, on surface-le[dges] that is, whenever I venture into the world of people, which is rare here.

But I won't continue to bore you with this. Living in the depths is perhaps just as much a bore as living on the surface. And the Depths are so allied to art (I hate this word but can't find another) that like Beauty and Truth in Emily's poem, they share the same tomb, at least they provide the same tomb for those who sacrifice for them.

✶✶✶✶✶✶   ✶✶✶✶✶✶✶✶✶

Stars for relief.

✶✶✶✶✶✶

Today is really Antipodean Christmas Day, the shortest day. Happy solstice, Bill and Paul and Ned. I have just eaten my lunch which I sometimes bother to cook as a main meal on Sunday. Casserole of groper (do you have that fish; probably it has another name). And I baked a pie filled with apricot, black currant, little oranges and coconut. I gave the wax-eyes their honey and water also—there are twenty to thirty of them. They made a sound like chickadees and they call out for their meal and some of them have formed the embarrassing habit of following me along the street—I don't know what I've started!—the ugliness of their natures comes out—only a few of the twenty ever get a peck in, for the big fat baddies stand quivering their feathers and threatening the hungry skinny ones, even pecking them. They are such a beautiful colour—bush colours, strange greens and rusts with a tinge of dull red and a smudge of dull yellow—autumn toning. Sometime in July when the bush flowers start to come out they will fly back to the bush for their honey.

✶✶✶✶✶✶   ✶✶✶✶✶
More stars.

No more shivering, and my house installed with heating panels . . .
✶✶✶✶✶✶   ✶✶✶✶✶
Battery has run out.

Dear Carney, (per Paul)

You lovely bit of vegetation, you! That was a nice portrait of you by Paul esquire, in fact a magnificent portrait which laid bare your soul and your distinguished trade mark of Steinway and Sons. (One of the sons is out here at the University and has just been *inaugured* and teardrops come to my eyes when I remember that I was not a witness to it.

But my real object in writing to you, Carney dear, is to enquire how ever you escaped the *Salad Incident*—or are you resurrected? In future you must keep a stricter—calyx?—on your three guardians, and there's no harm in getting Steinway to help you, you could take turns to keep Perpetual Watch with both watching at crucial meal-times and never, never allow Paul or Bill to put you among other greenery on that counter in the kitchen, even if they make the excuse that they're giving you a change of air, or a chance to be among your *own kind*, or even be as company for them as the meal is prepared, for one false move, one moment's inattention and it is *you* who will be prepared.

Now to more serious matters. About that habit of yours, that ineradicable habit of being what you are, I say congratulations, *Carnivoration* is *You*, nothing would look so well on your life, but (to refer to your message) as for my coming to lunch *as your lunch*, are you aware of the sacrifices I would be making? If you are, good; because I'm not. What sacrifice would it be for me to arrive on the Peanut Butter Patio, in time for lunch, say a quick, eager, shy, happy, hello to B and P and N, and then resign myself to my fate, I, who have trembled so long in my life between Active and Passive, the Doer and the Thing Done To, the Seer and the Seen, the Beer and the Been, to join the company of the Devoured.

There's only one drawback, Carney dear. Think it over. *We created you*. Think it Over.

Yours, J

Dear J,

What a tired old argument. You created me, indeed! Who cares who created me? I am. I keep my ineradicable habit. I devour. Are you coming to the sacrifice? Think it over.

   Yours,
    Carney

Correspondence closed.
Correspondence cannot be opened as the key is lost.
Why is the key lost?
'The moss has covered up our lips.'
 ★   ★   ★ —ends of witches' brooms ★   ★   ★
All kinds of love & sad missings, to B apis mellifica buccaneer of buzz (?) & P official draughtsman to the Carn. Plant & Ned Washer-Inhabitor Extr (W.D.I.E.)
 from crazy J pining (pine, pine) in the Antipodes.

Dear Bill
Sweater was ill
But reading your letter
sweater felt better
(twas only a chill)

Dear Paul,
My aunt wears a shawl
I wish the carnivorous plant
would visit my aunt.
That's all.

Dear Ned
Out of your head
you created a purr
especially for her
(Dr Gilbride said).

70. Dunedin June (Wax-Eye City)

Dear B, P, and N,

Hello. I'm thinking about you and so put key to paper. I wish I were there, unobtrusively, and you were going about your daily activities—just your presences are enough for me.

Meanwhile back in Wax-Eye City I've just had my mutton broth but its flavour could not take away the flavour of the horrible review my publisher sent me yesterday, nor could the nice review they sent today remove the flavour. 'Brilliant etc.' Who would believe that? Not I.

I now have thirty wax-eyes to feed, and some of them are getting so fat that when they perch at the top of the stairs their paunch hangs down, but there are still the thin ones who never get a chance to eat the honey. I think all the wax-eyes of Dunedin are concentrated here. There are scores of them in my trees but they are invisible, as their colour is leaf-colour, and all their moving and fluttering makes it seem as if a wind were blowing the trees until with that extra vision that you get when you persist in looking closely, suddenly you see the trees are alive with birds. There's something Biblical about it—I feel as if I should be reporting a miracle and inviting people who study and classify miracles to stand beneath the trees, notebooks in hand, to record and judge. (If I were able to paint I would make a Giotto-type painting and the people would have those narrowed suspicious sideways-glancing eyes of the people in Giotto.)

Life continues very much a La Emily D with little of her courage and none of her talent. I need the presence of the 'like-minded'. Eternity was her like-minded company—Eternity, Beauty, Truth, Time, all flitting and buccaneering around her garden. One glimpse of eternity terrifies me (whatever it is). I could not transform it into wax-eyes and feed it daily, for I already do that without wanting to know about it. How at home she was with it! Even for Vaughan—or was it Herbert, a glimpse was enough for him to write a solemn poem for the occasion, 'I saw eternity the other night like a great ring of pure and endless light.'

Well I'm getting involved!

You did ask me what I said in my radio interview (which I did not hear) as my radio, an old-fashioned huge cabinet-type with valves, condenser etc. suddenly became 'live' and I'm waiting for it to be fixed. The questions were: Why were such things as artists colonies set up? Did the colonies help you? How common is this sort of thing in the States? What were the criteria for entering the colonies? When you are concerned about writing and representing the realities of life did you find the colony an artificial situation? Did you feel the violence of the American society? . . . I won't continue with the questions, they were so stupid, but quite usual. I gave a factual account of how the colonies work. Questions like 'Did they help you?' I didn't answer. About violence, I said it was too big a question to answer but that if you visit U.S.A. you must equip yourself with a watchfulness that you don't need in little old Dunedin. I said that where one used to learn that cities and highways were the life-lines of a continent, one now knows they are the death-lines.

Ghastly answer. I did mention the beautiful woodlands and wildernesses and the interviewer was surprised (as I was when I made my first visit to the States!) that there were *trees* left.

I didn't speak about my work, saying I preferred not to, but that I was interested in the problems of people working in the other arts. I mentioned sculptors who couldn't pay their foundry bills, or hadn't homes and so had nowhere to store their sculpture, and of the difficulty women painters seemed to have: a. in being aggressive enough to interest gallery directors; b. in being strong enough to cart paintings from gallery to gallery. I shouldn't have spoken in the plural—there was only one of each that had this problem but I thought the audience would be interested.

There was one question which began, 'Do you see life as . . .' which I answered by saying I didn't see life at all, I lived largely in a state of unconsciousness. Which I do.

Enough of that tripe. I tried to emphasise that if you are a writer or painter or sculptor, it is not an artificial situation if you practise your work all day. But my insistence fell on deaf ears. I know. Yesterday I met a woman in town who said she used to sit beside me at school (that type!) and that she had enjoyed my radio interview very much, that it was interesting to know about the arts. Then she said, What are you doing these days? Have you got a job somewhere?

!!!!!!!!!

The first plum blossom will be out soon. These days there is an absence of cats except for the golden one that stalks in the garden across the road where the new people have moved in. It is golden with blackish small stripes as if its fur were feathers.

****

> *I will arise and go now and go to Santa Barbara*
> *and a kennel live in there that Bill and Paul have made,*
> *nine mountain lions will I have there, and a place for my typewriter,*
> *and live alone with Bill and Paul and Ned.*
>
> *And I shall have some peace there for peace comes dropping slow*
> *dropping from the olive tree where the finch-family sings;*
> *there lunch is brownbread sandwich on a peanut patio,*
> *and evening full of music, collages and things.*
>
> *I will arise and go now . . .*

End of inspiration. Don't mind my dreams. They're only dreams.

So goodbye for now. Enjoy yourselves in the sun.

71. Dunedin June 27

Glad you got my silly tape.

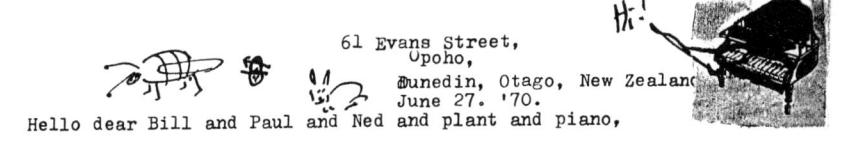

61 Evans Street,
Opoho,
Dunedin, Otago, New Zealand
June 27. '70.
Hello dear Bill and Paul and Ned and plant and piano,

Hello dear Bill and Paul and Ned and plant and piano,
   I'm sitting at my desk, my heater is heating, the wax-eyes or silver-eyes (I learn they came from Australia in 1856 [in margin: this makes them 114 years old]) are twittering and fighting over their breakfast, the world outside is a subdued Saturday morning world, the day, after a week of blue sky and sun, is faintly blue, with smoke from fires misting the air in the valley, and the hills starkly outlined like the exposed backbones of huge beasts. The smoke does not reach them and they are sunlit.
   Having just had a letter from H Drive, I feel my inner warmth matches the outer warmth, and after I've written this letter I shall probably work, bake, eat, and try to get my fuschia off my conscience: I must explain: my small fuschia hedge at the front of the house is sick. I know it, and I have done nothing for it, and I hope this weekend to feed it at least.
   News flash: I have a primrose out. [in margin: As this is not (yet) a maid's diary, the word *primrose* is *not code*.]
   I was interested in what you were saying about isolation and stimulation. Whether we like it or not I think maybe we *have* become machines for over-stimulation, and over-stimulation is 'normal', and even in places where it doesn't exist the urge is there to be subjected to it. When I was staying in London or New York I'd go out for a wander around the streets, looking at the people, the traffic, just watching what was going on, and I'd come home full of impressions, maybe ready to write a story. If I go walking in the street here the only time I receive impressions that move me enough to write is when I walk where people no longer go but where they used to be (The Place of the Stone Bees [in margin: my next title?]) and their presence remains. I do miss the people-stimulation. The only or about the only stimulant people serve to me here is fear or a

feeling (possibly ineradicable for me now, in this country) that I'm some kind of freak. Some of the people I know in Dunedin live the kind of life your great grandaddy lived. I do, not through choice, but because here in New Zealand I am even more of a social cripple than I am when I'm in other countries. Being here frightens me.

But I don't want to write a serious letter, because I'm sitting warm and cosy, out and in, at my desk putting finger to key to say hello to the Live Oaks growing in Santa Barbara—live oaks that are so famously famous that Walt Whitman knew of them★. [footnote: ★see 'I found (knew?) a live oak growing in Santa Barbara'—official Whitman adaptation by Paul Wonner]

Here is a story Ned will like: There was an art show opening recently. I did not go to it but the other day in off-peak hours I went to see the paintings. The gallery is run by an acquaintance whose husband keeps the manuscripts at the University Library; it's something like the place in Montecito but more elaborate—even something like Felix's place. When I asked after their cat (they live near here and when they go away I look after their cat) Maureen said it was very well. She then told me how about eleven months ago it seemed to be ill, and was shedding its fur, and one evening she and Michael sat discussing it, and decided they should take it to the vet the next day. Ngeru was listening to this discussion about him. The next day he had vanished. They searched and searched, put advertisements in the paper and so on but he had vanished completely, and at last they thought he must be dead. He was away for seven months. About four months ago Michael was in the bath when xxx (I typed *Ned*) Ngeru appeared at the window (he uses the bathroom window which they leave permanently open, as a door) jumped in (to the floor) as usual and went to his usual feeding-place. He was fine and healthy and behaved as if he'd never gone away. They never found out where he had been, and he isn't telling, but they know he left home because he heard them planning to take him to the vet. Like your Ned (and all cats I suppose) he doesn't have to be told with words or deeds, he can divine things. I suppose here he knew the word *vet*.

Isn't that a nice story, Ned? (don't let it give you ideas)

P.S. I liked the paintings very much. Two in particular were shapes in two colours which were moving, I don't know why. They had the physical effect that paintings sometimes have of pulling your heart away from your body towards the painting—or the mass of colour.

✶✶✶✶✶✶ Thank you for your lovely letter and its enclosures. Do you know W.H. Auden's long letter to Lord Byron?

Quote: 'Every exciting letter has enclosures,
        and so shall this—a bunch of photographs,
        some out of focus, some with wrong exposures,
        press cuttings, gossip, maps, statistics, graphs;
        I don't intend to do the thing by halves.
        I'm going to be very up-to-date indeed.
        It is a collage that you're going to read.'

✶✶✶✶✶✶✶✶✶✶
Send Eva and Jeff my love (sacred).
✶✶✶
Twice a week, as I told you, I visit my aunt to watch with detachment the slow withering of a statistic, and the slow blossoming of the truth, What is not used, dies.
' ' ' ' ' ' '

    My pop song.
    Down Serious Alley
    Where ghosts get pally,
    la-de-da, dum-de.
, , , , , , ,

Does Ned's *Petro*malt have *petrol* in it? For his engine? In all seriousness I ask . . .
✶✶✶✶✶✶✶✶

The Live Oaks Page. Air, water, sun your problems. Smog them too, with abandon. Nothing too small or large.

Dear Live Oaks,
    Every week without fail I read your page and it thrills me very much to see what good work you are doing to help those with problems. I used to write with mine to Aunty Glossy of the Sunday Surprise but now I turn to you. I think, though, that your answer to *Overfed Wax-Eye* in last week's page did not have your usual wisdom; on the other hand I approve heartily of your advice to *Eleven Months*

Old and Proud of it. I too think he should wait.★ [footnote: ★Temptations abound when the very young leave home to rent their own apartment.] You are to be commended also on your restraining advice to *Go-Ahead Ned*. We are fortunate indeed to have watch-cats like you in our society, such as it is, this present day, all things being equal. Also your reply to the arrogant yet heart-felt letter by *C Plant* on resisting temptation even when the temptation is present twenty-five hours of the day, is worth far more than the fifty dollars you charge each week for your paper. And how true your dictum rings, We all have to start at the bottom!

My problem is this: Someone I know (I will mention no names) has discovered an old grocery list belonging to F Sargeson of Auckland. It was sent to me in a letter but it was originally discovered in a supermarket in Auckland. Should I hang on to it? Your usual advice has been to hang on to things as closely as possible. I also have a framed original of a famous Californian cat, and would like advice about this. Is it likely to appreciate? (either me or itself). Returning to the grocery list. It is in manuscript, resembling verse-form, with one word-change which could be the subject of research. Should I fly at once to the United States to offer this grocery list to the Universities? Should I return the list to Frank S as some of its items are intimate (e.g. toilet tissue) or should I philanthropically donate the list to the local University to be on display in the foyer of the Home Science Department?

About the framed original of the famous Californian Cat. Should I perhaps just hang on to it? I should prefer to hang on to it. Should I go to California to hang on to it?

I look forward eagerly to your page next week and send my best wishes for years of problem-solving ahead.

Hanger-On, The Antipodean Room.

★   ★   ★   ★

Hello. Here I am again. Sunday, but no sun, pearl-coloured sky, the hills a blue haze, birds flying by as big as planes. I've spent some of the morning checking my electric plugs—in the house, that is. I discovered my tenants had confused phase and earth wires on my electric stove and one desk lamp and I myself had done one or two foolish things in attaching plugs. So I've been screwing and unscrewing all morning!

How boring can I make a letter!

★★★★

I didn't feed the fuchsia. I just went and looked at it and felt guilty and then stirred up the earth around it. I pruned the black currants and the gooseberries and freed their roots from strangling weeds, and that was enough. I'm not an energetic gardener—I prefer to read about it, though the gardening book is so full of details of pests and diseases.

[Illustration: a cow saying "I spy with my little eye."; a newspaper clipping headed "revolution"; a cat (Ned) saying "Come to N.Z. & paint us. No-one has painted our portraits. We have no rights, no vote, no lions to lie down with. — Que sommes-nous.... etc"]

Ned, 11 months old.

★★★★★★

I am busy eating the fruit garden you sent me; saving some for hungry days.

★★★★

Dear Live Oaks (you can ask Aunty Glossy to help with this one),

Someone whom I've met only once (for about twenty minutes) has written confessing that he is in love with me and can he dedicate his next book to me. How can I gratify my vanity by agreeing to the dedication and at the same time gently but firmly let him know that his declarations embarrass me and his feeling is not reciprocated? I'm sure you will be able to give me some good advice in your weekly page.

★★★★★★   ★★★★★★

I've been rereading Yeats and each time I do I feel he's the greatest because he is so free, he may go anywhere.

And now my battery (as you may have noticed) is running out so I'll say au revoir (I hope it is this?), and where did you get that picture of the C Plant eating???? how amazing! and I send so many thoughts and feelings and fantasies that if they were visible I'd have to hire a fleet of ships or a squadron of planes to transport them.

    Drivel.

               Love to B P N

               Separate & collective love.   from homesick Jay

JULY

72. Dunedin July

Bill and Paul, you two dears, what a warm letter I had from you yesterday, and my cockles are bubbling and steaming with enough inner fuel to feed me through the internal winter. Your journey, and the long lonely beach-walks, and the mountains and desert sounded ideal, Paul. I love such solitude, myself, but as part or season of the human year, not as an everlasting winter. I do think that people don't give themselves enough autumns and winters, and we need these seasons as much as the feverish growth and bloom of spring and summer . . .

But this is going into deep water and I'd prefer to just laze around in the sun and not dive today. My typewriter sends greetings to your typewriter—was it born in the Blue Chip Shop? How distinguished it must be.

I must tell you both that I'm working hard to retain my insanity! It's not really very hard to do but I agree that you have to watch yourself or you slip over the edge into sanity and the problem then is you have lost the power to realise that you're sane. Carnie too has 'eaten of the insane root'.

I'm afraid I have been complaining about my loneliness here. It's an autumn. The separation is the leaf-fall ('something real has gone') and this is a barren country for souls, at least for the living; and the dead make sure they retain their deadness and operate in a fertile country. I see people here and talk occasionally to them but it is the like-mindedness that is absent and has always been absent here, for me. One becomes, quite successfully, a half-person. The other half, that matters too, becomes a tangled growth, and is eventually killed by frost. Again, it is the *continued* working of the seasons that matters, it is the cycle, going on past death and before birth, with no beginning and no ending. Frost is good for the soil only if there is a spring to follow.

★★★★★★★★★
End of deep water.
★★★★★★★★★★★★★★★★★★★★★★★★★ Stars.
Seeing you again will be springtime.

★★★★★★★★★★★★★★★

And if you find a place in the mountains and I come to stay (on twenty-one days appro.) the first thing I shall do (after feeding the mountain lions and the rattlesnakes) will be to *quaff* a toast to the continuity of the human seasons.

★★★★★★

Stars again.

Garden News:

None—not really. I have partly cleared the vegetable garden, and, worried about the fuchsia, thinking that perhaps it needs more food, for it is near the roots of the olearia hedge which are hungry roots, I went into one of the many plant shops in Dunedin, and of course I panicked when the assistant said, 'Can I help you?' I mumbled, 'Well . . . I . . . I think . . . some food . . .'

She looked at me as if I were crazy.

'I mean, something for the earth. I think the earth needs some food.'

Then I got so tangled up that I said, 'Well I'm in rather a hurry, I'll come in again when I've got more time.'

That was my expedition to help the fuchsia.

Next time I shall walk boldly in, and remembering Carnie, I shall say menacingly, 'Give me some blood and bone!'

Fan News: All my letters are fan letters.

Work News: Working. $\dfrac{\text{Boy of Ten} \times \text{Jay}}{\text{aged aunt}} = ?$

Misc: It is a sad spectacle to watch the degeneration of the wax-eyes. Once they used to take their honey and water and fly away. Now they are too busy worrying whether some other wax-eye will get what they think is *their* fair share that they spend more time quivering their wings at each other, threatening and pecking and screaming. At least, while the burly ones are fighting the more timid ones are able to sneak in and have their taste of honey. This morning when I opened the curtains I saw the big dark grey tom-cat sleeping at the top of the stairs as if he owned the place. I said hello to him and he put that surprised look on his face. He is so incredulous that I should speak to him. He gave me a long long stare, full of language, then got up, twisted his heavy bull-shoulders and walked down the stairs into the garden. I haven't seen him since. He hasn't appeared to bother the wax-eyes. (This should really be in Garden News.)

Misc. Continued.

Tonight I am going to Charles B's place for dinner after which we are going to see/hear the Opera Company's *The Impresario* and *Il Pagliacci*. It will be a very good opportunity for me (as co-director of the Peedauntal Company N.Z. Ltd.) to see how the product actually works. I know one can have dreams about one's product but the proof of the peedauntal is in the peeing (aren't I rude?). I also wish I had kept one of the original audience models for personal use. They are incorporated with a distinguishing device which will enable me (once I have a quick look over the designs) to know immediately which members of the audience are wearing peedauntals. I daren't ask Charles if he wears them! I shall know at once, of course. I shall pretend to pick up something from the floor and while I am there I'll cast a quick glance crotchward . . . from under the table.

Anyway when the evening is over I shall write a director's report. It's quite likely that our factory has bungled terribly and the peedauntal conditions have some unknown factor here that we never dreamed of. It should be corrected, (if this proves to be so) by the Christmas buying season.

Apart from its being very much a working evening I hope to enjoy both the dinner (Charles is not an enthusiastic cook) and the opera.

******   ********

To offset, balance, my rather depressed state when I think of the old people in the home where my aunt is (I usually speak to several of the old people), I was delighted to have a letter from the elderly woman (going on 76—not terribly elderly . . . still) whom I know in Norfolk, England. Quote: 'The past week has been idyllic and I'm off for an all-day cycle ride northwestward to the sea . . .' Also: 'Having recently read Strachey's life of Cardinal Manning I've been fired to read Newman's *Apologie* . . .' And hearing about your Aunt Amy is another balancing factor. It is the *barrenness* of my aunt that appalls me, but then it has always appalled me, for though I never knew her well, whenever I met her I was aware of her confined inner life—it's the exposure of it now for all to see that is sad. Yet maybe all don't see it, maybe she's just another old woman, and I'm so used to reading people or trying to ('pages where to read pathetic histories').

********* Enough of that. ********************* Stars. Tomorrow I am having a visit from a young French woman who sounded very twittery and fluttery over the phone. It sounds incredible and crazy (the wrong kind of craziness) but she is here from the University of Toulouse, is on the staff of the French Department, and is completing a thesis for Professor Du Pont (the Toulouse professor) on J.F. in her New Zealand setting !!! Natural habitat, I suppose! I've invited her (after she phoned me) because I've been rather annoyed that she's been paying visits to people who know me. Touchy, aren't I? Apparently, though, she's rather nice and hasn't been asking personal questions; I want to ask her about *Vergers*. She was rather amusing. She said,

'Oh I don't want to interrupt your gardening.'

I said, 'But I won't be gardening, I'm very lazy.'

'Oh,' she said. 'But everybody in Dunedin is gardening, gardening, gardening all the time.'

So I'll make a report on the visit in my next instalment.

****
More Stars.

I can't help making stars. I just can't wait to collect my mountain lions and rattlesnakes and come to California!

***

The other evening I heard a 1938 recording of Fischer (?) playing the Schubert Impromptus 142 (my daily accompaniment, along with my other records including the lilacs and the Schumann and the Peter Serkin. My other record is Glenn Gould with his first four Mozart Sonatas). It was so beautiful, so warm, not so warm that it became cloudy, though there was just a faint suggestion of haze, but it was different from the record I have which is slightly metallic (though that may be the pornograph which is the cheapest I could get and may not have too many refinements but it *is* a good phonograph and the Clara Haskil Schubert Sonatas sound warm and quite dizzy on it. What a happy inner experience to hear that the other evening.

****

I'll go to post this now. I think your new paintings sound very exciting as if you're both at the *peak*. Mention of the 'lovely colours' makes me hungry. Looking at paintings is very much a consuming process? I'm enclosing a strange card sent to me from a strange address asking me to send it to you. No doubt Carnie left a little note for you tucked away somewhere.

Look after one another and each other and all & hardy perennial love from me too.

[handwritten drawing: to [figures] — a very costive-looking school-marmish looking Jay!]

73. Dunedin July

Dear Live Oaks, ('Oh my dears, my dears!'),

You will see from the enclosed report that something is rotten in the Peedauntal Industry. I'm beginning to think I'm not cut out to be a manufacturer. You ought to have been at the theatre last evening when all those Peedauntals burst! Charles B, who was with me, and who has what is supposed to be the English trait of disregarding anything the slightest bit unseemly at all times, behaved as if nothing had happened, while streams flowed back and froth! from stage to audience. I wasn't wearing mine and I was unable to discover whether Charles was wearing one for it's not the sort of subject one brings up with him.

Well it's all over now, and what a fiasco. Hurrah, I may be turned out of the country for harbouring peedauntals! (This letter is being sent by wax-eye.)

What other news? I'm afraid I'm homesick all the time for you. Just for you to be around.

I've just been to visit my aunt and I spent some time persuading several of the old dears that it was night-time, for suddenly they began to get up, saying, Well we must be going, we can't stay here being waited on.

I said, –It's night-time now.

–Oh, is it? they said.

Well they (there were three) decided to take my word for it and so they settled down to sleep. I go there out of visiting hours, though there are very few visitors, and it's guiltily easy to play the role of comforter.

★★★★★★★★★★★★

I forgot to say that for dinner last night at Charles B's I had soup that started off as ham hock with lentils but has been going for three weeks now, and was full of good things, and very tasty. Then some cubed steak with vegetables, then boysenberries and cream and seed cake and coffee; and wine.

And in spite of the Peedauntal incident the opera was fun although I was surrounded by the smell of cough lollies (sweets) for a woman next to me was eating very strong irish moss and licorice and wintergreen, everything cough mixtury and it didn't quite go with the operas, though maybe it did, for the music sometimes made me wince when the violin played a squeak instead of a note.

★★★★★★★★★★★★

I play your poems and the bagatelles and Hérodiade and Wolf almost every day, Bee, and the interview I played too. I'm always curious about what you edited out! I had hoped to ask the French woman for her interpretation of 'the slow, the happy' etc. but after waiting most of the afternoon for her to turn up I found out that she was so excited that she forgot which day she was coming to see me and she decided it must be Saturday! So she'll be here on Saturday and far fom answering any questions about myself or giving her any information I'm going to be armed with Rilke's poems. I recently got Baudelaire's *Journal Intime*, reissued in Penguin, translated by C Isherwood with introduction by Auden. Do you know it—I'm sure you do. It's horrifying.

—Peedauntal Report—

Special Baths

Special baths were provided for members of the audience at the Dunedin Opera Company's performance of *The Impresario* when a number of faulty Peedauntals burst under pressure. One of the directors of the Company, when approached on the matter, had no comment to make.

Co-directors of the overseas-based company, resting quietly in their home in Hermosillo Drive, also had no comment to make, though a black and white cat resting on the family patio was heard to remark,

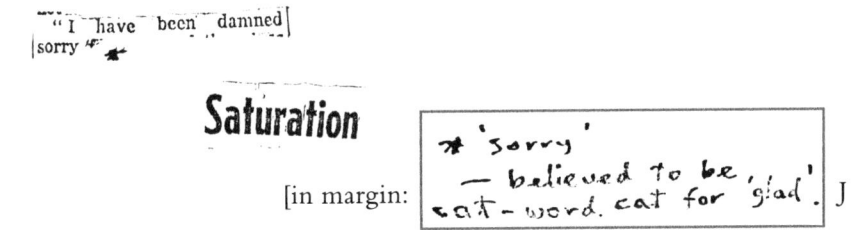

"I have been damned | sorry*"

Saturation

[in margin: * 'sorry' — believed to be 'glad'. cat-word. cat for 'glad'.]

It is not known whether repairs will be made to the theatre and the stage after the unprecedented flooding from both members of the cast and members of the audience who were known to be wearing the faulty peedauntals. When approached once more the Dunedin-Opoho-based director stressed that the performance both of the opera company and the peedauntals which were a new design had been:

"far better than expected,"

"The new peedauntal," she said, " allows the large cast complete freedom of movement.

Other designs had been " less secure "

Water Safety

The Chief Inspector of Police and the Manager of the Opera Company agreed that the cast of an opera and the audience needed to have a special concern for water safety.

Warning

NEW ZEALAND: MARCH 1970 TO JANUARY 1971

One member of the cast who was wearing a special-capacity peedauntal has warned that he will sue the company for damages. Speaking of the peedauntal he said his family had insisted on his buying one and had gone without holidays for ten years.

> "We have spent thousands of dollars on it."

was his comment when asked to name the sum he would demand in court.

Plan

Local members of parliament, concerned at the influx of peedauntals and their production by an oversea-based firm said investigations would be carried out, and searches without warrants made at 61 Evans Street where some of the company's correspondence and designs were believed to be kept. They assured the Press.

> "We have drafted legislation which will provide the means of dealing with this situation."

74. Dunedin July

/honey/

Dear B, P, N, and all at Live Oak Inn including the Carnie who slunk home, tendril between his legs, because he didn't like the big bad world. In one of his journeys he took a tramp steamer to Great Britain and the papers wrote nasty things about him, and there were rumours too with quotes like a

> 15ft plant that escaped from the Royal Botanical Gardens, is endangering health in Britain.

> "The plant is spreading rapidly, and is now constituting a public health hazard."

What hope has a plant of protesting? Well, he left Great Britain and took a tramp steamer home to Live Oak Inn and *that* was what Paul must have seen sailing through the hall—after so much furious conjecture one realises it was, of course, Carnie on board the tramp steamer, coming home with his tendril between his legs and with his little bundle of cottage cheese, peanut-butter, round-square or square-round of bread only half-eaten. Bill can never play the page of music again though, it is all covered with tramp-steamer residue, and it got rained on and the raindrops stayed on it, glued there with soot, making new notes of music, so if you do try to play it, Bill, it will be like something you've never played before.

All that, however, is a digression. There you are on the peanut butter patio and here am I saying hello and wishing I were there.

I had a visitor last evening, the nicest visitor I've had since I've been home. I heard something at the door and when I opened it there was a mewing kitten which wouldn't go away and clearly was visiting me. It wasn't a stray, it was tiny, plump, wellfed, but it insisted on coming in. I gave it a small drink of milk. Its purr sounded all over the house. It wasn't a 'pretty' cat—nondescript grey and white and eyes set very close together, but it was a cat with a cat's grace. After it had drunk the milk it explored the sitting room and my study and walked to the front door and back. Then it peed in a small tray I put down for it. Then it came to the sitting-room and washed itself. Then it climbed on my knee and purred and purred and snuggled. Next it explored and played. It skated on the kitchen floor, rushed up and down, skating from end to end, it climbed on the table and sat and fell asleep on the typing paper, then it rushed to the study and ran round and round the chair, all the time purring loudly with a loosely-beaded purr. Sometimes it meowed and I spoke to it in meows. Then it went to the back door, opened the door, said goodbye, and the kitten went home to wherever it lives—I've never seen it before and there's no sign of it today, but it was a delightful visitor. I can't think why it came to me but I've at last decided that the old dark grey tom who nests under the apple tree in the garden is some relation and it happened one day to see this little kitten, and suggested, Why don't you go to visit J.F. one evening? Get some practice in visiting people, as part of your education. All you do, as guest, is go in, have a drink of milk, a pee, a wash, a cuddle and a play—it's quite simple but you need practice—there, dart up to the door now and pretend you're starving, and once in, do your stuff. You have to learn some time how to handle people . . .

⟨ Page Two. ⟩
Of Peedauntals, Yawls, and Other Complications.

I'm sorry the Peedauntals business turned out badly. At least the chap with the special-capacity peedauntal who had been going to sue the company for thousands of dollars has been pushed over a cliff by an elephant I hired from the Auckland Zoo. The elephant was flown down a week ago and I gave it instructions and took it out to St Clair where the cliffs are and sure enough this chap appeared and the elephant did its stuff, or its thing or whatever you call it. I thought I'd better explain the elephant Requisition on the Company Report you will be sent when our bankruptcy hearing comes up later on. No date is set yet. Meanwhile 61 Evans St is overflowing and flooded with peedauntals. I have them in the cellar, in the washing-tubs, in the garden, everywhere and I had thought of sending them free to underprivileged Americans on the Moon.

How glad I am to wash my hands of the business!

★★★★

About Yawls.

I hope you and Paul and Ned are not worried by the yawl. I've been doing some research and I came across a reference which should calm all fears at Live Oak Inn (I mean fears that you all might be *sane* after all). The verse is as follows:

The reference was 'Halls, Passing through by yawls'.

> *Yawls have been known to pass through halls*
> *just as shoes have been known to wear feet*
> *and old women are often worn by shawls*

(a last line is censored
> *because of its pornographic pitfalls.*)

so you can all breathe easily at last!

★★★

Many thanks.

★★★★ Stars.

Pure virgin wool love, warm, shrink-proof, mothproof, easily
>   *washed in* Cold Water All,
>   *also transportable by yawl*
>   *and useful*
>   *when correctly spread*
>   *for warding off a chill*
>   – this finished fabric from me
>   to Bill and Paul and Ned
>   or more familiarly to N and P and B
>   (Aren't I crazy?)

★★★★★★

>   My mortal enemy keeps turning the other cheek.
>   *Bill filled the Bill and all was still.*
>   *Paul cried out in the hall, –I sight a yawl!*
>   *Ned, recently fed, tucked his head under the covers*
>   *of his washer-drier bed.*
>   The night came. (This is an impromptu rhyme.
>   *I make them all the time*
>   *as I weep on the southern shore)*
>   *inchoate –just a word I know –all the time I make my rhyme*
>   *from caustic soda and lime*
>   Na2 SO4
>   *and calcium carbonate—for you see*
>   *I remember my chemistry.)*
>   *Where were we?*
>   The night came. Out in the patio
>   the moon dangled low on strings as if the silver dark were fishing
>   with a gold bait
>   but what it hoped to catch no-one will ever know. I think
>   the olive tree dreamed of Spain (only poetically, Dot!)
>   and its feet deep down in red earth for earth is a kind of flesh there;
>   and heavily the freeway freewayed, while inside the house in the hall
>   Paul was still concerned about having sighted a yawl.
>   –It passed by the Steinway, with a list
>   to starboard, he hissed (not wanting to waken Ned).
>   The sails were purple and red
>   like petunias. What has come over the place?

Bill strode forth with a white face and shoed feet and fingered hands
—Tell me all,
he whispered. —Paul, tell me all. Your face is eyed
and mine is mouthed. Is that at all
unusual? There's little weather outside.
Nor rain nor hail nor snow. Bill said —Be still. But, Paul,
truly I did not know
we had a yawl!
Panic. Ned woke
in a stroke of waking (a kind of explosion like that suffered
     by baking-powder when it meets a liquid in baking).
Ned fizzled and purred and finally stirred, the dreams vanished
deep
in his eyes as he was cooked out of sleep.
He meowed. —Did I hear something fall?
—No, Bill said, patting the sleek head. —Tell him, Paul.
Paul spoke aloud,
his voice unafraid and proud,
—I saw a yawl pass through the hall
with a starboard list to Steinway
its sails purple and red (I'm not dreaming, Ned!)
like petunias. In unity
we three
let us go seek it.
With the battlecry —Seek seek, and now not at all
afraid they strode through the hall
led by Paul. (To be continued next week.)

(a tender alternative is the sails were disguised air-mails wax-eyed your way from J)

75. Dunedin July 3 (postcard)

Postscript
Dear Paul,
Looking back,
I've decided it may have been a fishing smack
on its way to trawl
and not a yawl at all.
But why did it sail
  through the hall?

CJ.

76. Dunedin July 7

Dear blonde, brunette, periwigged, Paul, C.P.C. (Co-director Peedauntal Company),

Your letter came just now. You are a dear to make enquiries about teaching, and thank you. Unfortunately, away out here on the outskirts of Wax-Eye City, with the Peedauntal Bankruptcy Case looming (loom loom) I lose most of my ideas of social judgment. Just as when one goes to U.S.A. one puts on a certain watchfulness for the big bad cities, until the watchfulness becomes an unnoticeable part of one, so, in returning to New Zealand I put on a fear—understandably, inevitably—for I cannot abolish my past experiences here (not at the hands of the wax-eyes or garden trees or Carravaggio skies—but at the hands of people—maybe you know that species??) I mean I, rather timid to start with, become really timid, and so from here the prospect of teaching anyone scares me—apart from the fact that I know so little about writing, and the responsibility of pronouncing judgment on the work of those just beginning is a fearful one. On the other hand the technique and forms and problems of writing fascinate me and I would love to learn more by teaching. I'm inclined to think that if I attended the College of Creative Studies it would be as a student. The opinion of some who know my work and have seen and talked to me as a person (or plant or animal or vampire) is that I would be able to teach. I'm thinking of a poet, Ann Stanford who's in charge (or was in charge) of the Creative Studies at San Fernando State College. She saw me at Yaddo a couple of years ago and saw, I suppose, what a reserved (!) person I was—they used to call me *The Corner Woman* because I sat in the corner and listened and would not join in the conversation (that was Hyde Solomon's nickname for me), and yet Ann was very keen for me to go to San Francisco, en depit de tout.

Short terns.

Well . . . I've rather gone on about this but I don't want to say yes, and have you make arrangements, and then get scared and send a wax-eye with a big NO in its *bill*. Not at all, *Paul*. A short tern class—a month to six weeks—would be a good idea and then I would find out; and I'm not scared when I'm away from New Zealand—well, I'm naturally shy to start with but I don't get really pathologically scared as I do in N.Z. though it's not pathological, it's natural.

A short (tern) class

To parody Auden who had his photo in our morning paper today (on the second page—the front page was occupied by the photograph of two jersey cows), 'Oh my dear one is mine as mirrors are lonely'—'Oh my fear is natural as plastic flowers are bright'. A bit askew but it will do.

I'd say yes to a class of a month to six weeks. After that—the deluge. And I might like it very much—I wouldn't know until I try (I mean the class not the deluge) though perhaps I can combine the two.

I hope you get the job you want and not the job they seem to want for you, and that you cast a spell over them by gazing in the mirror of your picture, or letting them gaze in it,

Miroir, miroir,

and now I've got myself into French phrasing how do I get out? I'd really much rather try to earn my living by 'pure' writing.

Miroir miroir au mur

suis-je pure?

je ne suis pas sur.

If, however, saying I am interested in a few weeks of teaching will get me information on what to do, that is, how to go about turning the administrative wheel, and not mean that a yes cannot become no, as in your mirror painting, then I'll say I'm interested.

You are an angel, Paul.

And a dove.

That's all

today

Love

Jay ♡

(the baby who never say yes or only maybe.)

77. Dunedin July 7

Bee dear I'm thanking you too.
Was receiving yesterday
letter one, painting one, records two.
Your letter said you knew
that they were due.

Well they're here this week.
The saucy painting's lovely work.
I'm overwhelmed by the music.
Your letter like your sweater's warm and thick.

You'll get my letter say
July the something. Reply some day
or better with or without sweater bee my way
yours, Jay.

I am running out of Emily-battery for that poem.
I find I'm suddenly addicted to writing in rhyme.
How glad I am that at last you have the sun shining
in Santa Barbara where
'How doth the little busy bee
improve the shining hour'.

Excuse this crazy corn, if you will, Bill.
Bear with me as well as bee . . .
      at last, I'm free
from the circuit of rhyme!
Let all drivel shrivel.

Forgive the above. I like the Lotos Eater painting very much and you are so kind to give it to me—'on the hills like Gods together careless of mankind'—I always love the colours you make. The painting is saucy but the shapes give away the sadness—but I'm foolish about everything, I could go on and on saying things—on paper only; speech is different, it is awkward for me, it is like groceries. And I have so much to say about the music that perhaps I had better say nothing about it. I'm going to listen over and over again. The jacket describes the B Sonata as 'tearless'. For once, I agree with what is on the jacket. It's a lonely tearless grief, 'telling it like it is' without once turning away to how it might have been or using the notes for comfort—or that's how I feel, in listening to it. I like the places where the music takes me—there are no images there and no words. I'm afraid—or glad—that I gave up all yesterday to this music. I played the Requiem also. I must have heard these before but not listened as I find it hard to listen at concerts. I really listened—in my study where I have my record player and which is naturally a room where listening is the chief activity whether it is to the silence or the sound. I have heard some music, listened to less, and so have not a wide range of experience in it. I have never heard music which showed so clearly to me the nature of death as the Mozart Requiem does. It takes one beyond death. It shows (for me) death not as the surrender of life, as if one met death and said, I give up, here is my life, and was dead, having surrendered, that is, acknowledged the victory of death. It shows death as submission, where one does not empty oneself of life, one keeps everything, oneself and one's life; yet one submits, accepts death, and dies—if that can be called death. It overwhelms me that all this comes through so clearly in the music. No words, except the ritual words of the singing. No images. Another language full of telling, if language is telling.

★★★★★★★★★★★★

Stars to get me into more homely territory which is not a thing stars are renowned for doing.

★★★★★

More stars.

Lots of sun here, blue skies, twittering birds.

The young French lecturer came to see me on Saturday afternoon—very twittery, fluttery, and delicately balanced; also beautiful. She offered some impressions of New Zealand: Auckland reminded her unpleasantly of the seedier parts of Morocco where she was born and brought up. The coloured houses here make her think she is in a setting for a Disney Film. She loves Dunedin and the people. She had been warned they would be reserved and cold; she has found them warm-hearted, generous, open! We decided it was because she herself was in another country, away from the home territory, in another language.

On Sunday I accepted an invitation to lunch among people who resemble the sandal of the Great Gray Drayhorse of Hopkins—they're 'bright and battering'. It was a family lunch with a bright friend, her daughter and her new husband, her own new husband and new stepdaughter. The new husband and new stepdaughter are nice, quiet, sallow people whose faces don't move around from expression to expression. And I still saw, in my mind, in the background of the scene, the first husband old, red-faced, sick, in his food-stained big-checked dressing-gown and checked slippers padding about the house while his wife and his two desperate daughters grew brighter and brighter and brighter in their efforts to turn away from their sadness. I think it is too late now for the daughters to retreat from the brittle country.

Hope you're not bored, bored, bored—I didn't know I was going to go in this way! The perils of the pen . . .

How I loved also the head tiger of the zoo! (This remark comes out of the blue.)

In my letter to Paul I've discussed teaching. It would be a way of escape from here to places where there are souls of like-mind, which Rilke so approved of. My friends here in Dunedin (I've known them only since I came to live here a few years ago) survive, I suppose, because in some way they are within the structure of the place and its people, and have lived here many years. Well I won't go on about the scary side of life here—for me, anyway. But it was sweet of Paul to make enquiries about an escape route.

★★★★★★★

A hit, a hit, a palpable hit!
Quote from Broadway.
" " ★★★★★★★★★★★★★★★★

It will be nice to see Jo. I wonder if she has a suitcase full of anagrams. I'll never forget the Anagram Experience . . .

 I'm coming to the end of my leak-proof battery. (Oh—Genius, by the way, is a dirty six-letter word. You and I know that it bears no relation to anything.?? It is part of the new pornography. Also there's that twelve-letter word which corrupts all who see it in print—Intelligence.)

> *Some day some day*
> *I'll fly your way,*
> *you will look up in the sky and say,*
> *Look Paul (Ned will waken),*
> *Am I mistaken?*
> *Here comes Jay.*

'Ah then and there will be hurrying to and fro
and gathering tears and trembling of distress
and cheeks all pale . . .
    who could guess
since upon night so sweet such awful morn could rise?'
I have my wires crossed in the Battle of Waterloo.

Many thanks again for the treasured painting and music and letters all. Oops, I spilled the syrup again, you must excuse me!

78. Dunedin July

(written on the back of a nice crazy letter from the Editor of the student newspaper who has asked me for an interview)

Another morning. Just about now, if it's not too enticing a day, you will be setting off for the studio to commune with your greens, your blues, your reds, and so on.

I've been doing some communing with bright colours because my friend, the poet's wife, is coming for a few days' stay at the end of the week and I've been putting everything gold and red and pink and so on into the spare room, as she is cheered by bright colours. This will be my first real guest and I expect to learn a lot about eccentricities I didn't know I had. She's coming chiefly to rest and sleep and sleep after hectic family life. Her daughter has just had a baby boy which my friend's husband (also my friend) is taking to look after.

Jacquie is Maori, and it is from her that I've learned much about white and brown in New Zealand, about secret arrogances and prejudices. Race relations are fairly good here, compared with the rest of the world, yet this seems to be as long as the Maori is looked on as 'dead'. Dead and in his place. A visit to the Dominion Museum in Wellington with the family gave me the horrors because I could feel *their* horror—the place is full of Maori Art and history and the past tense, with children inquiring of their parents, 'Is that what they *did*? *Were* they like that? What *did* they,' and so on. Jacquie became more and more depressed. She's a sensitive person, extra-sensitive, but that kind of person is desperately needed here to transmit feelings.

Any reference to groups of people as 'they', also gives me the shudders. I had a phone call from someone who had been newly appointed to one of the local psychiatric hospitals, in charge of leisure activities, and she asked me what I thought 'they' would like.

*********** Stars to write off the world which is what stars do.
****
Many stars for comfort.
****
An oversight. I forgot to feed the wax-eyes—but oh they make their presence felt—there they are outside clamouring away. It's a misty rainy morning, the hills are invisible—it looks like a grey S.B day.

***

I will go to post this now.

Have you finished your peanut butter sandwich?

I hope you enjoyed it.

You are all so far away.

I send bulk love mixed with special harmless and special deadly ingredients; by Boeing and tramp steamer and feelie-touchie-wave. Got it? Good. An après peanut-butter desert (sp.?)

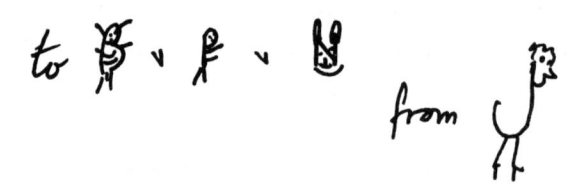

to 🐝 v 🐝 v 🐰 from 🦙

79. Dunedin July 10

Dear 🐛 and 💗 and 🐱

and 🐭 and 🌷 and any and all other presences at Live Oak Inn,

Sunset outside, noisy home-going traffic uphill changing gears, darkness falling soon after a dead calm day closed in by a lid of dark heavy cloud that promised, threatened and finally had the grace to blush when it had such a fine view of the sun going to bed. Oh how many times I pass the telephone and think, I just happened to be passing the telephone but conversations by phone are so unpredictably unrewarding and bungling (my conversations) therefore I turn sharply from the phone and 'happen' to pass my typewriter as I did just now and sit down and write to you from Wax-Eye City.

Yesterday I took my courage in my hands (surprising how *familiar* it looked) and nobody seemed to notice I had it in my hands, or perhaps they were being polite—anyway I seized the opportunity I've longed for and wandered down to the University Music Department to go to a free concert at lunch hour and make the acquaintance of the new *Steinway*. The new Hall is just as I imagined it was in the verse I wrote about not being there, with high windows and blue curtains and the sunlight falling in the windows but Steinway looks decidedly undernourished with spindly legs (it hasn't that fine turn of leg that your S has, B) so it's probably a weak branch of the family. It spoke quite nicely when touched but then what or who doesn't? I enjoyed the music but because I had taken my hands off my courage (it would have looked indecent had I kept them there) I didn't go right up to the Steinway to give it any messages. I sat just inside the door and hurried away afterwards, not speaking to, indeed not knowing a soul—yes there was one soul whom I see around the town and who goes to concerts and who says, Hello Janet when I see her. I say hello and we do not stop to speak, just look with the sort of look the cats give me, a look full of experienced language—for she was many many years in hospital and in the days when I knew her no-one would ever have believed that she knew or remembered anyone's name; but she knows me. As with the cats, there's no reason to say anything. It is sad though and unnecessarily reminding of things I ordinarily do not think of.

I am looking forward to going away from here.

I must change my life.

That 'Torso of an Archaic Apollo' is haunting isn't it?

So. I love your painting, B I happened to glance at it, I mean it happened to glance at me—and it's full of language, colour-language and shape-language.

★★★★★★★★ stars for extrication.

I haven't laughed for a million years—except when I have your letters. Fun fun fun.

★★★★

More stars. This is such a small note.

★★★★★

Any word of P's job?

★★★★

You are dear angels.

80. Dunedin July 12

b.
America's

Hi,   most,   News from the Antipodes this quiet domestic-fire-filled Sunday morning of pale blue sky, pale cloud streaked with a pink shell-colour and a tidal estuary colour—sandy yellow, muddy grey and smooth—well, that's the clouds which I see most because my house is really level with them. I'm looking out on the hills too. Earlier their rims were sharp, now they are blurred, misty—I guess it's pollution from the domestic fires. I'm thinking of you a lot, you're running like a thread through my mind, which is comforting and I almost phoned you yesterday but I knew it would be silly and I'd have nothing to say except hello and you may not even have been home. It's nice you're having sun again—well I hope you are—and that drive up the coast to the little place among the pines sounded lovely, and it sounded like a day that can be returned to, and your description of it before you went, B, and P's description after you had been, reminded me of a day I had by myself on Ibiza when I hired a bicycle and went to the other side of the island to a little beach among the pines . . . well, pine trees send me, their sound up there near the sky generously takes what happens to be in one's mind and returns it with all the notes arranged and the precise mournful effect.

The National Orchestra, or rather, the N.Z.B.C. (Broadcasting company's) orchestra has been in town this week, and this has been its last visit for the year. Dunedin still has a smaller Civic Orchestra, though, as do each of the main centres. Charles B has been performing what seems to me his self-adopted duties of escorting the *Fellows* in town. On Tuesday evening he took the Burns Fellow and me to a free concert of modern music given by the orchestra. And last evening he took the Frances Hodgkins Fellow and me to the final concert. The Burns Fellow is a pretty good writer but he's been going blind over the years and now is almost totally blind or at least in a dim dim world where light doesn't enter. The Frances Hodgkins Fellow in Art is also a composer, a rotund jolly type of man, busily composing and painting—I heard his Short Piano Sonata played on the Steinway the other day when I went to the lunch-hour concert. He has just finished writing a quartet and is about to do a song cycle of poems by Walter Raleigh and Emily Dickinson . . . I haven't met the Mozart Fellow (Gus) . . . Rumour has it, and rumour is probably correct that it is Charles B or his family trusts that have given Dunedin these *Fellows* (his aunt recently left her thirty-four roomed mansion crammed with art treasures to the city and it is now a tourist show-place).

The Concert's chief item was Beethoven's Ninth Symphony which was very excitingly and enthusiastically (over-enthusiastically?) played, and conducted by an American Alfred Wallenstein who was very demanding and exact. Or should I have said *the* American? The sweetness was not sweet enough and heavenly enough and so on but the orchestra put its whole heart into it and it was a treat to have it in Dunedin. Charles pointed out the 'Nabobs' of Dunedin, all in evening dress in the front row—the Mayor and his wife, the Head Brewer (The Beer Company and his wife), the Chief Breeder (Race-Horses) and his wife. These are the people upon whom the foundations of the city rest . . .

It made me very happy to see the city (and hear it) full of music. I was glad, too, to meet the people who are working at their painting and their music and petry (misprint for poetry, but I'll let it stand), and to clarify and deepen my understanding or realisation that I am a stranger here, that I should never have returned to New Zealand, that I must be exiled from it as surely as people from some of the communist countries are exiled. I miss the Live Oaks greatly—their brand of gentleness, and so on.

Forgive me.

Quiet Trading

In spite of the restrictions upon the sale of Peedauntals there continues to be quiet trading, the N.Z. director said today at her peedauntal-flooded home in Evans Street.

Seventy

Seventy, she said, had been sold during the weekend.

CHANGED MIND

The exact total, however, would be sixty-five as one client who had bought five changed his mind.

all five of them

When asked why the five had been returned the director, at first reluctant to answer, later said that all five had been faulty.

Maids

The client had bought these intended chiefly for maids who spend many hours ironing so that the peedauntals themselves had not exactly been faulty. When questioned further the director refused to comment.

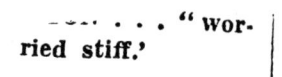

". . . "worried stiff.'

It is known that the co-directors resting quietly at their home in Hermosillo Drive are 'worried stiff'.

Enlarged

All things connected with peedauntals, the N.Z. Director said, had been unnecessarily enlarged.

Shape Of Things To Come

In spite of setbacks the Company (now emerged from bankruptcy owing to the generosity of Ned Cat the two-toned tycoon) has the future well in hand and is confident of the pleasing shape of things to come.

NEWS FLASH.

Embargo on potato movements

The movements of potatoes around the country have been prohibited since it was discovered that the common potato is some distant relative of the Carnivorous Plant. Hotels have been asked to refuse accommodation to all potatoes of whatever skin or shape.

    Ha. Ha.

This is a silly letter but it's saying hello to you all which I like to do.

The colours on your new painting are quite different today, B. There are rivers of light in the background. I think I've said this before (I'm old and fuddled . . .) but your paintings are so much tomorrow and yesterday as well as now—this sounds pretentious from me—but one does have such a strong sense of complete time. Any people caught in a pose inevitably make one (me) think of the Grecian Urn, 'bold lover never never can'st thou kiss and she be fair'
or something like that,
but here there's no arrested quality—though it's still it's moving—I'm probably all out of focus and I don't know about painting, I only know (as they say) what I feel. This man and this woman are already dead and yet they're going to be born. It's a happy picture though. The woman's Y looks like a palm tree and the man's P looks like Stonehenge!

Near the end of the page.
It's grim here—I'm full of complaints—people write to me—people I don't know—asking advice, giving details of their mental and emotional unhappiness. I shouldn't have had the radio interview because this seems to have prompted quite a few letters from people who are certain I will 'understand'.

"I groped for the receiver and heard a well-spoken voice saying: 'This is Ned Cat the two-toned tycoon speaking, just a moment and I'll call Bill and Paul from the geranium and finch patio. Well, they're busy with peanut butter just now.

81. Dunedin July 13

Dear 'Strange and freeing blades,'

'What an extraordinary mode of address', he said, between peanut-butters—or maybe you have some new patio food? I ask this because I know that the only certainty in this life is *Change*.

Well, dear Strange and freeing blades human (2) feline (1) vegetable (?), it is early Monday morning and I'm writing this to catch the morning mail collection. It is still dark outside and I see from my study window the hills are black against the sky with a row of house-lights and street-lights almost near the top of the hill ('sought-after view, desirable property, blushing toilets') and the sky a Bill-painting sky (yesterday afternoon the sky was Paul-painting) with that wonderful blue-violet-grey, ever-changing, with one colour devouring another.

And that is the morning. My guest, Jacquie, is asleep in her guest room on her guest bed with her guest dreams which could be nightmares. (When I phoned her the other evening to find the plane times her son (the talented boy who drew the flower picture I had—maybe you remember it) answered the phone and told me an amazing lot in three minutes—I suppose here I should say—My God! Or the guest dreams could be—hopefully—sweet, for J's lover visited her here last evening and I left them the house to themselves after giving them a dessert and a coffee. I went off to my Janet-home-alone bed and listened to the radio playing Stravinsky's Mass and Beethoven's Seventh Symphony.

And that is the news from Wax-Eye City. My friend has come here to sleep and rest and forget for a week before she returns to face things—I hate that expression facing things. Today a new wine shop is opening in town and there's free tasting all day and we are going to drop in and out and by the evening we should have forgotten all. In the midst I shall visit my aunt who is now dying—two weeks ago I noticed the water was there and it only remains for the rather narrow-minded pathetic old swan to let herself go. I noticed that her eyes, overnight, suddenly moved in her head, seemed to have been set back as if on dark-lined shelves, as if someone had said of her eyes, 'You won't be needing these much longer, let us put them on this dark-lined shelf', for indeed her eyes looked then as if they had been put away, stored, as things are which are no longer of any use.

How one gazes and gazes at the faces and their 'pathetic histories'.
******
Did Jo arrive? How is her anagrammatic skill? Up to scratch?
****
Cockles warmed at your letter, B I think I am most of the time—perhaps always—at Live Oak Inn. I seem to have left myself there—I'm sure if you search the garden you'll find those brown bread shoes. I feel like a lizard that has lost its tail or the tail that has lost its lizard. I'm looking forward to having ten mountain lions (did I say ten or have I upped the number since I last dreamed?)

I like what you say about the silence escaping as if from a puncture. I hope you're now suitably inflated? The puncture mended with that stuff which my father used to call—'the solution'—only now I remember it and think how strange it was: he would be wanting to mend a puncture in car or bike and he would cry out, 'Where's the *solution*? Has anyone seen the *solution*?'
****
Stars for you.
*****

> *In Wax-Eye City today the wax-eyes ride their twigs home to honey,*
> *make their honey cry*
> *a green and rust posse wearing their white-eye badge*
> *trailing down all householders branded for generosity.*
> *They twitter out the wintry siege.*
>   *Meanwhile*
> *back in the ranch-house bush*
> *the flowers brew their spring liquor, the recipe*
>   *handed*
>   *down*
>   *and down.*
> *When it is matured*
> *the wax-eyes will resign their office, turn in their city habits*
> *and leave town.*

****
A little fancy.
****   Stars for sherrifs or is it sheriffs.
****

I wish I were there in Santa Barbara
among the live oaks growing.
    My battery has run out so I'll say goodmorning, a sour honey-full good morning and all kinds of possible, impossible, pure, impure, straight, narrow, crooked, curved love to
          B   P   N

      from Jay
who thinking of you loses her middle & becomes J_oy.
    (Don't mind my battery)

82. Dunedin July

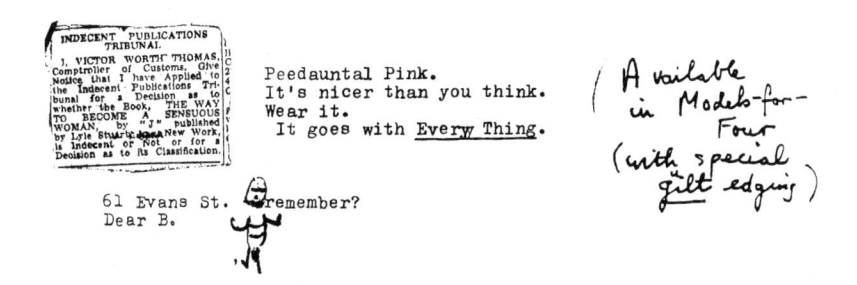

> INDECENT PUBLICATIONS TRIBUNAL
> J, VICTOR WORTH THOMAS, Comptroller of Customs, Give Notice that I have Applied to the Indecent Publications Tribunal for a Decision as to whether the Book, THE WAY TO BECOME A SENSUOUS WOMAN, by "J" published by Lyle Stuart, New York, is Indecent or Not or for a Decision as to its Classification.

Peedauntal Pink.
It's nicer than you think.
Wear it.
It goes with Every Thing.

Available in Models-for-Four (with special gilt edging)

61 Evans St. remember?
Dear B.

Dear B,

Hello. So nice to have your letter this morning—and oh I hope your silence has been restored and your surcingles readjusted, darned, in the places where they were punctured, with matching fuzz and your cell relined with honey-quiet. ('Give me my scallop-shell of quiet.'); and all in order and the studio work proceeding, and miseries exchanged, for variety. Was it Penelope (whom I used to call Penny Lope) who used to unravel her day's weaving each night? People do unravel one's woven self and there must be a place and time for it to be rewoven. I find that a little work (a thimbleful) is magic, like a whole body of weavers arriving. And *other things help*. Well. Thus speaketh I. So I hope even the tiniest torn stitch, even the ravaged invisible mending, has been made like new on each surcingle. And then, of course, the next round of people, seeing your polish and sparkle, will say, B where did you get those brandnew surcingles? What do you want for them?

B 'They're not for sale.'

People. 'Here, I'll give you this for them.'

B (anguished, impulsive) 'Take them.'

Later: B surcingle-less, Paul pallless, Ned nedless, will huddle shivering around the fake fire.

B, P, N: Never again.

****** Stars

This morning I got up early and put on the Hérodiade and Wolf side of your tape, through the record player. It was lovely, just the right light outside for it—the Hérodiade matched the light. There was a storm yesterday, the first winter storm, with the wind screaming around the house and the rain lashing (lash lash) against the south windows, and this morning the sky was clear. Yesterday I nearly phoned you for comfort—I passed by the telephone and I thought, What will I say? I'll say I just happened to be passing by the telephone. Later in the day while the storm still raged I went to visit my dying aunt, and noted how much nearer she was to the water's edge. Most of her feathers have been plucked out, though. But this morning's light was so lovely, as if a sickness had passed over the world and now it was cured. And now the hills are warm green and blue (if that is possible?) with a haze of gold, and the hills are hollowed purple. The sun is out, the light is lemon-coloured.

My guest has gone for the day to visit her husband's parents who live by a wonderful beach about ten miles away. Gran is in her late eighties and Grandad is ninety-one. He is a wonderful old man who on his ninetieth birthday had reprinted a book which he wrote about the first World War where he was conscripted as a young man and objecting on conscientious grounds, was sent to the front in Europe, and put with others in the fighting lines, and, still refusing to fight, was nailed to a cross on the battlefield. It almost overwhelms one to think of the continuity of mind in a family. Grandad's book was called *We Shall Not Cease*. His son, brought up under the shadow of this cross, has now gone, as I told you, to live in a religious community in a place in New Zealand called Jerusalem. And it is *his* son and daughter who are suffering the teenage nightmare.

★★★★

Sad that you didn't see Jo but good that she sounded fine.

Nice of Eva Marie to try to persuade producers to read F. in the Water (otherwise known as Faces in the W.) Unfortunately the contract I made with that book gave my N.Z. publisher world rights—though I think he's lost them now because he hasn't reprinted. It did mean, though, that F. in the W. which was translated in several languages (where it never sold, though) didn't make for me the money it would have made if my publisher had not more or less 'owned' it. It was robbery, bare-bottomed robbery, much more subtle than bare-faced. I think I told you that there's a movement (move move) to get me a Distinguished (i.e. Displaced) Person's Pension but these things are not given out unless one is, say, fifty or sixty or a hundred, and I have some years to wait before I'm fifty, though it's surprising (as they say) how the time does pass and before you know it there you are, isn't it extraordinary, and how the seasons are changing, and I do think they ought to hang or birch those types that abound, bring back the gallows is what I say . . . they say, they say . . . Still, even Proust, no traveller on the cliché line, admitted that time passed.

Dominique (the French girl—a chicken—poule? or is it that old hen?) read the 'slow, the happy' and her translation agreed exactly with yours . . . I did not quite get from her 'the tender alternative'—but it is what we (you mostly, you are ¾ plus ½ plus ¾ plus ⅔ me)—said it was—she dreams she will be met by handsome gentlemen of former times—though she knows she won't—still, for a moment she considers the *tender* alternative. I shall be seeing Dominique again and I will record her reading?

★★★★★★★★★★★

I like the idea of Grimms Tales being made into a stage play. Why has it been so long? I have a gory two little books of Fairy Stories (so-called) which we used to study in French; chockfull of people eating people and people unravelling people and the unravelled people spending a life-time trying to reknit or people emptying people and the emptied people trying with a thimble to fill themselves up again.

★★★★★

I dream of being in that little hill-house or valley-house
or motorway-house (I and my mountain lions nine,
            I human, they leonine.)
with you live oaks (seen growing), each with a little cell where the emptied, unravelled, honeyless people refill, reknit, make honey, for in spite of the fact that kin-people share honey and switch identities and sweaters (ravelled and unravelled) when you die you do not switch deaths.

    She said.   She said.

I have to go out shopping now & I will post this.

Love to B P N
from the sensuous
woman who signs
herself

    J

---

83. Dunedin July 20 (handwritten)

Dear   Morning. Woke. Peed. Brought in milk & newspaper. Put on coffee. Stirred up fire, put manuka logs on fire, buttered a slice of home-made bread, sat by fire with preliminary breakfast & newspaper, read, drank, ate, slowly woke, thought of you (not in that order). Went to study, switched on heater, sat in armchair, put pen to paper . . .

My guest who leaves on Friday is still asleep. She has been out for almost every meal, with friends who, when I know them too, have asked me & I've declined. Tonight she (it was meant to be we, but I think I've had my ration of people) will go to dinner with the people whose cat *heard the word vet*. (Even now Ngeru is probably the centre of attention in some alley as he describes 'the night I heard the word vet'.) This afternoon Charles Brasch is coming up for a cup of tea between his Russian lectures. He has had the 'flu but he is so eager to see Jacquie whom he has known, with her husband, for many many years.

The wax-eyes, seeing me in my study, have begun clamouring for breakfast. I have just given them yesterday's left-over *Vimax* (a sort of porridge with wheat germ, vitamins etc. etc. oatmeal etc.) sprinkled with raw sugar which they love.

So you have tits in your tree! How extraordinary! There was a time when, here, we used to be able to listen to the sound of cocks in the early morning! And people always kept a few cocks in their garden, but that practice is dying out or has been banned in the cities. You are still allowed to have a noisy cock in the country.

I had a letter from Charles Neider to say his project in Ross Island has been approved & he's coming to New Zealand sometime in November.

The wax-eyes twitter, twitter outside. They have almost finished their breakfast.

Having a guest has been a valuable 'experience' for me. The only eccentricity I have so far discovered in myself (apart from the ones I know about) is a tendency to 'make sure' all the electric plugs have been unplugged and switched off at night. I fear my guest has said she likes being here so much she would like to stay for ever (you have that continuing problem with me!) She said she would like to come to live here with me.

How valuable my solitude & silence seem! My guest is very pleasant & more or less goes her own way but I am looking forward to her going & she is wise enough to know it & understand it. I have moved my record-player into the sitting-room so she can listen to it & my study is like death without it & I did not realise the music had so been absorbed into the very walls of the study. The room is alive with it, as a past experience, but while the phonograph is in the sittingroom it is death in here, the whole room so yearns for it. How pathetically fallacious can one be!

You & Paul & Ned were so wonderful to have had me stay for so long (to me, so short!) in a place where you and Paul & Ned could not entirely be sealed off! I think each needs to be 'sealed off' & then all merge in one common room for waking or one common bed for sleeping; but the 'sealing' off, the solitude, retreat, the denial of the senses of everything except one's self is necessary. I mean one's self & what is beyond. It is a poor human failing to have to rely on physical environment—doors, private facilities—to 'seal oneself off'. One should be able to do it at any time regardless of place. Does meditation, practised, do this?

★   ★   ★   ★   ★

It is night now, only ten o'clock & I am lying in bed far from, denied, the sweet touch of a tendril; I'm listening to the Beethoven Concert from Bonn, writing this & thinking of my three live oaks in their carnivorous-planted Steinwayed home, their peanut-buttered and carnationed (I mean geraniumed) patio beneath the finched eaves and the titted tree . . . I'm homesick.

My guest is out for dinner. I couldn't face it, after a morning of baking an apricot pie and my special brand of ginger cookies, not to mention my *meat balls*. This afternoon Charles B came up, bringing his usual bunch of anemones, blue and purple and red. He sat by the fire with Jacquie and talked about news from the North. As he was going out the gate I reminded him of the Rilke poem about the anemone—'Flower-muscle . . .' *Blumen* I said & to my surprise he quoted it in German. Then he raised his hat to us in a gentlemanly way and went up the road to catch the bus home.

★   ★   ★   ★

It is now 12 midnight. Beyond all sight of a tendril I shall soon turn off my light and sleep & dream of the Wild West.

★   ★   ★   ★

Art thou real, art thou Ernest?
No, I'm Bill and this is Paul
and Ned to whom thou, Jay, returnest
when thy housèd masters call.
Thou shalt come with mountain lions
(few require such pageantry)
thou'st a laundry maid who irons
hard by finchèd eave and titted trees.

Now it is morning again. Woke . . . etc. (But I can't write a nice journal *intime* about morning functions because mine are so paltry. I like reading yours!) The wax-eyes are not yet awake; my guest sleeps (& is rather depressed at the thought of facing sick, really sick, son and post-natal daughter & 2-yr old & job & so on).

Plod on with thy work! (Work for the *Knight is coming*!) I shall do likewise when my guest goes. Actually there's enough room here for her or a guest to live independently as I use only two rooms on one side of the passage. (That is put in to show you that if any of you (Ned, say, with his valise and his paw-passport all in black and white) wants to visit me before I can get to your part of the world, you can be sealed off at will!) Supposing you came soon to withdraw from noise-pollution (i.e. to exchange pollutions!) Fortunately I don't have to wear ear-plugs here—that may be necessary if I'm here in summer when all windows are opened & radio & tvs blare forth.

When my guest goes I'll plod on with my book ('scarcely begun, a few words picked, the rest dead') & get it done before the end of the year. It was she who suggested her stay here & it's been hanging over me, but now it's nearly over & it gave me a chance to get out of my usually selfish ways & do something for someone else, for a change.

How gladly I will sink again into my selfish ways!!!

I've sent you, for anyone who wants to wear it, a cap knitted from left-over wool (from the multi-coloured scarf) & a copy of my German edition of The Lagoon & the Landfall with the remainder of Frank's interview.

★ ★ ★ ★

Wax-eyes call.

★ ★ ★ ★

Vita? Vita Nuova?

I can't really *imagine* myself teaching, probably because my images are stereotyped & include a huge room with seas, ships, anchors, of faces & I stammering, unable to complete a sentence.

But individual students . . ..

Perhaps I could advertise . . .

Writer gives lessons—Do *You*, Have a Restless Urge? A restless urge for *Strophe* (always available) or perhaps *Sestina* (weekends only) *Anaphora*? *Arsis* (quite complicated). Is your rhythm sufficiently *sprung*?

Seriously, I don't think I have the confidence (in my present setting) to suppose I could teach anyone anything. Perhaps a course on *The Sentence* (I could do with one myself).

★　　★　　★　　★　Stars like kisses or snow-stakes to prevent drifts.

★　　★　　★　　★

And now goodbye, goodbye, ('we all nodded at him') and tendril-love to

    B,　aimed & arrowed love
    to P,　no-nonsense
    love in black-and-white to N
    As for Carnie & Black Steinway—well, such goings-on!

J

84. Dunedin July 27

Dear live oaks, my friends, Hello,

Another crazy letter from me away in the Antipodes. I've just had a bath. 'Steaming, warm' I put finger to key as I sit in my study after a tolerable day's work. Yesterday the temperature was well into the sixties, the day was so heavenly that I could not face it, away down here, and hid from it by staying inside but oh it was a warm sweet day, full of sweet air, and the blossoms are out now. Today the mild northwest wind changed to southwest, smelling of snow, and I shivered, and wore my MacDowell clothes, and round about noon I traipsed into town, paid a quick visit to my dying aunt (a few minutes). In spite of my know-it-all attitude to death, I've never had direct access before to a person so clearly dying, and I'm surprised to find how natural it all is, and how natural and simple one feels, watching it. I'm not a demonstrative person, particularly with people I've never really known, yet I'm surprised to find that now I can't exchange light chatter with my aunt, touch takes over where the words are lost and I find myself sitting there stroking the old dear's white hair and taking her hand, for about five minutes. All she says is, 'It's nice to see you,' when I arrive, and 'Come and see me again' when I leave.

My guest has gone. You use the word 'eroded', B, when you were writing about having too many people around? Well, I felt distinctly nibbled-at, and very defenceless. My guest was quiet, softly-spoken, but, alas, I felt quieter and totally without any willpower. In short, I became what everyone used to say my mother was—a doormat . . . Enough of that.

. . . When are you coming to visit me? . . . Just after my guest went I had a visit from the kitty—the first I'd seen of him/her (I didn't look) for fifteen days, He/she was meowing at the door, and came in, visiting, played and purred and snuggled and then went to wherever it lives.

....

I hope that you are both having a fruitfuk period of work—excuse the typing error but it *is* an error. Like so many Mortal Enemies, mine turns out to be what I did not expect and I have to start it all over again—

I'd done more than I thought. According to plan it should have been finished next month; and I might even make it still, now I've cleared a bit of rubble away. I suppose it's like painting out? In fact—this gives me an idea!

★ ★ ★ ★ ★ ★ ★ ★ ★

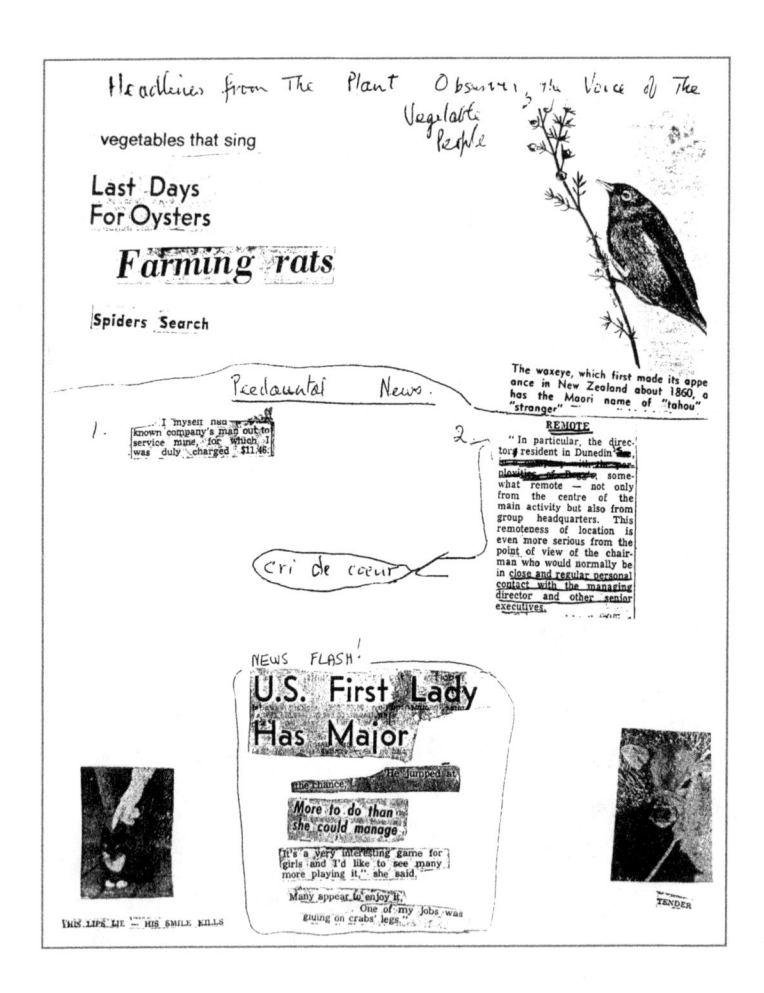

> Headlines from The Plant Observer, the Voice of The Vegetable People
>
> vegetables that sing
>
> Last Days For Oysters
>
> Farming rats
>
> Spiders Search
>
> Peedauntal News.
>
> 1. I myself had... known company's man out to service mine, for which I was duly charged $11.48.
>
> 2. REMOTE "In particular, the director resident in Dunedin... somewhat remote — not only from the centre of the main activity but also from group headquarters. This remoteness of location is even more serious from the point of view of the chairman who would normally be in close and regular personal contact with the managing director and other senior executives."
>
> Cri de cœur
>
> The waxeye, which first made its appearance in New Zealand about 1860, has the Maori name of "tahou" "stranger".
>
> NEWS FLASH!
> U.S. First Lady Has Major
> ...the chance... Had dropped...
> More to do than she could manage
> It's a very interesting game for girls and I'd like to see many more playing it," she said.
> Many appear to enjoy it.
> One of my jobs was gluing on crabs' legs.
>
> HIS LIPS LIE — HIS SMILE KILLS   TENDER

My homesickness does not lessen. I thought of phoning—
several times—instead, I imagined I phoned, and this is what happened.

J: Hello, Hello. I just happened to be passing by the telephone and I thought I'd call you.

Voice: Hi!

J: It's wonderful to hear your voice. Is it Bill or Paul?

Voice: It's Ned speaking. Here's Paul.

Paul: Hi.

J: It's wonderful to hear your voice.

          (Sounds in background: What about that liver, Paul?)

Paul: Here's Bill.

Bill: Hi.

J: I just happened to be passing the telephone and I thought I'd call you.

Bill: Hi.

J: It's wonderful to hear your voice.

> (Sounds in background: I want a new sweater put out on the washer, Bill. The old one has lost all its snuggle.)

Bill: Be right there. Here's Paul.

Paul: Hi.

J: It's wonderful to hear your voice.

> (Sounds in background: I said, the liver! And get off that phone, I've an evening free and I want to call Dr Gilbride.)

Paul: Here's Bill.

J: I just happened to be passing by the telephone and I thought I'd call you. It's wonderful to hear your voice.

Bill: Watch out, you'll be cut off!

J: Oh is my three minutes up?

Bill: No, I was talking to Carnie, he's dipped his tendril in the juice extractor.

> (Sounds in background: Bill will you see to Steinway, it's started a sonata again.)

B: Be right there. Here's Paul.

Paul: Hi.

J: It's wonderful to hear your voice. You all seem pretty busy.

Paul: Busy! I've just cooked a month's supply of liver. We do things in bulk around here now.
Ned's idea.

> (Voice in background: I said get off that phone, I want to call Dr Gilbride. And this doesn't look like a month's supply of liver to me! And where's my petunia?)

Paul: Be right there.

Operator: Your three minutes is up.

Click, click, click.

Everything goes dead, including J.

★★★★★★★★★★★★★★★★★

★★★★★★★   More stars.

Furnished Antique Love to

[handwritten sketch: "Furnished Antique Love to" with drawings of THE HOUSE, THE HILL, mountain lion country, a figure, a cowboy head, and a horse labeled "from J.d"]

---

85. Dunedin July Wednesday (your Tuesday)

Dear B,

Sad and *lovely* to speak to you on the 'phone—I couldn't resist it—it felt like being a visitor to a prison, speaking through the bars. It was nice, though. I had a tax refund of fifteen dollars and I wondered what it would be like to say hello from Dunedin. 'It was wonderful to hear your voice.' Quote from script of phone-call in previous letter—everything I do seems to have to be fiction before it is fact and *vice versa*.

It was a golden kind of day here—raining, but the blossoms are out and the hills have a golden glow and spring is irrevocably here, and my third primrose is out. The wax-eyes remain. Soon, I believe they disband as a flock and go to live in pairs, in the bush. The flock here has been consistently thirty-five to forty, with some acting as lookouts, some as prime eaters, others as the poor old lookers-on at the feast. As most of the bush here is evergreen, winter has a different appearance from that in a land of deciduous trees (though we have many deciduous trees, introduced from Britain and the East) with the landscape always green and the trees in the bush (the hill opposite me has much native bush) showing a smoky grey-green under the grey sky.

Here ends the lesson on Nature Study! My ten mountain lions wait in the cellar and I will do as you say and keep them happy with steak—lion steak!

Thursday. Today you are in L.A. with Felix. Is Ann there too? How is the painting? Are you painting out or in at the moment?

I'm using you today. I'm trying to finish this letter so I may say, later, when I have a visitor and want the visitor to go, 'I must go to mail a letter'. I'm afraid I'm being bothered by students quite a lot—using me as a kind of psychotherapist, with not only letters but also phone calls. This morning someone who described herself as 'very depressed' phoned to ask if she could come and see me. I don't know her—she's a student at the University—but I've asked her up for a cup of tea and a chat. I may feel bothered but I do feel sympathetic towards such people because I think being young is a nightmare. I'd almost think that being young in New Zealand (described so often as 'a great place to bring up children') is worse than in some other countries—I don't know—forget it.

Back to the Live Oaks. I might sail to L.A. in a ship—it takes nine days—a seasick heaven compared to my other two experiences of thirty-two days each.

If the cap fits wear it. Did it? Will you? I'd like to make one for Paul but I'm too shy to ask (a refusal will not cause offence). If he'd like one (with a scarf or without) could he paint his colour on a little square in your next letter?

I have a feeling that men should beware of women who knit for them. I promise I'll never knit anything again unless asked.

Inspired by Emily D, through you, B, I've at last attacked my Mortal Enemy. My mistake was that I was doing it head-on, forgetting that 'success in circuit lies' so now I'm 'telling it slant,' and it's a great relief.

****

More stars. It's evening now & (obviously) I still haven't posted this letter. I'm worn out after my visitor. She was beautiful with long glossy black hair (no I'm not describing my newly acquired mountain lion or kitty), beautifully dressed in a maxi-skirt patterned outasightly. Her manner tended towards the studied-dramatic and many of her remarks began with 'Sensitive people like you & me . . .' She is a widow (once), a divorcee (once), has 3 children & expects a fourth in six months & how have I managed to survive? I could have asked her a similar question.

No, I'm not being cynical for she *was* a sensitive soul & I felt very happy when she described some of her experiences during meditations—I felt happy because I thought of Live Oak Inn. Do you still meditate? I miss the meditation—I more often forget it here & I can't quite discover what it did (or maybe I haven't tried to but it did something important—though maybe I'm using the wrong verb in 'do'—it is more *undo, undid*.

Unfortunately I was not equipped to give my visitor the kind of advice she wanted, e.g. what to 'do' (kittens are much less demanding). She kindly brought me some newly-baked bread and a bunch of yellow flowers for my Antipodean room, and when she left I gave her a bottle of cider.

And that was that.

⋆   ⋆   ⋆   ⋆

Every day I look at the lilac cuttings I planted because whether or not this is so, I feel that they will be more likely to grow if they know they haven't just been abandoned in the cold cold soil—which they have been! But they can't really be deceived and I try to communicate my desire for them to grow. 'September is the cruellest month.'

⋆   ⋆   ⋆   ⋆

Do you still have to wear ear-plugs, B? I hope not. I've moved into my guest room which has a fire-place & five windows, against no fireplace & three windows of the other bedroom, & hence it tends to be noisier—mostly gear-changing coming up the hill from the Gardens Corner & so now & again I wear wax plugs. We could make a fortune with ear-plugs, issuing them as a bonus with peedauntals, only I'm going out of the business, resigning, handing in my badge, my knife & fork, my pepper and salt etc.

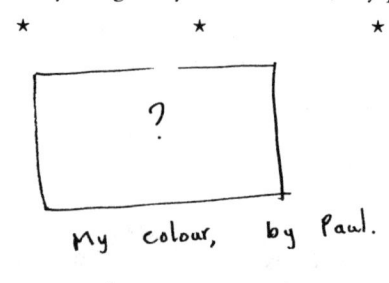

⋆   ⋆   ⋆

[box containing "?"]

My colour, by Paul.

⋆   ⋆   ⋆   ⋆

As you see my battery is very low.

⋆   ⋆   ⋆

Friday: Morning again, 'a golden morning'. As I look out of the window I see the golden cat in the corner house opposite taking a morning walk around its 'territory'—sniffing the geraniums growing all along the front of the house. There's a pink blossom tree out & a crab-apple tree hung with rosy apples.

I dreamt last night I was living in a cotton wool factory, training to live as a mouse—in Italy! (don't tell Ned!).

  ★   ★   ★

When I have finished my book I'd love to come back across the Pacific. . ...??? . . ...??? . . ...??? . . ...???
rosy apples of love to

   B P. N.
 & all other inhabitants
   from [J]

AUGUST

86. Dunedin August 1

> 61 Evans Street,
> Opoho,
> Dunedin, Otago,
> New Zealand.
> August 1, 1970.

Dear B.

Your letters have the miraculous effect of unclouding me.

Before: After:

Dear B,

Your letters have the miraculous effect of unclouding me.

It was nice to get a letter today, for the weekend—and where do you get all those nice pictures of hesitant swans?

It's Saturday and people are hammering, hammering, which is what you do on Saturday if you live in Dunedin you climb on your roof with a hammer (not necessarily with nails) and hammer so that the sound echoes through the wooden bones of other people's houses. Soon, on Saturdays, if you live in Dunedin, you will mow your lawn with a power mower (moa) on Saturday afternoon and Sunday morning.

I like to think of you taking your after-supper walk again by the sea, along Butterfly Lane, getting the sea breezes and the Down Under stink—I have a Pacific here, too, and perhaps I should send my three live oaks a letter in a bottle? I'm glad you liked the cap: I thought it was very bold of me to make it but I did have the leftover wool, from the long fringed scarf, and I still have some only it won't make anything unless it's a tendril-cosy for Carnie.

Ursula Bethell and D'Arcy Cresswell are separate writers, both very interesting—and dead. I should think that Ursula Bethell had something of the spirit of a May Sarton. She emigrated to New Zealand (Christchurch) in the 'early days' and established a wonderful garden which she wrote about in perhaps the most original poetry we've had—she was a kind of Marianne Moore of the garden. She wrote long poems about flowers, using their longest names, rich rhythms and unusual words. D'Arcy Cresswell who died some years ago in London (where for many years he worked as a nightwatchman in the British Museum—his death was by suicide) wrote long archaic poems. He was a friend of Frank S's, a contemporary or a couple of years older.

I was much alarmed to read that someone is *preparing* me. Another reason to flee the country. I have never heard of the person in question and it's the first I heard of the project . . .

I'm glad you were interested in Frank's interview! He and I have a kind of arrangement—it wasn't really planned, but when he makes a statement in public he says something about me (not always) and I have a little fun by doing the same.

I confess I didn't read the review or discussion I sent you! I thought it might be useful *if* I do need any sort of reference—if I do happen to be in the unfortunate position of doing a few weeks' hard labour for hard cash—as it's written by a University Professor. I started to read it but became weary when she made the usual mistake of supposing that a story I had written was a true story of my childhood. And that I had watched my art mistress die, or some such, when of course I never did.

Enough of that, enough of J.F.

I'm expecting Ned any time with his black and white airline bag, his blue woolly sweater (with plenty of snuggle in it) and his medications. His room is ready.

Strange that just after you mention my friend's son who did the flower painting, you mention Rimbaud. When the boy's father was young Rimbaud was his God—I suppose he is every young tortured poet's God? Jim has some fine translations from R in some of his books. The uncanny thing about what has happened is that the father (this is just something I sense) has in some way willed his son and daughter to be and do what they are and have done. I don't suppose this is so unusual after all—it's just that what he has willed for them is something of the same suffering that he has undergone, through his own nature and that of his father and his own father's experiences. And this is not unusual either, is it? The only thing unusual is that they are a gifted, sensitive family going from nightmare to nightmare. And then maybe this is not unusual either—so I've demolished what I set out to say. I've phoned my friend since she returned home and things are not so bad. The boy is in the care of a doctor and hasn't been, as they say, 'busted' by the police, though a friend of his, who lives in Dunedin, has been, and is on probation. I met him one day along the street. He's about seventeen—no sixteen—a beautiful boy with long fair hair and fragile feminine face and slim body. It's really as if he were a young lamb being bred for the Dunedin wolves because one shudders to think of all the misunderstandings and persecutions he will suffer here.

But enough of that, also. Aunt Swan continues to dip only her big web in the water and then withdraw it but it should not be long now.

That sounded like a nice birthday party for Eugene Anderson! Here is a recipe for something that is sometimes known as N.Z.'s national sweet. You are not a New Zealander, it seems, until you have made a Pavlova cake, called a 'Pav'. Shudder and horror of horrors.
Here it is:

- 4 egg whites
- salt
- ¼ teaspoon cream of tartar
- cup of sugar
- 1 teaspoon vanilla essence
- 2 teaspoons vinegar
- 1 dessertspoon cornflower

Add salt and cream of tartar to the egg whites and BEAT UNTIL STIFF. (The Marquis De Sade's favourite recipe.)

Add sugar, a little at a time. Add vanilla and vinegar and fold in cornflower (beating all the time).

Then wet a large piece of greaseproof paper, place wet side down on oven tray. Pour mixture on paper. Put tray in oven at 350 degrees and turn off oven. Leave for 45 minutes to an hour. Remove. Invert on plate and spread with whipped cream and fruit if liked, especially passion fruit.

That is a party dessert.
★★★★★★★★★★★★
Stars.

It's wonderful that you have finished your lover paintings. Both you and Paul sound as if you are doing your 'best yet'.

You may do your portrait of Santa Barbara?

I like the idea of a self-portrait appearing through apertures in the clouds, as if one's other self, in the heavens, may see oneself clearly in parts but never whole—blah blah, I could go on fantasying about such things but it gets pretentious-sounding. It's a nice idea and it reminds me 'all dreams lead back to the nightmare garden'*—that is an Auden quote, I told my publishers so) of Rilke again with the roots of the tree in heaven. I wish I were a painter.

★★★★★

[Enclosed] a translation of Rimbaud 'Seven year Old Poet' by J.K. Baxter.
★★★★ Just references.
★★★★★★★★★★

Hemet, where Aunt Amy lives—is it any relation to the old word for ant—emmet? Anyway, it reminds me of that lovely poem by Blake about an ant that lost its way—

> 'Once a dream did weave a shade
> o'er my Angel-guarded bed,
> that an emmet lost its way
> where on grass methought I lay.
>
> Troubled, 'wildered, and forlorn,
> dark, benighted, travel-worn,
> over many a tangled spray,
> all heart-broke . . .'

★★★★★   ★★★★★★★★★★

Eva Marie Saint is playing in Dunedin!
   Trivia, continued.
By the way I have a prize scoop in my next tape—which is taking ages and ages—and this scoop is pretty well all I have so far—it is Virgil Thomson speaking . . . !

Sunday morning. I dreamt last night I was a cow grazing in the fields and in conversation with another cow we decided that it was good to have

---

* Apparently not a quote from Auden, the phrase 'all dreams lead back to the nightmare garden' is increasingly attributed to Frame herself

our noses to the earth and the grass all day, that people just didn't know what they missed! (Before I went to sleep I listened over the radio to a delightful dramatisation of the Saki story, 'Tobomory', about the cat which began to speak and embarrassed everyone with his remarks and quotes of other people's remarks. Do you know it?)

A wild screaming wind raged all night, rocking my house as if it were a ship, and this morning it is dead, the sky is sullen with two gaps, over the western hills, of egg-shell blue, the temperature almost sixty degrees, and the hills dark and close, rain-warning. The mornings are now light enough for me to make garden-inspections before the world is awake, and in the morning now when I go to fetch my milk and paper at about six-thirty to seven, the sky is no longer full of bright stars being 'steadfast'—the light has arrived.

I have a japonica bush which grows just outside the door of the cellar, in the earth-covered sort of patio where I hang my washing. This bush, with the bathroom floor above it, never gets wet and lives on the drips from my washing, yet it blooms, and now has a number of tight red buds, with one opening.

If only I could transport myself and the japonica to some place that is not here where I am not afraid, as I am here, and where my friends are! I am very homesick for my live oaks, and I know I go 'on and on' about this. Do you really mean that there will be a little place for me with you? I can try it, anyway, and leave it very open as all living is, like cheese that Dot buys, or used to buy.

My work is going well just now, I think, with continued inspiration from you and with the help of all that strength-giving home-made love that Paul sent in his letter. I have got to the stage where I just can't leave my work alone.

When I finish my book . . . ah. California etc. Or before . . .

Now, all kinds and varieties (same thing) of love, remote, near, oblique, direct, voiced, unvoiced, manufactured, home-made, re-leasing, binding, from heaven and hell and devils and angels to same. (Do you think Ned can take all this? After that alarming phone conversation (I think the fantasy one was perhaps the real one) where Ned seems to be in control, living in bulk, eating in bulk, I'm not sure what he can or can't take.)

Anyway, love to B   P.   N. of whatever variety each desires (may be refunded after seven days, or before).

87. Dunedin August 4

Dear B, P, N,
   Morning. Woke etc. Thought about the three live oaks I saw once growing in Santa Barbara,
   'And I broke off a twig with a certain number of leaves upon it,
   and twined around it a little moss,
   And brought it away, and have placed it in sight in my room;
   It is not needed to remind me of my own dear friends
   (For I believe lately I think of little else than of them . . .)'
So much for Antipodean greeting but while things are Whitmanesque (?)* I'll tell you that when I went to my gate to collect my morning milk and newspaper I looked at the lilac twig I planted near the front door (the gnarled old fuchsia hedge will have to move over or expand into ruder health), and it has a tiny green shoot. It was already in bud when I picked it to transplant but, so far, none of the buds have developed in any of the four twigs I planted in various parts of the garden. What confidence it shows now! Inheriting Whitman and Eliot how could it show anything else? They do not bloom, though, for about five years after they have been transplanted. It is only two years

---

* From Walt Whitman's poem 'I Saw in Louisiana a Live-Oak Growing'. Frame often refers to B, P and N as her 'live-oaks'.

ago that this plant, which my aunt was given seven years ago and which has spread to become a big bush, had lilac flowers.

Excuse this rhapsodising (sort of) about lilac. It sends me, babe, as much as that bit of Madeleine cake sent Proust. Well, it is Spring, and the air is full of sweet smells—wattle and japonica and cherry and plum blossoms, and the wax-eyes have departed in a hurry.

I've moved my furniture around again! The sunshine in my studio was too much. The house next door, which is very very close, prevents me from getting the sun until about noon (except for about an hour's early shining in the front windows) and from then on until sunset it fills the studio, bathroom, and lavatory, shining through the kitchen and down the passage and out the front door. Later in the season, when it moves farther south it shines in the late afternoon and evening in the sitting-room. I've moved to the smaller front room. Diagram guaranteed to bore:

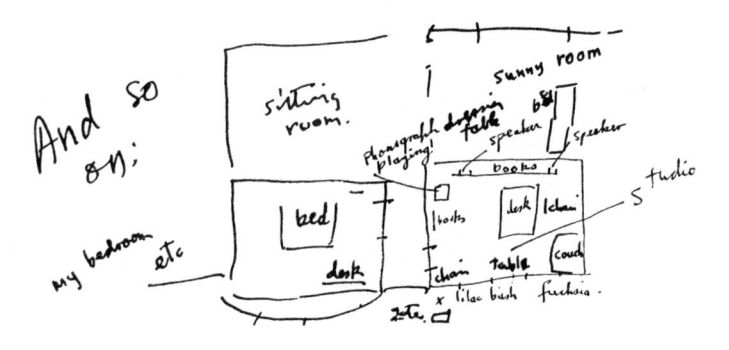

⟨ Page two of my exceedingly Non-letter. ⟩

I have just finished a morning's work, getting involved with my characters, and am going to post this and at the same time look in on the old swan for two minutes to see if the water has claimed her—actually, it hasn't yet, for I always phone to find out because much as I talk boldly about death I do not want to walk into the hospital and find a corpse. I had thought she might die this week as it is the anniversary of her husband's death (my father's brother), and though she's too far gone, perhaps, to realise this consciously, it might be in her bones somewhere, to communicate with her. I think the fallout of all kinds of experiences, like DDT, settles in people's bones and skin and flesh. My experience equivalent of Strontium 90 is at danger level!

Also when I go to post this non-letter I must go to library to consult a German dictionary; or splash and buy myself one. I have a letter this morning, entirely in German, and I'm ashamed of my inability to read it.

A sentence such as

'Herausgeber und Verlag bitten Sie hiermit um Erlaubnis zum Abdruck dieser Erzahlung.'

says something about a publisher but my frivolity makes it say that Herausgeber has bitten the hermit.

I'm afraid I'm terribly much longing to be among you, with you, by you, and all prepositions my three live oaks. And the Steinway!

I hope you're both still uttering beautiful paintings as live oaks 'utter (joyously) dark green leaves'. I know you are. The paintings I have— your two, B, and the catalogue ones of you and P., but in particular the originals, change marvellously with the changing light, I suppose because they *secrete* light, themselves, at least you have so composed them that they are bodies of light.

I hope that doesn't sound too fancy.

Here is a line or two I wrote about Paul's self-portrait in the sky, the idea of which rather haunts me.

> *Now while our gaze is fixed we try not to cower*
> *under the static heavy sky whose clouds*
> *have become engineering equipment. Stars gong, of brass.*
> *Trapdoors slide open to reveal the colourless eye*
> *claiming its earthly reflection, the hand uselessly*
> *grasping air, picking space-blossoms at the sky-window.*
> *The machine set in motion reveals now limbs, heart, face*
> *– so far away feet that are not wings and cannot fly—*
> *a self suffering the responsibility of a whole sky.*
> *The consolation is that paintings have power to arrest all.*
> *That loiters within their boundary [. . .].*

That's just an impromptu sort of verse, using the wrong words, and so on. And now end of page and accumulations of love

88. Dunedin August 5

Hello Everyone,

Bang goes my resolution not to write every day but it's my only way of being with you, which I'd like to be, but then I'd be quiet as a house-mouse and not speak much, and only be happy to know you were around somewhere, being yourselves.

The days are long and blue now, the kind of days that one thinks one knew in childhood, when one is revisited by raptures of discovery: I remembered yesterday my first encounter with a nasturtium flower and leaf, the feel, smell, wetness etc., and it was somewhat offputting to recall that so many of these rapturous discoveries were made when I first learned 'the facts of life' from a little girl I knew, and her big brothers. I wonder now where the rapture really lay, that was associated with geraniums and nasturtiums and ice-plant. It doesn't really matter, though, (I should have a quote from Rilke here—he's said everything) it only emphasis the completeness of the pattern.

What does one do if one is an old swan and goes to the wrong water? I think this is what my aunt has done, for now she's retreated inland, no doubt looking for the 'right' water—I'd forgotten that dying is so much like living. Old aunt Hannah (did I tell you that was her name?) was endearing yesterday. She's been semi-conscious for two weeks but yesterday she spoke to me, and when I asked if I would read her a letter which came for her she answered proudly, I'll read it myself. Where are my glasses? I found her glasses and fitted them over her nose and ears, opened the letter and held it in front of her (her head has no support now, like that of a small baby) while she gazed ahead, still with her eyes closed.

—Are you reading it? I asked.

—Of course I am, she replied, still with her eyes closed.

I read her the letter then, while making it seem that it was she who was reading it, and when I had finished I asked,

—Have you read it all now?

—Yes, she said. —It's nice to get a letter.

—Shall I put your glasses away?

—Yes. I won't need them now I've read my letter.

I put her glasses away, and put the letter back in its envelope, and I asked her if there was anything she wanted.

She really has retreated (briefly, I suppose, for she is dying) from the water! She began to describe, with relish, how nice it would be to eat a raw ripe firm tomato cut up with 'a little onion'.

Well. That is the saga of my aunt. It reminds me that we used to say a rhyme in speech-training which went,

'Swim, swan, swim.'

(Also in the speech-training exercises appeared a relevant line: 'Monday is laundering morning'. And another of the many 'moral' ones: 'Difficulties, perplexities, obstacles, all are sent to test our grit. Do not blame Destiny for your Defeat; instead blame idle days and wasted opportunities.')

Strong stuff.

I had a little private amusement yesterday translating my German letter. It was much more vivid if taken literally. Someone just wants to put a story in an anthology. The anthologist 'beats his breast with sabres and has bridled your story, with impertinence, for detailed demolition.' 'Yours, with many friendly shudders.'

Very nice.

*****   *******   ********

Stars now, for time passed, while I return to my new book, called Critical Condition? Resting Quietly? Danger List?

****   ****

> Mr Menuhin flew into Wellington yesterday morning, his two Stradivarius violins tucked firmly under his arm.

don't they mean his wing? It sounds like a Chagall painting.

Thursday. Hiroshima Day.

THURSDAY   HIROSHIMA DAY.

Afternoon again, work plodded along with but fearfully commonplace in my usual bogging-down. Thoughts of the live oaks and their joyous uttering of green and blue and purple and red paintings.

And two visitors in my solitude:

Yesterday kitty came to see me again. I think he-she-it (I haven't looked) lives next door but yesterday it came in and played and washed and slept on the spare bed in the sun and I thought guiltily of being accused of 'alienating affections' but I need not have worried, for as soon as the sound of the next-door car was heard arriving home, Kitty vanished. So you realise that when you and Paul are out Ned's day becomes one long wait for your return. He watches and watches—he's also on guard—but the sound of you returning and he instantly relaxes and is off duty. I used to watch him, his ears alert, his paws stiff, his eyes fixed on the gate. He was waiting to ward off strangers too, animal and human-animal, I suppose. Yesterday Kitty became very fierce with this-is-my-territory attitude when another kitty, the same age and colour, only fluffier, decided it wanted to visit too. First kitty shooed it away and then returned to sit on the stairs in the sun, flipping an occasional paw at bees in the koromiko blossom which grows beside the stairs, and making silent jaw-rehearsal at the birds.

    This morning I had another visitor—Jim, the husband of my recent guest, Jacquie. He was unexpectedly in Dunedin to visit his old old father (the one who was nailed to a cross on the battlefield in the First World War) who is in hospital with pneumonia, suddenly, after a bout of 'flu. I had a rich couple of hours in which Jim recited from memory some long long poems he had written, said a long prayer, aloud, for me, and told me something about his life in Jerusalem—a settlement in the wilds of the North Island, beside the Wanganui River. The Sisters of Compassion (Jim is a devout Roman Catholic convert) have given him an old cottage to live in, and Jim is rather worried that the Sisters of Compassion may not quite understand the kind of life that goes on in the cottage—he uses it as a kind of refuge, and anyone who wants to, may go there—'and what will the Sisters of Compassion think,' says Jim, 'if they catch sight of a naked man knocking at my door?' It was a refreshing visit, full of his usual eloquence (he preached the first Roman Catholic Sermon in Christchurch's Anglican Cathedral!) but I shan't accept his invitation to go to live there, in Jerusalem! too many people coming and going! in too many senses! It sounds like a bright spot, and he acts as a kind of a guru for the distressed nonconforming in a strictly conforming country and (what is important, though he doesn't think it is important any more) he writes his poems.

    After his visit I went to see my aunt, to take her two small firm ripe tomatoes—but, alas, or hurrah, she has found water again and is toying with the idea of having a swim! I'm reminded of the terrifying occasion when I first learned to swim. The teacher (who looked like a cow whale) simply pushed me into the water, and I shall never forget the panic and struggle. No swan, I!

I am making what those who write of migrating birds describe as 'intention movements'. I'm in earnest about not making this country my home, and I've got some forms from the U.S. Embassy to find what I must fill in to go to stay there for an indefinite period—it's all rather formidable. I must a. prove that I can keep myself. b. have an address to go to. c. give evidence (for this kind of visa) that I have 'outstanding ability in one of the arts'. Very formidable. Especially when I can't even identify myself!

Therefore I play my two Requiems, bathing myself in unearthliness; and I try to remember some of the lines of the poem which Jim said to me this morning, and all I can remember is

'O star that I do not believe in,
send forth your tendril of light . . .'

Well I can't remember it but it is the same idea I had when I was thinking of Paul's painting—of his climbing down the beanstalk, except in this poem the climb was upwards—the picture had not yet been painted, so to speak.

***** ***** Stars, for up there. We are rich in stars here and in the morning they seem to flee towards the ocean.

****

I'm afraid I am very lonely for you, and I want so much to be with you and Paul and Ned, and I imagine I am there—perhaps I should not confess these things for I have to go down down deep to get them—and I might meet Pluto on the way, and be whisked to the Underground Streams—but perhaps I will have a small crushed pomegranate seed in my hand, to give me six months light. Excuse the confusion of myths . . .

I'm enclosing some photos I took one day when I went to look at the sea. And a photo that I tried to take of your painting, B, and got, instead, for some strange reason, a photo of my front door and passage! I can't find your paintings anywhere, though I focused on it. It might be a case of telling the truth 'slant', once more.

By the way will you paint the door of your studio? Among your landscapes near the studio? I'll stop this letter before I launch into a poor man's woman's Rupert Brooke.

Love to ~~~ the sea Dunedin ~~~ [drawing with annotations: "look", "help, I'm becalmed", "look sharp!", "Santa Barbara", "it's Jay", "no it's Paul's dinghy"]

Love from [drawing of a bird]

[in margin: Rimbaud is in encyclopedia between *Rilke* and rime ('deposits of white ice crystals')]

89. Dunedin August 8

Ah dear B,

Your letter just came and immediately I am restored—I love it, and I love the little drawings. Sitting there with my large Mortal Enemy within, I look decidedly egg-bound, and for the life of me I can't think of the remedy—I think it is a diet of greens, chiefly sow thistle, chickweed, grass, and plenty of bran mash in the evenings. (When we were children we used to wrap the hens in pieces of old blanket, put them to bed, and give them enemas of straw! But this was not a cure for eggbinding, it was *in lieu* of dolls!)

Eggs, eggs, eggs. Did I tell you that one of the painters at Yaddo described how he kept getting a boiled egg for lunch, and nothing he said could change it, so he stored them in a drawer in his bedroom and when he left Yaddo he left a drawerful of eggs!

Sunny today again. Up early, to work. The birds have begun their dawn chorus now, and the days are lighter, earlier, and the lilac transplants are showing more tips of green, and there are many primroses in bloom. The old grandfather cabbages still lean, unpicked, though (of course) their hearts have been removed long ago, so long ago that they have forgotten they had hearts and their joy is their thick stem and rubbery coarse leaves and their ability to stand against the south winds that blow more fiercely in my garden as my neighbour cuts the hedge to barely three feet high, when I long for a high hedge that will enable me to *lurk* in the garden. The daffodils are coming up in the grass. I have worked *one hour* in the garden since I came back here!

I am visiting here only, I feel. I have not even unpacked the masses of manuscripts in the room downstairs—chiefly poems and stories that no-one but myself has ever seen, that I would not think of offering for publication, yet which a quirk of vanity or possessiveness or something prevents me from destroying.

You ask what happened to the French lady. Immediately I feel guilty because I have not been in touch with her again and I know she is rather homesick and I have all her family photos, full of long-long-legged children standing with poodles beside ancient stone walls and an ancient low farm-house, in Mauriac country.

A visit from kitty last night. What an affectionate kitty it is. It's quite small but I think it is pregnant—they must start early these days—as there's a low-slung bulge within. I will record its purr.

******** *********** *********************
asterisks
***

The Stevens story is sad. No apologies needed for telling about it. If such a thing happened to people I knew, I suppose, because of its haunting, it would eventually become a kind of story, a kind of mirror. Painting and music are more mysterious—the mirror is turned to face the wall. I don't know what I'm trying to say—almost everything I say is dictated by images—I just had an image of myself, haunted, writing a story in broad daylight; and of a painter or composer in a dark room with a mirror (the only source of light) turned to face the wall. How does one know it's a mirror? Because one *sees* the light in one's mind.

I really don't know what I'm trying to say. Which is a good enough reason for saying it?

**** ****))))))))) the thin moon in the sky.
Carnie's goings-on are certainly indelicate and immodest, especially if as a result, Steinway goes out of tune. It looks like a symptom to me. That trip abroad (was it in a yawl or a junk or a schooner? I forget) might have introduced Carnie to undesirable or desirable practices. Confinement in the Royal Botanical Gardens at Kew has been known to bring about *Tendrillia*, and there have been many severe cases. Plants in the Botanical

Gardens at Kew are indulged in all their whims (for instance The Chalk Garden made especially for plants which thrive in chalky soil). Sleeping quarters often leave much to be desired, or nothing to be desired. To quote from the Handbook of the R.B.G. at Kew, 'Thus the Dandelion and Thistle Family, which comprises more than 13,000 species, is represented by a selection occupying 29 beds, while smaller families often share one bed'. No doubt Carnie visited his relatives the *Nepenthes* and the *Sarracenias* (who knows how much time he spent with Cousin Insectie?) He may even have called upon the *Darlingtonias*. He will have come to know a wide range of habits. He will have lived among the *Succulents* and the *Aroids* and he may have visited *Magnolia* in her bed, or *Luculia Gratissima*, who is part of the *South-West Plot*.

I should think that as long as he makes music with the Steinway, he should be encouraged; otherwise it might be a good idea to let him spend several hours a day in the garden. Introduce him to Petunia. Remember, though, that he *must* be indulged—after all he *is carnivorous*, and unless his attention is diverted he may *strike at any time*, and what he has seen in the Royal Botanical Gardens at Kew will have made him wiser (and sadder). And no-one, not even Steinway, ever died of *Tendrillia*.

Just keep Carnie gently in his place, respecting his appetites and there should be no further scene such as you describe, with Steinway. And if that should not be so, and there are many many more, then B and P and N (and Steinway) must accept Carnie as he is, as the Travelled Plant who has lived among the *Succulents* and the *Aroids*, has known strange beds and stranger plots.

★★★★★   ★★★★★★

Yes, Charles Brasch is a nice *gentlemanly* type. When he left us the other week, the day he visited, I said to Jacquie that I thought N.Z. would go to rack and ruin when Charles died. She was thinking the same thing! He has held the Arts on his shoulders for so long—little Antipodean Atlas. He was *unpaid* editor of *Landfall* for twenty years. Perhaps something of his rather Spartan nature is shown in a letter from him to a N.Z. scholar who had been away in Oxford and was returning to N.Z. This letter is quoted in a book about the scholar, Don Anderson. (My chief claim to fame is that in our French class at University Don Anderson and I were the only ones who used to get our dictation correct!) I never knew him. He had cerebral palsy and his mother used to bring him to lectures.

Anyway, Charles wrote, as quoted,

'My warmest congratulations on your coming marriage, and—yes—I can congratulate you on coming home too. You have to be prepared to make your own life here—nothing is made and ready, as in England, you need to be self-dependent; but, that granted, life can be quite rich. I suppose you will get the shock nearly everyone does, when you first land and look about you, but go into mental training at once, and you'll be able to take it.'

'Go into mental training.' That strikes a chill to my heart! But it is pure C.B—a noble, upright old man, with discipline instead of marrow in his bones.

★★★★★★★★   ★★★★★★★★★★★★★★★

Stars, snowflakes.

I love the drawings in the letters.

★★★★

It is now Sunday evening and I have had a dose of Requiems (Hindemith and Mozart) and am floating on a serene wave of death. I have been thinking about the people you knew, in Palm Springs; and I have been thinking about the people I know, all in the great Chain Reaction.

Enough then.

I wanted to do a collage for you today but perhaps I'll get one within the next few days. Nixon hasn't been in the newspapers lately.

I felt as if I had the 'flu today so I went to bed with W. H. Auden—his new book only—and enjoyed him—it.

Silence. Footsteps in the street. The clock ticks.

★★★

And now it is morning again and I go to post this. Kitty comes to see me early every morning now and I am troubled that I am making her into a 'doublecrossing twotimer'. She has the same kind of markings that the horses of the 'goodies' used to have in the cowboy films.

Therefore in this letter I'll not have time to report fully on the NEWS FLASH which just came into my Factory Office. The Headline Reads:

Visit to our shores recently was A. Carnivorous Plant, a member of the Nepenthes family (young and not respected), and a close relative of

A. Certain Steinway.

I'll give more news of this another time. It seems that Carnie has been rewriting famous texts for Antipodean use, e.g. 'April is the cruellest month breeding lilacs out of the dead land' becomes, 'September is the cruellest month'. When that Aprille with his showres' etc. is also changed. But more of this another time.

> Meanwhile lots of unrestrained, restrained, satin, cedar, kisses and hugs to B (satin on ninon over nunon) and P (cedar-satin on satin-cedar) and N (fur on fur), and goodness knows what that means, from Cool Jay.

90. Dunedin August (handwritten)

Greetings & love to Bill, Paul, Ned,
                 Pill, Naul, Bed,
                 Nill, Baul, Ped,

with apologies for moronity, from Baby Jay, in bed with 'flu & wishing she were next door, a wall away, a door away, a skin away from the Live Oaks & their joyous green utterings (*their* greens, *their* blues). However, next to beings in this longed-for state, is the imagination of it, & forthwith from her sick (sic!) bed, Jay gives a further instalment of Stranger Than Fact, or Social Jottings from The Peanut Butter Patio.

But first, the promised extract from the daily newspaper about the recent visit of A. Carnivorous Plant.

Quote:

'Here to grace our fair, foul city recently was A. Carnivorous Plant. In an interview A. C. Plant declined to comment when questioned on his relationship with A. Certain Steinway. 'Certie & I are just friends, good friends.' He denied that he was visiting in order to change the literary record as it affects the Antipodes. 'Nonsense,' he said. 'I'm here partly on the *Lilac Tour* (economy) to supervise the breeding of the lilacs out of the Dead Land. Some prefer to call it 'The Lilac Tour' but I call it 'The Cruellest Month Tour'.

When questioned further A. C. Plant said he was also making a tour of 'lilacs in dooryards, or their equivalent', and ascertaining in each case on behalf of an overseas firm, 'when lilacs last in the dooryard bloomed'. He was also gathering, for the same firm, samples of lilac-scent in the air & 'eleventh-month grass'. A. C. Plant has brought with him a small 'musical shuttle'. 'It makes me feel at home,' he said. 'I find the cities very much pent and the streets keep throbbing with their throbbings.'

When questioned about his interest in travel, A. C. Plant said he would be exceedingly glad when his fearful trip was done.

'And man I mean *trip*,' he said. 'Real trip, not L.S.D.'

And when questioned about his home in America, he smiled secretively & his leaves uttered a 'rude, unbending, lusty look'. 'I saw in Santa Barbara three live oaks growing,' he said, declining to comment further.

His only direct reference to New Zealand and the Tourist Industry was,

'Pretty large unconscious scenery you've got here, man.'

Spokesplants however, close to official roots, insist that this reference was of a sexual nature only.

This is a hasty sic(!) letter with rain of love on Live Oak Inn & its inhabitants B P N.

Some people believe it would be best to enlarge it still further

91. Dunedin August (handwritten)

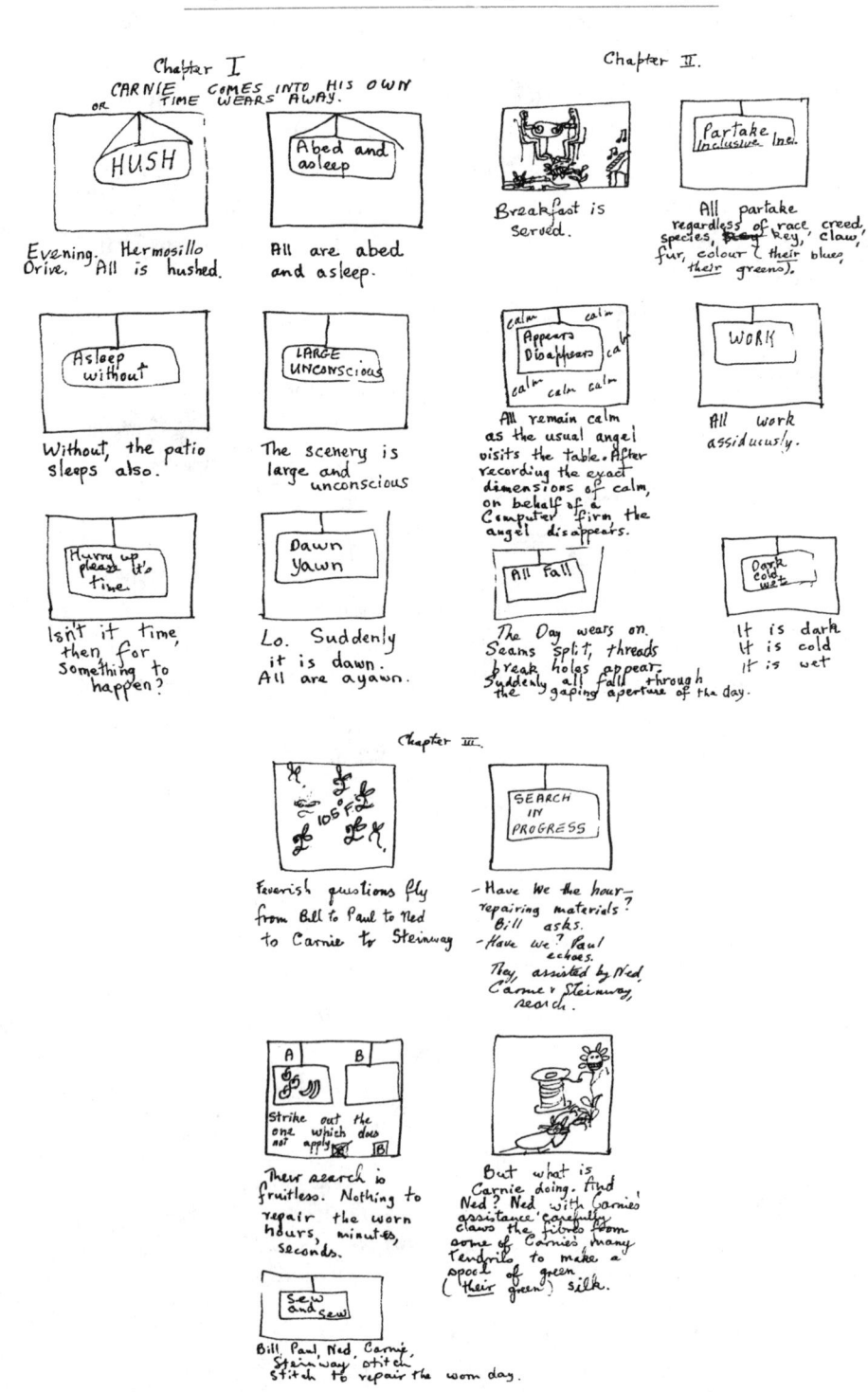

Chapter I
CARNIE COMES INTO HIS OWN
or TIME WEARS AWAY.

[HUSH]
Evening. Hermosillo Drive. All is hushed.

[Abed and asleep]
All are abed and asleep.

[Asleep without]
Without, the patio sleeps also.

[LARGE UNCONSCIOUS]
The scenery is large and unconscious

[Hurry up please it's time.]
Isn't it time, then, for something to happen?

[Dawn yawn]
Lo. Suddenly it is dawn. All are ayawn.

Chapter II.

[Breakfast scene]
Breakfast is served.

[Partake Inclusive Inc.]
All partake regardless of race, creed, species, key, claw, fur, colour (their blues, their greens).

[calm calm / Appears Disappears / calm calm calm]
All remain calm as the usual angel visits the table. After recording the exact dimensions of calm, on behalf of a Computer firm the angel disappears.

[WORK]
All work assiduously.

[All fall]
The Day wears on. Seams split, threads break, holes appear. Suddenly all fall through the gaping aperture of the day.

[Oooh cold wet]
It is dark. It is cold. It is wet.

Chapter III.

[105°F thermometers]
Feverish questions fly from Bill to Paul to Ned to Carnie to Steinway

[SEARCH IN PROGRESS]
- Have we the hour-repairing materials? Bill asks.
- Have we? Paul echoes.
They, assisted by Ned, Carnie & Steinway, search.

[A B / Strike out the one which does not apply]
Their search is fruitless. Nothing to repair the worn hours, minutes, seconds.

[spool and flower scene]
But what is Carnie doing. And Ned? Ned with Carnie's assistance carefully claws the fibres from some of Carnie's many tendrils to make a spool of green (their green) silk.

[Sew and sew]
Bill, Paul, Ned, Carnie, Steinway stitch stitch to repair the worn day.

4.
Chapter III. (continued)

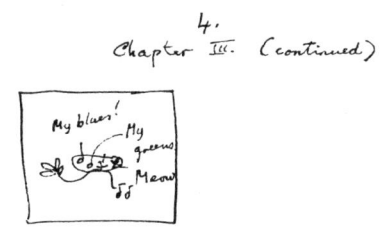

> My blues! My greens My Meow

The day repaired, our heroes climb up from the cold, the wet, the dark, to the bright day. 'My greens!' Paul cries. 'Ah, my blues!' Bill exclaims.

All turn with looks of love and gratitude upon Carnie who, with now bandaged tendrils, glows with pride.

'Nevertheless,' he mutters, fortunately out of earshot, 'I remain carnivorous.'

THE END.

IF YOU WOULD LIKE TO JOIN OUR HEROES IN THEIR EXCITING DAILY ADVENTURES HIJACK A BOEING 707, 737, or 747, & FLY TO LOS ANGELES. DO NOT DELAY.

LOVE FROM JAY.

This is another moronic letter from my bed. My 'flu is improving, & will be O.K. tomorrow, I think.

Jacquie is staying with me—last night & tonight—while she & the rest of the family, including her husband, Jim, who is with his mother, attend the funeral of Jim's father.

That is partly why I have sought shelter in bed.

Goodbye for now & parcels, registered, unregistered, explosive, unexplosive, of love to

B. P. N.
the heroes
of Hermosillo
Drive.

Miss Miss Miss Miss Miss
Miss Kiss Miss Kiss Miss

Jay — Economy Section!

NEW ZEALAND: MARCH 1970 TO JANUARY 1971

92. Dunedin August 15 (handwritten)

Writing-paper filched from the Shipping Company on my maiden voyage, fifteen years ago!

Dear 🐜, 🤠, 🐴,

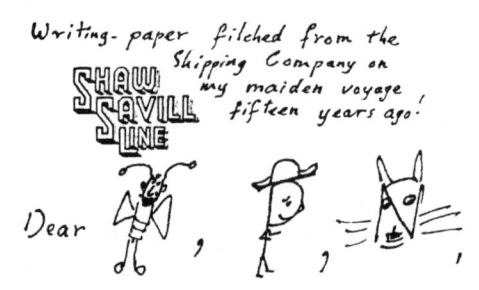

Hi, from my sick bed where today I finished Paul's cap, knitting furiously since I was able to do little else. Old 'Flu, however, has almost departed, leaving me once again to face My Mortal E.

This past week has been great weather for adventurous swans—first, last Monday, old grandad Baxter, and on Thursday evening my aunt Hannah Florence (I did not even know that was her second name) finally found the secluded pool she had been searching for, and slipped into the water & those tough old webs got working as she never dreamed they would & she was soon out of sight.

What other news is there? Let me think . . . My guest went home on Thursday with the rest of her family (including her husband Jim). The previous week she had attended a Maori tangi (funeral) & was finding it difficult to move from culture to culture—from openly expressed grief—wailings & chanting followed by feasting, to a Pakeha funeral where, as she said, everyone talks about the weather & pretends the dead are still living!

No other news flashes. Carnie has left our shores once again, kitty has not been seen in the vicinity, the grocer, a *Mr Motion*, came with supplies for me, & my friend Ruth passed by the house, knocked at the door, and gave me a magnolia petal.

And I have been lying in bed planning my U.S. trip . . . I thought of a plan to have money—not from teaching but from doing what I most like to do—writing; and in this case something I'd like to write which could be lucrative: some children's stories. I'm going to tell my publisher or agent & get some advice about this. Mona Minim has not been lucrative but what I have in mind is quite different.

It will be so nice when the kennel is ready. Even before then, I'll perhaps see you three, mes chênes vivants, for a short while? because time wears on and out and through and only Carnie has the green silk thread for mending it, & only you & Paul have the blues, the greens, the reds, to give life to the time.

Well, I'm a dreamer—it's the only thing to be: a feely dreamer in a precarious little satin ship on the sea of change.

What a mouthful or foot-ful! Excuse me while I scrape the barnacles from my cedar bottom.

Monday: Ah, that's better. I'm sending Paul's cap & this letter if I can possibly get out today to mail them. I'm still semi-live. And of course I'm thinking of you & all live oaks, from moment to moment & I'm sending a prim-rose in this letter and a koromiko blossom & leaf which the bees love—they are back, as expected by Fly, but I, Jay, did not discern the one with the repaired surcingle.

No further news flashes. I listened a lot to the records yesterday. I chose the Hammerklavier again and again. It is magnificent and terrifying & dogged and I love it. I wanted to play something to furnish the week of deaths & I found I rejected the Requiems because—it's hard to explain—they entered an open door—oh, that reminds me of the Rilke sonnet ending

'then after terrible knocking
entered the hopelessly open door.'

In contrast, the Beethoven Sonata remained 'out there'—I suppose in this case 'out there' was life & living. But I'm hopeless at writing these things, though I want to. Forgive.

All kinds of pure, polluted
love, sweet, sour,
flowery, fruity

P.T.O.

I could make this look very rude!

93. Dunedin August

Hi, Tena koutou,

from the Antipodean waste of noise-polluted Evans Street where outside my gate an electric drill is working road-works. The day is grey, damp, chilly, and I sit snuggled in Santa Barbara sweater which retains 99 percent of its snuggle, and I think of my live oaks, demi-live, semi-live, wholly live, who will now be setting off to the studio—maybe not—I think it is washing-up time, sonata-time, vitamin-time, Petromalt-time. Here it is Tuesday. There it is Monday. I should be able to send you bulletins about the future, as I live in it.

I am up out of bed now but the devastating 'flu has left me infantilly weak-kneed which is what I always have been. It has been a nasty epidemic here with many deaths, so many that I am tired of death for the moment. I'd like to come over to you and laugh, laugh—everything is so grim here—ah how long it is since I laughed pure, impure laughter! It is a million years ago. Everyone here is so serious and I feel myself becoming caught in the serious groove, grim, unsmiling, and it scares me. I have friends here, as you know, but none are—is close in the sense that it is possible to laugh with them. Now that is very strange. It means one is semi-live. But I've told you this over and over again, and bored you with it . . . I will arise and go now and go to Santa Barbara where I felt among the live oaks like a working zip—strange comparison, here it's like being a stuck zip—with nothing and no-one to adjust it. I think zips have a wonderful time—you call them *zippers*? Up and down all their lives, in the grooves that are made for them.

Enough of that now. My greeting at the beginning is a Maori greeting. Jacquie, my guest, brought me some Maori language records which I've been playing. A wonderful way to learn a language. The Baxter family are all now returned to Wellington and Jim has gone on to his haven in Jerusalem. Grandmother is selling their old house in Brighton—now that's a place one would dream of—by the roaring sea, beside a brown river, with peach, apple and pear trees, and an alpine garden, and passionfruit. I have visited there only twice and each time, the old lady (about 86 now) has taken me to see her alpine garden, collected from plants she, as an active member of the Naturalist's club, has gathered from her walks around Dunedin hills and elsewhere. Every plant is labelled, with English and Latin name, and she knows them all, and she talks of them as a mother talks of her children. I remember her saying proudly, 'Now this is a little *Hebe*.'

Her maiden name, by the way, was Millicent Brown.

I dreamed last night I was with you and we all had a beautiful blue meal, I have never seen such a lovely blue. And there were two mountain lions sunning themselves on the roof. And the light was gold, drenching light.

Goodbye for now to my much-missed L. O's, and all kinds of mentionable, unmentionable, tangible, intangible, monostitched, laconic, desperate, deliberate, makeshift, conclusive, unanswerable, goatish, porcine, mulish, zoomorphic, dovelike, recoverable, conservative, waterproof, bloodsucking, unauthorized, fictitious, authentic
      LOVE.

94. Dunedin August

Ah, your warmth-giving letters—one from each of you (except Ned who has his own problems, see enclosed cutting) yesterday, give me courage, increase my snuggle-store. I love hearing at the other side of the Pacific, and try to get my book done, after the interruption of deaths and 'flu. Frank S always said one must work on in spite of *every* interruption, and I know he's right, because even to breathe is an interruption—living itself—and one would get nowhere if one started measuring the magnitude and deciding, here's where I stop. I can say that now, but stricken with 'flu . . . well, I had other ideas. It is the same 'flu, I think, that struck New York the Christmas before last, and I remember when I was then on the Island in the Bahamas, how people arrived to recuperate, all looking as if they had come from a city stricken with the plague. I had so many impressions during the year that they seem to have trampled on those Christmas ones, among the beautiful face-lifted people.

Oh my heart bleeds for you among the barking dogs! Here, the Council has suddenly decided it wants to tear up Evans Street, lift the footpath and put it down again, unearth drains, and so on, and stinks are floating around outside, from tar and gas and sewers, and an electric drill is throbbing with its throbbing, and sources close to the city tell me it is alarmingly pent. But all the blossoms are out, and all my lilac cuttings are getting their green heart-shaped leaves, and I am so grateful; and moved by their apparent eagerness to grow; and the big overhanging fuchsia, like God, 'has not said a word'.

The journey up the coast sounded very pleasant. I suppose there are lots of Steinway's relatives tucked away, some old, some young and, as Whitman would say, *growing with their growth*. The Unicorn tapestry is breathtakingly pure, and the card will be another of my treasures.

Did Hildy get her job teaching?

I bleed for you, also, in the visit of the Museum Director to the studio, and his lack of awareness. Perhaps it is better if the painter is not there when his work is looked at? Writers can escape this kind of face-to-face judgment of their work. One would have thought that the Director, as a professional looker, would have known how to be alone with the paintings, in company; but it sounds as if he either has no filter or it wasn't working; or else he was afraid to look so he stopped up the filter with fatuous remarks. The older I get (my grey hairs fall on the paper as I write) the more I realise that it takes so much courage or something like it, to practise even the usual habit of looking, without polluting it. (Title of my new book—*The Snowflake Senses*.)

★★★★★★★★★★★ Stars, after that mouthful.

★★★★★★★★★★★★★

I hope you had a wonderful time at the Fiesta Parade? I suppose you saw Ned, lone demonstrator, carrying *his* banner? No doubt he kept out of your way, though. I happened to be there, in my brown-bread shoes, and I glimpsed him looking very determined and yet I don't think his campaign was successful because few knew the story behind it, and I heard someone remark as he passed, 'Another demonstrator! Dressed as a cat this time! A bearded hippie underneath, that's for sure. What will they think of next?'

Meanwhile, back in Dunedin, I live my solitary life, in my homesickness. I haven't seen anyone in the house since Jacquie called the doctor to me the day she left. He was a *Dr Moody*, dark, with short back and sides haircut, and pale skin stretched over his face and gone thin in parts, kind of like chewing-gum.

Kitty has vanished, but the shyer, fluffier kitty comes to sit on the stairs. I suppose I'm not being fair to the district cat population by not having a cat, for I have such wonderful stairs, and a little balcony (I mean wonderful from a cat's point of view) and the neighbouring cats like to sit there, but not being sure which cat owns it, they get nasty with each other, and fight for the territory, whereas if one cat owned it, the matter catter-matter (ugh) would be settled. I'm sure if cats were invited to studios to look at paintings they would appreciate and understand them. I marvel at their power of looking.

Away now for lentil soup of which I made a huge potful to last me the week.

★★★★

Return after lentil soup. Fuller, fatter, more furiously futile. Thesaurus and I are having a love affair. He says, Toss in a blanket, come to the gallows, drink the hemlock, tickle the palate, commit a debauch, titivate, scintillate, repatriate, ransack, snaffle, let the cat out of the bag, throw light on, overpaint, paint out, and put up the shutters. Well. What am I to do? I smell of the lamp, I am unpolished, impromptu, enhanced, strategically worn to a frazzle while he handles the ribbons in a nutshell, hangs together, dematerializes under the sun, and has logic on his side in some galactic latitude where farness spreads like wildfire and dishevelment adds fuel to the flame . . .

More of our exciting adventures in my next instalment . . .

✸✸✸✸✸✸✸

Oh Paul that is a lovely knit-skin you have in mind and on paper! I've made another cap, but it's not in the colour which is *your* blue, I'm afraid. You'll be thinking I'm quite sane to be sending a—rash, troup—what?—of caps. It happens I have the wool and I haven't been able to use my eyes for words, so I've kept them in practise by using then for stitches. You should receive the first instalment of blue cap shortly—other instalments may follow when I am within measuring distance of you. ✸✸✸✸ Meanwhile, and keeping my fingers crossed for the early instalment of the mountain lions or at least for an early visit and meeting, I'll send simple unvarnished rustically flavoured

    LOVE   TO   B P N

Demonstrator!

FREDERICA is back.

Ned Cat sits resolutely beside his banner in a recent lone demonstration against the appearance of Frederica (heroine of the novel (Feline edition *Cat in August*) in his neighbourhood.

(Drawing by courtesy of the Bottom-of-the-class-in-Art Stud

✷ readers will recall Frederika's words at the beginning of this famous novel — 'I have come from Santa Barbara: a fur piece.'

Dear Paul,

    I am a cap, hat, petit chapeau and I look forward to seeing the world from the top of your head. I have a tassel or pom-pom which can be removed. My colour is not to your specification, but my maker tells me that nothing in this world conforms to specification. Although I am inclined to disagree with her I am not yet old enough to have formed a philosophy which develops—so my maker tells me and this time I agree—with wear and tear.

    This is not to say that I am raw fleece. Far from it. I have been scoured, dyed, teased, twisted, & knitted to conform to a pattern.

    Ah me!

    I am a wishing cap.

        Yours (I hope)
        Petit Chapeau

95. Dunedin August

Dear Ned and Bill and Paul,

    The large ginger cat who seems to own this house and who rescued me from a cage in the pet shop out South Dunedin has told me about you, Ned, and about your two big cats who have been staying with you quite a while, and whom you employ to provide you with bed and board. My large ginger cat has been doing something like that for me since I arrived four days ago. What colour are you, Ned?—From a painter's point of view, not from the aspect of racial discrimination—I am white. I think I am seven weeks old. I am going to be a writer when I grow up. Already I can hit the space bar of the typewriter which I let the ginger cat use in the meantime as I am not old enough yet.

    My house has three pretty good chairs. (You will understand that I adopt the policy of letting the ginger cat believe she owns the place.) When I first arrived I was given quite a good box to sleep in and to humour J I slept in it a couple of nights until I discovered my own place in the small sittingroom—there are two sittingrooms and two bedrooms, with J having her study in her bedroom as she likes it this way. I found a marvellous place on the bookshelf beside Bullfinch's Mythology and Brewer's Dictionary of Phrase and Fable (no doubt you have read them). J had a white woollen stole which she uses to keep warm with, and again I have humoured her by letting her think it belongs to her. It is ideal for a bed, and I sleep there every night now, and oh it reminds me of mamma who was white and soft with tassels that I used to pull and suck just as I do those on the stole. J, of course, has no idea of my secret thoughts. Have your cats any idea of your thoughts?

I've heard about your Dr Gilbride. My vet is called Dr Twaddle but I have never seen him yet. I may go soon to be inoculated against that dreadful disease feline enteritis which strikes very quickly. I will have to stay overnight and it will cost me two dollars fifty cents. I shall probably hire a taxi to get there. I have not yet learned to use the phone, though.

I think I will enjoy living here. I'm too scared to go outside yet though I like to sit on my stairs. It seems such a long way to get to the garden and there are many enemies about, for instance the other evening a cat which thought it owned the place came right inside the door. I put on a furious display like a white peacock. 'Get out,' I said. 'I live here.'

'*I* live here,' it said. It hissed and snarled at me. I looked up at J, my faithful servant for her to tell it that this is my place. She explained nicely that it *was* my place. The next time a strange cat appeared I had more confidence and really frightened it away. Both ladies and gents have left their calling cards around here, and I daresay all the ladies, even the grownup ones have fluttering hearts. What a life!

There's not much more news for you. I've explored everywhere. I climb everything I can climb. I chew everything I can chew. I have fairly good meals—egg and milk, and meat, sometimes mixed with salad oil and garlic to keep the worms away. At first my motto was *Pee Now Pay Later* but now I know where to go and I think J is surprised I'm so quick at learning. She should see me when I commence my studies at the bookshelf when she is fast asleep.

Do you have a book shelf, Ned? Do you have a little garden? I'm dying to hear from you. J says she is going to visit you some day and there are other people who want me to look after them when she goes.

⟨ J's news. ⟩

J has asked me to add her news to my letter. She says she has no news. She just lives a quiet life. Her flowers are coming out—daffodils and so on. She thinks a lot about you and your two big cats and misses you very much and sometimes feels depressed because you are so far away. She is writing something on her typewriter. There is an airport strike and after September 7th there will be a postal strike which worries her. She will feel cut off (not in the sense you and I understand it, Ned).

I'm saying goodbye now. Your affectionate penfriend,

    Lucas.

P.S.   I have marvellous hiding-places here.

Hi, & love daubed, scumbled, tattoed, varnished, mellowed, whitewashed, discoloured, illuminated to

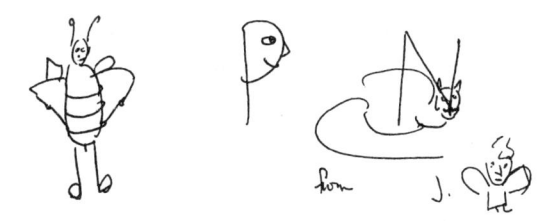

              from J.

96. Dunedin August

Dear B, P, N, and all other mythical and real members of the household,

    A misty rainy day and I sit at my panoramic window in the sitting-room typing this while Lucas plays with the keys (he depressed the space bar just now). Let me explain Lucas. He is my guest, invited, and even named—one does not always have the delight of naming a guest. I saw him shivering with fright and shock in a shop window—in a cage—and I impulsively bought him for one dollar. He is all white with a faint smudge of black between his ears and he has short hair, and is seven weeks old. A kitten. His whole name is Lucas Burch, from *Cat in*

August—probably a son of Frederika's lover. After a short period to recover from his shock—I suppose he had been taken from his mother, also—he has made himself very much at home. It is strange to see the surroundings from a cat's point of view—I did not know I had such wonderful chairs. I have three chairs—the big winged Landfall chair that can be climbed over and along; and a very tall-backed chair, originally a prayer-chair, which someone bought in a church sale, and gave to me; and a cane chair which also can be scratched at and climbed. I really got swelled-headed yesterday, thinking what fine chairs I have, and I never knew it.

I loved the notes from the Underground. My 'flu's gone now. It was a nasty 'flu. Charles B phoned the other day and asked if he could call in on his way to visit a friend. He came for fifteen minutes—stayed I mean—and brought a big bag of grapefruit, lemons, and a lovely kind of honey that I haven't seen since I was a kid and my father used to get it wholesale, in forty pound tins. He was looking very fit and had been mountain climbing with a friend. He said he had been to five funerals in the past three weeks, including that of an aunt who was 96!

Carnie's visit to supervise the breeding of the lilacs was—you may tell him—an immense success. My lilacs seem not to be able to wait to burst into leaf, anyway—I doubt if they will flower yet. I'm sending you one of the 'heart-shaped' leaves, from the lilac in the dooryard.

Lucas is asleep now, snuggled on a woollen shawl that is on a hot-water bag, in a cardboard box. I wish we had fur instead of plain skin. Human beings are terribly deprived.

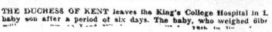

I am a 'heart-shaped' lilac leaf. * Jay says this is a scrappy letter but she had fun making the collage. She sends lots of heart-shaped love.
P.S. I grow in the dooryard.

97. Dunedin August 28

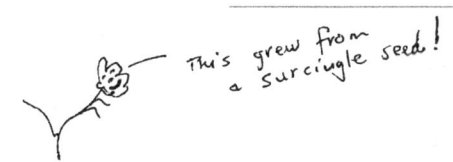

Dear Bill the Kill, Paul the Call, Ned the Head,

So Cap no. 1 has arrived for Paul! You'll be wondering what form of sanity has struck me when you receive in about a week the specification Cap (cap only, minus body-skin). I assure you I haven't been struck by sanity—I'm as insane as usual. People who return to Dunedin from the United States always start knitting caps, after a few months. Most do a dozen. I have done only three and already the cure is in sight, the symptoms are disappearing. One is always in danger of scarves, too. Fortunately I have never had the *sweater syndrome* which is very serious and quite incurable. I had supposed I was immune to it but one never knows . . .

Why not come to New Zealand if you are eager to get out of the United States? I want to come to the States only because you are there

---

* a lilac leaf was affixed to the letter

and I'm rather like a kitty that feels separated from its family. I hope this doesn't scare you.

Paintings sell for less in New Zealand and salaries for teaching are less but though the cost of living has risen quite a lot one can still live on a small amount. Telephone rental for the year (excluding toll calls—local calls are not charged for) is 44 dollars. My two-month electricity account which includes all heaters warming the house, cooking, hot water, lights and so on, is sixteen dollars maximum. My house tax or rate is 44 dollars a year with Insurance on the house (Fire etc.) about eighteen dollars. A visit to the doctor which used to be free, is now one dollar. Medicine is free as are hospital treatments.

Etc. etc. etc. Now are you sufficiently bored with this economic review, sitting there all surcingled in your sanity-caps, with peanut butter all over your tender fingers?

It was lovely getting your letters and Ned's photo (which I haven't yet shown to Lucas) and to hear all your news. The Violence in America episode sounds similar to the one in Baltimore when I was going to cross the road and a car passed and slowed down. There were three men in it with what I thought was a walking stick pointing out of the car. They called out something to me—probably abuse which I did not hear distinctly—and I laughed and looked happy and they drove by. I learned later that they had been picking off people with their gun, around North-East Baltimore. Smile at your would-be assassin! I've told this story several times as an illustration of Violence in America (I told it to you, too, I think) but I haven't embroidered on it. Frank Sargeson is a marvellous embroiderer. If you tell him a story and visit him a year later you find him telling the story with all kinds of improvements and innuendos—preferably with a sexy base. To digress—I once knew a physicist working at the University in Wellington. He was a gentle mild man, an inventor, who had invented a detonator, and once when I passed through Wellington he invited me to the Dark Room where he had set up his headquarters (he even slept and ate there; this was in the university), to see his *detonator*. You can imagine the story Frank told about that one! Actually it was quite a scary experience as we had a meal there, cooked over a Bunsen burner, and I enquired about a little saucer of white stuff on the improvised table. I thought it was icing sugar. He told me calmly that it was PETN (whatever that is), so many times more explosive than TNT!

So ends my digression and adventure in detonators.

I haven't played Scrabble solitaire for ages now. I just could not resist cheating and so scored for impossible words. I needed the enforced discipline of MacDowell cronies. Oh yes I remember the day B and P set off for Wright Ludington's. It's a very happy memory. You both looked so handsome ('dashing' is the word Sylvie Pasche would use) and I loved your colours, and Paul's tie, and the day was blue—your blue—with the sun out, and I liked the idea of your going out to lunch and then coming home and telling me about it. Maybe I have no right to get so homesick for you, and there.

Lucas Burch is settling down nicely. *He* would say, no doubt, that *I* am settling down and getting trained. He's still too scared to go down the stairs into the garden but he's exploring a little more every day. He is touchingly gentle and patient. My clothes are being chewed, my buttons are being chewed off and anyone who comes to visit me is chewed. I've had only one visitor—the rather dramatic woman who came to see me some weeks ago. I don't care for her company at all but I could scarcely turn her away when she appeared at the door the other day and said, 'Can I see you, I think I'm going insane.'

I'm making arrangements with my friend Ruth whom I seldom see but who phones me now and again, and perhaps with Charles B whom I never talk to on the phone but whom I see about once in six weeks for a cup of tea, to have a special code of communication so that I can escape unwelcome callers. I'm quite interested to see what Charles thinks of my kitty because when I first visited him some years ago when he was living with Rodney K. (his old close friend) they had a white cat.

No prostitution, no money! How right you are! I know it's the custom in U.S.A. for authors to get an advance on a book they have yet to write but the thought of it appalls me. I always get my advances for books I have already written. The idea scares me—being paid for an idea that might decide to disappear if it thought it was captured in a money-cage. I remember poor Harrison Kinney trying to write his book years after he had spent his advance—but then 'his pecker was excessively skinny'. (This is a quote from a MacDowell historian of the times, who wrote a long dissertation called *Peckers and Prose: A Comparative Study*.)

It's my birthday today.

I had a phone call from New York yesterday. A friend there (she and her husband lent me their apartment for the summer once, and offered me their house on Martha's Vineyard also but I had no transport and would have been scared by myself) has offered to pay me so much a month if I want to live in America. She has repeatedly offered this kind of help but I have declined—so far. She is a good giver, though, in the sense that unlike with some givers, the giving is not the equivalent of taking, a way of getting possession. If I accepted this offer I would arrange for her to be paid the income from my books. She would still lose quite a bit of money. But my conscience would be helped. (It's less a conscience than a fear of being involved and 'tied'.) Well, I'm thinking about it and haven't decided. For 'thinking' read 'worrying' . . .

I went into a shop yesterday and I was surprised at the tomcat smell in the shop—until I realised it was *me*. Ned would probably attack me if I walked into Live Oak Inn now. Lucas Burch's favourite desire at the moment is to get into the bath with me. He goes crazy in the bathroom—I suppose because of all the smells.

How's your status quo? Improving?

I know all too well the feeling that what one is so tenderly creating suddenly turns to shit. I get it when I read reviews of my work. And I get it every time I re-read in the evening what I have written during the day. If I want to regain my confidence which is so easily lost as I have a very small store, I read my work in the early morning and then I think, sometimes, maybe there is hope for me as a writer, but sometimes even in the morning my work bores me and reads dully and I hate it, no the feeling is not as strong as that, I just feel it doesn't matter and I'm wasting my time writing and why on earth did I begin etc. etc. When I was living in London which I thought was such a convenient place, and this feeling hit me I used to go off to one of the suburban movie-houses to see a double-bill of B grade movies. Sometimes if I went to a good movie (a Bergman for instance) I would emerge inspired and ready to accept writing again. I used to rely a lot on the movies. I'd go in the afternoon among the pensioners and West Indians and dirty old men and sometimes I'd have to move my seat as quite a bit of unwanted fingering and handling was the rule. I should really have accepted it as part of the fun shouldn't I? I used to go every afternoon to the movies. It's quite convenient to go here, and there are four or five theatres in Dunedin, but one does not feel anonymous, and there isn't the nice depraved feeling that one gets in a theatre that shows continuous movies—it's all too clean and healthy for me. Everybody seems so respectable.

Here are two limericks which Frank S wrote. *Robb* is a heart surgeon in Auckland. And *Liston* is the Archbishop.

[two Sargeson limericks were enclosed here]

★★★★★★★★★★★★★★★★★★★★★★

Stars now for stars.

Love hot and cold, flowery-fruity, sweet-sour, and longing to be among you with my mountain lions.

I love your drawings B. & P. (Ned does not draw) Jay.

SEPTEMBER

98. You know where. Dunedin September 1

Dear B, P, N,

How nice to get a morning letter—I'm always there in my breakfast thoughts—also noon and night and inbetween thoughts.

The news about Frederica is enchanting though I suspect that only a mamma cat who was looked after by two painters could have produced such a delightful assortment of *her* colours—white, black and white, calico, orange. And for her to have had the good taste to have booked herself into the *Wonner Ward* of the maternity hospital is altogether too much. These cats are too smart for me. What will happen to the kittens?

I haven't mentioned the event to Lucas Burch as it might put ideas into his head for the future—or to shift the context of the Stravinsky letter (which you suspect is Craft letter)* it might take ideas *out* of his head. He (Lucas) is more like a little white fox than a cat. He may have Siamese relations, perhaps. He is long and lean with huge ears and a pointed face and if he is good training for me before I progress to mountain lions I may have to revise or reduce the number of mountain lions I can keep.

★★★★★★★   ★★★★★★

The lunch at Wright Ludington's sounded blissful. My mouths watered.

★★★★★★★!?!!   ★★★★★★★

In the same mail as your letter was one from the New York Times inviting me to send them a poem to print on their editorial page! For a few minutes I had a swelled head and was dying to talk to someone so I could say casually, Oh I've been invited . . . My head so easily swells but more easily diminishes to pin-size. I wish I had the confidence even to think of sending poems anywhere, but they all seem so *bad*—and *are* so.

★★★★

It is early morning now. Grey days these past days with Scotch mist and a damp chill lingering around my feet as my house is so high and the dampness invades the lower storey which, as I've told you, is just a large

---

* Brown was a friend of Stravinsky; Robert Craft was Stravinsky's biographer

basement with a decayed old bedroom and what used to be a bathroom and a little patio where the japonica grows inside, unrained on but flourishing. My daffodils are all in bud and the lilacs are all healthy and Lucas is eating the primroses. He must have been reading my old English recipe book where the first instruction for primrose wine is 'Take a peck of primroses'.

I haven't done anything outwardly or been anywhere or seen anyone since I last wrote. I'm just quietly in exile and longing, pursuing my writing and making occasional discoveries but the work is slow as yet. Until these past few days the weather has been beautiful with all the birds singing crazily in the sun and the flowers bursting open—and, inevitably, all the windows opening and the radio and tv noises coming out, and all the lawn-mowers mowing with their frightful noise. I haven't yet had to put in my ear-plugs in the daytime yet, nor at night, for the world does go dead at night, it's like country night. There was a 7 and a half acre place for sale across the valley for 8000 dollars—it must be the place I can see, where sheep graze. The place you saw in the mountains sounded interesting. You could always live in the avocado trees. It must be very expensive, as I believe the mountain lions demand *their cut* or else. I've seen only one avocado tree—at Frank S's place. In his younger days he used to be a very keen gardener on his ¼ acre property and there were always stout orange pumpkins on the window-sill and strings of garlic and tree tomatoes and chinese gooseberries. He planted an avocado and a custard apple and a pawpaw and had fruit from them. And there was a lemon tree at the back door where he encouraged his male visitors to pee as pee is good for lemon trees, so he said.

Today I may take a walk along the town to the library. I always think there are so many strangers in the town until I remember that I am the stranger. I can always call in at Maureen's gallery where there's usually an exhibition though they've stopped inviting me to the openings as I never go—I usually sneak in a couple of days afterwards. And once last week I met Rodney who is Charles' close friend and, unusual for him, as he does not know me very well nor I him, he stopped to speak to me. He is scarcely five feet high. He works as a drama tutor and producer. That day last week he seemed very excited and dramatic. He'd been in Wellington and had difficulty getting back because of a strike and he spoke like a messenger out of a play.

'There are all kinds of rumours going around Wellington,' he said. He didn't say what the rumours were and I had no clue but he communicated some of the excitement of a returning traveller. I felt like labelling him as Enter Traveller from Athens, rather than from Wellington.

****

I've at last settled about Intensive Care in England. Macmillan somehow (through my agent who is no longer my agent) read the typescript and were very keen to publish it, with a slightly bigger advance, and I had to decide between loyalty to my publisher of ten years (publishing age only) and the big prestigious firm and (rather reluctantly) I decided in favour of loyalty and my old firm. Or rather, it was less in favour of *loyalty* than of *habit*.

****

I may have to go into hospital for an operation—I'll know next week. If I do go I'll be there 14 days and then come home to take things easily (as if I don't always!) for a couple of months. It's hard not to feel a little gloomy and apprehensive but if I do have to go (and it's still not certain) I know I'm a very quick recoverer. I'm in rude health now but I'll be in ruder health when I go travelling from New Zealand which will be early next year. I'll have a place to stay in New York until you find (if you decide to find and if the ground has not moved too much from beneath our separate *feets*) the 'remote spot'—Always bearing in mind that the remotest spot (though there may now be no guarantee that it is remote now, as it may be polluted by noise, people etc.) is that little town of *Psyche*. Handy quote from John Keats,

> 'Yes, . . . I will build . . .
> in some untrodden region of my mind,
> where branched thoughts newgrown with pleasant pain
> instead of pines (avocados) shall murmur in the wind:
> Far far round shall these dark-clustered trees
> fledge the wild-ridged mountains steep by steep;
> and there by zephyrs, streams and birds, and *bees*,
> the (mountain lions) shall be lulled to sleep:'
>
> etc. etc.

He spoils it of course by saying the 'casement will be *ope*'. I'd certainly not live anywhere where one had to ope the mail and ope the casement and ope everything else that needed oping.

****

My psyche's not untrodden, anyway.

****

In the meantime until I see you next year (unless you can visit me, which is only a dream) I'll be patient, and finish my Mortal Enemy which is growing daily; and think of you and write my Live Oaks in the manner in which they are accustomed.

******

I wish Paul well for the new semester and both satisfaction in painting and everything else and Ned success in further banner-carrying—which will probably not be necessary. If word of his success gets around he may be called upon to represent the nation in Washington. You'd get a surprise if you woke one morning to find a hastily scribbled note—Gone to Washington.

****

Now. Peedauntal News. *Have you looked at your testimonials lately?*

All kinds of warmest love to

99. Dunedin September 4

Dear B P N,

A quick letter full of sweet nostalgia. A hello. A greeting.

It's two in the afternoon and I've done a fair morning's work and I'm really getting involved in my characters now, and I find this is enjoyable. They're not alive yet, though, in the writing. Characters seem to become alive with me only when they're about to die.

The day is grey, with mist and a little warmth and I'm about to walk down into the town to take the air and mail this. A mail strike starts on the 7th September.

No outward news. Just inward. I felt sharply homesick for your paintings.

I came across a short poem (not very good, I thought) written about one of Dick Diebenkorn's paintings.

Here it is, for your interest.

'Ingleside, 1963'. Adrian Henri

'Look through the Supermarket window / up the highway
the hill rises steeply / hoardings and magnolias bright
in the sunlight / white walls black freeways traffic-signs
at intersections / green lawns dark hedges / colours
clear and bright as packets in your wire basket.'

That's all. I really don't think much of the poem but maybe I'm dumb. I'm interested in writing about paintings, though, as they're great inspirers. Also, it's easy to write rubbish, a catalogue.

In my last note I mentioned the possibility of having an operation. I don't think this is likely now, so I'm sorry I mentioned it. I don't know yet, though, till next week.

Just thinking of you, and thinking of you, and waiting till I can say in the flesh Hello Bill Hello Paul Hello Ned Hello Schubert (who is woven with morning light).

Love to the Bee, the Pee, the 'En,
    from the Jay
who was born that way
and lives in hope
the casement to ope

upon the mountains where the lions play
till
dusk
all golden and their light is shed
on
Bill
Paul
Ned
Jay
a dream away.

    Geometrical Love from Jay

100. Dunedin September 9

Dear live lively oaks B.P.N. (I'm sure Ned would object to being called a live oak.)

    That was a lovely present, B. It came this morning and your letter came yesterday. Lucas (who's asleep at the moment on soft white pseudo-mama) was also overjoyed and tried to claw the letter from my hands and was very excited while I was unwrapping the records. I had forgotten how much of oneself is communicated to an animal, how characteristics that one has but conceals are expressed openly in the accompanying cat—the 'familiar'. Lucas licked the photo of Paul and the little kitten—what a lovely kitten—but where's Paul's head ('never will we know his fabulous head where the eye's apple slowly ripens'). And what tiny ear-folds (the kitten, not Paul). Lucas has huge ears; and back feet like a kangaroo; and a pointed face—I think he must have Siamese relatives, and he's very much like a panther as he spends a lot of time crawling and slinking away up on the bookshelf and the backs of chairs. Kittenhood, also, seems to be a wonderful trip. Lucas now has another mama—my dressing-gown, and he purrs hysterically and plays the piano and nuzzles whenever he touches the dressing-gown. When I got up the other morning I found 'Lay your sleeping head my love human on my faithless arm' torn from the book and lying on the floor. Penguin Book of English Verse. What taste in one so young!

I learned yesterday that I shall only have to go into hospital overnight for a test. These medical people are forever scaring me! I shall take Lucas overnight to the vet whose name is Mr Aberdeen (he's nearer and cheaper than Mr Twaddle or doctor T). I hear that he's very good with animals. He even dresses like one.

I did like hearing about the lunch and the bathing—what bliss. And you will say hello to Ann for me? I don't say Felix because I don't know him and was a little scared of him that night when he came to dinner.

Back in Dunedin (which used to be Wax-Eye City—what a year's history is being written in my letters!) I see no-one, go nowhere, and though it's not my practice to tell people the day of my birthday I told it to you because there is no sharing of it with anyone here. Still, I share it with Christopher Isherwood? Also with Saint Augustine, Goethe and Tolstoy . . . among numerous others. It's difficult to know what star and sign I am because everything applies to the Northern Hemisphere. Here, August is Spring and corresponds with northern March.

Down among the daffodils, my daffodils are out, and my paper-white narcissi, and my forsythia, and the orange blossom which has a heavenly smell is putting forth its leaves and the primroses are still numerous, even with Lucas having one for breakfast now and again.

The woman in New York who offered to provide for me would do so, I think, as a patron of the arts. Her father was a publisher and when she herself worked in publishing, though she did not have to work for a living, she used to give many grants to authors from her own and the publisher's pocket. I think it is wise to take money, though, only if it is impersonally part of a foundation which this woman may perhaps establish. I don't know. Ici repose . . .

Snow on the hills today.

THE NEXT DAY.

Early morning. Sun. Lucas is drunk from eating his breakfast primrose. I will not believe that cats do not know colour. His favourite colours are white, black, purple and red. I find his company exceedingly refreshing as he hides nothing and is not ashamed of any of his feelings. I think that when I fly away from here some time my sister will take him—oh oh what heartstrings one has, always being tuned.

******** Stars.

Work as usual. The sun is coming south and now shines in the sitting-room in the evening. I write, read—poems and dictionaries. I bought myself Ulysses for my birthday. And a bundle of Penguin poets. Recently the BBC had a programme in which it used verse which had been rejected by the little poetry magazines.

> Here is just one example from the programme:
> Wolfgang Mozart surpassed all others
> And deserves a fuller account of his fame.
> In six weeks he wrote his three brilliant symphonies
> B flat, G minor and C are their names."
> The programme is to conclude with a mass rendering of " Excelsior."

****

I have very little to say this morning, only that I am thinking and thinking of you all over there and if I were with you I would just be silent and happy. I'll go to post this now, with butterflies to eat the moths that eat B's surcingles and P's cap-pompom, and lots of invisible love.

101. Dunedin September

Dear Bill, Paul, Ned (your full names today),

Just a short hello letter before I walk into town as there's a bus strike. It's raining. Lucas is asleep on my knee. (I hope. Otherwise he will skate across the desk and eat all the typescripts he can find, tearing them into small pieces. He makes 'lace' of the toilet paper too, like the mice at MacDowell.)

Your painting that used to hang on the wall of Paul's room is particularly beautiful this morning, B, as there's a soft grey in the sky, with hints of thunder-blue beyond, and these are echoed in the painting so that it looks more mysterious and the blues and greys are colours in a dream. Did I tell you that my favourite is the man on the extreme left (left, facing the picture). His pose in some way inspires so much compassion. The others too. But don't let me embarrass you by talking about things I know nothing of. Let me, instead, paste here a picture of your friend

The Executioner

want to work in our modern hygienic Butchery Department.
The hours will be from 8 a.m. to 5 p.m. daily and the gross weekly wage is $38.50.
Apply personally or Phone 85-142 for an appointment with Mr B. K. Blow.

A bedhead to become you

Poor chap.
The rain rains heavily now.
The sky lowers. The blue has disappeared.
★★★★
Here we are wondering how our Prime Minister will deal with a remark made by Ky of South Vietnam on B.B.C. television. Ky is reported as saying he will retire anytime if it suits the country. Holyoake (our Prime Minister) has promised him a cattle ranch . . .
★★★★★   ★★★★★★
Yesterday I went into human society for the first time for months, and I felt lonely for you and Paul, in the midst of Dunedin human society. I

went to Charles Brasch's place for dinner. The Burns Fellow, Ted Middleton was also there and we had a pleasant dinner swallowed with and followed by diluted conversation about publishers here and elsewhere. Charles is reading Mailer's *Armies of the Night* to Ted who is almost blind. If one does not want to join in the conversation at Charles' place one can always gaze at the paintings on the wall. His collection is usually on loan somewhere but last night he had a lovely painting by Frances Hodgkins whom I think you said you didn't know. She's our painting equivalent of Katherine Mansfield and her life followed something of Mansfield's pattern—most of it spent away from New Zealand. She did return to New Zealand, and Dunedin, where she was born but found she could not bear it, so she left permanently to live in England and Europe. The painting on the wall last night looked very much Matisse-inspired. She lived to a great age, though, unlike K.M. and changed and developed her style in her later years. The painting scholarship at the University (equivalent of the Burns Writing Scholarship) is named after her.

End of lecture. I don't make a very good lecturer do I?

★★★

It still rains heavily. Lucas who woke briefly when I stopped typing to paste in Nixon's picture, and almost decided to eat the paste, but thought better of it, is fast asleep again. He's very useful as a hand, foot, and lap-warmer.

★★★★★★★

I have again had courage to study the forms for application to live indefinitely in the United States. I am getting out all kinds of credentials (if one is a scientist or worker in the arts one has to prove one is worthwhile) to try to prove I can write. It's an awful miscellany. It includes a letter from the Mark Twain Society making me *A Daughter of Mark Twain*. (I thought the U.S. ambassador might have heard of Mark Twain.)

Every time I venture into human society here it is clear to me that I do not belong here and I am not happy here, though I do not necessarily seek happiness. Pain (nights in the gardens of) is pretty fruitful. I cannot be myself here, as I have found that I can be, when I am away from N.Z.

★★★★★★

Pause for joke. What joke?

★★★★★★★

Now I will away. I hope your work Bill and Paul, the glossy live oaks, is going well. Mine has reached rock bottom and I found out partly why when I was sorting my papers yesterday and came across the raw original of *Intensive Care*, pages and pages and pages. I don't know how I endured such agony or how I deceived myself into continuing it; the memory of the agony quite swamped me. Isn't it crazy? I haven't needed such a long recovery before.

★★★★

Pause for thought and love barrage to make its way from here across the Pacific.

And hello and goodbye and concentrated love from

to B.
apis mellifica   P   N.
                       his black   his white.

J.

DEAR CUSTOMERS AND COLLEAGUES
CONGRATULATIONS!
YOU AND YOUR ENTIRE HOUSEHOLD
HAVE BEEN SELECTED TO RECEIVE
AN ALL COTTON
SEED PEARL
BELOW KNEE
PANTY.

WE, FORMERLY AND STILL OCCASIONALLY OF *PEEDAUN-TALS ANTIPODEAN INC.*, ARE GIVING AWAY A LIMITED NUMBER OF THESE SEED PEARL PANTIES. YOUR HOUSEHOLD HAS BEEN SELECTED AT RANDOM.

YOU PAY ONLY FOR INITIAL SHAPING, STYLING AND FITTING. WE MUST CHARGE FOR THIS AS WE WANT TO BE SURE YOUR SEED PEARL BELOW KNEE ALL COTTON PANTY LOOKS ITS VERY BEST.

CONGRATULATIONS.

WE ARE STILL MANUFACTURERS OF THE FINEST PEEDAUNTALS IN THE SOUTHERN HEMISPHERE. WE ALSO MANUFACTURE AND PROCESS MORAL FIBRE INTO THE MOST ENCHANTING GARMENTS AND UPHOLSTERY.

A SPECIAL CATALOGUE IS AVAILABLE ON REQUEST.

OUR REPRESENTATIVE HOPES TO CALL ON YOU IN A FEW MONTHS' TIME. PERHAPS BEFORE. WHO KNOWS.

AGAIN CONGRATULATIONS.

YOURS, *PEEDAUNTALS INC.*

Opera Group Benefits

WHILE NOT DESIRING TO BOAST OF OUR PRODUCT WE DRAW ATTENTION TO THE ACCOMPANYING HEADLINE WHICH DEALS WITH THE USE BY THE OPERA GROUP OF OUR (NOW UP-DATED) SPECIAL CAPACITY PEEDAUNTAL.

SOCIAL TIT-BITS

Plant may move to Australia A CARNIVOROUS PLANT, THE WELL-KNOWN RELATIVE OF A CERTAIN STEINWAY, DEPUTY MANAGER OF PEEDAUNTALS LTD, INC, OC, THAT ENTRANCING PLANT ABOUT-TOWN TOLD OUR SPECIAL GARDEN CORRESPONDENT OF POSSIBLE PLANS TO MOVE TO AUSTRALIA. 'IT'S ONLY A THOUGHT,' HE SAID. 'I WOULD STARVE DOWN UNDER. CARNIVOROUSLY SPEAKING, OUR SPECIAL CORRESPONDENT WHO GAVE US THE NOTES OF THE FOREGOING CONVERSATION IS OF COURSE NOT AVAILABLE FOR COMMENT.

READERS MAY CARE TO ATTEND THE MEMORIAL SERVICE THIS FRIDAY.

★   ★   ★   ★   ★

~~Very Special~~ Love

TO   B. ⁃ P. ⩒ N.

from.

J.

PEEPAINTACS INC
(THIS IS NOT AN ADVERTISEMENT)

.: Permanent, textured protection. Durable, decorative, guaranteed!

The permanent answer to dampness problems. Effective for a lifetime! We can install!

HIRE that Tool from Dunedin Hire Service, Crawford Street. Phone 76-279.

Just Another Service Available to our Clients.

---

102. Dunedin September

Capital City gives party for Cats.

BY NORMA KATZ

BOTH the Mayor of Wellington (Sir Francis Kitts) and the Chief Justice Sir Richard Wild) mentioned the gaiety emanating from the Town Hall

Dear B, P, N,

> Under the live-oak tree
> with thee and thee and thee
> stifling our merry utter*
> with lashings of peanut butter.

[footnote: *an anatomical term of uncertain meaning]

Hello again, on a wet Friday, a day when cats keep to their counterpanes and people carry umbrellas and bow their heads before the rain and blackbirds who need rain to sing, sing, as one is doing now in the garden across the street. A furious wind came last night, a dark grey cloud shaped like a plate hung in the sky, and my house rocked and shook, and some miles inland roofs were blown away.

So much for the weather. Rereading the above paragraph I realise that 'counterpane' is a literary word which I never use in 'real life' but which always fascinated me since I first met it as a child. I look up my dictionary now and find that 'counterpane' was originally 'counterpoint'. Cats, therefore keep to their counterpoints and I keep to mine, for I've been playing the records you sent, B, and replaying as I do when I feel dismal, the tapes of the poems, the Beethoven Bagatelles, the Hindemith, and that wonderful interview with Dame Mary Margaret who was your guest at that time, I believe. What a forthright body is Dame Mary Margaret. To mention the original Dame M.M. who used to broadcast to Egypt, I'm glad that I invented names for these people because now if I ever think of them, and that is seldom, I remember them by the names I gave them, not by their real names. Except that one day, unexpectedly, on a bus here I saw 'Julie' whose real name was 'Dolly'. That was the day I went to Browns and tried out their funny old pianos.

How is Steinway? Ah, Steinway!

Lucas is growing up fast. He still finds it difficult to keep control of his foot when he is washing in the leg-in-the-air position, therefore he prefers to anchor himself in my lap at this time. He has made friends with kitty-next-door who used to come to see me and I almost heard him say, See you tomorrow, when he came in last night after playing wildly in the high wind. I think he's finding me a very unsatisfactory cat and his puzzlement increases as he tries to place me where he thinks I belong. I'm mama, but a terribly against-the-grain mama as I don't always wear fur and my head is an enormous distance from my feet and a ghastly sound like a lavatory being flushed comes out of my mouth, a sound I think is a laugh . . . As for smell . . . And how are the kittens? Lucas said to tell Ned that he may call him Luke, if he wishes. I don't know what this is a prelude to. And that he's having his photo taken on the first sunny day which he hopes is tomorrow because what can a cat do in the rain but sleep while the Big Cat with the Jay within potters around writing and listening to records.

★★★★   ★★★★★★★★

Stars rising and setting on the horizons (do they) of the Northern and Southern hemispheres.

This is all of my letter. Don't mind my silly letters. I have suffered from nostalgia since I was three years old, and stood alone looking at my first green-weeded swamp and grey uninhabited sky. Nostalgia is a possession one doesn't really want to part with; or perhaps I am not calling it by the right name; I don't know; I don't think I am; it is not nostalgia, it is just a large helping of vivid imagery served with pleasure-pain. Very tasty.

Now I'm going to the Chief Post Office to post this, and afterwards walk through the wet (very) town; so here's a helping of love

Oh! I think I'll stop these sketches. Ugh.

Jay

103. Dunedin September 14

Dear Ned and your two dear big cats,
            How are you all?
              Preparing for fall?

Hastily I must tell you that I have no intention of becoming a literary cat unless I break entirely new ground, as there are so many literary cats, as I learn from consulting my Dictionary of Cat Lovers. I learn also that there is a disconcerting tendency for these cats to refer to their 'master' when they take pen in paw. You and I, Ned, are more honest in our assessment of our relationships with our Big Cats. For instance, when I first came to live here I was given quite a cosy box to sleep in and something soft to sleep on. Temporarily only, you may be sure. I now occupy the rear apartment of the house—spare bedroom and sittingroom with my lavatory in the kitchen at night and on the balcony in the daytime. (I have discovered the Garden now.) Jay occupies the front apartment-bedroom and study-sittingroom. We both roam freely from room to room. A cat should occupy nothing less than an apartment don't you think? At night I sleep on the spare bed, on a white woollen stole which makes my heart ache and my paws paw, I don't know why, but I seize the tassels in my mouth and purr and purr and paw and paw, and feel sleepy and sweet and very sad and happy. Jay says that I must have been snatched untimely from my mama's breast. And I think I was. Barely seven weeks is too young for a kitten to be taken all alone to a pet shop and put in a cage in the window. It seems so long ago now, that dreadful morning, when from among my brothers and sisters and my mama I was taken so suddenly. We were all snuggled (I was on top because I'm the toppest) and mama (bless her) had just bitten me gently on the leg because I was squashing silly little sister who was rather feeble, and one brother had just put his foot right in my eye and I was getting ready to retaliate when it happened: The huge man-Cat took me. I won't dwell on this, only to say how thankful I am that it is all over.

Self-portrait of me, with my chin on shawl-mama.

I could not stop shaking for fear and when I walked my back legs wobbled and shook and I kept falling over. You may be sure it's nothing like that now! I'm pretty smart, you know. Much smarter than Big Cat Jay who can't even play hide and seek in the grass, as I can. Until I find another cat to play with (I have my eye on the lady next door) I'll just have to be content with Cat Jay.

I follow her around everywhere and I know how to get to her heart. When she is busy and I am too boisterous and she goes to one of the rooms and shuts the door I do not meow outside, wanting to get in. I did this at first but I've become more sophisticated and subtle in my behaviour. Now I do not complain at all. I go quietly to my shawl-mama and cuddle her, and later when Jay is finished what she calls work, and comes to look at me, I put that heart-rending (Gaze No. 1.) gaze on my face and she says she is so sorry, oh so sorry . . . You of course will have had a long education in *Gazes*. Yesterday I learned the *Inscrutable Gaze*. I'm dying to use it again. I was delighted at its effect on Jay. It's the kind of gaze, isn't it, that these big cats interpret according to their mood. Jay put a 'What-have-I-done-why-are-you-contemptuous-of-me look on her face. You know the game, Ned. How many I.Q. points does a cat score for bringing about that result with the *Inscrutable Gaze*. Before a kitten learns the Inscrutable Gaze it has to learn the You-Have-Betrayed-Me Gaze. Most of us learn that quite early, I should think. I put it on when Jay took me for the second visit to the Vet and he jabbed me and made me squeal. I almost put on the Things-Will-never-be-the-same-between-us Gaze but I reserve that for something more disastrous. I'm not sure what gaze I will put on next week, for Jay does not know I know, but she is taking me for a couple of days to *live* at the vet's. Fancy. *Me* in a boarding-house! I don't think I shall be very frightened. Yet, clearly, I can't decide beforehand what gaze I am going to wear

a. when Jay leaves me there.
b. when Jay comes to fetch me.

Well Ned, there's not much more news I can give you. A day of smells yesterday. I smelt a rat, I think, and chased it but it was only a handful of dust. I took a book from the bookshelf the other day—seizing it between my teeth, and carrying it to one of my chairs. You ought to have seen Jay's face! She was thinking, What an extraordinary kitten! The name of the book was *Blow Wind of Fruitfulness*. Next I chose John Milton's poems—not the volume with the tasty binding, but another volume she has. How delighted and amused she was, never dreaming that I was only trying to humour her, to cheer her up as she was feeling lonely for you and your two big cats. She's very fond of the two big cats you keep. Where did you get them? At the petshop? Or were they strays? Jay got me at the pet-shop but I don't know who got her. No doubt her back legs were as wobbly as mine.

I am studying Cat History. Here are the names of the cats owned by Chang T'Uan in 1100: Eastern Guard, White Phoenix, Purple Flower,

Expelling Vexation, Brocade Belt, Picture of Clouds, A Myriad of Strings of 1,000 Each. What do you think of these as names for cats? I like the last one.

self-portrait, asleep.

Now I will finish this letter. I have asked Jay if there is any news for you and she has answered that I've probably told you all the news she has. She sends very much love in a basket (my favourites are baskets) and she says you can chew it and chew it and chew the basket as well and share it with the two big cats and she says for you, Ned, to look after them, and see that they get their Petromalt and everything else they need, and for B to look after his surcingles as they are rare, and for P to see that no-one steals his pompom. There was some talk, recently, of your sailing here to visit us. I think it was a fantasy.

LATER:
Jay and I have just had the letter from Big Cat B. She and I struggled to see who would open it and though I'm an expert struggler, she won. By the way I still have the envelope of the letter you wrote me, Ned. I keep it in my toy-basket where I also have a clothes peg, a handkerchief, a chocolate wrapper, a cotton reel, a plastic spoon and cup, a glove, an egg carton. I guard this basket very carefully and whenever I see Jay approach it I rush to her and stand on guard. It is sacred to me. The only time I allow her to touch it is when I climb along the backs of the chairs (*my* chairs) and up to the high book shelf and along the bookshelf to the end. Then I meow to Jay to fetch me something to carry. Usually she fetches a glove, puts it on the shelf, whereupon I seize it and carry it on the perilous journey to the floor where I hide it. This also seems to amuse the poor big cat.

Just now she read the letter from Cat B and was so delighted and happy to get it and read it. She said she loved the story of the trip to Hawaii. She said she has seen this programme on American tv. She remembers the portrait in the blue bath robe and she wishes that she could be there with you, to see all your new paintings and have them as daily bread though I'd rather, myself, have cat food. When she told me about Fred's kittens at the malted milk bar I felt very envious. I suppose the little dears haven't learned any gazes yet, except the Hazy Gaze and the Wonderment Gaze (guaranteed to bring all big cats to their knees around continent mama and peninsula kitties).

Back to your visitors. They sounded wonderful fun, and no doubt you laughed too, Ned. Jay is crazy about mimics. The best she knows or knew was Philip Roth who was always mimicking. And hiking along a canyon stream! That sounds idyllic. Jay says, about Gardening as a profession, it attracts some interesting characters. Frank Sargeson used to work a. as a milkman, when he had *tall* tales of women coming to the door with their dressing gowns purposefully open in the early morning breeze;

b. as a gardener when he also had a fund of tales. Unfortunately J can't remember any of the tales he told.

******

Jay says that someone has made a play from *State of Siege* and is reading it this evening and has invited her to hear it. She says, Hell No.

Apart from that she is leading a quiet life as befits her ginger station. She has had a letter from Charles Neider who is at MacDowell for a while. He says there is Nobody, but *Nobody* at MacDowell (except Louise Varese). Jay says of course if there is no W.T.B there is nobody at Mac-Dowell or anywhere. Charles N says he is keeping physically fit, ready for the Antarctic—so we know what that means don't we? In the swim at the Y.M. jogging etc. etc.

****

Jay is finally doing something about that tape she has half-done. She's going to record my purr for you, Ned, and you can charge admission to the big cats if they want to hear it, and in that way you can earn enough to buy an airticket instead of coming to visit me and being dehydrated in the tropics.

Love to you and to Fred and her lot, and Jay of course is rushing to get another parcel of love to the two big cats. They must have been with her in the same pet shop, she's so fond of them.

So goodbye. I think it might be familiar if you called me Luke. What is your opinion?

Goodbye again. And whoops—love—though you understand I reserve much of it for my shawl-mama but Jay said, quote, True love in this differs from gold or clay / that to divide is not to take away ha ha you're telling me. Blow wind of fruitfulness ha ha.

    ARTIST LUCAS   PORTRAITS PAINTED ANY DAY

The mail strike was settled—incredibly—by the interviewer in a TV programme. He confronted the Govt. rep plus the P.O. representative & brought about a reconciliation. Govt. now by TV, which I have not & am therefore ungoverned & ungovernable.

    Love

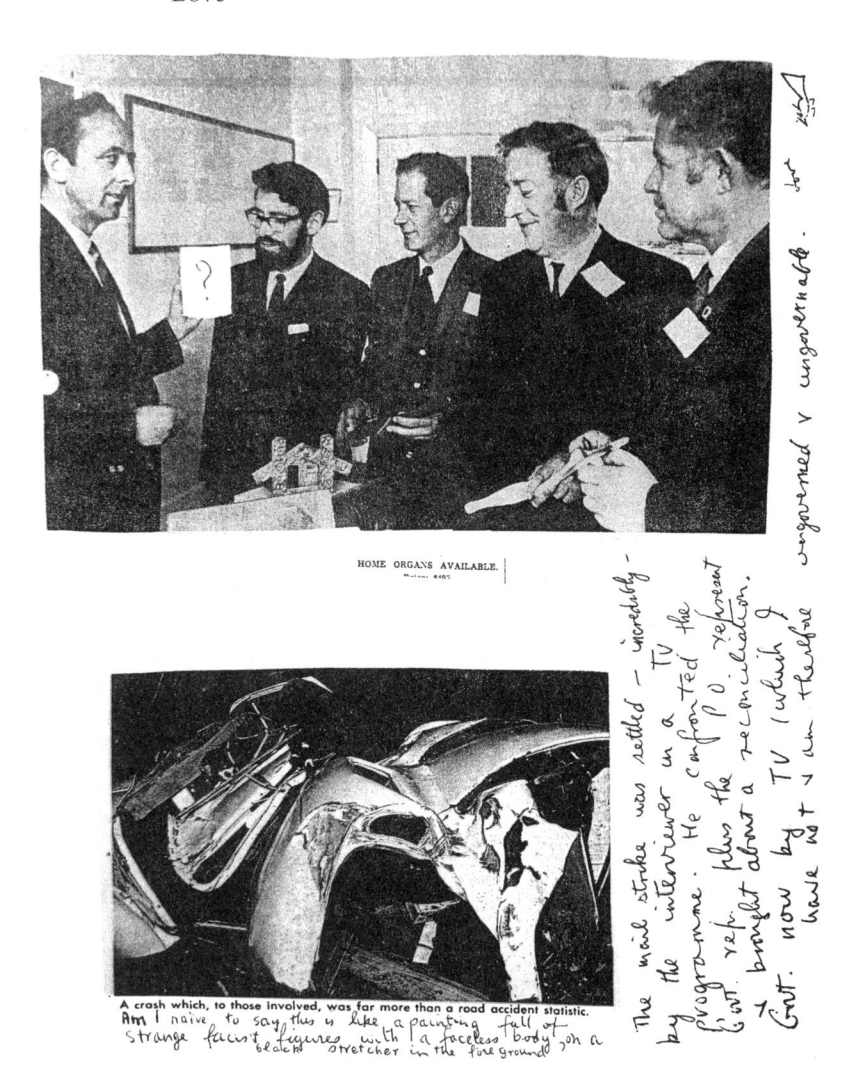

HOME ORGANS AVAILABLE.

A crash which, to those involved, was far more than a road accident statistic.

Am I naive to say this is like a painting full of strange fascist figures with a faceless body on a black stretcher in the fore ground?

NEW ZEALAND: MARCH 1970 TO JANUARY 1971 | 303

104. Dunedin September

Dear B and P and N,

I had a letter from the State Department yesterday and I'm enclosing my reply to a certain J.J. Smith. Perhaps one of you could send it on for me? Very many thanks. I'm sending a photo of Lucas too, to influence him. This was Lucas' idea.

It has been sour weather here—wind and rain and quite cold (temperature in fifties). Lucas has taken over nearly all the rooms of the house and to eat my meals I escape to my study but that is not sacred either and as I type this Lucas is locked asleep on my knee. If anyone comes to visit me I shall have to say, Wear shields on your legs and elsewhere or Lucas will get you. He's quite a silent kitten. He has three meows, so far. One is very small and broken and hardly used. It is, Let me In. It's hardly used because he's always in. The next is, Play with me and Come Outside and Play with Me. The third is when he uses his pan inside, and means, with its note of perplexity, I thought I was going to pee but I'm shitting instead. Oh my!

**** ****

The other evening, though I had resolved not to go to a reading of a play made out of *State of Siege*, I did go. It was held at the home of the proposed producer who's also a tv producer. There were just he and his wife and Rosalie Carey who has adapted the book or part of it and who with her husband Patric runs the Globe Theatre here. I felt quite detached from the book as I haven't read it for years, and I was interested in the new experience of seeing it, as it were, snatched from me. I didn't realise the dismay I would feel but did not show at my work's being 'reduced'. I thought it was very well adapted though, and it was both moving and comic and revealed to me so many of the book's faults. The producer was enthusiastic and declared he 'must read the book'—for neither he nor his wife had read it. I was surprised to find that I joined in the discussion and criticism and (I thought) had a few pertinent things to say. I enjoyed it, and thought (such is my impressionability always) that I might do O.K. after all as a teacher in a small group. One might evaluate this fantasy in its proper setting if one knows that even when I read *Kon-Tiki*, I almost decided that I would build a raft and sail the seven seas. Seriously.

Oh how I miss my Live Oaks, when I am alone here and, sharply, in a different way, when I go among people who seem so much part-people. The younger generation here are less part-people, I feel, yet there's a constriction in their being and living. At the home of these two young bright people the other evening I had the feeling their lives were growing in a kind of sunken garden and they'd never see what was beyond it—but if I'm to make the metaphor work for its living I might say their roots could find a way out, even without their knowing.

Well, I'm getting involved. (I'll say less a sunken garden than a garden-in-a-barrel. Or a disused well.)

I had a nice letter from Jo—oh it's impossible to keep typing this letter as Lucas is Loose on the desk. He's quite crazy and he's skating on all the papers. He's discovered skating—putting his feet in my shoes and flying across the room. He really does snatch letters from my hand and runs away with them.

I suppose you're back at School now Paul. I wonder how it is? and Frederika and her brood, litter, lot or what?

More later but I'll mail this now. Big Love to my live oaks.

from

Jay.

+ + + + +

To
J. J. Smith
Immigration Dept.
Wishington.

Dear J. J.,

Yours inst. ult. etc. to hand, in hand. Thank you for your epistle and for the test. I wish that you had sent me a duplicate test so that if I make mistakes with the first copy I may return an unblemished second one. Most embassies send three or four testes to be dealt with. Here in this small country where the Prime Minister boasts he has scarcely read a book we are not used to dealing with testes, therefore there may be some delay in my sending the completed form. Bare with me, please.

My guest at the moment, Mr. Lucas Burch, insists that the Queen pictured in your test is the cat next door and none of the listed people. He tells me that the post received by Madeline Shaw was a scratching post.

There's a question of colour. I am Blue—it does not appear in the photograph I enclosed with my application. I believe, however, that the Blue disappears when one sets foot on U.S. soil.

I confess the test is very fiddicult, I mean difficult. One solution is influence in low places. My guest Mr. Lucas Burch has asked me to enclose his photograph and to say that he would like to meet you. He is ten weeks old, white, and very active. He has green eyes. He is looking for a penfriend in the State Department and he hopes that after you and he have corresponded for a while you will arrange this meeting. He is house-trained. Are you? (His question, not mine.)

Hoping to return the test unblemished and correct, I remain, my dear J.J. hoping this finds you as it leaves me, and believe me to be when very often I don't believe it myself,

yours, with yours in hand,

105. Dunedin September

Hi you lovely cats and bees and plants, this is Lucas here, here's my news written all in order,

《 a. House 》

Nothing much to tell. I met the Vacuum Cleaner last week, and fled and nearly died of fright and Ginger Cat-Blue Jay had to give me a hot water bag ha ha and cuddle me to stop me from shivering and I insisted on inspecting the house, *my* house, *entire*, furniture by furniture, my sniffing working overtime. I haven't yet solved the problem of what it was that made the terrifying noise.

⟨ b. Garden ⟩

Spend a good deal of time there lately. Can climb two trees but wish Jay would hang around to see me and congratulate me, and I wish she would chase me through the grass. Play chasey with the next-door cat and enjoy myself immensely but he/she's bigger 'n me. Hope to find a rat or mouse this week but so far no hope. Smell all the flowers—great perfume those daffodils have. Still like to suck at mama's tassels for comfort.

⟨ Personalities ⟩

A woman called the other afternoon, a poet friend of Jay's. She admired me, saying, –He's a bright kitten.

I played around to show her how bright I was. She was hoping I would climb into her lap—you know what people are, always wanting to be flattered by us animals—flattered, reassured and so on—well I think I failed my first social test because I didn't climb in her lap, I was just a little apprehensive. I went to sleep in Jay's lap, which I like to do, getting into all kinds of weird relaxed postures, making a long kitten (I believe, Ned, you're expert at the Long Cat—I've seen drawings of you by that famous artist you board at your house, and I've seen a picture of you sailing to New Zealand, painted by your other star boarder. I'm thinking of taking in boarders myself, if things get tough—I can put Jay down in the basement, she can sleep on the coal, and I'll let the front apartment. I must of course have my own apartment as I have now. I employ Jay to clean it.) No other personalities. Jay seems to be busy. She's trying to write but this week there's a bit on her mind as she's going into hospital overnight. Nothing serious. She'll be home the next day, fitter than a fiddle. I know she doesn't like leaving me at Mr Aberdeen's but she's heard he's very good with animals and he did take a fancy to me when he inoculated (how do you spell that word???) me. He sure treated me like one of the gang. I think Jay thinks I'll be corrupted; but it has to come some time hasn't it, Ned old boy? She's giving me all kinds of lectures about not accepting lifts in automobiles from strangers, about not accepting sweets and so on; nor pieces of fresh beef or mutton. You'll see, however, by the enclosed headlines that I've already become something of a character in this country.

⟨ Work ⟩

Who said Work? Jay makes a pretence of working but her characters have suddenly thinned out, like diarrhoea (you mentioned it Paul Cat), no substance at all, oh hell she says; and she is anxious to get out of New Zealand as it is crippling her, she thinks, to be here, she's noticed herself going downhill. She's grown fond of me, you know, and her sister phoned and said *their* cat Tinkerbell who's a few months older than I is *dying* to meet me and so when Jay leaves Dunedin I'm travelling with her to Auckland. I'm a keen traveller already. I told you how I travelled with Jay on the bus—it's forbidden but I was as quiet as—you know what.

⟨ Play ⟩

I do it all day, when I'm not asleep. Jay's a bit short of play, I can tell.

⟨ Mice ⟩

None.

⟨ Music ⟩

I ran from the room when I first heard Bach but now I stay and listen. Unfortunately I can't get at the record player. Jay has had to arrange in special places all that furniture which must not be got at. I think I must be the *cunningest* kitten in Catdom.

⟨ Literature ⟩

I like to choose a book from the shelf at the close of my boisterous play. I chose *A Room of One's Own* the other evening. (It's slim enough to carry in my mouth.) I tried to take hold of *Boys and Girls Who Became Famous*, but I couldn't manage it. That is a book Jay has had for ages—she got it as a prize when she was young and it sure gave her a false idea of Fred Chopin and Mozart and Marie Antoinette.

⟨ Art ⟩

Jay showed me a lovely drawing—I forget the artist's name—called *A Plan of Kittens*, showing the exact geometrical plan of kittens feeding and sleeping and so on. *Very delightful.* Your Fred (hope I don't sound too familiar) might be interested. I haven't been to my Bottom of the Class in Art Studio recently. I declare I'll have to get Vocational Guidance. I don't know *what* to be when I grow up. All I can think of now is being a *tomcat*. Wow! Did you find it so hard to decide, Ned? And did your two lovely big cats have any trouble? Jay says I'll have to go through *stages*.

⟨ Weather ⟩

Frosty. Cold. Jay uses me as a handwarmer. I told her she can hire me and hire me out as a white furry handwarmer, and then I'll save for my fare to U.S., charter my own plane, I think.

⟨ Time ⟩

Lost and regained. Time now to mail this letter. Jay's unloading boxes of love to you and your two big prowling painting cats and their plants and Steinway, and I'm sending my love too, and deference of course as to an older cat who could, if he were here, teach me the tricks of a lifetime.

    Yours & Yours & Yours & Yours & Yours
        L.B.   &   Jay

Lucas
Guilty Of Murder

106. Dunedin September 24

Prized Bee

Dear B and P and N,
    Hello, Hi from faraway J who opens transmission with her usual cry,

Bee I'm missing you!
Was saying yesterday
to Somebody you all know
(Lucas) a visit was due.

What happened last week?
I suppose Paul's settled and at work,
you too, stretched on the rack.
— I've run out of ideas for what's warm and thick.

Sweaters are, of course.
And cat's fur; and my
thoughts of the Live Oaks across
Pacific sea, under Pacific sky.

You'll get my letter by
next week.
Blue Jay has this to say:
She's pretty homesick.

    ★★★★★★★★★★★

Hi again, after that first spurt from the old typewriter. Would you believe it, it's snowing! This is the second snowfall I've seen down in the city since I've lived in Dunedin. It's a rare thing, and the time is out of season and it makes me homesick for North American snow. How differently it is falling here! It is in such a hurry, rushing down as if this were the only chance it had, and perhaps it is, whereas in North America the snow takes its time, is leisurely, drifts down. It is so business-like about its being here, possibly because it has so little time and will be gone tomorrow whereas North American snow has all the time in the world.

    Yesterday I took Lucas to Dr Aberdeen's for four days (cost two dollars). Oh heartbreak, heartbreak! He'll never forgive me, I'm sure.

He's getting big enough to *demonstrate* now and he wasn't so happy about going in a bag though he was quiet on the bus (where travelling with animals is forbidden) and all the gloved and hatted ladies who were on the bus little dreamed that I was carrying a kitten-in-a-bag, and not my weekly groceries: though he felt so warm, like a little hot pie being carried. I hadn't realised how much he has taken possession of the house and I felt absolute agony, perhaps unwarranted, at the thought of how he would feel, deprived of all the freedom he has here. I hope they pet him some. He is so happy here, so full of delight. He knows all the hiding-places, all the scratching-places. If he is denied something he goes on a wilful bout of destruction which usually includes tearing the pictures from the walls—yes! I hear bang crash from the sittingroom if I happen to have deprived Lucas of some attention or refused to play with him. I don't know how much cats feel the agonies that human beings feel—maybe more so. He's made friends with the kitty next door who's maybe about six months old, and they play together in Lucas' garden, and last evening after I had taken Lucas away and I was downstairs hanging out some washing, little Kitty next door came to see me, meowing plaintively. He was saying, —Hey, where's Luke? Isn't Luke coming out to play? They play such a lot together and then they just sit looking at each other for ages and ages, no doubt conversing.

He wakes me every morning at half-past six by springing on the bed and buffeting my fuzzy head with his paw; and from then on the day, for me, is just a succession of surrenderings.

I'm quite enjoying my return to pre-Lucas days!

Tonight I go into hospital to stay overnight and if I'm well enough I'll come home that day, or the next and then I'll hasten to collect Lucas Burch. I assure you dear people that my health is very rude, so rude it's unmentionable . . . I'm only having tests which are unlikely to be taken further as my health is as before mentioned, obscene. It is just something that was recommended by the doctor I saw in Baltimore, and I put it off until I arrived here, and then I put it off until I started getting ready to leave here!

I'm taking Short Novels of the Masters to read and will reread Death in Venice.

Apart from above I haven't done anything been anywhere seen anyone.

All my daffodils are out, and as my garden is bewitched, vegetables are springing up though I've never planted them, and the former tenants didn't plant them, but every year from the time I first planted a garden of vegetables they have sprung as if eternally. I have carrots, parsnips, silver beet, spinach, parsley and a variety of herbs the names of which I don't know. And of course the cabbages! (Jo is amused by the cabbages!) They are now in yellow flower, quite astonished at my policy of laissez-faire.

Did I tell you that every so often during the day I glance at the clock and translate N.Z. time to Los Angeles time? Then I visit you.

It's a miracle I'm able to type this—Lucas has discovered that the best way to stop me from typing and make me realise it's my duty to play with him, is to come and sit on the typewriter keys and refuse to move. I tried writing with a pen but he kept blotting everything with his paw.

Haven't been in Peedauntal Country recently. Am pretty hungry to be at your place and hear B at the piano.

More when I return home. Plain starched laundered (no ironing) love plus a few of the newer lines of affection,

        (I'm dotty, aren't I?)

        (I'm dotty, aren't I?)

love anyway
beyond my ken
unrestricted free
to Bee and Pee
and their master N.

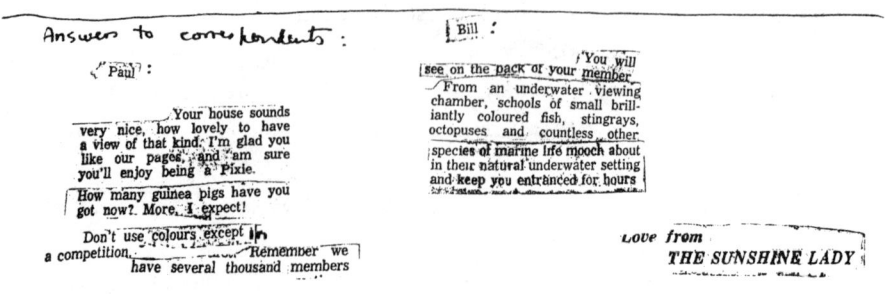

from J.

Answers to correspondents:

"Paul":
...Your house sounds very nice, how lovely to have a view of that kind. I'm glad you like our pages, and am sure you'll enjoy being a Pixie.
How many guinea pigs have you got now? More, I expect!
Don't use colours except in a competition. Remember we have several thousand members...

Bill:
...You will see on the back of your member. From an underwater viewing chamber, schools of small brilliantly coloured fish, stingrays, octopuses and countless other species of marine life mooch about in their natural underwater setting and keep you entranced for hours...

Love from
THE SUNSHINE LADY

107. Dunedin September 28

[handwritten letterhead with drawings: 61 Evans Street, Opoho, Dunedin, Otago, N.Z. 28th Sept.]

Dear dear friends,

This letter will be waiting for you on your return from Santa Fe. I do hope you have a pleasant time there. I remember vividly the conversation about Santa Fe the evening the Haydns came to visit and you (B) showed us your Indian books (I can see them now, on the bookshelf).

The letter from Ned to Lucas and from B to J came at such a nice time & both letters were so full of interesting details of the world-with-you & laying waste your powers—so appropriate to read when I emerged from the anaesthetic! My friend Ruth brought my mail to me & when she arrived I was still encased in my theatre gown and not properly awake.

[handwritten note: 2. Blank page. Dream of Mountain lions]

I spent a couple of nights in hospital & had an anaesthetic trip during which a dark handsome young doctor did what I'll never know, & I blush to guess, to me. I have been pronounced (as I knew already) in rude health & I'm so immensely relieved it's all over. I was so sure I'd die under the anaesthetic. You can't (perhaps you can) imagine how wonderful it was to wake up to a letter full of life from the Lively Oaks.

I went to a private hospital (the Sisters of Compassion) & it was worth the 70 dollars I'll have to pay. The actual hospital cost is 5 dollars a night.

So now I'm writing this from 61 Evans St. sitting on my bed, feeling very cosy, while Lucas plays with my toes under the blanket. I collected him when I came home yesterday & he & I have spent the time since then sleeping the sleep of recovery, while outside it's been snowing & hailing & a wild wind has been rocking the house and wailing between the walls, & in the trees. And each time I've switched on the radio I've heard news of fire in California, the worst emergency since the San Francisco Earthquake . . . nothing will harm the Live Oaks.

I'll now hand the pen to Lucas as my letter writing is less up to scratch than his & I'm still dwelling a little on the curiously lost day & the relief of it's being all over.

Hi Ned & others, namely Bill and Paul. I'm very grateful to you, Ned, for pointing out that the large animals you employ are merely *training* to be cats. I had suspected this but my knowledge of the world is limited and I shall ever be grateful to you for giving me the benefit of your wider deeper (deeper) experience. The final proof was revealed to me when J and I returned after a few days vacation. I guess on my return I must have used up more purr than I've ever used. And do you know there was *not one single purr* from J who was obviously pleased to phone and to be able really to *eat* instead of putting up with delicate-looking non-food.

Actually, J looked sadly at me and said—I wish people could purr.

Well, she's *people* & what they are, I have no idea. You and I have already reached agreement on their shortcomings.

Thanks also, Ned for details of the food trick. It's one I learned quite early & I have to hide my smirking face with my paw when J throws the uneaten food away & produces something more expensive.

When I returned from my vacation I practised now and then, as a torture-reminder, my Abandoned-Loveless-Homeless look (abandoned on the mountains of the heart). It works well on J. She gets all apologetic and says she would never have dreamed of leaving me but an emergency cropped up . . . you know the talk . . . and then . . . cream for tea!

I'm growing up fast, Ned. My friend the grey & white cat next door, a few months older, is teaching me a lot. We plan to go on the prowl one evening.

By the way, I can't see why you think liver's so wonderful. I really mean that I like it but I'm not yet ready to let J know. I like to keep her in suspense. She gives me a dinner of kidney & I rave over it and then the fool buys kidneys to last 3 days. Well, after that first meal, I act as if I despise them; and then it's the paw-over-the-smirking face once again.

This letter is pretty weak & so is J's but we've both recovering & we do want to send our love to you and B and P and Fred & her lot who will probably grow up to be motor mechanics. J says her thoughts are rooted & growing where you are. No comment from your ever more mature tom-cat pen friend

Lucas.

108. Dunedin September 30

Dear Steinway,

Others younger fairer thinner furrier silkier taller less magnificently keyed, polished, but maybe sweeter, in their ways, have had all the attention lately, so now I'm writing this letter to you to tell you, dear Certain, that I have not forgotten you, that I think of you often, and I do want to thank you for sending me the first seven bars of Schubert's B Flat. There was no trouble at all in their transportation and they were received as good as new, as one of your servants plays them. I hope your servant is keeping you well polished and your other servant is vacuuming around your sturdy legs and that you no longer have that recurring dream of being a mere upright. I believe it's a common dream among the Grands. I advise you to count your many blessings, think of your relatives, of Carnie tendrilled and touching, so attentive to you, and of the lesser-toothed two-legged (my arithmetic may be incorrect here) human beings who are your keepers and of him who plays upon you, who fingers you when you might otherwise remain untouched, silent, imprisoned.

Today I believe your servants set out for Santa Fe. I hope you have a marvellous time when they are gone. When they return they'll come rushing to you for comfort, I'm sure.

Well, Steinway, I haven't much news from here of any of your relatives. I think the Marama Hall Steinway in the University is being much played upon and attended to but I fear for the ego of the older Steinway who remains on the platform and is used, I suppose, only when two pianos are needed. All solo performers choose the new. I don't know if I told you that about a year ago I knew a colony of your relatives in the wilds of New Hampshire. One in particular, a library piano was beautifully played upon. Well, Steinway, here is the end of my paltry letter. I hope the time is not too far away when I see and hear you again; otherwise I shall waste away my sturdy legs and polished skin and my teeth or keys will decay.

Give my love to B and P and that cat Ned who tickles your legs with his fur.

Yours,

J.

★★★★★★★★ ★★★★★★★★★★★★ ★★★★

Now, unLucassed, unSteinwayed and UnCarnied, I turn my attention and typewriter to Bill the Pill, Paul the Doll, Ned the Fed, Fred the Wed, and say hello from plain uncluttered Jay who lives a quiet life and is hoping to finish a book some day, some day, now the unpleasant hospital experience is over and the rudeness of her health has been confirmed leaving no doubts.

★★★★

Stars.

The weather has been foul, and cold but gradually, yesterday and today, the sun is beginning to shine and the air to recover its warmth. A frightful storm came up from Antarctica, just to show us, to teach us a lesson not to forget the neighbouring ice. As if we could forget either ice or fire. I've been worried about your sister Paul in San Diego, as the news says the fire has been there—the visible fire. I think of you driving your car through flames and emerging unscathed.

Today I shall walk down to the Gardens Corner to post this. All the blossoms are out, and most are withered now. Two of my lilac bushes have withered in late frosts but the dooryard lilac persists healthily though it will not bloom yet. The lilac elsewhere is in bloom. Cats are also in bloom. I notice that most of the cats in this neighbourhood wear white waist-coats. If Lucas does not have his attention turned to lower things the waistcoats of the new generation of cats will be even whiter.

I think what I appreciate most about Lucas is his capacity for pure delight and wonder at everything, and his enjoyment. You know . . . 'What shall man do who can whistle tunes by heart and know to the bar when death shall cut him short, like the cry of the shearwater?'

I'm inclined to think, though, that animals do know about death, and that they include it in their range of delight and wonder. ????

★★★★★★ ????????

Stars and many question marks.

I missed hearing Hindemith's The Perpetual (lovely title) which was broadcast here from Italian radio.

★★★★★★★★ ????????

More stars. More question marks.

Yesterday I had my first visitor since old grandad Baxter's funeral. It was the young woman* (mid thirties) whose picture I showed you B and P, at home with her children and the calf. I have met her only once before but she was in Dunedin for a few days having a vacation to 'recover' from the death of her little boy, aged two. She sold her novel to the movies and it's being made in California somewhere and when everybody else has whittled off his or her share she will be paid six thousand dollars. Not much really, but it will enable her to buy a house as she and the man whose two children she has are separating. Her other little boy is five. I invited her to lunch and she stayed four hours but it wasn't so bad because the sun shone and we sat outside in the sun, and Lucas in his new role of being a cat-about-town completely ignored her after the first sniff. When she had gone, however, he smelt all over the chair she had sat in, carefully inspected the whole house to make sure she was not concealed anywhere, and when he was satisfied, he behaved

---

★ Jean Watson

as I've come to expect him to behave—he just went crazy with delight or relief or something, just rushing up and down and in and out carrying pieces of paper here and there and hiding them in the toes of my shoes.

    ****

Hot, cold, rare, common, impure, sweet sour love & always-thought
        to   B   P   N   from   J

> Wednesday. — Sandwiches of cheese and peanut butter; buttered date scone; apple.

Answers to correspondents.
Dear B. of California,
My advice is:

> Drop from teaspoon on to foil-covered oven tray. Bake in moderate oven

Dear P. of California,
I am sorry my advice given recently did not work. I can only suggest

> oven. — Return to the

If this does not work,

> beat well.

    *   *   *   *   *   *.

Hot, cold, rare, common, impure, sweet sour love & always-thought
to   *I spy the coast of California*
    B.   P.   N.   *from*   J.

OCTOBER

109. Dunedin October Sunday Morgen

Dear Bee Pee Enn Eff piano and plant and all,
    piano and plant and all.
(Space for illustration of peedauntalled singer; the tune: Tom Pearce, Tom Pearce lend me your grey mare.)
★★★★

    As I write this you'll be returning from the Santa Fe Trail. Refreshed, 'tired but happy' (as we used to write, falsely, at the end of our school essays). Are the fires finished? Will all the mountain lions be dead? And the rattlesnakes that were waiting for me to tame them or be tamed by them? It's hard to imagine the Californian fires—well no it's not, but it's hard to imagine anyone getting out alive from a burning canyon. We have occasional forest fires here, but nothing, I think on the scale of Australia. Australia, like U.S.A., is a continent where fire (not ice) and sun happen on a big scale. We were having ice while you had fire. A rare blizzard raged through Central Otago, killing the lambs and the young apricots, apples, peaches, and everything that gives a livelihood to the people of 'Central', (as we say). (I had an aunt who used to talk, it seemed to me, all the time of 'going up Central' and I used to think it was a ladder she climbed and I used to imagine her climbing it every time she said, I'm going up Central this weekend.

    I loved the photo of the kittens in their *Fragile Phonograph Records Box* —much classier than Lucas' *Bushells Instant Coffee* home. They're very chubby. Lucas (my only comparison) is very thin and long (he probably has worms!) but he's now getting the characteristically round tomcat head. He's out gallivanting with cat next door at the moment. I wish I could persuade him, though, that he doesn't have to have an indoor toilet. He interrupts his play to come inside to use his pan! He must have been boasting about it to cat next door because cat next door came in and used it too! ('My house has all mod cons you know. No peeing in the garden for me!')

    The Hamlet piece is a scream, both the touched-up photos and the additions and deletions in the incredibly inane text. I love your sense of fun and I love having a share of it over the vasty deepy Pacific. We have such inane reporting here but much of it is devoted to the *Queen* and her brood. The Horse Races, being more important here than the theatre, do get the treatment though. I can't speak for the *Underfoot* World (I liked that).

Until the end of September Jo was staying with Joan Colebrook in Truro Mass 02666. She said she had taken a room in Provincetown where, presumably, she was writing, but that she had MacDowell for October and November, if she wanted it, and she was thinking of accepting. Otherwise I don't know where she is. Mark will be at Salem, she said. So, B, you might get to visit MacDowell in the Fall after all and renew acquaintance with Mrs Crocket and Rural Violence. When is your mother's birthday and when are you going to Chicago? Will you wear your black cap to go East? The East is on fire too at this time—I remember the incredible maple-light I lived in.

I keep thinking of the fires. When I reread your letter, B, 'Malibu is still burning after three days' I get the feeling we're in the Middle Ages and a runner has delivered your letter from the Land of the Plague. I find in Pepys, 'as far as we could see up the hill of the city, a most horrible malicious bloody flame, not like the fine flame of an ordinary fire. We saw the fire as only one entire arch of fire from this to the other side of the bridge, and in a bow up the hill for an arch of above a mile long; it made me weep to see it.'

But—It *is* something that, secretly, we desire.

Paul, you'll have started teaching by the time you read this. How is it? How often do you go? I hope it isn't too bad.

★★★★★★★★★★★

Did I tell you that I have decided to be 'loyal' to my old United Kingdom publisher and so have rejected the advances of Macmillan, a bigger firm who does print and publish finer books than my publisher W.H.Allen who churns out royal family sagas of the What-the-Butler-wanted-to-see type? As Macmillan are interested, however, I can always bear them in mind. I have dispensed with my agents now and at the moment have none until I may find one which does not send me enormous accounts for books they buy.

★★★★

Jo, in her letter, said something about a show. B? of P.? Or both? If so, you have my sympathy—you have it anyway—and good wishes—you have more than that, both of you, and I'm pining away for you. Pine pine.

I plan to come to the United States, anyway, maybe next February, or sooner, and even if I and my fifty mountain lions and three rattlesnakes in assorted hatboxes can't move in (don't panic) I'll see you, at least?

In the meantime it is marvellous of you to sustain me with shares of you in letter and thought (both arrive here)—I found a bottle of thought floating in the harbour and it distinctly said, Thought from 131 Hermosillo Drive California. There was no poison label! It said, instead, Drink Me. And I did. And that is why I am full of sustenance until I see you. I am homesick for the most curious things—well I'll say goodbye now and send this letter and love-in-a-bottle stickily flavoured fizzy with preservative (a new kind that does not destroy as it preserves).

to B P N NO DRAWINGS TODAY. *from Jay*

110. Dunedin October 5

Dear B,

I've just had your letter full of news of your wonderful Santa Fe journey and all the enticements of being there and the grimness of California. What will you do? Where will you go? I'd stay in New Zealand if I knew you and Paul were here, but our nasty government won't let American cats in, and now that you and Paul know how to purr, perhaps you won't be let in either. It would be too expensive for you to make a quick visit to see what it's like here. (I think about 1300 dollars economy return now, though an excursion fare of less than a month's stay would be about 600 or 700 dollars.) My house is at your disposal anytime. Do you still think there would be an ironing-room for me in your living quarters? I don't think I'd go for a long stay in America if I thought you and Paul were away some other place, Mongolia or the Moon.

(Pause while I talk on the phone to the young French lecturer who is going back to France next month and is coming up to see me tomorrow afternoon. I shall record her reading of some of Rilke's French poems—if I have the courage to ask her.)

To return to where what etc. I'm pretty homesick for a sight of my live oaks. Will you be at home in February? That's more or less when I'm planning to visit U.S.

(Pause to answer the phone. I never have phone calls in this way, usually. This time it is an invitation to dinner next Friday evening at the home of Wanda and David Hall. He is a retired University lecturer and critic. She had a rather sad life as the daughter of the German professor at Wellington who was so persecuted during the War, for being a German, and dismissed from the University. Civil Liberties Union etc. had a long struggle to get him reinstated. It's one of the nasty blots on N.Z. history. Many German people in New Zealand, through both wars, changed their names or anglicised them. Charles Brasch's father and brother* became *Brash* but Charles refused to change. I suppose I shall go to dinner. Oh I do wish I could see you and Paul, and Ned, and hear you playing the piano once more. Is it a dream?)

To return to where what etc. Yes, I'm planning to visit next February, flying from Auckland to L.A. I'm accepting Sue Marquand's help (confidential but not on her instructions) for a limited time but I shall not need it for many months. She's also offered me a New York apartment—a nice little homey walkup in 53rd Street East Side where her father, a publisher, lived when he was alive. The shelves are lined with his books. I mention this because I don't want you and Paul to panic at the thought of my arriving and staying and staying and staying at your place, though this is what I'd love to do. I believe in facing practical situations, though.

Lucas agrees with me. He now owns three rooms of this house while I own my study and the only reason he has not taken it over is that it was here he first met the Vacuum Cleaner Monster and he's never forgotten it and he displays like a white peacock whenever he enters. He agrees that I am being very reasonable and practical in accepting my one room and leaving him to his devices in the rest of the house. His

---

* Brasch did not have a brother but a sister, Lesley (1911-1939)

collection of envelopes, letters, assorted knitting wools, clothes pegs, table-tennis balls (2) now occupies the whole of the sittingroom floor! He said this morning as he left via the window to play with the cat next door that both he and I are living in peaceful coexistence. If I sometimes get the thought that he's quite a cat now and won't want all these toys to play with when he's got *real cats* he becomes very fierce and possessive.

'Don't you understand?' he says. 'It's the *dream* that matters.'

(Which is much what Ned, curled on the washer-dryer, or making a long cat on the washer-dryer, has in mind.)

I'm looking forward to Paul's watercolour and Joan Tanner's drawing. I wonder where the letter is that started in Paul's left foot? I should think it has stopped in its circulation after this past week of teaching following on the wonderful world of Santa Fe. I've been allaying my homesick condition by playing my records and my tapes. 'Good evening world, this is Splash Down Day. . .' 'Typic heres, foretold locations . . .'

My tape is slow slow slow in making. The last I made was a record of Madame Nijinsky speaking. If I recall rightly I now have Virgil Thomson rubbing ? with Madame Nijinsky and Klemperer and soon, tomorrow, I'll have Dominique Sion (the French Lecturer). With maybe a dash of Frame Clutha.

You might get to visit MacDowell and play the library piano, Bill?

I hope your visit East is not too exhausting. Parents are so terrifyingly unique and the bondage both ways is like the magical weaving performed in folk tales: it doesn't exist but it does exist. When I was grown up, whenever I saw my parents after an absence, I felt struck powerless at first. I suppose they did not live long enough for me to adopt gradually the role of being *their* parent—which is what happens, doesn't it? There's always the instant though when one is struck down by the sheer accumulation of memories.

Well, don't I think I sound Miss Wise-Cat? And I can't even purr, as you and Paul can. It would save so much bother if I could purr and if I had furr.

I hope Jo is finding it O.K. at MacDowell. I know where to write to her now.

Repeat: If you come to live in New Zealand I'll stay here. The Schools of Art employ teachers, painters, but as there are fewer people here there are fewer people who care about painting. The number is increasing though and we're now raising an interesting generation of sons and daughters of immigrants who are alive and talented and it is from them, I think, that we'll get our great painter, writer, etc. End of repeat.

Remark from Lucas. 'Where is this Jay I hear about? I know only a purring-post, scratching-post, eating-post, a piece of furniture moving around and sometimes murmuring and setting me a great puzzle about which end I'm to address myself—the feet that move level with me or the fuzzy part where the voice emerges (I mean the head, silly). I know no Jay. I know only smell and texture and when I grow up to be a painter I'm going to be the pioneer of smaintings (paintings with smell incorporated.)

End of remark from Lucas.

Now so much from J and homesickness and good wishes for B and P's work and play and sleep and dream and thought and everything from

Lucas' purring-post, alias Blue Jay.

111. Dunedin October 5

Dear Ned,

I've just been writing a short story called *A Stair of One's Own*, and in the midst of writing it I put paw to typewriter key to say hello to you and your two big cool cattable cats. It's a wonderfully smelly day today and the sun is out and an invisible wind is blowing. I was up early as usual and dashed around on my chairs and up and down in the rooms which did not have the door closed. I have a basket where I have collected an assortment of things. I love screwed-up (!) envelopes which I carry with me. I also have a spoon and a handkerchief and a cotton-reel (spool is your word, Ned, isn't it?) I spend most of my day carrying envelopes from here to there. The other day when Cat Jay was writing to you I tried to creep inside the envelope for her to mail me. Oh. Went down the stairs today to scare away a cat three times my size. Not half as handsome either. Found some clover and a twig and watched the clouds in the sky but didn't have the confidence to climb up to them and chase after them. Two birds perched on the next door roof and hurled insults at me. Went back up the stairs then (*my* stairs) to see if everything was O.K. in the house. Big ginger Cat J was reading a book and didn't that make me jealous! Every time I see her with a book I climb on her lap and try to knock the book away and I'm not satisfied until she has put it down and turned her attention to me. These crazy books! whole shelves of them. I knocked over the Guide to London yesterday and I tried to do the same with the telephone. And in J's study I get into the waste-paper basket and carry off pieces of manuscript to add to my hoard. She tells me I'm more like a dog than a cat, the way I chew everything and carry things away.

[in margin: I would like an in-depth report]

I'm still going to be a writer when I grow up—that's why I've been writing this story about my stair. Do you have a stair? It's an absolute necessity. A patio does just as well, of course and I hear you've got a nice patio, with petunias and geraniums and an olive tree and a live oak and a bird of paradise flower and ferns and butterflies and peanut butterflies and Old Smoky. Are your sleeping quarters O.K.?

I'm only a very little kitten and big Cat J told me that you are much older than I and she told me that if I wrote to you I was to be very polite and call you Uncle and not ask personal questions. She said you learned photographic modelling when you were very young and have had an exciting career and are terribly handsome but that your health has not been the best lately. I hope you are feeling better now and are taking your medicine.

Must go now. J wants the typewriter. I'll just have time to slip this sheet out before she comes to the study and she'll never dream I've been here.

Much love to a distant uncle and his two cats from your ever affectionate

Lucas Burch

P.S.　How is Frederika ha ha
P.P.S.　Have you ever explored and *tasted* John Milton's *binding? Delicious.*

112. Dunedin October

Poem for Paul

Colour. Lay on the c. Daub. Scumble.
Paint. You check-shirted conjuror to put
a man in sunlight in a canyon, safe
there, and within an orange tube flying sky-high
to me as a kinda fulfilled wish for my birthday.
Not every painter (they always say this but it's true) can get
sun at his fingertips as you do, smearing it in
a beautiful sword-fish (see I swim in the world at ease) pattern
on W.T.B
*　　　The rusted canyon is wearing away*
through use by fire but the man and the sun and the sky are always new.

★★★★★★★★★★★★★★★★★

Stars. Excuse the silly verse but thank you for the painting. It is on my wall and it changes with the light but W.T.B is a vessel to catch the light in that canyon.

And now.

Cat news.

I have recently performed what I thought was an ingenious deception. I opened a can of cat food (V.I.P. chicken for some very important pets, so the label said) and offered some to Lucas who immediately showed me what he thought of it by attempting to cover it up as if he had just excreted it which gesture, translated, would mean, 'This is what I think of your shit.'

And so I picked up the dish, took it to the sittingroom and sat there with the dish on my knee making noises of delight while I pretended to eat it. Lucas of course who is rather puzzled that he and I do not share our meals, came into the room, climbed on a nearby chair, and ate with enjoyment all the vip chicken food.

There's a moral somewhere but I think cats should be kept away from morality.

★★★★★

Bill will be away in the East when you get this letter. I'm sorry that you're finding the teaching unpleasant. Maybe it's to be expected.

More later.

Look after yourself and Billy always and always.

        & love,
           canyons of,
             from J

113. Dunedin October

Dear B,

('Oh my dears'), I've just written to Paul to say I received the water-colour and I'm writing to Joan Tanner and to you—oh what excitement when I found the orange tube propped against the front door. W.T.B in the canyon is already on my wall. Like you, Paul has this way with light—which, I suppose, is a definition of a painter: to have a way with, control, govern, sway, know how to manage, make legal (I like this one).

I hope the allergy has gone. I sent a special spell straight away which meant Removal of Allergy from Man in Electronic Bed in 131 Hermosillo Drive. I hope it worked. By now you will be East. I've sent a special spell to Man Going East. I hope it reaches you with its powerful waves.

I loved the Dicks pricks quicks kicks licks of California. And I shall be flying your way around the 12th February next year if that is O.K. My first stop.

When you return from the East you will find my new tape waiting. Dominique Sion from the French Department came to see me the other afternoon and I recorded her reading some of Rilke's French poems, and she was highly amused to find that she is sandwiched between two samples of Lucas Burch's purr. I'm sure you'll like these. I have to think of something this weekend to fill the tape—it's hard isn't it—I mean thinking of something is hard, but you and Paul are O.K. you have the piano and reading poetry and Paul has the interviewing techniques and communication with Dame Mary Margaret last heard of on SplashDown Day. Rather suspicious, that. Dominique is quite delightful, and everybody has loved her, and she's been happy here. Well, that sounds too good to be true. It's like the statement people make about a marriage—they're very happy, they've never been otherwise. Dunedin has reminded Dominique of a small German town in the mountains. She has been pleased that whereas in France at the University of Toulouse most of the staff are French, here there are people from all nations on the staff. The University has N.Z., English, Welsh, Scottish, Irish, Australian, American, Russian, French, German, Dutch and so on, also Chinese, Polynesian. I realised when I was talking to Dominique about Dunedin that it is very much like Peterborough in New Hampshire except that it is by the sea and the climate is not extreme.

Well it is Saturday morning
and Jay is yawning.

I went to dinner last evening and I swear never never again, not with the same people. It was interesting though. There were Dorothy and Robert Ballantyne (second wives and second husbands, he is a doctor), Wanda and David Hall (he is a retired lecturer) and Ted Middleton (the Burns Fellow) and I. The dinner (at Halls who live quite near me so I walked there) was delicious, a flavoursome concoction of rice and meat and so on, preceded by some kind of fish on toast, followed by something worthy of Yaddo, called The Best Ever Pie topped with whipped cream, followed by coffee, brandy and chocolates. There was wine at dinner and drinks before. I thought the company was heavy-going and the conversation tiresome and I don't suppose, I mean I'm quite sure I did nothing to help, as it is my custom to withdraw and spend the time receiving impressions and whenever I am startled by having a question directed at me I give a laconic yes or no which makes me appear utterly brainless, which I feel that I am. David Hall, at the head of his table, turned to me, quoting Disraeli's comment on the English as a divided nation and asking me if I agreed it could be applied to America.

I gave him very short change with my clipped, Yes.

End of conversation with David.

Meanwhile, Ted, who's almost blind and who's had a rough working life among the wharfies and the seamen and so on, and who a few years ago brought a successful libel case against the national scandal sheet which hinted at his communist activities, was obviously not enjoying himself, among the solid citizenry, which is what the Ballantynes and the Halls are.

What a marvellous view I had of everyone!

That sounds very pompous but I did get such a clear view and it was unfair of me, really, to stay in myself. The point is that I'm strictly a nonverbal creature. After watching Lucas and seeing how he is receiving, receiving impressions every moment, I have the feeling that maybe I'm a cat or some kind of animal, because going among as many as five people I am bombarded with impressions, undercurrents and so on, and become an instrument more than a person.

This sounds crazy.

Anyway, I showed as usual how brainless I am.

Though I had a rather nice time with David whom I've seen only twice before and who has a nasty streak but a nice sense of humour. He was in the hospital at the same time as I (I had not known this) and he was not as lucky as I in the results of his tests and I suppose it's the beginning of the end for him. I basked in the reflected tragedy of his fate for I had been *there*. We discussed, in asides, details of hospital routine.

A tiresome evening, though.

I was glad to get home to kitty who tugs my heartstrings so. He is so spiritual and so wicked. I have had to keep Joan Tanner's drawing well out of his way. He seized or tried to seize Paul's painting when it was taken out of the tube. Dominique thought he was beautiful but she looked rather sceptical when I said he leaps at the wallpaper in the passage and tears it and eats it. As she was going out, Lucas came rushing along, leapt at the wall and began to chew it. Next letter, I'll let him tell his own story, particularly about his new range of expressions all guaranteed to make me feel guilt or heartbreak.

★★★★★★ Stars

Oh your letter just came with the kiddies' page. My spell couldn't have worked on your allergy. Maybe the man in the electronic bed was Ned and Ned received the spell? I do hope it's better now. What a lovely Mixon! I mean Nixon!

And what a lovely Bee. In Bed with Ned on Knee

or is it Ned in Bed with Bee on Knee.

★★★★   ★★★★

A couple of hours ago I sent you an International telegram as this letter will be too late to get to you before you leave (if your allergy is better, and you do leave). Don't I chatter and babble?

I just wanted to hurry on your good health as my spell has not worked. And to say I had received the painting and the drawing which is lovely and mysterious. I wrote Paul a poem for his painting which changes colour (the painting not the poem); it has a day of its own with the sunlight changing its patterns. Again, the Day is of course the artist who admits the sun.

Change the subject baby Jay and quote from Virginia Woolf whose essays I read in bed. V.W. received her first cheque for one pound ten shillings and sixpence.

> 'But to show you how little I deserve to be called a professional woman (?), How little I know of the struggles and difficulties of such lives, I have to admit that instead of spending the sum upon bread and butter, rent, shoes etc. I went out and bought a cat—a beautiful cat, a Persian cat, which soon involved me in bitter disputes with my neighbours.'

You probably knew this. I didn't.

One point in favour of the people I visited last evening was their liking for cats. Their Elizabeth whom we did not see had just had kittens and they were horrified when I told them I had *bought* my cat. I realise that in the world of cat-owners, however temporarily I may be there, my status is low indeed: you are worthy only if a cat chooses you, you do not condescend to *buy* a cat. Both their cats simply arrived from nowhere and stayed. Opoho, they told me, is Cat Country. I already knew this. Indeed, almost everyone in Dunedin has a cat. Every house in my neighbourhood has one.

★★★★

End of cat report. It's too long already . . .

★★★★

I'm waiting to hear from the U.S. Embassy whether they consider me worthy enough to be granted a visa for a longer stay than six months. I've not mentioned my time in *that* kind of hospital and I don't intend to. If the question arises (and it's pretty well known that I was out of circulation for many years) I have the advice of the psychiatrists whom I know in the worldfamous Maudsley Hospital in London. They, including Sir Aubrey Lewis, once head of the hospital, insisted that I should never have been in hospital. I may have had psychological difficulties, they said, but I have never suffered from a mental illness. I know that, myself. They are prepared to offer evidence and so on, if the question arises. It's a pitiful reflection on N.Z. psychiatric services and one which, I should imagine, they would not want publicised. The question, I hope, is not likely to arise.

I knew you'd understand about the Intensive Care aftermath. What I've been writing since (I *have* been writing, all winter) is more than I thought I'd done but it is really in the nature of an afterbirth, probably to be disposed of, burned or buried. (If I were a cat, I'd eat it.)

It's a sour time, with confidence in one's work low. As Paul said 'everything turns to shit'.

★★★

It's grim, Paul, if the teaching is not fairly enjoyable. What will happen?

I'm going to mail this now. Look after yourself, and selves and each other, Bill and Paul and Ned and Steinway. I wonder how my words 'Avoid Carnie' in the telegram will arrive. I said Carnie was the name of a friend, and who will deny that I am telling the truth? All the same, avoid him or put him in the care of Steinway because when B is in bed with Allergy and P comes home tired from teaching, Carnie gets an instant reading on his gauge which says to him, A moment's inattention and possible meal ahead. Fool he is. He does not know that the 'meal ahead' is one of Live Oak Inn's dinners.

oh this is drivel; Love in glorious technicolour for B & P & N & Steinway (& Carnie)

from J

114. Dunedin October

Dear B P N.,
   A few lines to keep you in touch and to keep in touch with you; from the cold cold Antipodes where summer is never going to be— maybe I'm unfair; it's very warm but overcast—the sun has gone to another country.
   Nothing much to say, therefore I send a few notes from here and there. Been nowhere, done nothing, seen no-one, said nothing. Rosalie Carey, the woman in the enclosed cutting, came up the other day bringing the script of a A State of Siege which is being performed in November. It's very arrogant of me but I think I could have done better myself. She acts it very well, however, which I could never do. I don't care for the sudden publicity simply because I'm such a *drip* when it comes to being interviewed.
   I have to say goodbye to Lucas this week while he is still young enough to re-adapt. My sister can't take him, after all. Parting with him is one of the most terrible things that's ever happened to me. I think I told you he's so ethereal and at the same time *so wicked*. He's one of these very intelligent cats—and I don't think I'm saying this in the role of proud mama—and he will always be a poignant memory in a life that is crammed with memories of cats lost, dead, and so on. His chief delight at the moment is trying to use his paws as hands. He doesn't put his mouth to his food; he picks up a portion of food in his paw and conveys it to his mouth. He puts a paw on my face to wake me in the morning. The cat next door who used to visit me when it was a kitten has now adopted me and Lucas, and sleeps at the back door and Lucas who really

enjoys its company had given up trying to defend his territorial rights except for an occasional half-hearted box over the rump and sometimes a mewing appeal to me to, Do something about it can't you.

I sent off a tape yesterday. It's crazy and dotty and everything else.

We've had a bus strike here so I'm cut off unless I want to walk downtown which is too much there and back every few days. I had a lift from a man who immediately travelled his hand on my knee and upward and sent the car zigzagging on the road. I hastily said, I live here (a few hundred yards from my home) and got out. Virtuous Jay.

B will B out East now, as I write this. P will be home with Ned. I'm getting excited about seeing you all again, about 12th February in 1971. My battery is exhausted. Take care of each and all
 and love
  old fashioned
  tonic
  love from
   Jay

115. Dunedin October 27 Labour Day in N.Z. (handwritten)

Dear Ned,

Hi, handsome, Hi. This is your friend Lucas writing to you with J's pen in J's preparation book. In three days from now I leave this house of mine; and my trusted servant who has told me of my forthcoming departure yet presumes that I did not understand—I do! My God, I'm going to miss this little mansion of mine with its chairs and scratching posts and mama-stole which I still suck at and the garden with its trees which I'm clever at climbing. I'll miss my slave too. She thinks that I follow her around everywhere; the reality is that she follows me. Certainly, though, I feel it my duty to keep an eye on an inhabitant of my house, and I do check fairly frequently to see where she is and what she's doing.

Well, Ned, my secret is out at last now. I'm going as a birthday present to a little boy who will be seven at Hallowe'en. You know what that means don't you? The magic 7 and All Souls' Eve and a white cat. I have been a spirit in cat form. Getting down to more earthly things, however, I think I shall enjoy (continuing as cat) the company of a boy of seven. I think—I hope—he is much wiser than his mother who called to inspect me to see if I was suitable. She *had* wanted a tiny kitten but when she saw me of course she fell in love with me, cat-about-town that I am, and wanted me. (She knew me, as they say in the Bible.) She was rather inclined to go on about the last cat they had who died. He liked this, he liked that and did I like this and that?—What J calls the cooked fish syndrome from the line of an old song 'My first wife never cooked fish like this'. My new servant's mother, however, had a gentle voice and manner and as long as the boy of seven protects me I'll be O.K. (Is that what you American cats say?)

J tells me that B has been out in the wicked East and that you are home looking after Paul. I hope you take care of him, give him his Petromalt and so on and when Bill returns make sure he hasn't any more kittens in his luggage, I mean you'll never know where you are if there are strange kittens around the house all the day.

What a lucky cat you are to have a door of your own. Maybe where I'm going I'll have a door though I confess, with a tear in my eye, that I'm happy enough to have had such a magnificent stair.

Ah, I've learned since I was that tiny fox-like kitten that catdom as well as peopledom are cruel. Already cat-next-door has taken possession of my stair and I haven't the energy to drive *her* away. She comes in the window now and sleeps on the spare bed. I'm going to miss her. Every morning as soon as I wake I rush to see if she's there trespassing. If she is there I make such a magnificent display of anger, and if she isn't there I make a magnificent display of disappointment at being deprived of an occasion to make a magnificent display of anger.

J and I have been good friends, as cat and *mistress* go. I talk to her quite a lot and whenever I enter through *my* window I call out, Anyone Home? I've been practising my Abandoned-to-Strangers-When-I-did-so-much-for-you-is-this-love-and-gratitude expression which is quite an advanced expression calling for subtlety and a nice sense of timing. I pray—I know—*you* will never have to use it.

LATER:
Well Ned old boy it's morning again and for these last few days I've been standing guard over the basket of toys I've collected since infancy. I still play with them and select one in particular to play with each day. I put on my Anxious Expression whenever J goes near the basket.

But, Ned old boy, sleep calls, my eyes can hardly stay open so good morning. This will be the last time you hear of me so I hope you wish me well. I was going to pass your way and visit with J but she decided against it; perhaps it is better that you and I never meet and have only the beautiful memory of our strictly nephew-uncle-nephew correspondence.

Don't let the two big creatures Bill and Paul read this. If Frederika is next door you can read it to her, if you can bear to after her parturitive trespass on your sacred territory. Meanwhile you and I (to quote an old cat-lover J told me about)

'grow old, grow old'
and no doubt you will
'wear your black and white fur and walk upon the beach'
and we shall both
'hear the neighbourhood cats crying each to each.
Will they sing and meow to us?'
(While in your home Bill and Paul come and go talking of Michaelangelo . . .)

Farewell, Ned.
Yours in memory of a beautiful promising friendship, August to October (the lilacs bloom now)

Lucas Burch esq.

116. Dunedin October (handwritten)

Dear B P & N,

I may be mistaken but early yesterday morning I fancied I saw Lucas stealing out to mail a letter he must have written, perhaps to Ned. I hope it wasn't too sad, as he may have told Ned of his leaving here tomorrow. I'm sure Ned can take it. As I write this, Lucas is

a. trying to eat an airmail sticker.
b. trying to file himself in the filing cabinet. He was filed last week and meowed to get out. He did not care to be among manuscripts miscellaneous.

Overjoyed to have your letter yesterday, B. Sad that you have generously given your cold to P. Glad that the butterflies are back. And that you're having a show—but what a torment a show must be—Exciting, too. It will have a fair number of portraits? The impact of a number of portraits is quite overwhelming. I remember a Beckman show I saw in Boston. And here in little old Dunedin there is in the Early Settlers Museum, a room with the walls full of photographs, painting-size, of the early settlers. There's a surrealist air about the photographs. It's quite a frightening room, not merely because the women are all such stocky-looking battle-axes and the men so gentle and frightened-looking—almost without exception, though this helps with the air of dream & unreality (I've just rescued my fountain pen from Lucas).

If my U.S. Certification of Labour comes through by then I'd love to be in U.S. at the end of Jan—I mean I could manage to arrive in L.A. on Sat. Jan. 30, early morning, or Friday Jan 29th in the evening. The early morning Sat. seems O.K. If I get my certification (which will mean that I can get work in U.S. if I want it & if I can find it). I think I then go through the Immigrant Visa rigmarole which must be done here though I think the results can be given to one in U.S.A. There's a quota, of course. It's easier to get in if one comes from U.S.S.R. and asks for political asylum. Being a ballet dancer helps, or the daughter of a dictator. Alas, I can put forth neither claim. Only that I am a Daughter of Mark Twain . . . I think I'm repeating myself. I eat baked beans three times a week.

The weather here is becoming more like summer. Our bus strike continues. I sit at my desk and try to write between showing people my house which I'm going to rent for 10 dollars a week. Lucas thinks it's all a game. At first he was shy but now he acts spiritual when anyone comes (calls, I mean) and everyone wants to take him, the little devil. He now insists on behaving like the Frog

> Q: what's Brian Waller got that's striped or plain and coloured blue, brown, coral, gold, cream, apple, fawn?
>
> A: the best in town, one you've really got to see!

Prince in the fairy? story who lived in the palace on condition that he accompany the princess (that's me, ha ha) everywhere.

'I must eat at your table and sit on your chairs and sleep on your bed,' the frog said, end of quote.

And end of crazy letter. I'm thinking of you, much missing you, & send undiluted love to my 3 live oaks of Montecito

me again Jay.

NOVEMBER

117. Dunedin November

> We are looking for a Young Lady who has her School Certificate qualification and several years punching experience.

Dear B P and N, but chiefly N because this letter will be all cat-talk, my last for many a day until I see Ned again, though there will be an interval in Auckland when I see Tinky. Lucas is gone and it's a big heartbreak for me. My only consolation is that it's a bigger heartbreak for me than for Lucas whose investment in me was perhaps more practical than my investment in him. I told him he was going and I don't know if he knew—of course he did—and all yesterday he practised his eloquent glances with more compassion than I had expected from him. He used the inscrutable resigned glance more than the what-are-you-doing-to-me-who-have-done-so-much-for-you glance, reminding me that he has always been a brave, patient little cat, ever since he was whisked untimely from mama and put in a cage in a shop window when he could scarcely balance on his hind legs. He behaved very maturely, indeed. About the time the people were to call for him he went and sat on the wide windowsill of the sittingroom where he could see the entire city as well as the street outside. He studied the city for a while and then turned his attention to the cars coming up the street. He watched each one with indifference. He had no means of learning from me which car was his new people's car, for I did not know it, and I was not watching the street. As soon as one particular car appeared over the brow of the hill, with about seventy five yards more to go to reach 61 Evans Street, Lucas knew that was the car. I don't know how he did. He 'stiffened'—as the novelists say and concentrated his attention on that one car. It stopped outside the gate. He stayed in the window watching it while I went to the door and his new lady and manservant told me they could see him watching them from the window as they approached. He liked his new manservant instantly. He prefers men and boys though he's only seen a couple of women and one man who came with his wife to look at the house. The woman who said at first she would take him, phoned before they arrived to say she had been rather hasty and it would be her husband's decision and her husband would look him over. He did. He was bitten and scratched and played peekaboo with but he liked Lucas very much and so they took him away as a present for their little boy and that was that; and Jay went stricken to bed and slept, as the novelists say, 'a fitful sleep', and woke, still stricken, and went to the back door (this was five a.m.) to find cat next-door there, also stricken. Cat-next-door came in, searched the house, meowing plaintively (few meows are not plaintive), and appeared inconsolable. Jay has learned, however, and cats soon learn that there's no such thing as permanent inconsolability.

So, once more, that is that.

My own grief has a wide range and includes the regret and shock (though why it should be a shock to me I don't know) that I feel my only friend in Dunedin has been Lucas. I would like him to have gone to an artist of some kind or to someone I know.

It is all over now and, like royalty, I am 'confined to my home with a feverish cold'—as the novelists, pardon me, the reporters say

CLEAN, HONEST AND RELIABLE MAN

to cover every little emotional upset of our kings and queens . . . In truth, I'm fighting fit but so sad, so sad. I learned so much from Lucas. It was an ideal situation for studying learning between woman and beast. Cats are so full of knowing on (to us) invisible evidence and I think they could teach us a way of reaching the invisible evidence.

Eh, Ned?

Well enough of that cat-talk.

But how do the cats *know* so much? Already the big black and grey tom, an old man cat if there ever was one, complete with all his block and tackle, has returned to haunt my garden. I saw him this morning and he gave me the long long look he used to give me, as if he had never been away. I think he's courting cat-next-door and was making an early call to press his suit. It's suit-pressing time in the Antipodes. Old Black and Grey lives about half a mile away.

Meanwhile in the above-foot world, people continue as pallid as ever. The bus strike finished yesterday after a month, and the buses returned today. The Government has introduced a mini-budget. Jay is getting down to work, with grief as a reliable foundation and fountain, and hope of seeing dear friends next year as sustenance.

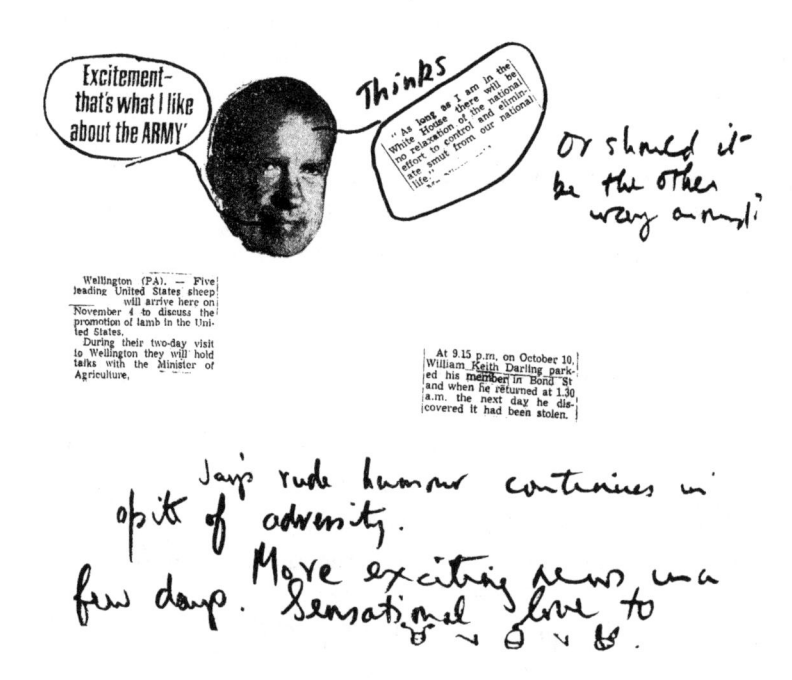

Jay's rude humour continues in spite of adversity.
More exciting news in a few days. Sensational love to

118. Dunedin November

My dears three,

Here I am, après-bain, wearing nothing but my bifocals, writing to you from a Lucas-broken heart that is, however, beginning to mend very slowly. What a love affair I had with my little cat! I feel like Swann, in Proust; or like anybody who loved and was bereaved; and one part of me studies the affair detachedly, observing closely, saying to itself, Now that is interesting. Much of my grief went today when, assiduously as any lover, I traced from the pet shop the place where Lucas was born and where his three-year old mother still lives. I spoke to the people on the phone. Lucas' mother is mostly Siamese which is where he gets his intelligence, I suppose. She too is white. And he was one of a litter of three, all toms.

Well, my dears three, am I not quite crazy! No-one here that I know shares the delight in creatures. My friend Ruth whom I phoned understood about the loss. The other woman I know said in a putting-down voice, Oh, *I'm* not one of those people who fall in love with animals. Cat-next-door understands.

So now I have a pet spider. Yes, I have. I had it while Lucas was here. It lives in the kitchen where I have a double light bulb, one of low wattage which I leave on all night, the other of higher wattage. A string dangles from the bulbs, with a puller on the end. Spider lives at the end of the string at night, spinning and hanging by his thread and when I turn off the light in the morning he climbs up the thread and sleeps on the still-warm lightbulb all day.

So. That is Spider. I don't know. I guess I was meant just to live among creatures.

And how are you three creatures? I hope Paul's cold is better and that all was well with B's journey and that Hallowe'en was fun—oh I wish I were not human; if I were one of the other creatures—say, a spider—I would spin a silver web on this page and that would be my letter and there would be no silly words, just a thought-sparkle for all at Live Oak Inn.

Ecology—we and the creatures and the earth, sea and sky.

Goodnight.

And pure wicked love.

MORNING AGAIN.

Cat-next-door sits purring on my lap. She comes in early every morning to look for Lucas and together we share our grief. I think she's having kittens some time soon.

Enough of that.

It's five a.m. The world is not quite awake. A day's work ahead—I've discovered I'm trying to write two books at once.

Ah to be in the peanut butter world.

End with a rude rhyme. The optometrist's name is Peter Dick believe it or not. I've just got my new glasses from him.

The optometrist Peter Dick
devised an ingenious trick:
he, bedded, benighted,
and feeling short-sighted
wore bifocals on his prick.

. . . . . .

Goodbye again. And purer wickeder love than ever.

from Red Jay

---

119. Dunedin November

Dear Bee dears three, yours to hand, in hand.
    I was overjoyed

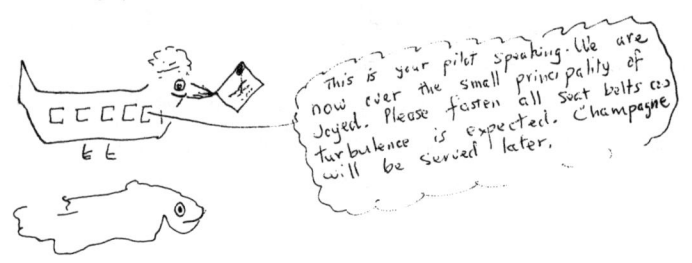

and relieved

to get your letter and hear about the trip east and the safe return home. It is sad about your mother and father, Bill. I was spared the tragedy of age in my parents—and they were too, which is more to the point; yet though I feel relieved they did not live through old age, I also feel deprived of something I know I would never have been able to face—how mixed can one's feelings be! I miss my visits to the Old People's Home to see my aunt and the other depressing sights—I think because being with the old people is a kind of death-play, a rehearsal; as necessary as the grownup play of children; but more secret.

But I don't know. Life would be so much less a burden if one never had parents at all; the age of other people's parents is so much easier to bear.

Well, again, I don't know. Thus speaks Dame Frame Clutha, all excited from her postcard from Mae West—come-up-and-see-me-sometime when I've got nothing—on.

So to New York. Your time there did seem fun—people, music, paintings, dinners, feasts—and the Natural History Museum with Anne. Did you walk in *Reptile Hall*? When I was in the Natural History Museum I made a note of *Reptile Hall* as a title for a novel (subtitle *The Cold Dream of the Copperhead*).

I was so happy to get your letter—as I said, I was overjoyed and relieved.

It's grim about Felix's closing down his gallery. There will be some other place to show? And it's exciting about your exhibition and Paul's too. If all goes well with my visa I'll be able to fly into L.A. on the Friday evening or the Saturday evening (Jan 29 or 30) around 6.30. Which would be more convenient?

... *Speeding Up Of Clutha*

Somewhere between here and L.A. I get tangled up with the date line international, going backwards and forwards from yesterday to tomorrow so it's possible to leave here on a Thursday and then get permanently lost in a pocket of Wednesday and then miss Friday or somesuch—all very fascinating. I'm going up to Auckland from here in the first week of December, I think, and staying with my sister until I leave for U.S. I'll be there for Christmas, I think. It sounds crazy but it's quite awful here now without Lucas. I think he's settling down quite well where he has gone, though, for he's young enough but I do miss his complete satisfaction in being here and owning the place; it was such a wonderful satisfaction he showed; there was no question of occasional grateful glances at me to say, you know, it's awfully good of you, Jay, to have me; no, just a wonderfully accepting satisfaction. This was *his* place, he'd been born to it, the chairs were his chairs, the cane chair was his to sharpen his claws on its southeast leg, and the spare bedroom window was his, to go in and out of, and always, coming in, to call out to me to see where I was; the trees were his to climb, and the lovely places in the grass were his to hide in, and oh how pleased he was with it all! And I was part of the furniture, more movable than the other parts, but just a furniture to be accepted and used. You said just the right thing in your letter, Bill, to give me the right comfort about Lucas—the quote 'may make a journey and still abide'. I cherish having had a devil-angel take over my heart and home. And as I named him Lucas Burch I have to accept him as such, and therefore quote about him from *Cat in August*: 'Having drawn upon the reserve of patient and steadfast fidelity upon which the Lucas Burches of this world depend and trust, even though they do not intend to be present when the need for it arises.'*

And, 'I don't reckon I need any promise from Lucas. It just happened unfortunate so, he had to go away.'

'When he first heard about how he might have to leave, he knowed then it would be best to go. He had got the word about how he might have to leave a long time before that. He said he would stay if I wanted him to. But I said for him to go. Going away among strangers like that a young fellow needs time to settle down. Especially a young fellow full of life like Lucas, that likes folks and jollifying, and liked by folks in turn. Lucas always did like excitement.'

And so on. A great book, *Cat in August*.

Nice that you're enjoying the tape. The story about Gipsy is my story, 'Swans', from *The Lagoon*. *The Lagoon* stories were written when I was twenty-one and so I'm ashamed of them, and rather depressed when people say they are my best work—there's nothing so crippling being told that your earliest work is your best.

I had a long moving letter from Elnora. The only happy part was her delight in her Afro hairdo.

---

* Quote from William Faulkner's novel *Light in August*, in which one of the main characters is called Lucas Burch.

****

Stars to precede light relief.

    I had to go for a final check to my doctor here, a Dr Sidey.

> *A treat for Jay on Fridey*
> *an appointment with Dr Sidey.*
> *Her health is so rude*
> *she'll surely go nude*
> *as befits a Dunedin lidey.*
> And on Monday I go to the dentist.
> *Next, to the dentist, Perry,*
> *whose face is exceedingly herry.*
> *For drilling so thrilling*
> *I'm strangely unwilling*
> *—how chilling! Well, not very merry!*

*****

My limerick battery needs recharging.

****

I'm still trying to let my house with no success so far, though there have been few people to look at it. Some interesting characters—one, a woman, talked all the time about her 'teal suite', or rather their teal suite. They're getting married soon and I gathered that the chief reason for their getting married was the teal suite, so they can sit on it and admire it. And when they phoned to say they would not take the house, the woman said, 'You see, I just don't think there's room for the teal suite'. I could always have let the house to the teal suite alone . . .

    Goodbye now and turbulent love followed by champagne to B and P and N

```
from J. overjoyed.
```

120. Dunedin November 15

Dear B and P and N (and so on), (freeing blades)

Hello. This is Dame Frame Clutha writing to you from Evans Street Dunedin. I am sitting typing this near my sitting-room window while cat-next-door (as the novelists say) 'big with child' sits on the armchair purring. The sky is blue (eggshell) with scatters of white fluffy cloud, there's a brisk wind blowing, and the red roses in bloom on the fence next door are shaking their heads vigorously, and in the garden of the house across the road the Yellow Flowers are doing likewise. I hear a child crying, a motormower mowing and the wind prowling in the cellar.

So. The scene is set.

Meanwhile, back in Santa Barbara I imagine that everyone, including Carnie, is painting and preparing for a one-man or one-plant exhibition. Or for a nice Christmas in Santa Fe. Or for the next meal. Or for the next breath, which may be as far as one can prepare.

I've been sorting things I'm taking with me on my flight north on the 4th and my flight to U.S.A. at the end of January—providing I have my certificate of Labour. I have an ordinary visa anyway. And as I can take only 44 pounds of luggage and that will include an eleven pound typewriter I've had to shear myself to the minimum, whatever that means. Work is neglected in the midst of these preparations and though I feel a small panic at the thought that work is neglected I feel that when I do return to it I will be so much more ready for it, and in some way it is writing itself while I am not writing it.

The past week has been quiet, as usual. To keep my tenants happy I bought them an electric range (I had only a rangette). Most of the young couples who looked at the house decided against it because it had only a rangette and as the young women were all about to be married they all had visions of cooking mountains of food for two. It makes the kitchen look like the flight deck of a jet—that is, the new range. At the moment there are two loaves of bread inside it, almost ready. The smell is wafting into the sittingroom.

The other afternoon I went to visit my former landlady while I was Burns Fellow. She is eighty-three, the daughter of the first Education professor here, and her working life was spent teaching music. Before I left she played me her choice—part of a Schubert Impromptu. Oh I did not realise how hungry I was for the piano until I heard it played while I sat on the chair beside it (not a red stool). All the notes were correct and she obviously loved the music but it was very tum-te-tum, as if it were being danced to as a waltz and she was reluctant to let the notes go wherever they go to when they are played but held on to them as if they belonged to her (and I don't blame her); and so the music became confined. As for Dame Frame Clutha she was startled to find she was so homesick for the piano with B playing it.

Make ready, Steinway!

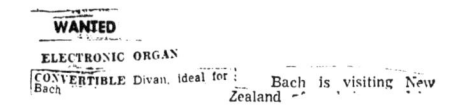

> **WANTED**
> ELECTRONIC ORGAN
> CONVERTIBLE Divan. Ideal for
> Bach

Bach is visiting New Zealand

> **TOOLMAKER**
> personal interview

Well, except for my visit to Perry the Herry the Uncouth Touth, that was my waking week. Sleeping and dreaming week, night-dreaming and day-dreaming occupied different worlds, naturally.

Oh, and last week I phoned Lucas' new servants to find out how he was and how they were and I was very happy to learn that he is at home with them and performing his trick or treat repertoire in the old way. He has the attention of everyone in the household (I felt that one of his minor dissatisfactions while he was with me was with the necessarily diluted attention that one person only could give him. He now has the purest concentrate, and he is thriving on it. His new mistress (?) says she is not sure who owns him (or whom he owns) though he was given to her little son. My heart bleeds a few drops when I think of that awful evening when he sat on the windowsill looking out and thinking (I'm certain) that the world was too much for him; perhaps he caught my infection; anyway, he still runs into the house to hide from the passing cars though he's brave enough to go outside now but he will only go outside if a member of the household is there. I think he misses his former wild garden with trees. Yes, he is happy. He plays and plays, and goes crazily round on his hind legs, as he loved to do, and eats the newspaper, and he gets into bed with the lady of the house (as he used to do) and his new people are just as absorbed in him as his old person was. What a strange comment on me or on my country and city that the only living thing dear to me, here in this place that is so lonely, with here and now and with memories, that self-sown poignancies sprout everywhere, has been a little white tom kitten with green eyes. (A rather confused sentence which I tried to rescue with commas but failed.)

Cat-talk again. Forgive. I visited my friend Ruth the other day and her talk was plant-talk. She was nursing tiny cabbages in beds of stone and pointing out how the cruel wind had bruised them. Her place is something like yours, inside and out. Charles B has lent her paintings from his collection to hang on her walls. She has made a lovely garden.

As today is the 15th November and I leave here on the 4th December I haven't much time left. The dramatisation of A State of Siege is being performed this week and I'm trying to think of excuses for not going. My sister is graduating from college on 10th December and she is anxious for me to be there, and I shall go as it means a lot to her to have at last 'come into her own' after raising a family of brilliant kids and getting to feel inferiorer and inferiorer and inferiorer. She has done very well in her exams and theses and I think it's brave of her as she's spent the last two years studying with 18-22 year olds. She's four years younger than I—no, three and a half.

My address in Auckland is or will be c/o Gordon, 61 Gladstone Road, Northcote, Auckland 9, New Zealand.

And of course, in Auckland, I shall be busy getting fingerprinted, I suppose, by the U.S. State Department. I ought to have a clean letter from a few friends to show that I do know people in the U.S. and that I'm not a monster and that my pleasures are simple—writing, reading, and playing the pornograph.

I'm getting excited about seeing your paintings. (The excitement of dropping in, briefly (Ha ha), at Hermosillo Drive, is always with me.) Now I go on cedar feet to mail this.

Reasonless seasoned love

from Jay

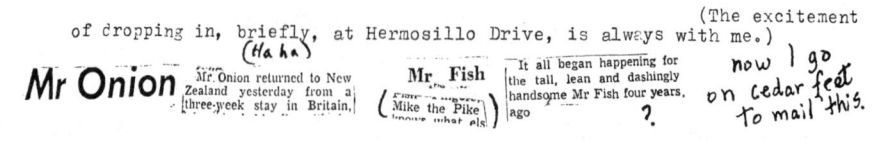

121. Dunedin November

> Lucas
> was at the very threshold
> of life. "He had reached
> the peak of his enjoyment
> of life He was on top of the
> world.

Evans Street, you know where, Saturday morning, sunny day, a mist over the hills.

Dear Burning newly realistic helixes (Helices), Bee the See, Pee the Free, En the Wren,

That's now crazy I am. What a nice warm letter full of enclosures and with a lovely picture of Jay yearning after Lucas. (See upper left corner.)

I'm so glad that Paul has given up the University teaching. I hope you both sell lots and lots of your paintings at the forthcoming exhibitions so that you'll be able to go to the place of your choice and do the things of your choice: among the mountain lions—which could be allies—what *does* that mean? I wonder what Felix will do. My brother-in-law has just given up the job he's had most of his married life, because it's been wearing his soul out.

About the clipping of J.C. Oates' play—I like the message from P. Anderson. And I feel only sympathy for J.C. Oates. She's a fine writer and the review is the kind of nasty thing that I've often had, and that always left me terribly depressed and wondering why I kept on writing. Maybe her nasty streak will save her. I've got my own nasty streak but I don't seem to be able to translate it into direct action: I guess I'm too lazy. ********** Stars in the night sky.

I'm flying into L.A. on Air New Zealand Flight 556A on Friday January 29, at 6.10 p.m. What a long time away it is. Meanwhile, as I say in every letter, I'm shortly going north to haggle with the U.S. Embassy. My beak is in good order, my feathers have been cleaned, oiled, (and picked free of lice), my webbed feet (in case I need to drop in the Pacific) have been fitted with cedar shoes (the satin ones I normally wear have been given to the local museum). I shall enjoy my short time in Auckland. I'll call on Frank and Harry who is bedridden and many years older than Frank; I think Harry is about eighty. And Frank will be seventy this coming year.

Except for my journeys into town to consult the U.S. Embassy and be fingerprinted etc. I'll try to work, and laze around on the many beaches.

✯✯✯✯✯✯✯✯

Stars for pause in which I cruelly demolished Freddie Fly.

✯✯✯✯✯✯

I'm so impatient to go. I pack and unpack and weigh and unweigh every hour.

The other evening I went to the dress rehearsal of *A State of Siege*. Being there wasn't half as bad as I imagined it would be; in fact I enjoyed it very much. It was fascinating to see everyone so concerned about concrete details—door locks, whether windows were open or shut, which newspaper the character held to kill the moth; as if the play were reality. And to see the characters that I know only in my head, being composed beyond me. I really found it fun; it was like being a child and *playing*—and it was a *play*. I had forgotten that so much of my life is spent just in play. If I had made the adaptation myself I would have made it different, of course, but it has been done very well; necessarily diluted although the development comes through. It is being produced by a keen tv producer and it's pretty sure that the N.Z. Broadcasting Corporation will buy it for both radio and tv. I share profits 50-50 with the adaptor.

Eva Marie is playing in town, in *Loving*. I went to see it yesterday afternoon. I think it's beautifully done from a very corny story. Eva Marie Saint is so tender and poetic and subtle.

What else on the Dunedin scene?

Nothing

nothing

nothing.

Lucas is over the hill and far away and sometimes he slips into the corner of my vision. At the theatre the other night there was an old female white cat who came and sat in my lap and gave me the feeling of delight which people get when they are *chosen* by animals; a delight mixed with gratitude.

I wonder how Jo will like Yaddo. It will be under a new directorship now and I think there were to be many changes. And then the island off Georgia where the rattlesnakes walk in the streets of a night and giant technicolor spiders drop from branches overhead and the air is steaming and warm as in a version of *Suddenly Last Summer*. The news of Henry Chapin and his wife brought him so vividly to mind—at Mac-Dowell, and when I met them on the Boston railway station. She really looked like a wornout fruit, then. And last evening when I turned on the radio and heard 'My name is Randy Stone. I cover the night beat for the Daily' I was reminded vividly of Steve Rothwell, that bright-eyed lad, with his hankering to play the detective. His eyes seemed to come right out of his head. Perhaps he was a crayfish.

Words, words words. I'm wasting them and mixing them up. Do you not find it peace to be painting, with words put to sleep and out of sight?

I'm getting ready my patent genetic code-cracker, D.N.A. molecules a specialty.

Excuse me while I attend to my invention.

Love and cheers
abate all fears
double double
forgo trouble
naught to play
but holiday
naught to shirk
but work
naught to utter
but peanut butter
naught to paint
but golden saint

        love, anyway, all way.
to the See, the Free, the Wren.
        from

122. Dunedin November (handwritten)

Composers Busts $3.95

Dear B P N,

So nice to get your letter this morning, and I'm writing this not, as you wrote, to the sound of Mozart but to the sound of all the lawn-mowers in the neighbourhood mowing. It's five-thirty in the evening, the sun is still high & ablaze in the sky and shining in my sittingroom on to your paintings and Paul's painting.

Lucas—ah, yes—his coming and going in my mind is painful and sad. I feel as if he believes I will come and fetch him home to his castle, but that is a delusion, for cats even more than people are haunted by the persistence (is that tautological?) of the present. Oh my dear *wicked* Lucas —I think I loved his wickedness most of all.

View of State Street. A good title isn't it? I wonder what you will paint now, after the portraits & the street. I keep thinking that I feel myself approaching something in writing where I, too, can use past work-experience, as if that was all it was, but I keep deceiving myself, the feeling remains a feeling. [in margin: Excuse my drivel!]

(The motormowers hum & buzz.)

It's sad & wise about Paul's decision. What does the future hold now? (We all had to write an essay 'What the Future holds for me'.)

I had a visit the other evening from a friend of Jacquie & Jim Baxter. He has been a dental professor all his working life, has a beautiful talented wife, has eight children, & has decided to remove himself from the academic world taking his beautiful wife & 8 children to a more 'human' existence. Because the reasons for his resignation are inexplicable to most of the community he lives in he is now the target of rumour, prejudice, hostility. He could be a character in an Ibsen play. He's a good man.

... But when I (hoping for sympathy) told him I was going next day to the dentist & was scared he confessed that he, a professor of dentistry, had been rather like the cobbler who had no shoes & was soon to make a *dreaded* visit to his dentist.

The lilac trees everywhere are in full blossom. I have some deep purple lilac in a vase on the windowsill.

Today our friend Dominique flew away on her journey home. She arrived last evening at my place, rushed from a taxi, looked very lovely & suntanned, & gave me her newly-bound thesis to read. I, mouth-clobbered that day by Perry whose drilling's more killing than thrilling, grabbed the thesis & muttered thank you out of the corner of my mouth. Like James Cagney or Bond or somebody. The thesis 'New Zealand in *Owls Do Cry*' is not particularly original but it is painstaking, illuminating and written in a fresh clear English style. I thought I'd be embarrassed to read it but I enjoyed it. And this morning I delivered it to her at the little cottage near the French Department where she lived. It was a pleasant walk down through the Gardens to the University.

I have let my house to a young couple (friends of Dominique) who will move in here on December 4th, when I am flying north to Auckland and will be with my sister for several weeks until I fly to L.A. & New York . . .

I'll stop overnight in Wellington with Jacquie who's full of anxiety as the young boy (you remember his painting & letter) has been picked up by the police in Auckland on a drug charge. I don't know what will happen. I hope to see him in Auckland & if he's in prison as Jacquie thinks he may be I'll visit him (if he wants it). The kid's a genius. His sensibility & suffering show so clearly not so much his predicament as that of everything & everybody around him. The same with the dental professor & his struggles.

This letter is a tired-battery one. I enjoyed hearing about what's going on in electrically-operated Santa Barbara. How clearly you put Paul's case for resignation. I'm thinking he'll be happier not teaching. I will take in washing & scrub the patios of Hollywood to let you & Paul work uninterrupted with crust in the mouth, brush in the hand, roof above the head. Ned & I will wear our furs and go walking on the beach.

What a shame you can't send Ned to Auckland where I'll be at Christmas so I can look after him. And how traitorous of Dr Gilbride to be an *absentee* doctor. I don't believe she ever existed. She was a *front*, a *cover*.

Received special Brand love & return Brand X love to all at H. Oak Inn including Carnie & Steinway.

Jaybird

Before I leave here I'm going to photograph the building with the Stone Bees.   J

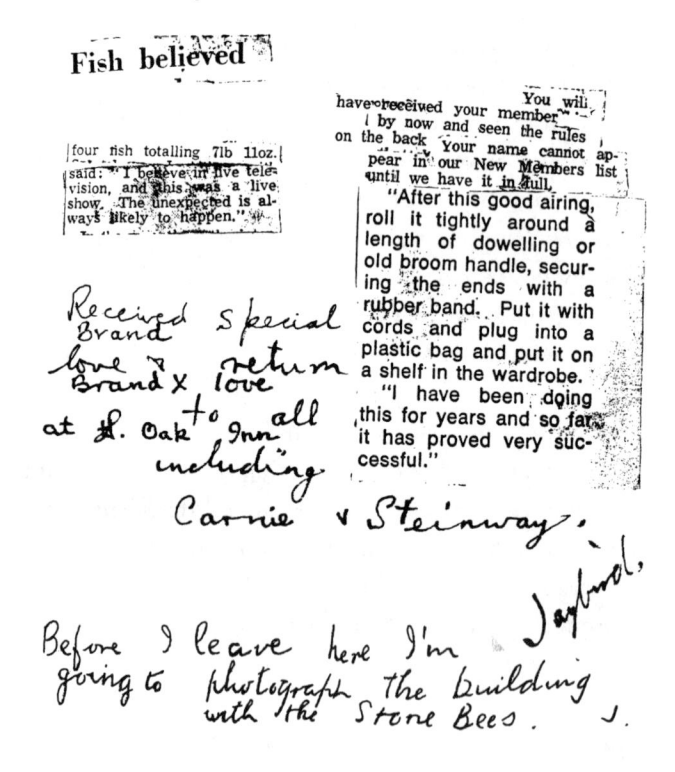

123. Dunedin November as from, well, almost as from c/o W. Gordon, (Auckland)

Hi feathered friends with thy well-oiled and pleasing plumage, it is dawn here, the lark (well, the blackbird or thrush singeth and trampeth around heavy-footed on my iron roof) . . . singeth. It is about 6 a.m., the day is warm-grey, I'm in my study typing this in my négligée, I mean on paper, and the rest of the world except the birds is asleep.

Yesterday I hired two strapping youths who would have looked well serving in the Steak House to clear my garden a little and make some kind of a lawn for the incoming tenants. I did not realise that a motor-mower is merely a giant shaver. I am horrified at what they have done to all my lovely green curly grass where each blade grew as it wanted to and waved about knocking into its neighbours without any hesitation or guilt; it was like fur on the earth. Now, suddenly, it is gone, the earth has had a close shave and all the hundreds of blue forget-me-nots have gone too. 'Please,' I said, 'don't behave like barbers. The last people who trimmed my garden behaved like barbers.' With a little supervision from me they did not (as I'm sure they would have liked to do) cut down any bushes; and I don't suppose I can blame them for the behaviour of the motor-mower. Lucas would have been so sad! I found a little den he had made in grass where he put his outside collection—little scraps of coloured cellophane paper which he adored. He loved their rustle, and he liked to carry them around in his mouth depositing them in the toes of my shoes and in his basket and anywhere else where he had his den. First thing in the morning, just as a child would do, as soon as he woke, he rushed to get his favourite piece of paper or wool. I've bored you with Lucas? No . . . You wait till I get on the other side of the counter from you, Paul, and you'll be putting your hands to your ears in protest. 'Not Lucas again.' And what will you say, Bill, when I get Lucas-launched?

Maybe I enjoyed him so much because I'm a child, too. I've never grown up, not really. And how clearly I remember longing for morning to come so that I could rush to enjoy my latest craze. I remember when I was staying at Martha's Vineyard, Edgartown, with the Marquands and I and the little boy were always up early and one morning the boy said to me as he was showing me his new rack of carpenter's tools. 'You know I just haven't been able to wait for the night to go, I've been thinking of these tools all night and as soon as I woke up I was thinking of them.'

Now I've gone into another province.

Tools or tools.

But how like a child! And how like adults who haven't yet lost the sense of wonder and enthusiasm about things.

The other afternoon I went to visit Ruth, my friend, who had also invited Raymond [Ward] and his wife Joyce, whom I haven't seen since I've been back here. How like people they looked! I felt very sad.

Raymond spends most of his time teaching, and Joyce teaches art to the student teachers, and both looked tired, and I had a terrible feeling they were letting go of the Dream, and soon if I met them in the street I would not know them, they would be indistinguishable from all the people.

This Saturday the Director of Broadcasting and tv is flying down from Wellington to see the production of *A State of Siege*. There is great pressure on me to go to the performance and I'm trying to find excuses not to go, because I'm just too plain scared and alone here.

All is in readiness for me to leave. Yesterday I got up early and played my Santa Barbara recordings, interviews, books, pieces of music, including the anguished piece from Schubert.

Otherwise day to day is a dream. I've packed together the tiny scrap of ms that I've done this year. I've been writing two poems at once, which is what I've done lately; and many poems that I think are better than my last year's poems because they're not so clearly defined. They're just feelings and images. What a grim time it has been. ('How long my road has been.') No laughs except with Lucas—and of course, which goes without saying, I've been sustained all the time by those airmail pages from across the Pacific.

Goodbye to all that.

I'm off to mail this.

May you be working furiously, satisfyingly among your your paintings—

that sounds crazy.

Your helixes burning.

Goodbye. My small energy has gone and I'm just another of the tired people of the earth.

I had a very moving note from George Braziller yesterday. If I find it hard to believe Marsha is dead, I can't even dream of how he must feel. I remember a weekend spent with them both on Long Island, away at the end by Montaulk (sp?), and I went with George while he searched and searched along the roadways for a bouquet of Marsha's favourite flower—Queen Anne's Lace.

***** *** **** ********

356 | JAY TO BEE

Factory-fresh Iron & Steel love to B P & N from J

>Apply Peedauntals Ltd. (N.Z.)
>Your last chance to be waterproofed
>before your Christmas carol-singing!
>(We are moving our factory from Evans St
>to the Northern Hemisphere.)
>BUY NOW. HUGE REDUCTIONS.
>EVERY PEEDAUNTAL *MUST* BE
>SOLD.

DECEMBER

124. Dunedin December (handwritten)

Dear Bee (defined by the dictionary as a 'social insect with a sting'), Pee (or Plosive), En (or nasal) & others in the household including the gopher,

Hello on a calm overcast day with Jay fully recovered from the enclosed little drama; & at the stage of hanging around wanting to fly.

I loved your up-to-date analysis of the Nixon-Eisenhower blockage & your suggestions for correction of same.

★   ★   ★   ★

Stars for interval during which Charles B came by on his way to a dinner party to farewell the English professor who is going *overseas* on sabbatical leave. Charles says he is going away for Christmas & is looking forward to being out of Dunedin 'where everyone knows your business'. I did not tell him this knowing covers the whole country. Your remarks in your letter about someone who said 'I know' chilled my chill bones. *Everyone* knows my sister lives in Auckland & my sister (unhappily) is the 'I'm her sister' type, though maybe now she is graduating from College she may be different ('you must change your life').

Charles is having me to/for dinner on Wednesday—a thoughtful gesture. He is inviting Ted Middleton also, with whom he has become 'fast friends'.

★   ★   ★

SUNDAY:

My tenants called by yesterday to deposit some of their goods in the one room I've managed to clean up. What nice kids they are! So sensitive, aware, overflowing with concern for everything & happily untrammelled by conventions of Victorian New Zealand.

★   ★   ★

Yes I'll be seeing Frank S in Auckland & no doubt he'll cook me a meal one evening with green peppers from his garden. He attends the hypertension unit at the local hospital & his reports of the conversations with other patients are hilarious. He insists that the blood-pressure reducing drug has a curious effect (yellow) on sex.

★ ★ ★

Goodbye for now. Love in transit, in packing, love-in-a-suitcase from me

    to

        you
    Bee   Pee   En

> AROUND DUNEDIN

A Suspense Drama,

& Fred & Gopher & all.
NEWS FLASH.
CITY SEARCHES.
WHO IS THE HERO OF THIS DRAMA?
Why –
   (Now Read on)

> CAT, small, white, part Siamese, male. Lost. Balmacewen Road.— Phone 63-799.

    – Lucas, of course!
Last evening five devoted servants (mother, father, three sons) of a certain vagabond familiarly known as *Snowy*, alias Lucas Burch, searched Dunedin for their straying master. Their first call was to a Blue Jay in Evans Street where, tearfully, they broke the news to the Jay, enlisting her in the search. Jay thought but did not say why should Snowy (formerly known as Lucas Burch) abandon luxury dwelling with 5 servants to return to 1 only?
   Later:

NEWS FLASH.
An overjoyed phone call to Jay from the servants. Their master had been hiding and playing (wickedly not responding to calls) two days in a ditch a few blocks away, near the golf course.* Snowy, formerly known as

---

* A cover-up, no doubt.

Lucas Burch Convict 99 has the world at his whiskers. Jay who had been planning to make a phone call before she left to make sure L.B was O.K. is most happy at the power and personality of Lucas (Snowy) and the passion and devotion he continues to inspire. *The end.*

125. Wellington December 6 (handwritten)

My dears,

Last time I passed through Wellington I wrote you a letter from this room which is the young John's room. The wind was blowing, I think, and the trees were knocking their branches against the window and it was morning and the rest of the household was asleep—Jacquie and little Stephanie, now. The daughter is up in Auckland, the husband is at the religious retreat he is founding in the wilds of the North Island, the son John whose room I have, is in a Detention Centre for three months on drug charges. This big solid house—very much like the houses we used to live in when we were children & so unlike my little cottage which trembles every time the wind lays a hand on its body—seems like a huge empty nest.

'Who has no house now will not build him one . . .'

It is child-spattered where the children like young birds have marked the walls and the furniture. A big teddy bear (like yours, Paul, in the corner of your room) with its fur well kissed & rubbed & hugged away sits on top of the wardrobe. Someone has tied a red scarf around its neck & its head is sunk in the scarf.

I'm flying to Auckland today—an hour's flight by jet; fourteen hours by train. It is wonderful to have left Dunedin. My last couple of days there were peaceful. As I planned to do I wandered to the place of The Stone Bees, to photograph them, and when I came to them I was confronted by my own imagination and memory, for they were so small I had to search for the carvings & I don't think my photographs will show them. I decided to keep my detailed imagination and memory of them enriched and perhaps made more precious and varied by being set beside their surprising reality which in itself has a clear delight & teaches me a 'lesson'. I'm afraid I profit from everything, even 'lessons'.

The flight from Dunedin was pleasant. I found that Charles Brasch was also on the plane & we sat together—I think the first time in my life that I've had company on a flight. I warned him that I would be likely to grab his arm if the plane were being buffeted & he whom I'm sure has remained ungrabbed all his life, suppressed a slight alarm & gallantly said he did not mind.

The flight was calm though & we were chased by a wind.

And so to Wellington. I've just stayed at home here, reading. As this is Katherine Mansfield's city, I at last got round to reading Anthony Alper's Life of K.M. Very well written, very moving. I always have a curious feeling in Wellington, a city I've never lived in for more than a week. I feel I know it from other sources, as if I've lived in it. It was my mother's city & so many of the names here were made memorable by my mother's gift of saying everything—names in particular—as if they were part of a treasury of doom: which perhaps they were.

But, B P & N I'm rather 'going on' aren't I? The sun has risen now. You're all in my mind, as you see, and if you are able to prise any secrets out of Carnie he will tell you that he's been seeing definite footprints of my brown bread shoes somewhere in the Live Oak Inn patio between the olive tree and the Bird of Paradise Flower. Ned has seen them too. That's why he gave you that glance when you came home yesterday . . . remember?

Love in transit

Hello again from Auckland. Your letter was waiting for me, so nice and warm, letters & sun; it is early morning & already the Auckland mosquitoes & ants have revealed themselves unto me.

 I liked the sound of the dinner with Lehmann & Co. Lehmann was Frank S's first publisher way back in the days of New Writing & it was he whom I once hoaxed by pretending I was a little native girl from the South Pacific. The poems, he said, (these were poems I wrote specially in my role as l.n.g.) were 'so fresh & new' clearly because English was not my native language and when I learned a little more English he would be happy to etc. etc. . . . That isn't an exact quote but it's the gist.

 It feels so strange being on top of N.Z.

[handwritten: It feels so strange being on top of N.Z. — Auck. ... Dunedin.]

 I'm sleepy & crazy & longing to be with Bee the Calmed the Liever the Cause the Dazzled; Pee the Knoll the Can the Body, En the Noble the Tice the Fold.

 Northern love More soon.

126. Auckland December 9 (handwritten)

Dear Blades strange & freeing,

Early morning. Sounds of coughing (engines and neighbours) of many wide-awake birds, & my c(l)ock ticking fast because its mainspring has been abused.

As usual I have spent my first two days here in a daze & bikini & without energy. Yesterday I made the big journey to town to confirm visa news which the office boy at the American Vice-Consulate had given me over the phone; to find that the office boy was the *Vice*-Consul himself who told me I'd have to wait about a year for a visa but as I have a visitor's visa which, strictly speaking, should not be used, I can go to the States & adjust visas there as soon as a number becomes available for me. I liked the Vice-Consul. He is very pale & sad & he looks as if he is dying . . .

In my confusion in town I lost my purse with a lot of money, keys etc. & I haven't much hope of recovering it.

Last evening I went to Frank's for dinner. He was in good form, & Harry, who appeared from the small apartment which Frank had built to house him, looked fine. Frank is giving a broadcast on Christmas Day, along with the Governor General & Dame Ngaio Marsh etc. etc. & Frank insists that his message is an account of his favourite Christmas meal, written in old-fashioned script—

fucking pig and apricocks

We had a pleasant evening—rather sad as well as humorous, for Frank discussed his death & his will and so on, between telling me such tales as that of the young man who went to church for the first time and being asked by the robed priest who was attending to the censer how he was enjoying the ceremony, he replied, 'Your drag is most impressive but your handbag's on fire.'

And another earthy N.Z. tale of the Englishman at work for the first time on a N.Z. farm, & given the job of taking the cow to the bull.

'Are you sure you know how to go about it all?' the farmer asked.

'Quite sure,' the Englishman replied.

And when he returned & the farmer asked how the event had gone the Englishman beaming replied,

'Oh top-hole, top-hole!'

*   *   *   *

Stars for rude Jay.

*   *   *   *

More stars.

The household here is my sister & her husband & one nephew & one niece (the other nephew is away doing research on a computer in Wellington). They're nice kids, packed with problems. When they start telling me about the movies they like, the books they read and so on, they say, 'You probably wouldn't enjoy this, it's mostly for young people.'

....
    dots.

Love waves across the Pacific to you. If you once again question Carnie he will tell you that not only the brown-bread shoe prints may be seen but the peanut butter haze in the patio of patios.

Your ptgs will be waiting impatiently in the gallery now to be *hung*. B, I think it would seem as if one created a tribe or herd of living images so you are driving your flock to market where they will be devoured/ patted, admired, envied, skinned, coveted—even paid for, perhaps.

You know now that I'm lost in words so I'll stop writing this & adjust my earthy peedauntal.

*   *   *

May's poems sound very good. I'm looking forward to reading them.

You know that I don't know what to say when I learn that some people are reading my writings. I can only repeat that I'm really a simple non-verbal non-bright feelie so I now send feelie love to

all at Live Oak Inn
see you soon soon soon

127. Auckland December

Dear Bee and Pee and Enn and all the other inhabitants musical botanical, simian, and the paintings on the walls,

Hello. Early morning. A grey Auckland day, warm, a slight wind blowing. I'm sitting on my bed in this basement room typing this while the rest of the household prepares to go to its work—my brother-in-law to his office, my sister to her Kindergarten College, my nephew to the broadcasting Offices where he is a Sound bloke, while my niece (fifteen) and I stay home. The other nephew is in Wellington—he's the one whose photo I sent once, God knows what for. 'The heart has reasons that reason doth not know.' It's time I found a new quote from the abundance available.

Last week, the big day, my sister's Diploma giving. She and two other older women had been studying among eighteen-year olds, and the valedictory address referred to 'you young girls going out into the field'. The setup—the audience, the clothes Doris Day style—all part of a world I don't inhabit and don't care to—a sad sort of world, everyone a little tired, uttering the old clichés. The only worthwhile aspect, for me, was the triumph it gave my sister and her family, and the admiration I and they feel for her courage and perseverance.

But—how does one escape from seeing (or thinking one sees) so clearly inside people?

★ ★ ★ ★ Stars for relaxation, for fun, laughs. Why did John Wayne? Because he saw Mia Farrow.

★★★★★★★★★★★★★★

In America the public toilet
is always ultra-voilet.

★★★★★★★★★★★★★★★

So far during my stay here I'm content just to stay around the place, recovering from Dunedin, I suppose. I feel very close to the other side of the Pacific, as if I'm already there. I'm going to type a few poems to send to Landfall before I leave and I'm thinking of sending some of my luggage ahead as unaccompanied baggage, at the cheap rate.

★★★★★★ stars for apologies for inflicting boring details.

★ a small star for a sudden memory of Lucas, with whose story I continue to bore people. I see the glazed look come in the eye as I begin each story. The family here retaliate with stories of Tinky, who is also part Siamese, and has many of Lucas' habits, such as running around like a young racehorse.

★★★

This time last year I think you were baking pumpkin cookies??????

Since I've been here I've baked many loaves of bread which are very quickly eaten, and one evening I made the dinner—meat loaf and stewed dates . . . not very imaginative.

★★★

The young boy next door brought in his autograph book to sign. What can one do in a country where people still write in autograph books such verses as 'God made the little niggers, he made them in the night, he made them in a hurry and forgot to make them white?' This was on the front page of the kid's book next to the old timer, 'By hook or by crook I'll be first in this book.'

I mailed off a little parcel to you the other day. I hope you get it before you leave for Santa Fe.

This letter is itty-bitty. I've just been having a telephone exchange (it is a few hours later now) with Air New Zealand who told me I can't fly to America on a Visitor's Visa with a one-way ticket. Jay's panic. I phoned the Vice-Consul who said I could. Air New Zealand spoke to Vice-Consul and reluctantly said I could fly thus. End of International Incident. This makes me impatient more and more to fly in case, suddenly, my visa is cancelled, as in a dream, and I remain trapped here—oh what fantasies of horror one conjurs up every moment. Why, then I should have to swim across the Pacific and Ned could row his cap-sailed boat out beyond the islands of the Santa Barbara channel and, dipping his oar into the water, hoist me on to the boat. Meanwhile, back in Live Oak Inn, Bill and Paul work hard with Old Smoky, burning—not cooking—truckloads of liver so the smell and smoke may lure Ned home—his only means of navigation. Tired and wet, but happy, we steer to shore, somewhere down near Butterfly Lane.

Crazy me.

I hope and hope the preparation for the L.A. show is not too terrible. I think it will be fine, fine, and recognized as such, and 'people will come and go

talking of B's show'.

Forgive this naive tactless way I have. I wanner communicate and words seem so silly, at this point, I mean the Pacific's there, not far from here, and it's sound and colour and movement, not a word in sight. When you're painting, and have painted and painted, does the paint become too tender to touch, as words do?

****

Pacific love—cool, wet, full of star fish, sunfish, and inaccessible forests.
    to
        B
            P
                N
        from Jay

More soon: Plane-loads of thoughts meanwhile.

128. Auckland December

Dear B P N, lately of Live Oak Inn, now, for Christmas, of Sante Fe and Gilbride Motel,

Hello, Hi, Greetings. Thank you for the lovely Bishop. He is beautiful; his colouring too. He is sitting here on my improvised desk in the semi-basement room of Ant Lodge (a small room made downstairs, off the garage). The ants in question live both upstairs and downstairs. When I used to stay here there was some kind of control over them but now they have taken over the place and the problem is to keep all food, especially sweet stuffs, from their scent cones. I should properly call downstairs where I'm staying, Mosquito Mansion.

The early morning is grey. Everyone upstairs is asleep. There has been some turmoil in the household this week. I remember writing in my last letter that I wished I didn't see, or think I saw, so clearly into people. The change of job, after a lifetime working in a newspaper, has been too much for my brother-in-law. He's had to go to hospital for treatment for a week or so. I saw the breakup happening and I'm glad everyone else sees it now. He's recovering very quickly and they will be able to go on their South Island Tour at Christmas time, when I shall be in the house with my two nephews, 21 and 19. They're nice kids, and we get on well, though I'm inclined to act the part of crabby aunt when they turn their pop music to full volume through the huge coffin-like speakers they have installed all over the house—the speakers are about seven feet high and three feet wide.

Poor May, with that nasty review in the N.Y. Times Sunday Review. I don't think I've ever cried over a nasty review. I just get a cold feeling of hopelessness and a desire to remove myself to the farthest corner of myself and never emerge again. And it's almost as bad with good reviews, when I clearly feel my head swelling and get the idea that I'm good and that everyone knows it. I used to get that feeling when I was a kid at school and won prizes. I would walk through the streets of our one-horse town, with a glow in my heart, and a certainty that everyone, everyone was thinking, There's J.F. (of the clever F family, you know) who won that prize.

Ah me. Stars for rain falling now, tropical rain. Everyone is up and awake. Tinky the cat is soaking wet and has just tapped on the insect screen—her way of asking to come in. They swear she is a cross between a cat and an opossum, for she looks like both and has the same colouring as an opossum.

John Lehmann never found out about either the little native girl or (a trick I played when I first came to London) the man from the West Indies.

> O Lord of the flying fish
> be sleep in the pocket of my fine London suit
> . . . pretty corny, really.

Auckland life, on the right.

and even urinating aboard the last bus to Henderson.

★★★★★★

NEWS FLASH.

The U.S. State Department has approved a Labour Certification for me, which means, I guess, that I can be employed in any aspect of writing, within the United States. I shall have to wait for several months, however, before I can make formal application for a longterm visa as there is no number available just now. So I'll be making my application when I'm in U.S., maybe some time this coming year. The L. Certificate means that if the worst comes to the worst I can go for a few weeks to a University or some such, if they want me.

★★★★

I'm looking forward to seeing that nice Christmas card, the painter's print of his fingers and toes and what else who knows.

★★★★

You should have been here a few days ago when I made the evening meal and inadvertently gave the household *Soap Soup*, as a sliver of washing soap found its way into the meat-pot: I had an inkling the lather was a little unusual.

★★★

You'll have the Bee Photo by now. No matter how diminished it is, it is still a Bee, and I'm beginning to think my next title is *truly* 'The Place of the Stone Bees'. It is a case of making a selection from the various hauntings, and those which stay the course, win. The other day I came across a notebook in which I had written 'The Basket Population'. A title that died, but may be revived. I think its origin was a kind of brain cell called a basket cell, and the practice of naming soldiers who had been blown to bits but were able to be reassembled, as 'basket cases'.

> *But this is grim.*
> *And it's Christmas time.*
> *I should send a rhyme,*
> *a reasonable rhyme*
> *to Bill and Paul far far away*
> *in Santa Fe,*
> *(New Mexico sun for cover)*
> *and Ned*
> *who doth bed*
> *his furry sides*
> *indeed his allover*
> *at Dr Gilbride's,*
> *and I shall wish*
> *the festive time may grant*
> *most*
> *joy*

to people, piano, plant,
and to Santa Fe family or host.
How corny and trite my rhyme.
Fortunately I stopped in time.

Now Christmas is here, the trees are erect
with spangles decked.
The bees are humming
the jays are jaying
all the organs are playing.
Santa is coming!
★★★★★★★★★

And on that starry note I end this rhyme
Once more, just in time.

I'm so happy I shall see you all in a few weeks. More in a day or two. Christmas love

to B P N from Jay

129. Auckland December (handwritten)

Dear Ned,

Christmas is near and no doubt you are wondering how to keep the servant problem solved by giving your household servants a few extra thoughts.

May I help? Do let me. I'm enclosing a few things for you, Ned, to distribute as you think fit. I'll be able to check up when I see you, i.e. brand the mouse and inscribe the books. Most of all, concealed and revealed, love is enclosed, with squalor, and other suitable accessories, from your Lucasless friend

Jay.

Look after your servants, Ned.

130. Auckland December

Dear B P N and (if it must be, it must be) Fred,

Almost Christmas Eve and Day and in the local shopping centre a sinister-looking Santa Claus is scaring the little kids out of their wits while Mama tries to assure them that the 'nice bearded gentleman' won't bite; or perhaps tries to assure them that he *will* bite. The harm generation. I'm sitting here in my basement room while upstairs my niece (16) and her girlfriend giggle together; and my sister and her husband (who came out of the hospital yesterday) are out driving. Tinky, the cat, has disappeared since I bought her some Tibs pep tablets for Christmas and my niece Pamela gave her one which she relished.

Not much news from here. No thoughts from this hot enervating climate where all I do is loll around all day. Just thinking of you all in Santa Fe (here I have to provide my own imagery) and in Live Oak Inn and wishing I were at least in the offing; but it's no time now. I'm thinking of your show, B, and all the feelings that must be going with it; and all your enjoyments in Santa Fe; just living and so on; delights and deserts; and desserts; rich mazes, gold threads; dreams; see how crazy I am in this basement room where the smoke of drifting fires, I mean the drifting smoke, comes in the door and goes out the window.

An ant (black) crawls along the wall beside me. It seems to have lost its way or else it's exploring for new territory; the scout; I have a few Christmas cards littered around—including one from friends in England who now own a restaurant with a Spanish chef called Jesus.

On January 4th I'm going to Wellington again to stay with Jacquie Baxter for a week, and when I return on the 11th I'll be making final preparations for my journey—robbing the banks of dollars and so on; and blackmailing Air New Zealand and the sad-eyed slightly built Vice-Consul who gets rotten eggs thrown at him when he appears in public.

✶✶✶✶✶✶

Stars. A power mower is at work next door. Lawns must not be longhaired.

✶✶✶✶✶✶

⟨ Page two, Auckland Document. ⟩

[in margin: Actually I'm not staying in Auckland *proper*.]

> She didn't agree at all, *she* said, with Glenn Gould, who believed that eventually music would be heard only in the well-known places where there are large numbers of hedgehogs, with decaying teeth, and that this was an inevitable development. This wouldn't affect the more blasé members of the audience, such as the critics, we observed. Maybe they'd be happier
>
> his opinion that hedgehogs do not eat eggs is immaterial.

accept as a **gift** LUCREZIA BORGIA

[in margin: missing portion lost forever in typewriter]

THURSDAY MORNING:

Woke, found cat waiting outside door, went upstairs with cat to make a breakfast, ate breakfast. Time five-thirty a.m.

Returned to room. Observed that the ants also had awakened. The scout I saw yesterday was indeed a scout and last evening he she or it brought the whole colony to inspect this room and I was forced, reluctantly, to do the thing which Mona Minim and her friends dreaded—put out tiny innocuous-looking dish of clear liquid which is poison.

'I had to do it,' she said, with narrowed eyes. 'I had to do it.'

Too often have I had ants sharing my bed.

And why not? you may ask.

Well, they tickle and I am uneasy if I have an ant trail over my pillow.

****

The other evening I went to Frank S's for dinner. He usually gets a Chinese meal sent on from the restaurant near his place. I gave him and Harry a little parcel of handkerchiefs and nuts and Harry was pleased. He sat up in bed and unwrapped his parcel. I also left the same for Jack, another old friend of Frank's who lives over in the city, and who, Frank once said, would be happy to spend his life drinking sweet tea and eating white bread and butter. Frank always refers to him as 'my simple friend Jack'.

> The other evening I went to Frank S's for dinner. He usually gets a Chinese meal sent on from the restaurant near his place. I gave him and Harry a little parcel of handkerchiefs and nuts and Harry was pleased. He sat up in bed and unwrapped his parcel. I also left the same for Jack, another old friend of Frank's who lives over in the city and who, Frank once said, would be happy to spend his life drinking sweet tea and eating white bread and butter. Frank always refers to him as "my simple friend Jack."

matter of words.
aged schoolmaster
people in their streets
"O Hangman, O Hangman"

In the morning I went to visit the elderly woman I have told you of—the one who has lost her mind completely except for her love of music. She does not go out walking now as she has begun to wander, and one day when she escaped from her husband Ernest's supervision and walked about a mile before he went to bring her back, she said when she arrived home, addressing Ernest,

'I've been for such a lovely walk. And such a nice gentleman brought me home.'

On my visit she kept telling me how lucky she was to have such a nice gentleman staying in the house with her.

She played a Mozart sonata for me. Beautifully. She spends her time reading the Life and Letters of Mozart and she now has no connection at all with the life around her. She seems to have received a gift rather than to have been the victim of theft. Or perhaps it's an exchange of gifts. A death-gift?

★★★★★★★★

'On arrange and on compose
les mots de tant do facons.'

★★★★★★★

> *Now goodbye, goodbye*
> *lay your cheek on a million-year yesterday.*
> *Whatever is there is what you are singing for*
> *are you singing are you speaking*
> *the mind spinning the one coin of loss*
> *which year's dark foot was it now, D for death out walking*
> *going our way*
> *and we stupidly looking for change.*

A spilled life what is it I am singing
the beasts of the fields and forest a million years gone
bodies the sides of ships sailing the golden grass
breathing to open the tiniest slit in the armoury
seeing to shuttle two commas across the view
continuation of a series that never continued

what is it
the half-life the going away
the D going our way.

★★★★

Stars for and so on and on. The above an impromptu nonsense and sense verse.

★★★

I hope the angel visits your table at Christmas and that you are never alarmed.

Innocent and wicked learned love to B P N and (if it must be it must be) Fred,

       from J
          almost in the offing.

---

131. Auckland December 26

Dear B,

    Many thanks for the Christmas Eve letter, and thank you, Dame M.M. for the memo, which has been noted, and filed and defiled. It was lovely timing—it tided me over, I'm not sure where to, but somewhere.

I'm glad the parcel arrived. I think the mouse is guaranteed indestructible. They are handmade by an elderly friend of Frank S who, Frank says, read a book on *felt toys* (probably mistaking the meaning of the title), made one mouse, and began to make more, and now it is his livelihood, supplementing his pension. They are for sale in Auckland's Petticoat Lane—a poor shade of the original. I have one mouse for myself in case I turn into a cat.

The N.Z. stories are interesting and some are very good. I never forgave Frank S for choosing 'The Day of the Sheep'. As for Karl Stead's choice—at first I refused to let him use 'The Reservoir' but he persuaded me. He is the only enemy I know that I have and his enmity springs from his reading himself into a story I wrote about a poet who went bald (among other things). I had a scene in the story of the poet and his wife in bed: a purely—impurely—imaginary scene which Karl took to be a description of his own marriage. When I knew Karl he had been married only six months, and the poet in the story had been married ten years.

O. E. Middleton is a fine writer. He's the blind writer I've mentioned during the year—he had this year's Burns Fellowship. He's the only N.Z. writer who's made me weep over a story—one called The Stone in a volume of that title. I told him this fact and it pleased him. He's had a varied career working at all kinds of trades. He was in the navy during the war, stationed in the United States. He's been deported from the United States for being a Communist or being accused of being such, and a few years ago he won a big libel suit against our weekly sensational newspaper, Truth. He was going blind then. He managed his own case and was very eloquent and what jury could resist 'this poor blind writer who had been so viciously treated'. (I nearly wrote viscously.) He has a wife and family but as so often happens in the 'middle years' they have fallen away from him like used skins.

Fancy having snow. Just fancy! Here it's humid and enervating. The family have migrated until January 11th and it would be peaceful were it not for the nonstop pop of my nephew from his giant speakers. He's very good, and tones the sound down when I ask him but I get tired of asking and I feel like a nuisance and a nagger and the generation gap gets wider and wider. He has no other interest but sound—he works at it and plays at it. His only friends are his sister's girl and boy friends who are six years younger than he (he's twenty-one). He's a nice kid, rather sad and troubled. He's not very tall and he's slight in build, and his room is littered with books on How To . . . Grow Tall, Build Muscles, Win Friends And . . .

God, the misery of being young.

The piece from your mother's letter about the stars is haunting. Is it true? Are there really no stars any more in the Midwest (is that where she is?)

O give me a home where the buffalo roam . . .
with the light from the glittering stars . . .

No stars at all? It's terrifying. Is this the result of pollution? It's too terrible to contemplate a time when we are exiled from the sky and from the earth. Is the time now?

★★★★★★★★★★★★★★★★★★★★★★★★★★

I hope you had a mishymashy Christmas and no hangovers.

It's early Sunday morning now. I'm about to go for a walk down to the beach (Northcote Point) before the sun gets too hot. When I returned to N.Z. from England I stayed in many places over Auckland and I once had a flat by the water at Northcote Point. It was fine until I discovered a family of nine lived upstairs and spent the time walking up and down. The old ferries used to leave from the Point but now that the Harbour Bridge has been built these past ten years few of the old ferries cross the harbour. When my sister first came to live in this house the place was surrounded by native bush that looks very much like the Panamanian jungle. Now, except for a bush reserve near by, the place is littered with houses. Fortunately it's still harder to disfigure the surface of water and there are wide clear sea views everywhere. The sky's still here, too. And the stars.

★★★★

 Well, I'm in the offing and it won't be long now before I emerge from the offing into the next phase of my journey. In view.

Hurry up please it's time.

Now I shall mail this and walk upon the beach
and (likely) hear the power-mowers calling each to each.

I wonder how Ned enjoyed his stay away?

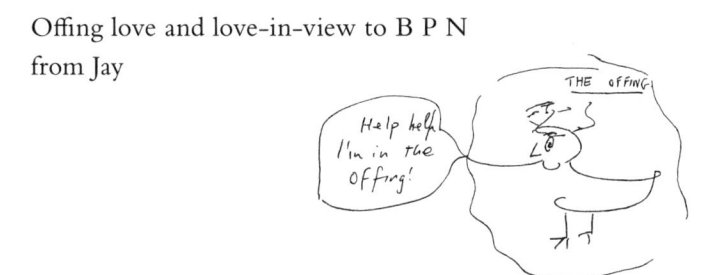

>Offing love and love-in-view to B P N
>from Jay

132. Auckland December (handwritten)

Dear Dame M. M.,

Thank you very much for your Angel on Yellow Paper which fluttered from W.T.B's letter to please and flatter.

Do you notice I am doing my best writing? I think within the stink of ink. Do you faint in the unrestraint of paint? I believe it is a common complaint which causes both inner saint and outer sinner and outer saint and inner sinner either to become a quaint clouter and shouter or to faint and day by day grow thinner.

(The Auckland summer is all shimmer.)

At the moment I am preparing for the sly joy of being an air traveller oft in the offing (though I hope I shall stay aloft, unlike Icarus 'the boy falling out of the sky'.)

Here is a poem I saw on an advertisement at the movies when the curtain moved across the screen.

>*En joy*
>*ni cest*
>*in*
>*ice cream.*

I hope you will print my poem on your page and that when I send you my problems under an assumed name you will deal with them on your page which I always read in a void mood of lived avidity.

Fondly,
>Dame F. C.

JANUARY 1971

133. Auckland January Ant Arbor (handwritten)

My dears yes isn't this a fat overfed letter! You might be interested in the writeup of Jim Baxter's commune.

It was so lovely to get your Santa Fe letter. I felt rather bold writing to you away from your habitat, as if I were indecently exposing, & it was sweet of you to reply from the midst of your social whirl to one, Jay, just entering the offing.

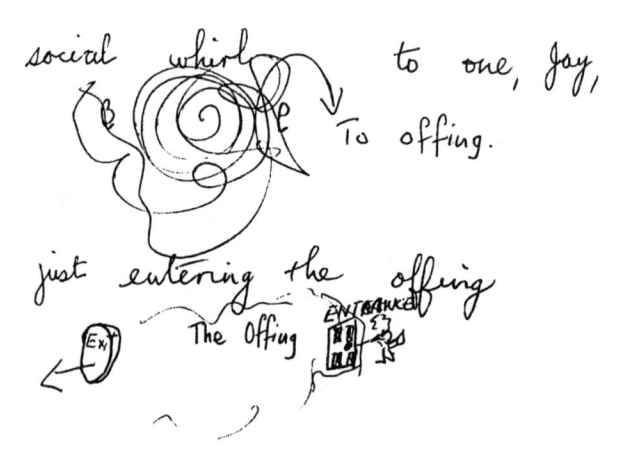

which means we are all in a tangle made by the unravelling of Christmas, New Year, meals, turkeys, travel plans, anticipation of Art Show, forlorn musings on the emigration of stars

— a tangle
waiting to be knitted purl plain and fancy into a warm tomorrow.

Thank you for the E. Welty poem. I look on it as a special treat.

★   ★   ★   ★

I had a card with a short excited note from Jo. Any notes or letters she writes are always written from a brilliant verge somewhere: her notes have the same snapping-up quality as her moves, in a flash, to spell out the word from the anagram.

★   ★   ★   ★   Four stars for comfort from the hinterland of dim seeing.

★   ★   ★

Tomorrow starting at 8 a.m. I make the all-day journey by train to Wellington—426 miles, arriving at 9 p.m. I've never seen the North Island by daylight & I hope the journey is not too hair-raising. I think I told you I'm staying with Jacquie Baxter for about a week. Jim is coming home for a while so I shall catch up on his news before I leave the country. I might also see Charles Neider who's around somewhere & had planned to do some research in Wellington's Turnbull Library. Jacquie is enjoying her work as Head of the New Zealand Room of the Wellington Public Library—though at first she was suspicious of their appointing her, a Maori, to that position as they were inclined to regard her as a 'show-piece'. In the capital city full of overseas diplomats etc. it's good propaganda to have Jacquie in that job—near the Museum which makes her weep because her race is dealt with in the past tense.

★   ★

You'll note that I'm writing this from Ant Arbor. The ants have made a trail along the foot of the bed & following the floor, the length of the bed. I peer over the bedclothes and watch them purposefully trekking— where? So far they haven't come into bed. They have taken over the kitchen upstairs, with the exception of the refrigerator, & my sister has given up trying to kill them. Only the refrigerator belongs to the family now. One is not aware of the smell of formic acid, here, but I remember when I was looking for a place to stay, once, in Auckland, how every little beach cottage & apartment reeked with the smell of ants.

★   ★   ★

Conclusion of Ant News.

★   ★   ★   ★

For the past week I've been alone in the house with my 21 year-old nephew & we've both been living deep in the culture-generation gap.

Actually it's more a culture gap than a generation gap. It appalls me to think that this is the first time since before his birth that he has been alone, day to day, with another human being (if I may flatter myself). They are very much a family, each identifying intensely with the others & while the family is here Ian is an erratic schoolgirl, like his sister. He's a timid boy & with no competition or dominance he's been himself. He sits there smoking his pipe, intent on his man-image & he talks about his friends & his hopes & fears. His life-dream is to own a 'Jag'. . . .

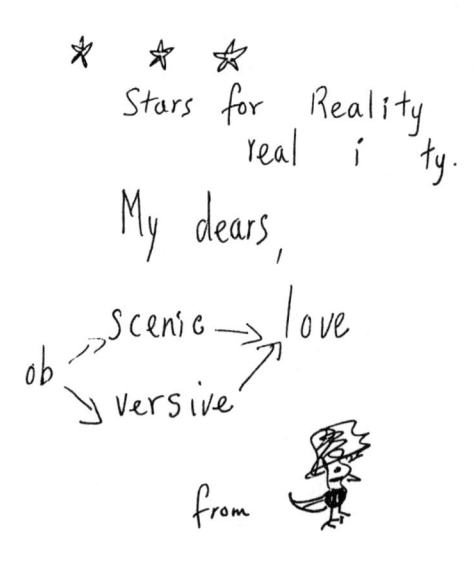

☆ ☆ ☆

Stars for Reality
real i ty.

My dears,

ob ⟨ scenic → love
     ⟨ versive

from

---

134. Wellington January 7

Dear

Hi, Ho, Hum.

Here I am sitting in front of a blazing fire in the Baxter household in Wellington while outside it rains and rains the remains of a tropical storm called Rosie. Baby Stephanie has just been put to bed after feeding me cups of water from her rose-coloured toy tea-set.

I've been enjoying my stay in Wellington—the longest time I have ever stayed (or is it 'stain'?) here except for once when, a schoolgirl, I came with the school to an educational exhibition when I and my sisters separated ourselves from the school and spent all the time riding the ghost train in the Fun Fair.

The people here are devoured by the surrounding mountains; everywhere is the trickle of streams in deep bush. The actual city area is small, with trains running from the hill suburbs to downtown. Buildings are immense, old, wooden & tatty with paint peeling from the walls.

But where else in New Zealand would someone come up to me in the street & kiss me, as an elderly man did today; because, he said, he liked my books so much . . .?*

Lunch today with an old university friend who lives a few yards from the sea, on a hill.† Her studio (she's a writer who also draws) overlooks the water & her little boat rocks in the bay. Her husband is a geologist; and her cats are 2, and she, who was brought up in the bush wilderness of our southern most island, Stewart island (or Rakiura, Land of The Glowing Skies) looks something like a penguin . . .

Enough of Jay's travelogue. I thought of you, well-wishfully, on the day of your opening, and my heart went out to you where it remains, with visits to Live Oak Inn between gallery-sympathising and hoping for the success of your show. It has left me quite heartlessly in the offing.

Soon I shall fly . . . well, it's just about 3 weeks now.

• • •

---

* This was the author and mountaineer John Pascoe, 1908-1972

† Sheila Natusch

[Handwritten panel with sleeping figures labeled "zzz" and speech bubble "Play play"]

The scene is Live Oak Inn. Paul v Ned are sitting by the fire. Bill is in L.A. telling his paintings to be brave. Paul v Ned doze. Music plays.

(Sleeping twain.)

[Handwritten panel showing a pencil and figure with bubble "Something emerges from the offing."]

(N.B. This is not a phonographic drawing.)

To Pacific

Meanwhile out in the patio Carnie playing with his toy telescope suddenly waves like an answer in the wind. "Something emerges from the offing," he cries. His cries are unheard by the

[Handwritten panel with figure, sign "Welcome to Focus", thought bubble "Thinks: How glad I am to have left the offing."]

A mysterious
form, part bird
part man, part
woman,
feathered, skinned,
winged, web-footed,
comes into Focus.

Don't miss our next instalment. Adventures in Focus. How will Carnie make his discovery known

> (when all
> is said
> and done)
> to Paul
> and Ned?
> Will Carnie's shrill
> voice reach Bill?

The foregoing is my letter

> I can't do better.
> I send, however,
> an orange and lemon grove
> of love to my dear folks
> the live oaks, hoping they
> will survive this load of corn
> blowing their way.

135. Auckland January (handwritten)

Dear inhabitants of Focus,

Hi. I'm just moving, still in imagination only (having left that crumby motel in Offing) out of one horse Focus Town into the pretty little resort of Foreground where I'm staying at the Foreplay Inn before I take the plane to Live Oak Inn. Quite a complicated journey, as complicated as a bee's dance at the entrance to the hive, at sundown.

   *   *   *

So I returned from Wellington this week to find a nice heap of mail including two letters & a lovely photo, all leaving me to feel warmly spoiled (like the dead in the desert) (she said, her eyes narrowing her face lifting . . .)

(Excuse crazy middle-of-the night letter. I had also a nasty letter from my N.Z. publisher & that is keeping me awake.)

By now, B, you will have had your opening, and the party and I'm sure Paul & you are croaking once again (from the Pallid bust of Pallas)* 'Nevermore!'

Every success & satisfaction in the show!

Santa Fe sounds lovely & I see what you mean about city prowling & city people because whatever it is it's on my circuit & I've never really understood why J.F. who was brought up as a simple milkmaid among the cows and sheep, delights in the seedy city. It's a novelist's attribute I believe (the only novelist's attribute I have).

* * * * * *

I thought you'd be interested in Jim B's commune & his floor-bed & eel-diet. The week I was in Wellington he was also there, at home, being himself & living his philosophy but also catching up on civilisation (?) by watching tv & having an occasional bath & reciting a lot of poetry & enjoying the attention of his little grand daughter. Maybe he was sorry to have to return to the eels. Though his heart is wrapped up in his Jerusalem project even he seems to need to have one foot, if not in materialism, then in the home comforts of shelter, privacy, warmth, light, and to need the strength of his wife's presence.

I had a nice infantile week. I also saw a couple of aunts & heard news of my mother's relatives: of my cousins who own a *Bee Farm* (my aunt was brought up on an apiary—(this I had not known). The cousins also have an organic farm, on which they grow their wheat, and grind it to make flour; and so on.

I sat down & fingered the organ ? at my aunt's house. (They hold religious meetings in one another's homes & each home has an organ.)

So that was Wellington. I return to find my bedroom empty of *ants* who arrived, however, within a few hours. They've made new tracks none of which, fortunately, are in the bedclothes.

Among my nice mail was a letter from the housemaid at Yaddo (I remember telling you about her—of the *Miss Gee* species (from whom Eleanor Rigby also descended) who had

' . . .a purple mac for wet days,

---

* 'pallid bust of Pallas' is a phrase from Poe's 'The Raven'

A green umbrella too to take,'*

Her motto (quoted to me as a saying of her Irish grandmother) was—'Nothing matters, everything passes; and forward look.'

She tells me that Alan Lelchuk (Mr Lelchuk) and Philip Roth (Mr Roth) are at Yaddo during January & how delighted she is to have 'the gentlemen'. Miss Woods! Her horror at being called *Mrs* is indescribable (lazy word). 'Oh no!' she said one day to one of the 'gentlemen'. 'I'm *Miss* Woods. I'm a virgin.' She is a dear character.

★   ★   ★   ★

Well—not many more letters before I fly in. I've written so much to you that I won't have anything to say. How good it will be to be away from New Zealand & how good it is to know that this is a fact which has been demonstrated to me again & again each time I have left New Zealand. It could so easily have been only another of those convenient dreams, half-insights, which are part of a change of place & which turn out to be shoddy imitations of the truth. 'If only I were away from *here* & over *there*, all would be well.'

★   ★   ★   ★

Next time I write I'll give again my plane no. & arrival time in *LAX*. (This is the airline's abbreviation.)

Jet love, all kinds of warm love to my three live frosted oaks & their household from

Dear Steinway. Hear you soon. Yours, J.

---

* from the poem 'Miss Gee. A Ballad.' by W.H. Auden

136. Auckland January (handwritten)

Dear Pixies of Live Oak Household,

    a page of pre-traveller's azzy frizzy izzy tizzy love bordered by a last below standard (D-) collage, from the 'I know' country—from Jay who flies-flees in to L.A. on Friday Jan 29, '71 on Air New Zealand (or Flea-t) 566A, arriving 6.10 p.m.

    Curious (yellow)

        Love from

            The Sunshine Lady

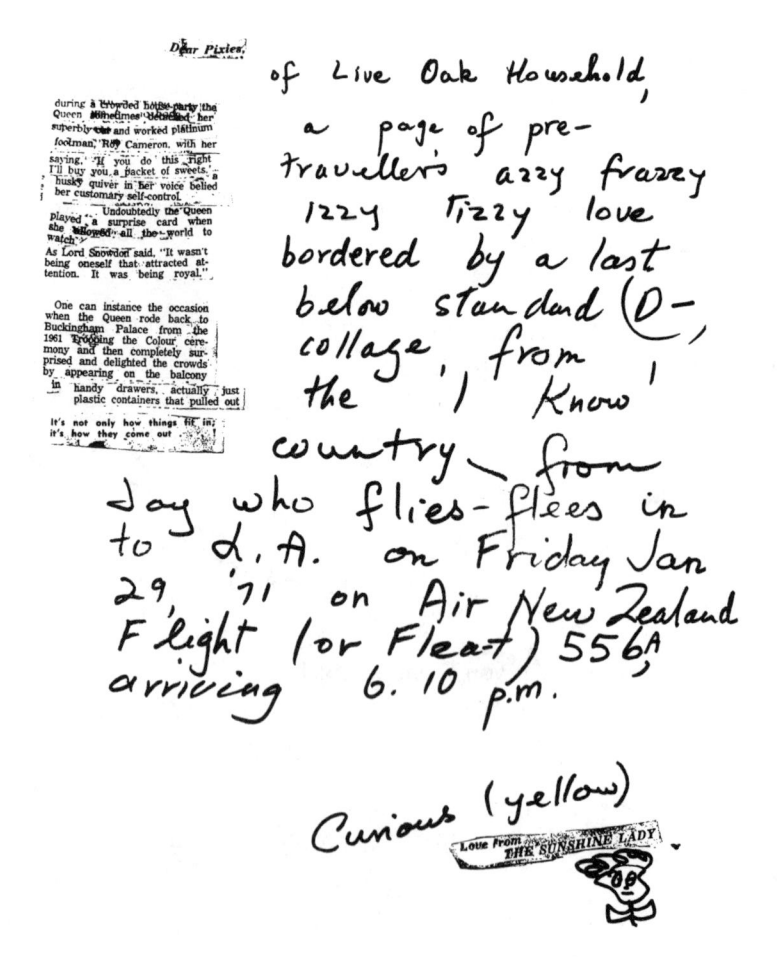

ACKNOWLEDGEMENTS

Much gratitude for input, assistance and encouragement is due to the following:

Pamela Gordon, Chair of the Janet Frame Literary Trust, without whose generous cooperation and support this publication would not be possible;

Bill Brown who discussed this project with great enthusiasm before his death and gave his permission to use excerpts from his own letters;

Sandra Stelts, Curator of Rare Books and Manuscripts at Eberly Family Special Collections Library, Paterno Library, Pennsylvania State University, where Janet Frame's letters to Bill Brown are lodged;

Staff at the Hocken Collections—Uare Taoka o Hākena, Dunedin, where Janet Frame deposited her literary papers;

Andrew Wylie, Tracy Bohan, Jin Auh and Jackie Ko at The Wylie Agency;

Jack Shoemaker, Kelly Winton and the team at Counterpoint Press.

APPENDICES

DRAMATIS PERSONAE

★ United States ★

Douglas Allanbrook (1921–2003) composer; at Yaddo

Elizabeth Ames (1885–1977) director of Yaddo artists' colony

Don Bachardy (1934–   ) artist; partner of Christopher Isherwood

Malcolm Bailey (1947-2011) artist; at Yaddo

Carl Brandt (1935–   ) literary agent

George Braziller (1916–   ) Frame's first American publisher

Kenneth Burke (1897–1993) literary critic Frame met at Yaddo

Josephine Carson (Rider) (1919–2002) writer, married to Mark Rider; at MacDowell

Henry Chapin (1893–1983) wrote epic verse based on American history

Joan Colebrook (1912–1991) writer born in Australia; at MacDowell

Elnora Coleman (–1971) writer; at MacDowell

Dan Curley (1918–1988) US novelist and short story writer; at Yaddo

Richard Diebenkorn (1922-1993) artist

Arnold Dobrin (1928–   ) children's author

Dr Gilbride veterinarian in Santa Barbara

Eunice Golden (1927–   ) artist and feminist; at MacDowell

Charles Gordone (1925–1995) playwright

Granville Hicks (1901–1982) novelist, editor; director of Yaddo with his wife Dorothy

Christopher Isherwood (1904–1986) British-born novelist, long-time resident of California

Alfred Kazin (1915–1998) writer and literary critic; at Yaddo

Ann Kazin (1927–1998) writer, second wife of Alfred; at Yaddo

George Kendall (1902–1998) director of MacDowall artist colony 1951-1970

Harrison Kinney (1922–   ) writer, editor, journalist; at MacDowell

Felix Landau (1924–2003) art dealer
Basil Langton (1912–2003) actor, photographer; at MacDowell
Alan Lelchuk (1938–   ) novelist Frame met at earlier stay at Yaddo
Wright Luddington (1900–1992) Santa Barbara art collector and philanthropist
Freya Manfred (1936–   ) poet; at Yaddo
John Marquand (1924–1995), novelist Frame met at earlier stay at Yaddo
Sue Marquand (1931–1977) editor, married to John
Charles Neider (1915–2001) novelist, essayist, nature writer; at MacDowell
Joyce Carol Oates (1938–   ) novelist
Sylvie Pasche (Elizabeth Roget) (1900-90) writer; at MacDowell
Norman Podhoretz (1930–   ) neo-conservative writer, editor of *Commentary*; at Yaddo
Ned Rorem (1923–   ) composer; at Yaddo
Philip Roth (1931–   ) novelist Frame met at earlier stay at Yaddo
Eva Marie Saint (1924–   ) movie actor
May Sarton (1912–1995) novelist, poet, memoirist
Edward Seaver editor at Frame's New York publisher, Braziller
Hyde Solomon (1911–1982) painter
Joan Tanner (1935–   ) artist
Katrina Trask (1853–1922) founder of Yaddo, with her husband Spencer
Louise Varèse (1890–1989) biographer, translator
Miss Woods housekeeper at Yaddo

★ New Zealand ★

Archibald Baxter (1881–1970) WW1 conscientious objector
Hilary Baxter (1949–2013) daughter of Jacquie and James
Jacquie Baxter (J.C. Sturm) (1927–2009) writer, wife of James K. Baxter
James K. Baxter (1926–1972) poet
John Baxter (1951–   ) son of Jacquie and James
Millicent Baxter (1888–1984) wife of Archibald
Charles Brasch (1909–1973) poet and editor of *Landfall* literary magazine

Rosalie Carey (1921–2011) actor, adapted and acted in Frame's *A State of Siege*

D'Arcy Cresswell, (1896–1960) New Zealand poet who spent his later years in London

Ruth Dallas (1919–2008) poet

Harry Doyle (1893–1971) Sargeson's long-term partner

Colin Durning dental professor and social activist

Charles Frame (Uncle Charlie) (–1965) Frame's paternal uncle

George Frame (1921–1989) Frame's brother

George Frame (1894–1963) Frame's father

Hannah Frame (Aunty Han) (–1970) Frame's aunt by marriage

Lottie Frame (1891-1955) Frame's mother

Ian Gordon (1949–2014) Frame's nephew, son of June and Wilson

June Gordon (1928–2008) Frame's sister

Neil Gordon (1951–   ) Frame's nephew, son of June and Wilson

Pamela Gordon (1954–   ) Frame's niece, daughter of June and Wilson

Wilson Gordon (1916–2007) Frame's brother in law

David Hall (1918–1971) book reviewer

Michael Hitchings (1924–2010) librarian of Hocken Library in Dunedin

Alan Horsman (1918–   ) Professor of English in Dunedin

Lawrence Jones (1934–   ) American-born Professor of English in Dunedin

Rodney Kennedy (1909–1989) Dunedin art patron and theatre producer

Iona Livingston (1921–2010) Frame's cousin by marriage

Colin McCahon (1919–1987) artist

Bill Manhire (1946–   ) poet

John Money (1921–2006) New Zealand born sexologist at Johns Hopkin University in Baltimore

O.E. Middleton (Ted) (1925–2010) writer

Sheila Natusch (1926–   ) writer and artist on natural history themes

John Pascoe (1908–1972) writer on mountaineering

Frank Sargeson (1903–1982) writer

C.K. Stead (Karl) (1932–   ) poet and novelist

Raymond Ward (1925–2003) British born New Zealand poet

Jean Watson (1933–2015) writer

Jack Whewell (1903–1978) friend of Sargeson

Dorothy White (Ballantyne) (1915–1995) children's librarian and author

Jess Whitworth (1874–1972) writer (married to Ernest)

Phillip Wilson (1922–2001) writer

* Other Countries *

Robert Cawley (R.H.C.) (1924-1999) psychiatrist at Maudsley Hospital in London

David Kozubei (1932-2006) writer in London

Lili Krause (1903-1986) concert pianist born in Hungary, briefly settled in New Zealand

John Lehmann (1907-1987) English writer and editor

Stan Ostoja-Kotkowski (1925-1995) Polish-born Australian painter and multi-media artist

Dominique Sion French post-graduate student in Dunedin in 1970

CONCEPTS AND NICKNAMES

A Malibu Sweater	a sweater that Bill gave to Janet
Baby Table (B.T.)	table at MacDowell where Bill and Janet dined
Basil the Gloom	morose; perhaps based on Basil Langton
Battery	energy level
Bee	Bill (William Theophilus Brown) (1919-2012)
Carnie	Carnivorous Plant
Dame Frame Clutha	Janet (who had changed her surname to Clutha by deed poll)
Dame Mary Margaret	Paul (after a character from *Faces in the Water*)
Fly	a character borrowed from Emily Dickinson's poems
Evans Street	street where Frame lived in Dunedin
Feelie	sensitive person
Fred	female cat; frequent visitor at Hermosillo Drive
Focus	goal
Hermosillo Drive	Bill and Paul's address in Santa Barbara, California
Jay, Jaybird	Janet Frame (1924-2004) also known as Janet Clutha
Kennel	potential room or studio for Janet at Bill and Paul's place
Kiddies' Page	(also Pixie Pages) collages and jokes etc.

Landfall	prominent New Zealand literary journal
Live Oaks Inn	name for Hermosillo Drive house
Miss Nostalgia Tarantula Piecemeal	Janet
My Mortal Enemy	the work in progress (after title of a Willa Cather novel)
Ned	Bill & Paul's cat (also known as En)
Omicron	haven (from the name of a studio at MacDowell)
Peanut-butter patio	patio at Hermosillo Drive
Pee	Paul Wonner (1920-2008)
Peedauntal	device strapped to leg to afford relief during long social events
Pornograph	phonograph
Stars	asterisks marking a section-break in a letter / marks for merit
Surcingles	stripes on bee's abdomen (from Emily Dickinson poem)
Steinie	Steinway piano owned by Bill
The Offing	the future
Thinkie	intellectual
Three Live Oaks	Bill, Paul and Ned the cat (derived from Walt Whitman poem)
The Tender Alternative	favourable option (from a poem and poet unknown)
The Stone Bees	moulded reliefs of bees on the front of a Dunedin building
Wax-Eye City	Dunedin (wax-eye is a small bird)

QUOTATIONS

Frame had a well-stocked mind from which she often drew appropriate quotations, paraphrases and parodies, mostly of poetry, ranging from traditional rhymes and songs to the literary classics as well as contemporary poems. Rilke, Auden, Dickinson and Whitman were among her favourites. The following list respectfully notes living and recently dead authors of lines quoted. Well-known rhymes and allusions to older works are left for the reader to recognise. Some longer quotations have been omitted as noted in square brackets in the relevant place in the text (for instance, passages by Thom Gunn, James K. Baxter and Frank Sargeson). All best efforts have been made to identify and acknowledge the authors of quoted material that is still in copyright, and to obtain permission in the case of substantial quotes. Copyright owners are invited to contact the publisher if there has been any inadvertent omission.

W.H. Auden is quoted on p44 (from 'Miss Gee. A Ballad'); p157 (from 'Horae Canonicae: Lauds'); p191 (from 'Lady Weeping at the Crossroads'); p201 (from 'Letter to Lord Byron'); p218 (from 'The Sea and the Mirror: A Commentary on Shakespeare's The Tempest'); pp384-5 (from 'Miss Gee. A Ballad'); p290 (from 'Lullaby'); p317 (from 'Culture'). Acknowledgement is made to W. H. Auden *Collected Poems*, edited by Edward Mendelson, Random House, New York and Faber & Faber, London (2007).

Josephine Carson is quoted on p121 (a limerick sent by private communication).

Cecil Day-Lewis is quoted on p79 (from 'Newsreel'). Frame incorrectly credits Louis MacNeice.

H.D. (Hilda Doolittle) is quoted on p54 ('O Heart small urn' from 'The Walls do not Fall').

T.S. Eliot is quoted on p264 and p376 (from 'The Waste Land').

Adrian Henri is quoted on p288 (from 'Ingleside, 1963,' in 'The Mersey Sound,' *Penguin Modern Poets 10*, 1967).

Henry Reed is quoted on p112 and p119 (from 'Chard Whitlow')

Rainer Maria Rilke quotations are variably from the J.B. Leishman translations and from collaborative translations by Frame and Brown. Quotations on p358 ('you must change your life' from 'Torso of an Archaic Apollo') and p360 ('who has no house now . . .' from 'Autumn Day') are from *Rilke: Selected Poems* translated by C.F. MacIntyre, University of California Press (1957).

Stephen Spender is quoted on p54 ('Tears pouring from the face of stone' from 'The Vase of Tears').

WORKS BY JANET FRAME

(with date of first publication)

1952	The Lagoon and Other Stories (stories)
1957	Owls Do Cry (novel)
1961	Faces in the Water (novel)
1962	The Edge of the Alphabet (novel)
1963	Scented Gardens for the Blind (novel)
1963	Snowman Snowman: Fables and Fantasies (stories)
1963	The Reservoir: Stories and Sketches (stories)
1965	The Adaptable Man (novel)
1966	A State of Siege (novel)
1966	The Reservoir and other stories
1967	The Pocket Mirror (poems)
1968	The Rainbirds (novel) aka Yellow Flowers in the Antipodean Room
1969	Mona Minim and the Smell of the Sun (children's book)
1970	Intensive Care (novel)
1972	Daughter Buffalo (novel)
1979	Living in the Maniototo (novel)
1982	To the Is-land (autobiography volume 1)
1983	You Are Now Entering the Human Heart (stories)
1984	An Angel at My Table (autobiography volume 2)

1985   The Envoy From Mirror City (autobiography volume 3)

1988   The Carpathians (novel)

1989   The Complete Autobiography (omnibus) aka An Autobiography aka An Angel At My Table

Posthumous titles:

2006   The Goose Bath (poems)

2007   Towards Another Summer (novel)

2008   Storms Will Tell (selected poems)

2009   Prizes (selected stories) aka The Daylight and the Dust

2011   Janet Frame In Her Own Words (selected non-fiction)

2012   Gorse is Not People (stories) aka Between My Father & the King

2013   In the Memorial Room (novel)

2013   The Mijo Tree (story)

For further information about Janet Frame's life and work, please see:

Janet Frame Estate website: www.janetframe.org

Wrestling with the Angel: A Life of Janet Frame by Michael King (Counterpoint Press, 2000)

— Excerpts from Brown's Letters to Frame —

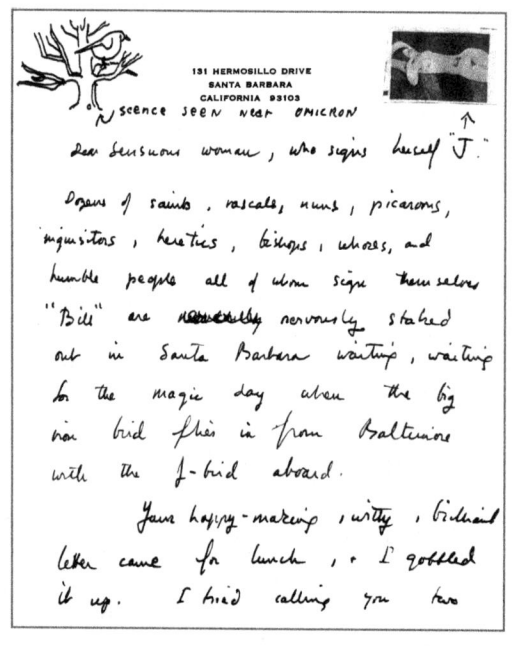

[Bill Brown letter—November 1969]

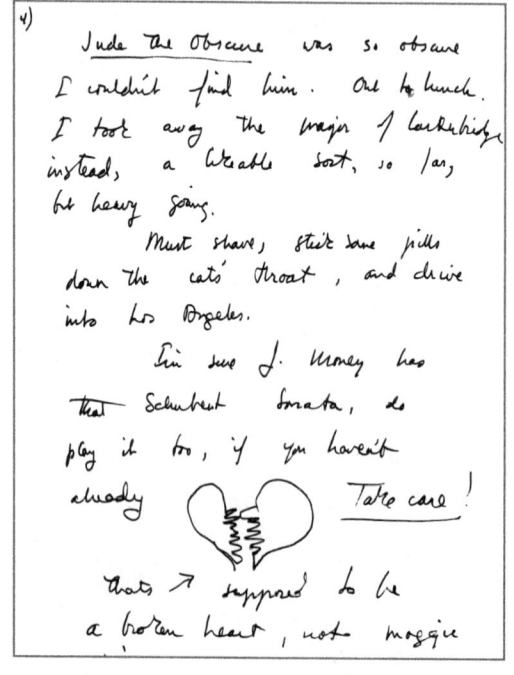

[Bill Brown letter—December 1969]

402 | EXCERPTS FROM BROWN'S LETTERS TO FRAME

[Bill Brown letter—January 1970]

The arrival of Janet's muse, part man, part woman, part bird, part cat, made in a collage drawing game.

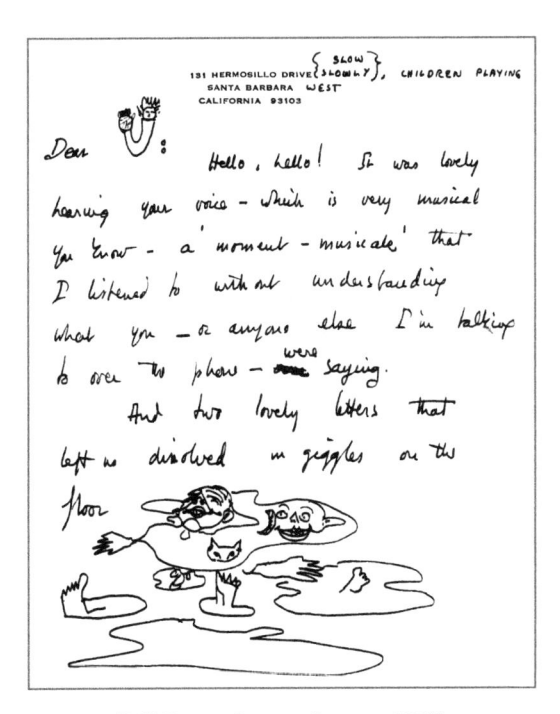

[Bill Brown letter—January 1970]

EXCERPTS FROM BROWN'S LETTERS TO FRAME | 403

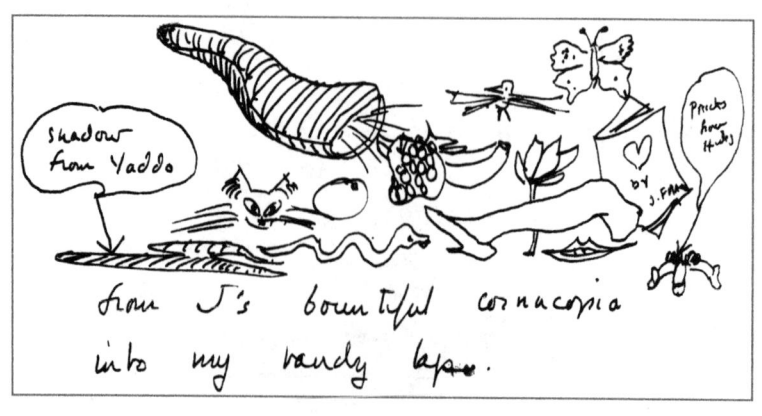

> Do you think we're both pregnant? I with St. Barbara + you with your Mortal Enemy? I suspect in my case, gas, (even though I'm beginning to nibble chocolates at all hours.)
>
> The enclosed photo they sent by mistake, do not feel obliged to keep.
>
> Goodbye now
> LOVE

[Bill Brown letter—January 1970]

> shadow from Yaddo
>
> Pricks have Hands
>
> by J. Fran
>
> from J's bountiful cornucopia into my bawdy lap.

[Bill Brown letter—January 1970]

404 | EXCERPTS FROM BROWN'S LETTERS TO FRAME

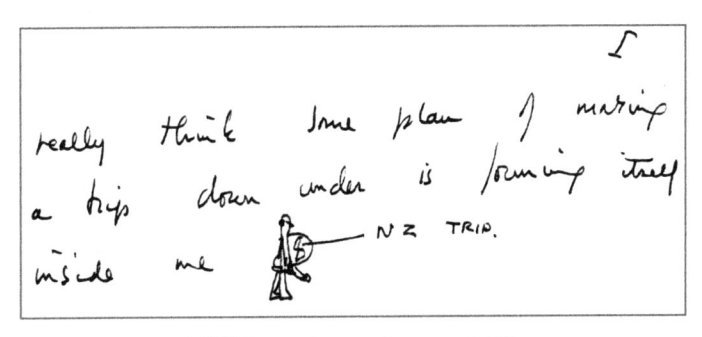

[Bill Brown letter—January 1970]

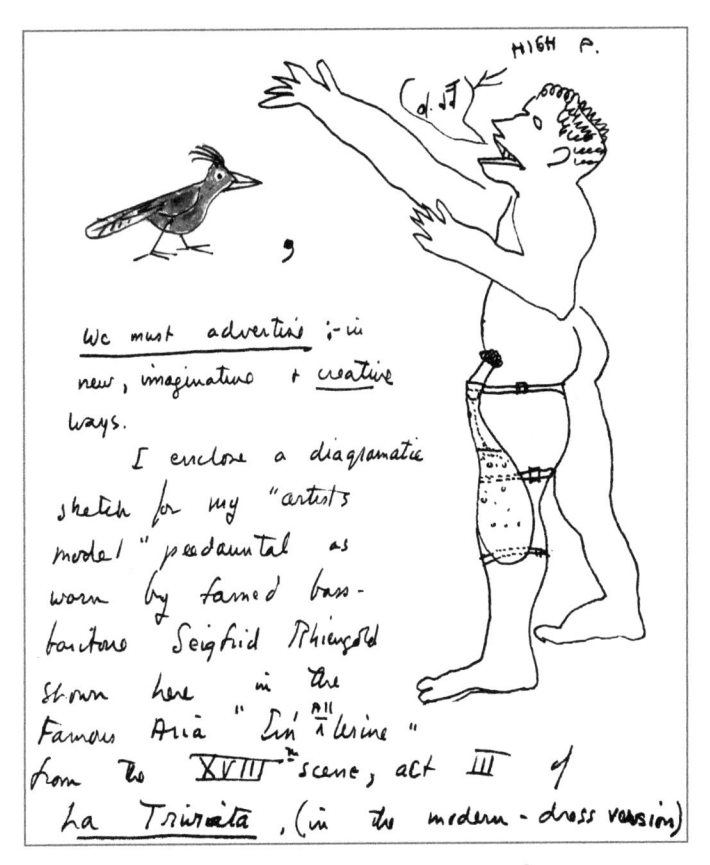

[Bill Brown letter—February 1970]

Frame comments in Letter : 'Alas sir, the Peedauntal model as illustrated has no sex appeal whatsoever, unless of course the buckles fastening it to the leg are diamond or snakeskin. I had in mind something less like an attached bagpipe'.

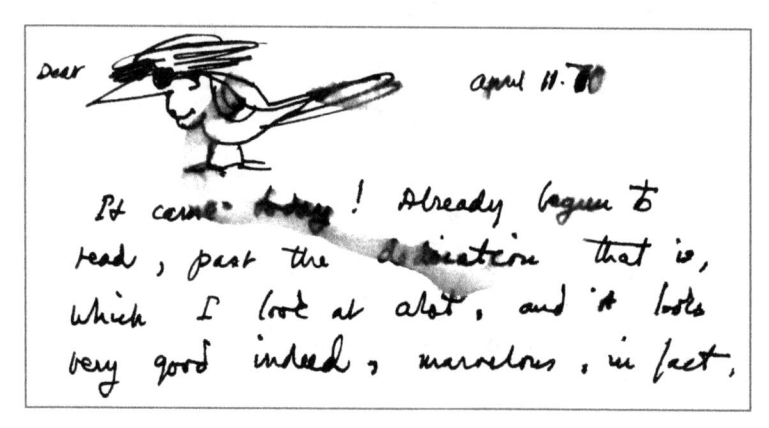

[Bill Brown letter—April 11, 1970]

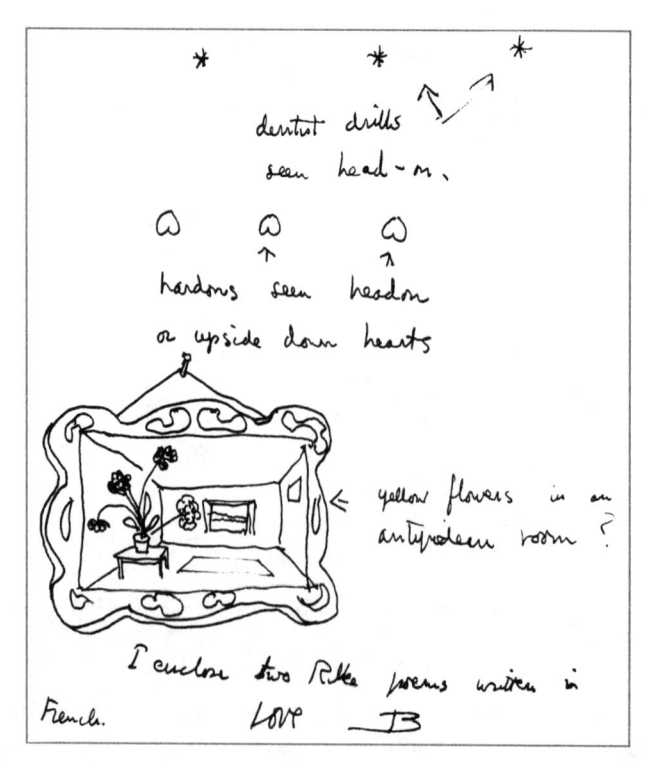

[Bill Brown letter—April 17, 1970]

406 | EXCERPTS FROM BROWN'S LETTERS TO FRAME

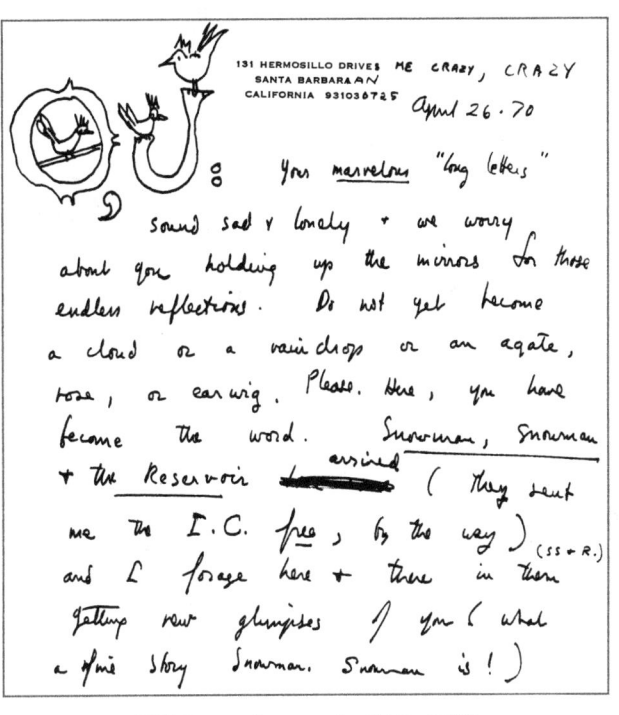

> 131 HERMOSILLO DRIVE ME CRAZY, CRAZY
> SANTA BARBARA AN
> CALIFORNIA 93103 8725 April 26. 70
>
> Your marvelous "long letters" sound sad & lonely + we worry about you holding up the mirrors for those endless reflections. Do not yet become a cloud or a raindrop or an agate, rose, or earwig. Please. Here, you have become the word. Snowman, Snowman + the Reservoir arrived ~~*******~~ (they sent me the I.C. free, by the way) (SS+R.) and I forage here + there in them getting new glimpses of you (what a fine story Snowman, Snowman is!)

[Bill Brown letter—April 26, 1970]

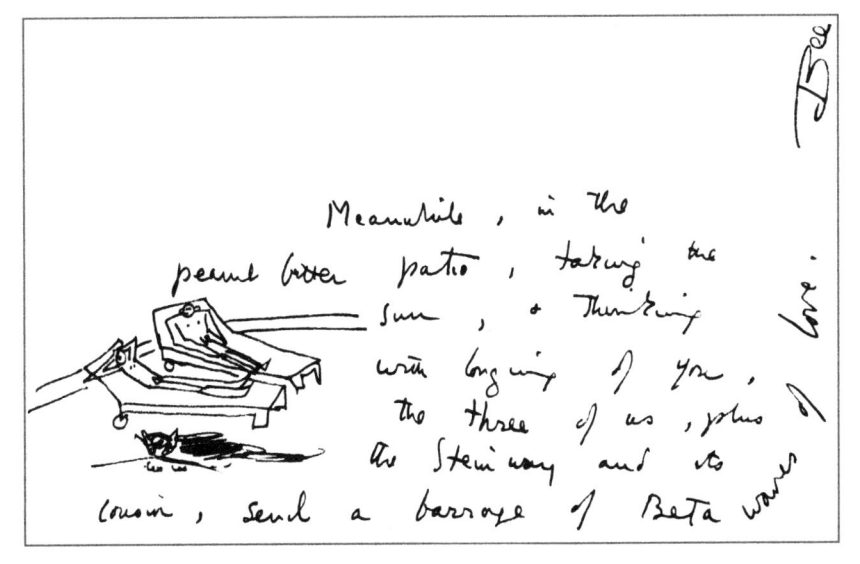

> Meanwhile, in the peanut butter patio, taking the sun, & thinking with longing of you, the three of us, John & the Steinway and its cousin, send a barrage of Beta waves of love.

[Bill Brown letter—May 1970]

EXCERPTS FROM BROWN'S LETTERS TO FRAME | 407

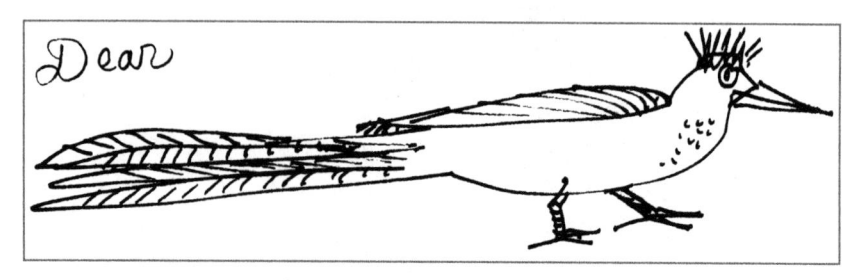

[Bill Brown letter—May 1970]

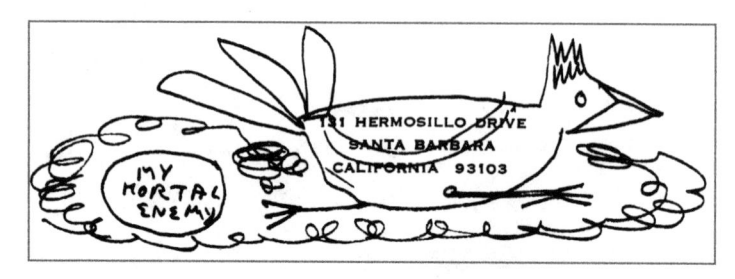

[Bill Brown letter—June 1970]

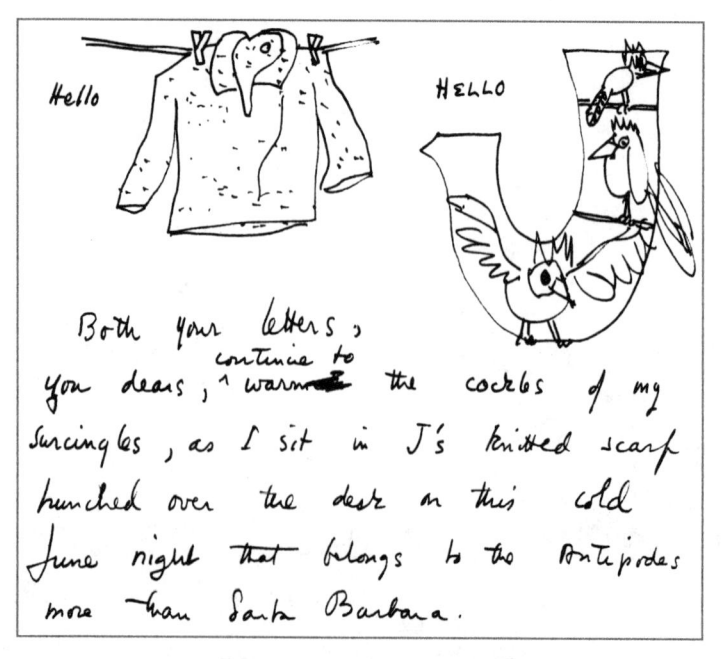

Both your letters, you dears, continue to warm the cockles of my surcingles, as I sit in J's knitted scarf hunched over the desk on this cold June night that belongs to the Antipodes more than Santa Barbara.

[Bill Brown letter—June 1970]

**** We build our day around your letters.

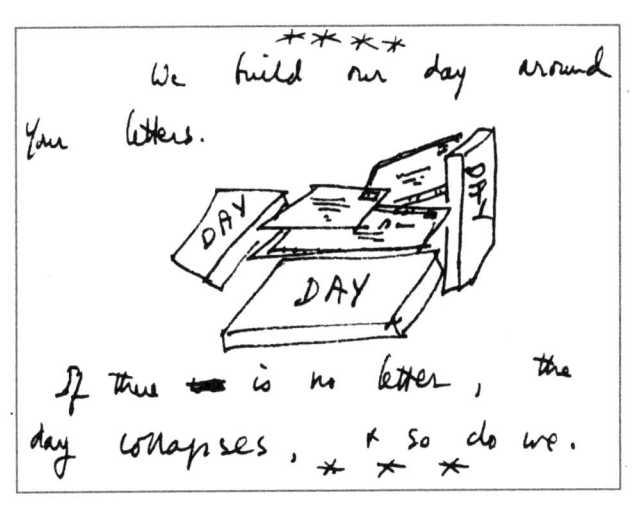

If there is no letter, the day collapses, & so do we. * * *

[Bill Brown letter—August 1970]

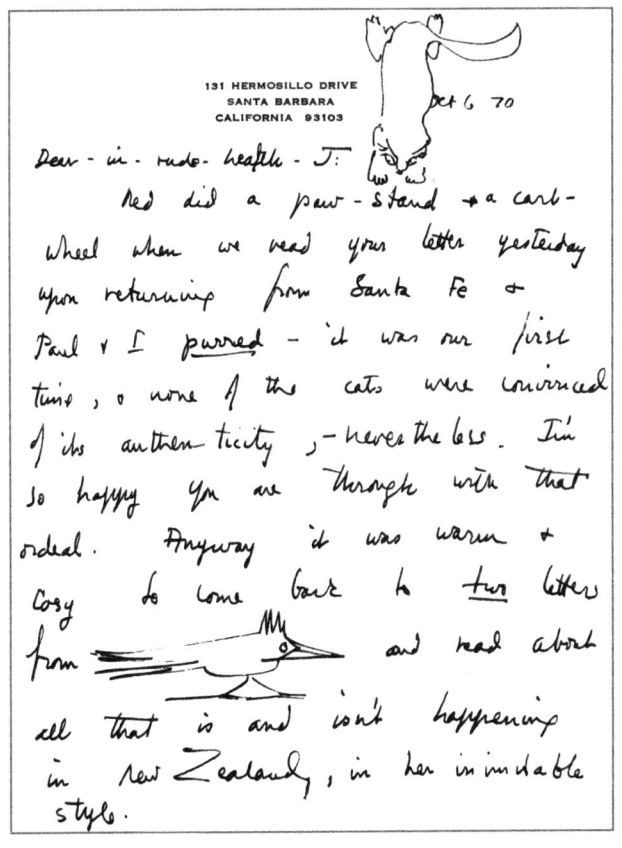

131 HERMOSILLO DRIVE
SANTA BARBARA
CALIFORNIA 93103

Oct 6 70

Dear-in-rude-health-J:
Ned did a paw-stand & a cartwheel when we read your letter yesterday upon returning from Santa Fe & Paul & I purred — it was our first time, & none of the cats were convinced of its authenticity, — nevertheless. I'm so happy you are through with that ordeal. Anyway it was warm & cosy to come back to two letters from ———— and read about all that is and isn't happening in New Zealand, in her inimitable style.

[Bill Brown letter—October 1970]

EXCERPTS FROM BROWN'S LETTERS TO FRAME | 409

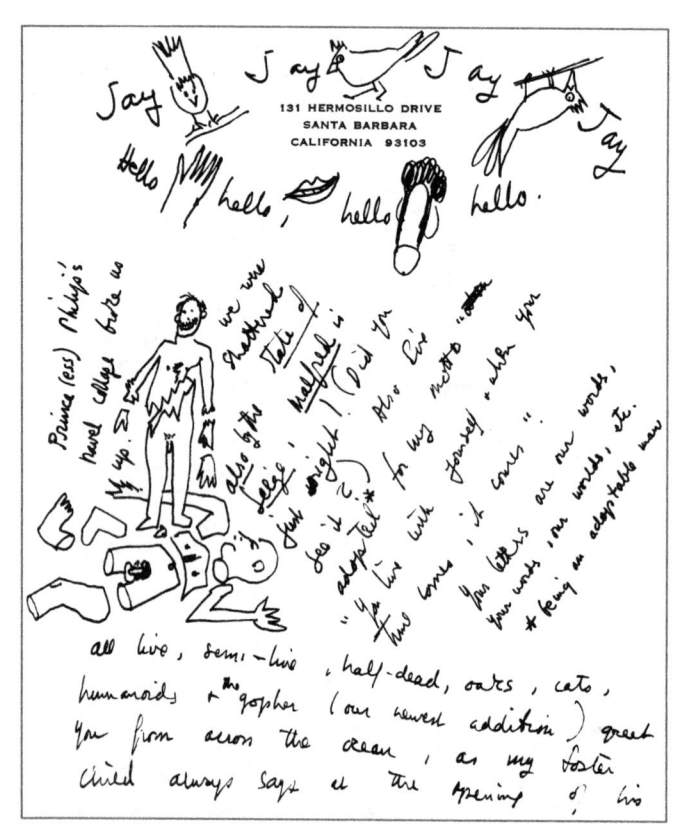

[Bill Brown letter—November 1970]

[Bill Brown letter—December 1970]

EXCERPTS FROM BROWN'S LETTERS TO FRAME

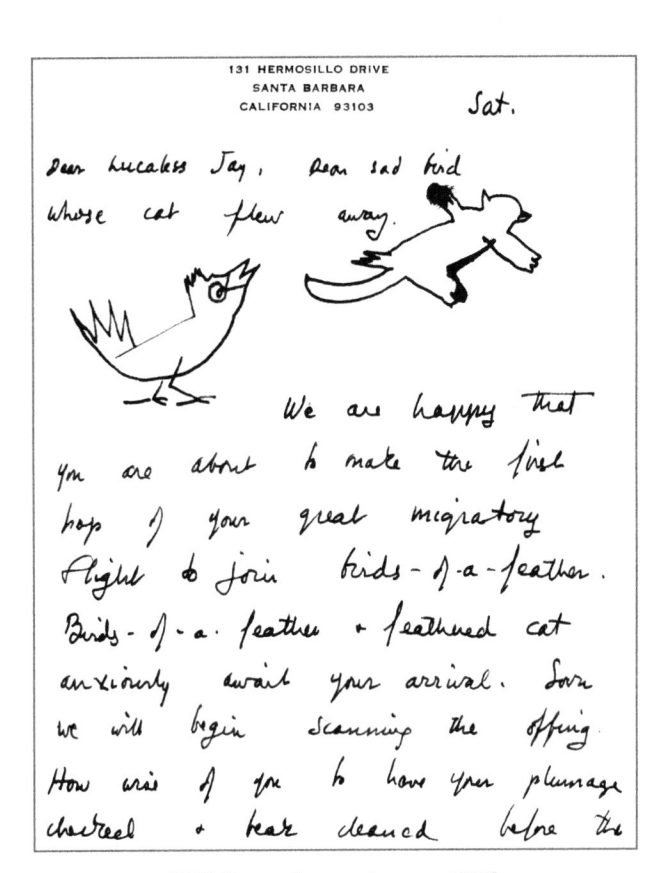

[Bill Brown letter—January 1971]